Rollback

Rollback

Repealing Big Government Before the Coming Fiscal Collapse

Thomas E. Woods, Jr.

Since 1947
**REGNERY
PUBLISHING, INC.**

An Eagle Publishing Company • Washington, DC

Library of Congress Cataloging-in-Publication Data

Woods, Thomas E.
  Rollback / Tom Woods.
    p. cm.
  ISBN 978-1-59698-141-6
   1. United States—Economic policy—2009. 2. United States—Economic conditions—2009. 3. Government spending policy—United States. I. Title.
  HC106.84.W66 2011
  336.73--dc22

 2010051713

Published in the United States by
Regnery Publishing, Inc.
One Massachusetts Avenue, NW
Washington, DC 20001
www.regnery.com

Manufactured in the United States of America

10 9 8 7 6 5 4 3 2 1

Distributed to the trade by:
Perseus Distribution
387 Park Avenue South
New York, NY 10016

To Heather

■　　■　　■　　■

There is no doubt that the real destroyer of the liberties of any people is he who spreads among them bounties, donations and largesse.

—Plutarch

The more corrupt the State, the more numerous the laws.

—Tacitus

Table of Contents

CHAPTER 1

Is It Already Too Late?

Nobody trusts the government, pollsters tell us. In April 2010, the Pew Research Center found that only 22 percent of Americans polled said they trusted the government at least most of the time.[1]

I wish I believed it. Most Americans seem to have a childlike confidence in government. They may be skeptical of the politician who insists he's been faithful to his wife, but they buy all the major claims government makes for itself. And although they know the government's finances can be dicey, they seem to console themselves that the experts are in charge, and that somehow everything will work out. Few entertain even the possibility of any sort of general collapse or default.

This confidence is about to be severely shaken. A systemic crisis is poised to strike an unprepared America, as the federal government is forced to renege on its impossible promises. It will no longer be the godlike dispenser of bounties, the miracle worker that summons bread from stones.

For even if (1) the robust economic recovery Americans have been waiting for finally arrives, (2) the federal debt becomes manageable, and (3) the nearly $1 trillion in annual interest payments on that debt—a permanent part of the federal budget within ten years—is a price Americans are willing to pay, we're still sunk. The federal entitlement programs on which generations of Americans have been taught to rely and to base their expectations for retirement will go bust in our lifetimes. The aging of the population guarantees it. The resources do not and will not exist to make good on these promises.

Most of the people reading this book will live through one of the most significant periods of change in American history. The scale of the coming, inevitable spending cuts will be unlike anything Americans have ever experienced during peacetime. Americans have never seen federal spending scaled back. Even when the newspapers speak of "budget cuts," they don't actually mean the budget will be lower than it was the previous year. They mean only that its *rate of growth* is falling. Government is never cut. But it will be.

Between now and the entitlement collapse, our representatives in government will keep trying to kick the can down the road. They will buy time with marginal reforms in the programs involved. When that time runs out, they'll try the same thing again. With default staring them in the face, they will try tax increases. They will try borrowing. They will try printing the money. None of these approaches will work, as I intend to show, though if employed vigorously enough they just might wreck the economy, including the dollar itself.

But in crisis there is opportunity.

Former White House Chief of Staff Rahm Emanuel, who notoriously observed that a crisis should never be allowed to go to waste, was on to something. Though his meaning was clear enough—that government should exploit crisis situations to ram through the laundry list of programs that would be politically prohibitive during times of calm—he arrived at the wrong conclusion. The coming fiscal crisis is an opportunity to take a careful second look at government, its claims, and its promises, and to see how much of it holds up to the harsh light of reason. Forget the comic-book rendition of government achievements we were all taught in sixth grade. This book paints a far different picture. And with that picture in mind, the unavoidable slashing of the federal budget that will have to take place is cast in rather a different light. Instead of a regrettable exercise undertaken out of grim necessity, it will be an enormous stride forward into a much brighter future.

The critical first step for checking the seemingly unstoppable federal advance is to stick a dagger through the heart of the myths by which government has secured the confidence and consent of the people. We know these myths by heart. Government acts on behalf of the public good. It keeps us safe. It protects us against monopolies. Without it, America would be populated by illiterates, half of us would be dead from quack medicine or exploding consumer products, and the other half would lead a feudal existence under the iron fist of private firms that worked us to the bone for a dollar a week.

But let's suppose that the federal government has in fact been an enemy of the people's welfare, and that the progress in our living standards has occurred *in spite* of its efforts. It pits individuals, firms, industries, regions, races, and age groups against each other in a zero-sum game of mutual plunder. It takes credit for improvements in material conditions that we in fact owe to the private sector, while refusing to accept responsibility for the countless failures and social ills to which its own programs have given rise. Rather than bringing about the "public good," whatever that means, it rules over us through a series of fiefdoms seeking bigger budgets and more power. Despite the veneer of public-interest rhetoric by which it hides its real nature, it is a mere parasite on productive activity and a net minus in the story of human welfare.

Now if this is a more accurate depiction of the federal government, and I intend to argue that it is, we are likely to have a different view of the consequences of the coming fiscal collapse. So an institution that has seized our wealth, held back the rise in our standard of living, and deceived schoolchildren into honoring it as the source of all progress, will have to be cut back? What's the catch? This is no calamity to be deplored. It is an opportunity to be seized. Still another purpose of this book, therefore, is to demonstrate that we would not only survive but even flourish in the absence of countless institutions we are routinely told we could not live without.

Americans have given government the benefit of the doubt because they have thoughtlessly accepted a schoolboy narrative of how much worse off we would all be without it. If the coming disaster is to be averted and future crises prevented from arising, the smiley-face version of government we learned in junior high needs to be dismantled and discarded forever. Chapter 4, for instance, spends some time discussing portions of the federal regulatory apparatus. It does so not because the regulatory agencies are themselves particularly expensive (their indirect costs on the private sector are another matter), but because they form a significant part of the mythological edifice that gives rise to the public's naïve confidence in government.

In speaking of averting the coming disaster, we can't fool ourselves into believing pain can be avoided. That horse has already left the stable. The federal government has made it impossible for us to escape unscathed. The only way to prevent the outright collapse on the horizon, a collapse that would surely be followed by emergency government policies that could destroy the dollar and with it the fortunes of the people, is by making severe cuts in the present. Some of these, as this book will argue, will be easy, and in spite of the predictable caterwauling by the interest groups involved, Americans would hardly notice them. Others will be more difficult, particularly since they will need to be so substantial and sudden. The best we can hope for is to endure some pain now in order to avoid a systemic crisis later. The more we can do in the present, the less severe will be the problem in the future, and the less likely our public servants will be to wipe Americans out completely in the course of trying to overcome it.

Finally, this book proposes some methods by which the expansion of federal power might be halted or reversed. Most of these approaches are unconventional, as the nature of the situation demands. Some will be derided as unrealistic, the usual complaint about suggestions that would actually work and are obviously necessary. What is truly unrealistic, on the other hand, is the long-term solvency of the federal government. A historic default is coming. Wrenching changes will have to be made to prevent it. Few people in public life dream of proposing such changes. Few Americans realize the depth of the problem. Everyone thinks it can be pushed off until tomorrow, even as midnight draws nearer.

In the short run, people's lives will be disrupted, in some cases severely, and there will be much human suffering for a generous people to alleviate. But in the long run, our prospects are much brighter. When the crisis at last subsides, we will emerge with a more just and humane society. We will have learned to care for each other as families and neighbors once did. We will no longer look superstitiously to one institution to devise solutions to the problems of 309 million people. Instead of seeking subsidies taken from our fellow Americans by threats of state violence, we will have to seek wealth peacefully, by discovering how we can best please our fellow man. The federal collapse will likewise yield us a far freer and more prosperous society, in place of the maze of subsidies, taxes, penalties, special privileges, and self-perpetuating bureaucracy that afflict us now.

Federal bankruptcy, in short, may turn out to be one of the best things that ever happened to America.

The Crisis

Since at least 2006, opinion makers have belligerently commanded our assent to certain claims about the health of the American economy. According to them, in that year everything was fine. The fundamentals of the economy, including the housing market, were sound. The stock market was booming. Dissenters were incorrigible "permabears" who refused to accept good news. In 2008, their tune changed. Unless unprecedented bouts of government intervention were approved, the world was about to descend into a black hole. Dissenters were laissez-faire ideologues who hadn't learned what the talking heads claimed were the lessons of the Great Depression. By early 2009, "green shoots" were popping up as prosperity began to return. There was a light at the end of the tunnel. Now dissenters were permabears who refused to accept good news, etc. And it continues.

The "green shoots" claim of early 2009 came from a *60 Minutes* interview with Ben Bernanke, chairman of the Federal Reserve System. Soon, that image was everywhere. Within months, a compliant media had taken a phrase no one had been using and made it central to discussions of the economy. A few hundred, then a few thousand articles featured it; in no time the phrase was generating millions of Internet hits.[2]

As 2010 went by, the "green shoots" grew more and more farcical. Employment figures, it turned out, had been artificially stimulated by job growth in health, education, and government itself, where state and federal money, rather than consumer demand and entrepreneurial risk-taking, was the driving force. Economist Nouriel Roubini laughed at the phantom "green shoots." The correct image for the economy, he said, was brown manure.[3] The light at the end of the tunnel was an oncoming train.

Whether the conventional wisdom has been right or wrong since 2006, it has studiously avoided mention of the Sword of Damocles hanging over these discussions. Even if modest economic recovery were to take hold in the United States, the federal government still faces a catastrophe whose proportions, in terms of the scope of the adjustments Americans will have to make in response to them, will exceed those of the recent financial crisis. In a moment of unusual candor, Bernanke himself drew attention to this coming crisis in a largely overlooked speech of October 4, 2010, saying in the understatement of the year that the federal budget was on an "unsustainable path."

Here's what he meant. Strictly speaking, the U.S. government's debt problem amounts to $14 trillion, the amount of the national debt (the sum of the accumulated deficits of the past). But although they do not technically involve the full faith and credit of the federal government, Social Security and Medicare—programs whose assistance millions of Americans have been taught to count on—are inadequately funded to meet the obligations of the future. To get the full picture of the obligations the U.S. government is facing, we have to add the amount of this entitlement shortfall to that $14 trillion.

Unfortunately, that extra amount is $111 trillion.[4]

The full future expense of these programs exceeds the total net worth of the U.S. economy.[5] That is what people usually mean when they say the United States is bankrupt.

In the early 2000s, well before the Obama deficits, commentators were warning that interest charges on the United States' debt would consume half the federal budget by the mid-2030s.[6] Today the Congressional Budget Office projects that by 2020 just the interest payments on the national debt will reach $925 billion per year. That is actually a rosy scenario, since it assumes a robust economy and stable interest rates. If the economic picture remains grim, or if interest rates should rise, that figure will grow much larger.[7]

But these deficits, staggering as they are, do not reflect the impending problem posed by the unfunded liabilities of Social Security and Medicare. Even if the federal budget were balanced and the deficit reduced from over $1 trillion to *zero*, when we factor in the unfunded liabilities problem, the U.S. government would still fall further into the hole by $2 trillion to $4 trillion a year.[8]

Of the $96.5 trillion in unfunded Medicare liabilities, $19.4 trillion was added by the "small government" George W. Bush administration's prescription drug benefit, known as Medicare Part D. The story of that bill's passage is the story of America in the twenty-first century. The White House did not want to risk the bill's passage by letting accurate estimates of its cost leak out. Richard Foster, Medicare's chief actuary, reported that its administrator, Bush appointee Thomas Scully, threatened him with his job if he revealed cost estimates to Congress—a claim that email correspondence from a Scully subordinate appeared to corroborate. The pharmaceutical industry was thrilled with the bill, which would yield perhaps an additional $100 billion in industry profits over the next eight years. Ten days after the bill's passage, Scully left to join a lobbying firm and represented several large pharmaceutical companies. The bill's principal author, Billy Tauzin, went on to head the drug companies' main lobbying organization, a position that paid $2.5 million per year.

In 2010, the Republican Party's "Pledge to America" promised to cut an unspecified $100 billion from the federal budget. The major budget busters were to be kept off the table entirely. America is staring default in the face, and the boldest proposal we hear is for trimming $100 billion. That's like taking three dollars off a trip to the moon.

Lawrence Kotlikoff is an economist at Boston University. He is a Democrat. His Establishment credentials are considerable. He estimates the fiscal gap at an astonishing $200 trillion. He thinks some relatively painless reforms can fix a $200 trillion problem, but he never tells us what they are. The truth is, there are no such reforms. If there were, they would have been implemented long ago. If there were, Kotlikoff would have disclosed them to us instead of hinting at their existence and never mentioning them again.

But listen to him. He is saying the sort of things people were once shouted down as alarmists for saying.

> We have 78 million baby boomers who, when fully retired, will collect benefits from Social Security, Medicare, and Medicaid that, on average, exceed per-capita GDP. The annual costs of these entitlements will total about $4 trillion in today's dollars. Yes, our economy will be bigger in 20 years, but not big enough to handle this size load year after year.
>
> This is what happens when you run a massive Ponzi scheme for six decades straight, taking ever larger resources from the young and

giving them to the old while promising the young their eventual turn at passing the generational buck.

It will all come to an end, he warns, "in a very nasty manner. The first possibility is massive benefit cuts visited on the baby boomers in retirement. The second is astronomical tax increases that leave the young with little incentive to work and save. And the third is the government simply printing vast quantities of money to cover its bills."[9]

More than likely, we'll see all three.[10]

Ronald Reagan's first White House budget director, David Stockman, noted in the summer of 2010 what had been happening for the past two years: nominal GDP had been rising at $4 billion per month, while federal debt had been increasing at $100 billion per month. That means the federal government has borrowed $25 for every dollar the GDP has increased. There's your big "stimulus." Never in American history have we seen the federal debt grow 25 times faster than the economy itself for two years running.[11]

Stockman also casts a skeptical eye on the prosperity of the past several decades. Since the last vestiges of the gold standard were abandoned in 1971, and with them the remaining restraints on how much money the Federal Reserve System (discussed in chapter 4) could create out of thin air, the economy has been taken for a ride that has looked like prosperity but has been more like a repeatedly stimulated sugar high. "It turns out," Stockman says, "that there was no miracle of economic growth, productivity and prosperity over the last several decades.…What we had, instead, was serial bubble after bubble—fueled by a tsunami of public and private debt and printing-press money."[12]

So it is an already rickety, debt-ridden economy that will have to face the coming fiscal crisis.

One of the key reasons for the looming collapse is the aging of the population, a phenomenon that is taking place across the developed world. It is the result of three major factors: (1) the unusually large "baby boom" generation that is currently proceeding through middle age; (2) falling fertility rates, which have resulted in fewer future taxpayers to make good on governments' extravagant promises; (3) medical advances that have increased human longevity, operating in tandem with rising prosperity that has made possible additional spending on health.[13] These impossible entitlement promises were built on the assumption that productivity would grow at unrealistic rates or that ever-larger hordes of new taxpayers would indefinitely continue to enter the world (rather as a chain letter depends on ever more people being added to the scheme all the time).

If current birth rates in America continue, by 2040 the number of people aged 80 and over will outnumber children under age 5. This has never happened before in history. In 1970 there were 3.7 million Americans aged 80 and over and 17.2 million under age 5. In 2040 those figures are expected to be 26.2 million and 25.0 million, respectively.[14] In 1940, people of college age in the United States outnumbered people 65 and over (9.6 million versus 9.0 million). By 2040, college-age Americans will have increased to 20.2 million. The number of senior citizens will have multiplied by over seven times, to 75.2 million.[15]

The retirement of the boomer generation in the United States is not simply a wrenching, one-time event, difficult as that would be. It presages a future in which the elder share of the population will continue to grow, until some unforeseen change compensates for it. The elder share will rise from 13 to 19 percent between 2010 and 2030, the years when the last of the boomers become seniors (age 65 and over). But by 2075, after the boomer generation has passed from the scene, the elder share will be an even higher 23 percent.[16]

Japan is feeling this demographic change the earliest and the most intensely. Life expectancy has reached 80 in Japan, and the average Japanese woman who reaches age 65 will live until 85. Extreme age is far more common than ever before. (One 100-year-old Japanese woman, ticketed for riding a motorcycle without a helmet, explained that her 79-year-old son, who was driving, was wearing her helmet.) Japan's cultural advantage in this situation—namely, a longstanding tradition whereby the extended family cares for its members—will help see it through the country's aging crisis, but the strain on public budgets and private households will nevertheless be great.[17]

Even as the elderly population is growing, the younger population is shrinking throughout most of the Western world, and barely holding steady in the United States. Birth rates have undergone a sharp and (at least to those issuing dire warnings of overpopulation) unexpected decline throughout the West since the 1970s. Replacement level, the figure a society needs to reach in order to maintain its population without immigration, is 2.1. The U.S. fertility rate is currently 2.0.

It will not be long before these demographic changes put serious strains on entitlement programs and change people's lives in drastic ways that they do not today anticipate. In 1960, there were 5.1 taxpaying workers funding each retiree. By 2030, that figure will fall to 2.2, which means every single working couple will need to support a retiree.[18]

Moreover, people over 65, but especially over 85, tend to incur disproportionately high medical bills, which an ever-shrinking base of current workers will somehow have to shoulder. Total per capita health spending for the "old-old" (85 and older) is three times higher than for the "young-old" (65 to 84).[19] Older Americans consume about four times as much in medical services as younger Americans, and seven times as much as children.[20]

Ah, say optimists, but various government programs, including the Obama health plan, will help to bring down health costs. (Such costs would have to come down quite a bit indeed in order to make possible all the additional health services demanded by a rapidly aging population.) Rarely do we hear specifics regarding these alleged cost reductions or how they will come about in the absence of some form of rationing of services, as will indeed begin happening more and more around the world. Additionally, as we'll see in chapter 2, the alleged savings from the Obama plan are an illusion. But let us suppose that these mysterious cost cuts will in fact occur. That still doesn't solve the problem, since for whatever reason Medicare's trustees *have already factored cost reductions into existing projections*. According to businessman and former U.S. Secretary of Commerce Pete Peterson:

> The official projections *already* build in a dramatic cost slowdown. The trustees assume that the growth in real per capita Medicare spending will decelerate from its historical rate of 5 percent per year to just 2 percent per year by the 2020s. The trustees fail to point to any change in medical technology, or health status, or social expectations that might account for the slowdown. The only justification they offer is that if Medicare spending did not slow down by then, it would rapidly take over our entire economy. Let us all take a collective gulp: *The unsustainable official cost projections already assume tough, perhaps even draconian cost-control measures that today we do not even contemplate.*[21]

Intensifying the problem is that while back in 1950 (when the demographics of Social Security were more sustainable than they are today) the average age at which people began collecting Social Security retirement benefits was 69; today it is 63. And while three out of five American men in their late sixties were still working, the figure today is only one in five.[22]

The aging of the rest of the world poses an additional difficulty for a U.S. government whose budget is increasingly financed by credit from foreign sources. Even in the unlikely event that the Treasury's credit rating remains perfectly strong over the long term, the challenges associated with global aging guarantee that those foreign sources are going to dry up. Savings will be needed at home, and will no longer be available to buy up Treasury securities. China, in addition to wanting to finance its own industrial expansion, likewise faces an aging problem. That means much less lending to the United States.[23]

Taxing our way out of this problem, as left-liberals might be inclined to propose, can't be done even if it were desirable. It would require raising payroll taxes by as much as 350 percent by 2040.[24] The Congressional Budget Office calculated that for the federal government to balance its budget while continuing on the same trajectory of expenditures, marginal income tax rates would need to skyrocket. The lowest marginal rate of 10 percent would have to rise to 26 percent. The 25 percent marginal rate would have to be increased to 66 percent. And the top rate of 35 percent would need to be raised all the way to 92 percent.[25] This presumes that tax rates at these levels would have no negative effects on economic activity, a rather heroic assumption.

Since the 1970s, mortgage payments, health insurance, and car payments have all increased in absolute terms. But not nearly as fast as taxes. Todd Zywicki, a law professor and bankruptcy expert, finds that "the increase in tax obligations is over three times as large as the increase in the mortgage payments and almost double the increase in the mortgage and automobile payments combined. Even the new expenditure on child care [as more and more households have seen both parents enter the workforce full time] is about a quarter less than the increase in taxes." He finds the tax bill for the typical middle-class family to have increased by 140 percent over the past generation. The fall in the real value of standard exemptions, combined with rising payroll, property, and state income and sales taxes, has put more and more pressure on average households.[26]

Leaving aside the moral objection to tax increases, raising taxes won't in fact solve the problem. For one thing, our public servants always seem to find something new on which to spend the additional money, and it isn't deficit reduction. But more to the point, tax policy can go only so far, given the natural brick wall it has run into for the past fifty years. Economist Jeffrey Rogers Hummel points out that federal tax revenue "has bumped up against 20 percent of GDP for well over half a century. That is quite an astonishing statistic when you think about all the changes in the tax code over the intervening years. Tax rates go up, tax rates go down, and the total bite out of the economy remains relatively constant. This suggests that 20 percent is some kind of structural-political limit for federal taxes in the United States."[27]

The public has been lulled to sleep about these problems in part because such topics are generally excluded from political discussion, and in part because people have been led to believe that their Social Security money is waiting for them in a "trust fund" in Washington. Only a small sliver of the public realizes the alleged trust fund is a fiction. The "trust fund" mythology actually exacerbates the problem, since it leads the public to believe the need to save is not really so urgent, since adequate savings for their future are already being accumulated in trust funds.

The money that the federal government takes in from payroll taxes earmarked for the Social Security program is not actually saved in a "trust fund." The federal government takes this money and hands it to current retirees. Current retirees, in other words, are not being paid back the money they themselves put in, plus interest from all the wise investments the government made with it. The government has already blown the money that current retirees put into the system all those years ago. The money they receive comes from workers today, who will in turn—according to the logic of the program, at least—be taken care of by a future generation of workers.

Now if the federal government takes in more in Social Security taxes than it pays out in benefits, it of course enjoys a surplus. Surely at least this surplus of receipts over outlays goes into a trust fund, right? Not exactly. The government takes this surplus and spends it on current expenditures. But don't worry— it drops an equivalent amount of IOUs into what it laughingly calls the "trust fund." We are then told everything is fine—why, the trust fund is full of government bonds it can cash in one day!

There's just one problem. When the Social Security "trust fund" begins cashing in these IOUs, where does the government get the money to honor them? By taxing the public. So it's rather misleading to say that the trust fund is just full of resources for when the time comes to start drawing it down. What it's full of are promises to tax the American public. But the public has already been taxed to pay for Social Security. The IOUs mean it has to be taxed again for the same thing. And this is how supporters of the program actually try to claim it's working just fine, and that anyone who points out the problems is a wicked plutocrat who doesn't care about the poor and suffering.

The political class avoids the truth about the trust fund like the plague. When Pete Peterson asked then-President Bill Clinton if he really thought a trust fund existed that could see Social Security through to 2037, the president replied, "You and I know that this is a pure cash-in, cash-out program and that it will be draining revenue from the Treasury decades before the formal bankruptcy date." But shortly thereafter, Peterson saw the President on CNN pointing to a chart purporting to show that the "trust funds" would "totally safeguard" Social Security until 2037.[28]

Even if Social Security can be saved yet again by another partial default—in the form of higher "premiums," lower benefits, and an older retirement age, program modifications a private insurer would be imprisoned for—it is Medicare that will sink the system. As we've seen, that is where the lion's share of the unfunded liabilities is coming from. The numbers do not add up. Or, put another way, they do add up—to default.

These are not the speculations of an incorrigible doomsayer. This scenario is going to occur. It does not rely on fanciful models or wild extrapolation. The people who will become elderly in the first half of the twenty-first century have been born and are progressing toward old age. But we are supposed to pretend this is not happening.

One participant in a federal commission appointed in 1994 to look into the entitlement problem later spoke of the obstacles to serious public discussion of the issue. The commission prepared a report detailing the cost projections for federal entitlement programs. The report warned that by 2030 the entire federal budget would be consumed by Social Security, Medicaid, Medicare, and federal civilian and military pensions. There would not be a dime available for any of the other areas of the federal budget, including education, child health, and the military. Before it even reached the stage at which reforms were proposed, the commissioners had received 350,000 preformatted "outraged" postcards from seniors. No matter how utterly impossible it is to maintain benefit levels where they are, and no matter how unjust the arrangement is to the younger population, the issue cannot even be discussed.[29] The commission's report fell into a black hole.[30]

The elderly are in fact by far the wealthiest segment of the population. Three-quarters of elderly homeowners have paid off their mortgages. Their median net worth is much higher than that of any other group. Their poverty rate is barely over 10 percent. The younger generation, which is expected to work to exhaustion to keep these programs afloat (only to watch them collapse anyway), isn't so lucky. A poll in May 2010 found an incredible 85 percent of college seniors saying they planned to move back in with their parents after graduating. Then they'll figure out how to cope with the $23,000 in debt with which the average college graduate begins his productive life.[31]

Their outlook continues to be grim. In late 2010, *60 Minutes* reported:

> The economic jam we're in has topped even the great depression in one respect. Never have we had a recession this deep with a recovery this flat. Unemployment has been at 9.5% or above for fourteen months. Congress did something that it's never done before. It extended unemployment benefits for 99 weeks. That cost more than $100 billion, a huge expense for a government in debt. But now, for many Americans, 99 weeks have passed and there is still no job in sight.[32]

Many of the states are going bust as well. California's budget shortfall has been legendary, but it's far from alone. In March 2010, it was reported that the Missouri state budget unveiled by Governor Jay Nixon may have overestimated revenues by as much as $1 billion. According to State Senator Kurt Schaefer, vice chairman of the Appropriations Committee, "This is a crisis in the state budget that we have never, ever seen before in the state of Missouri....We are way beyond cutting a few hundred thousand here, a few hundred thousand there. This is a whole-scale restructuring that's going to have to occur."[33] In Washington state, lawmakers were confronted with a $2.8 billion shortfall, and public unions that refused to budge on pay or benefits.[34] In Indiana, month after month for nearly two years revenues fell short of projections, leaving the state $869 million below its initial expectation.[35]

In New York, the *New York Times* found in May 2010 that 3,700 retired public workers were receiving six-figure pension payouts (which are tax exempt) every year. (The state has tried to obscure the huge pension payouts by averaging them in with those of people who worked in government part time or for only a few years.) The pension system is becoming an enormous strain on New York's budget. So in 2010 the governor supported a plan that would bail out the pension fund by borrowing from…the pension fund.[36]

Seven states—Connecticut, Hawaii, Indiana, Louisiana, New Jersey, and Oklahoma—will see their pension systems fail by 2020, with another thirteen by 2025. (Federal pensions are themselves underfunded by about $1 trillion.) That is assuming the pension funds earn an annual return of 8 percent. If they do not, the bust will come all the sooner. None of this, it goes without saying, has stopped these states from continuing to expand their payrolls.[37]

Dozens of cities are contemplating bankruptcy. Miami came close. Its pension expenditures ballooned from $16 million in 2000 to $70 million in 2009. Meanwhile, with the average salary of a Miami city resident at $29,000, the average Miami city employee salary was $76,000.[38] The city government avoided bankruptcy through a series of salary and pension cuts, and increased health-insurance deductibles, for city employees. But next year the budget shortfall is projected to be even larger than it was this year, which means drastic measures remain on the table.[39]

"The Worst-Run Big City in the U.S.," a story that ran in *SF Weekly* in late 2009, tells the almost unbelievable story of San Francisco, a city in which "despite its spending more money per capita on homelessness than any comparable city, its homeless problem is worse than any comparable city's. Despite its spending more money per capita, period, than almost any city in the nation, San Francisco has poorly managed, budget-busting capital projects, overlapping social programs no one is sure are working, and a transportation system where the only thing running ahead of schedule is the size of its deficit."[40]

Detroit is in a class by itself. Here was the very model of subsidies, welfare programs, and regulation. And all of a sudden, it simply collapsed. Half the population has fled since 1950. One-quarter of the city's schools are closing.

The money is gone. The city's budget deficit is approaching half a billion dollars. But home prices tell the real story. Median sales prices of homes in Detroit went from $41,000 in 1994 to $98,000 in 2003. By early 2009 the median price was $13,600. That was bottom, right? Wrong. By March 2010 it was at $7,000.[41] In relation to the scale of the collapse, the story of Detroit went completely unreported.

But guess who's doing well? The tax-eaters.

At a time when private-sector workers have seen jobs slashed and salaries frozen or cut, government employees never had it better. Washington, D.C., has seen demand for new homes rise faster than in any other major American city, and its median household income of $85,824 (as of 2008) is the highest of the country's twenty-five largest metropolitan areas.[42] "Federal workers are enjoying an extraordinary boom time—in pay and hiring—during a recession that has cost 7.3 million jobs in the private sector," wrote *USA Today* in December 2009. The average federal worker's salary at the time of *USA Today*'s report was $71,206, while private-sector employees were earning an average of $40,331. The number of six-figure federal salaries jumped from 14 percent to 19 percent in the first year and a half of the recession. Nearly 1,700 employees of the Department of Transportation were earning more than $170,000 by that time. At the beginning of the recession, by contrast, exactly one person in the Department of Transportation earned such a salary.[43]

They'd better enjoy it while they can. When Americans find themselves faced with a choice between unplugging Granny and cutting federal salaries, jobs, and departments, Granny will be safe. Our so-called public servants won't be.

CHAPTER 2

Barack Obama and "Change We Can Believe In"

T he looming fiscal crisis didn't originate with Barack Obama, but he sure hasn't helped. The nearly $900 billion "economic stimulus" package passed during his first weeks in office raised an outcry, to be sure, but nothing the president has introduced so far has attracted as much ire and opposition as the health plan that critics refer to derisively as Obamacare. We'll start there.

The assorted perversities of American health care are represented by Obamacare supporters as a failure of the market economy to supply these essential goods and services rationally and affordably. In particular, they point to the fact that the United States spends far more on medical care per capita than does any other country. Cost growth continues to far outpace inflation. The problem with this argument is that the American system of health-care provision is not actually a free-market one at all. The federal government accounts for nearly 50 percent of all American health-care expenditures. Various government regulations, in turn, have interfered with the system and contributed to increasing demand for medical services while decreasing their supply. The shift to third-party payers (insurance companies) has made Americans largely insensitive to price, thereby pushing prices ever higher. A staggering regulatory apparatus, as well as significant barriers to entry into the medical field, keeps supply down and cost up.

We can begin by clearing away a common objection. Critics of the American health-care system say that, for all its high costs, it can't even deliver the same life expectancy or infant mortality rates of countries that spend less on health, and that these failings prove the free market has not worked. This criticism is untrue, even if we overlook the false claim that the United States has a free-market health-care system. Homicides and car accidents, which are higher in the United States than in most Western countries, are not the fault of the health-care system. In fact, Americans who don't die in homicides or car accidents have a longer life expectancy than people in any other Western country.[1] As for infant mortality, the United States counts every baby who shows any signs of life as having been born alive. Other countries are not so generous—in France and Belgium, for example, a baby born at less than twenty-six weeks is registered as dead. In Switzerland, a baby has to be at least thirty centimeters long to be classified as living.[2] In this way, babies with an unusually high chance of death are simply removed from the statistics entirely, which makes countries that manipulate their statistics this way appear to be doing better in terms of infant mortality than the United States.

How We Got Here

In the early twentieth century, health insurance was hardly used. The treatments available to patients were at times limited or even nonexistent, so the market for insurance was largely undeveloped. Some people did acquire sickness insurance, but that was an income maintenance program during times of illness, not a program aimed at providing for one's medical costs. Programs comparable to modern health insurance policies gained some steam during the 1930s, but really began to pick up in the next two decades, when government policies made them artificially attractive.

Once the United States entered World War II, businesses on the home front found it difficult to attract the labor they needed because the draft had taken 11 million Americans out of the workforce, and the federal government had imposed wage and price controls. Those controls made it illegal for businesses to attract additional labor by offering higher wages. Businesses found a way around this restriction in the form of employer-supplied medical insurance. The wage-control authorities did not consider this benefit to be a wage increase, and thus it was not subject to taxation like regular wages. This is the origin of what became the tax exemption for employer-provided medical care.

After the war ended, labor unions began to make employer-financed medical insurance part of their contract demands. Nonunion employers likewise felt compelled to provide it, in the hope that they could thereby avoid the unionization of their workplaces.[3] Here again we see the role of non-market forces in bringing about the present reliance on employer-supplied medical insurance: the special legal privileges labor unions enjoy, and the lengths to which employers are willing to go in trying to preserve a free labor market in their corner of the economy, derive from statutory interventions into the free market and are not part of the market itself.[4]

That establishment of health care as a company-offered benefit seems innocuous enough. But as a result, medical care gradually became an expense Americans paid for only minimally out of pocket. People became accustomed to having most costs covered by a third party, so slowly but surely they came to disregard price altogether when evaluating medical products and services. If employers are paying health costs (beyond the employee's deductible) for their employees through an insurance company, those employees will be less mindful of cost than if they bore it themselves. Likewise, suppliers of health care have an incentive to offer high-cost treatments with marginal benefits because someone else is picking up the bill. The predictable result, since neither suppliers nor consumers have an incentive to keep costs down, has been ongoing price increases. Naturally businesses tend to push back when their costs rise, but for privacy reasons they find it more difficult to pry into the merits of a particular medical procedure performed on an employee than, say, to uncover why that employee purchased a first-class plane ticket on the company credit card.[5]

Vijay Boyapati, a former Google engineer, tells a story that could be multiplied millions of times over, regarding the effects on price when perverse incentives, and then normal ones, are in place. He wanted to have a small epidermoid cyst removed from his back. This is what happened:

The first practice I visited was a dermatologist's office, which deals primarily with insured customers and can afford to charge exorbitant rates. I explained to the assistant on my first consulting visit that I didn't have health insurance—I choose not to—and asked how much the procedure would cost if I paid cash. She quoted me $700 for a riskless procedure that takes about 15 to 20 minutes to perform, and would not in this instance be performed by the dermatologist, but by the assistant herself....The fact that there are very basic procedures that cost the equivalent of $2,100 an hour is a glaring sign that the market's normal price mechanism has been broken.

On the recommendation of a friend, I decided to visit another medical practice, Country Doctor, which deals mostly with lower-income patients who do not have health insurance. Because its customers pay out of pocket, Country Doctor has a much stronger incentive to charge prices that its customers are willing to pay up front. When I had the procedure to remove the cyst done at Country Doctor, it was performed by an actual doctor, and it cost less than $50.[6]

Medicare and Medicaid, created in 1965, are also examples of third-party payment. Medicaid, the means-tested program for the poor, and Medicare, a program to provide for the medical needs of American seniors regardless of income, artificially stimulated demand for medical services on the part of consumers who were not themselves bearing the cost. In 1960, government covered 21 percent of total medical expenditures, with consumers bearing 55 percent. In 2000, government covered 43 percent and consumers only 17 percent.[7] Naturally, costs rose dramatically under these conditions.

The federal government tried to push some of the costs it was bearing onto others. Doctors and hospitals, receiving only partial reimbursement from Medicare and Medicaid, began to compensate for their losses by charging private insurers more. Private insurance costs, in turn, began to skyrocket, a phenomenon that subsequently gave rise to so-called "managed care," the bureaucratic mess that everyone dislikes for its efforts to drive down costs by denying certain kinds of care.[8]

Why Higher Costs?

While some forms of government intervention, such as the ones we have examined thus far, produce an artificial stimulus to demand, others lead to higher medical costs as a result of artificial restrictions on supply. The American Medical Association, for example, restricts the number of medical candidates by means of its accreditation process for medical schools, with its decisions ratified by state governments. Nineteen states are limited to having *a single medical school*. We're supposed to believe this restrictive policy was developed with only the public good in mind?

The supply of medical services is also kept down by "certificate-of-need" (CON) regulation. Such regulation allows existing hospitals themselves to decide whether a "need" exists for additional hospitals in a particular area. Were such a privilege granted to existing firms in any other industry, its anti-competitive nature would be evident. Not surprisingly, CON regulation, which has also been used to block competition in related health professions like home health care and nursing, has been found to increase medical costs.

Additional restrictions on market competition contribute still further to rising costs. For example, Americans are prohibited from purchasing medical insurance originating in states other than their own. Mandates that states impose on insurance companies put upward pressure on policy prices. Each of these mandates requires that insurance companies in a particular state provide coverage for a particular disorder or kind of treatment. Each mandate results in higher premiums and less consumer choice. People have no way to choose policies that suit them and must instead "insure" against the need for hair implants or massage therapy—two examples of state mandates—whether they want to or not. As of 2009, Rhode Island led the nation in mandates with 70. Idaho, with 13, had the fewest. That year there were a total of 2,133 mandates across the states, up from just 252 in 1979. These mandates make it difficult for people to find low-cost, high-deductible policies that can insure them against medical catastrophes. That's one of the reasons so many people have chosen to forego insurance coverage in the first place. A young person finds it silly to spend $300 per month on medical services he won't need or use, just so he can save 80 percent on routine doctor visits.[9]

The Obama plan establishes state-based exchanges where small businesses and uninsured individuals can purchase insurance. Not one of the plans offered at these exchanges provides only catastrophic coverage, the sensible option that would be available to consumers on the free market. Instead, they all cover even routine health expenses, thereby causing individuals to be as heedless of cost as ever, and continuing the perversion of the concept of "insurance" whereby people are to be "insured" against events like checkups that are certain to occur. High-deductible, catastrophic plans are also penalized by the establishment of deductible caps and the prohibition of co-payments for preventative care, which will make such policies more expensive. Meanwhile, research finds that high-deductible, catastrophic plans put strong downward pressure on health-care costs, lead consumers to be much more cost conscious, and still deliver the same amount of necessary care that people who hold more standard insurance policies receive.[10]

Given the ongoing rise in medical costs and the countless stories of personal hardship to which those costs have given rise, critics of the present system have claimed that additional government involvement is necessary. But if earlier government interventions have tended to push prices up, additional interventions in the same direction are likely to intensify the problem. The Austrian economist Ludwig von Mises once described how government intervention tends to feed on itself: the first intervention causes problems that still further interventions are enacted to resolve, and so on, until the economy becomes a maze of regulation and control. Never considered is the mere repeal of the initial interventions.

The most obvious problem with the recently enacted health-care legislation is the incentive structure it creates for the uninsured, and indeed even for many of the presently insured. Individuals are subject to financial penalties for not purchasing health insurance policies that meet government standards. But the penalties are far lower than the cost of purchasing such policies. That means it is less expensive for people to remain (or become) uninsured and simply pay the corresponding penalty. They can get away with doing so because under the new law, insurers are required to (1) enroll everyone who applies ("guaranteed issue"), (2) cover pre-existing conditions, and (3) adopt a policy known as "community rating," in which they must charge the same premium to all, with minor exceptions for geographical area, age, and whether the plan covers an individual or a family. (And insurance companies are regulated in how large the differential can be between, say, very young and very old customers; the elderly, whose medical bills are far higher and of greater quantity than those of the young, may be charged a premium only twice as high.) It therefore makes sense for people not to purchase health insurance, wait until they become ill, and then purchase an insurance plan—their current illness being a "pre-existing condition" that insurance companies would be required to cover.

This is a suicidal business model—or perhaps homicidal, since the insurance companies did not elect to impose it on themselves. No insurance company can survive without being allowed to pool risks appropriately and charge premiums based on relevant actuarial estimates. Profit-seeking insurance cannot operate according to a business model designed for a social-welfare agency funded by taxation. Requiring insurance companies to cover "pre-existing conditions," moreover, is like demanding that homeowners be able to take out fire insurance on a burning building. Cynics suspect that advocates of this plan understand perfectly well the impossible burden it will place on insurance companies (the bogeymen we are supposed to hate, who are in fact earning a mere 2.2 cents on the dollar in profit), and must be intelligent enough to foresee the coming collapse—and, as night follows day, nationalization—of the insurance industry.

In 2006, Massachusetts instituted an individual mandate along with guaranteed issue and community rating. The result was major losses among insurers, which led to lower payments to hospitals and large group practices. Insurers and hospitals found themselves on the verge of going out of business. Residents, meanwhile, faced an ongoing rise in premiums. State Treasurer Timothy Cahill said the program had been a "fiscal train wreck," costing more than $4 billion—over 11 times the initial projection.[11]

Now the whole country gets to try out this approach.

On top of this, insurance companies will not be allowed to impose lifetime limits on coverage—e.g., $2 million or $6 million, as in many popular plans. The insured must be allowed to consume as much as they need, forever. Insurance companies will also be forced to cover the children of the insured until age twenty-six. Some "children"! All of this means higher premiums, naturally, and less consumer choice. By October 2010 some health insurance premium rates in Connecticut had already risen 47 percent in response to the new law, and Well-Point, the country's largest insurer, found the average premium for a 25-year-old man likely to rise by 155 percent in Richmond, Virginia, and by 300 percent in Louisville, Kentucky.[12] But that hardly seems the point, which is how juvenile all these provisions are: why, if we want a particular outcome, let's have our congressman demand it! Resources are unlimited! Demand your share!

Meanwhile, the Obama plan will add another 18 million people to Medicaid, a jointly run federal-state medical care program for those with low incomes. In other words, states drowning in red ink are about to be thrown an anchor.

Other anchors are being thrown to taxpayers and businesses. The so-called "rich"—who have no rights and exist only to be plundered—will find their Medicare taxes jump by 60 percent, and will be hit with a new tax on "unearned income," based on the Marxist view that income not derived from physical labor is not really "earned." Health insurance companies and pharmaceutical manufacturers will also be hit with higher taxes, and a new tax on medical devices will be imposed. "Cadillac" health-care plans, which offer consumers more than the federal government thinks they ought to have, will be subject to a new 40 percent tax. And the annual tax deduction for medical expenses—a deduction half of whose beneficiaries earn under $50,000 per year—is being reduced.[13]

In 2014, firms with fifty or more employees will be fined if they do not offer workers a health insurance plan that meets with the federal government's approval. (Smaller firms are exempted, but skeptics say the exemptions will be short lived: the federal government, facing rising costs and revenue shortfalls, could very well lower the threshold to twenty-five or even ten employees.) As *Barron's* puts it, if you want to expand your business under these conditions, you might follow one of these strategies: "a) asking your full-timers, at say 35 hours, to work 40 or 45; b) firing a few workers and outsourcing their services to another firm; c) hiring more workers off the books; d) not expanding at all."[14]

What about all the "savings" the program is supposed to yield us? The alleged savings are the product of accounting tricks. They result from the fact that the program begins taxing people in 2011 but doesn't begin paying out benefits until 2014. If we start our measurement of costs in 2014, we find the program's alleged savings are nowhere to be found, and that in fact—although estimates range from several hundred billion to several trillion—it promises to be enormously expensive over the following ten years.[15]

The Obama plan also suffers from critical omissions. It does nothing to reduce the regulatory burden that reduces both the supply and the efficiency of health-care services. It does not promote competition between states. It does nothing at all to reduce costs. It does not address the cost implications of low deductibles and co-payments and of excessive reliance on third-party payment in general. If anything, it accentuates this reliance by imposing penalties on employers who do not provide health coverage to their employees. It is precisely the employer provision of health care and its tax deductibility that has encouraged the system of third-party payment. It seems significant that in Switzerland, whose health-care system is so often praised, the percentage of medical costs that people bear out of pocket is two and a half times as great as it is in the United States. And in the United States, those sectors of the industry whose services are not typically covered under standard insurance plans—including LASIK surgery and most plastic surgery—have seen costs come down, even as technological innovation has increased.[16] With consumers bearing the costs of these services themselves, they have been much more conscious of price differentials, thereby forcing providers to become competitive on price.

Medicare, meanwhile, which is supposed to provide medical care for the elderly, is itself in serious need of reform, underfunded to the tune of tens of trillions of dollars. And yet with the program's unsustainable trajectory becoming clearer every year, a Republican Congress under President George W. Bush pushed through so-called Medicare Part D, which established a prescription drug benefit for seniors that added tens of trillions more to the total. Most Americans, seeing such a program proposed, can be forgiven for assuming it must have been addressing a pervasive problem, since why else would the federal government get involved? In fact, a 2002 government survey of seniors found 86.4 percent saying that getting the prescription drug they needed over the past six months had been "not a problem," 9.4 percent "a small problem," and a mere 4.2 percent "a big problem." Three-quarters of American seniors already had prescription drug coverage through various private and other outlets.[17]

We now know that the estimated cost of the program was deliberately understated; the program, moreover, was structured in such a way that future expansions of coverage were inevitable. But even in the absence of any modification, Pete Peterson warns that "by the year 2030, incredibly, the federal government will be spending as much on prescription drugs for Medicare enrollees (as a share of GDP) as everything it now spends on nonhealth benefits for needy working-age Americans—including means-tested cash welfare, food stamps, unemployment compensation, child nutrition, foster care, and the refundable portions of the earned income tax credit and child tax credit."[18] It has been estimated that nearly $20 trillion of the staggering unfunded liabilities facing the U.S. government is attributable to Medicare Part D.

What did people do before these programs existed? Historian David Beito has documented the previously neglected role of fraternal organizations in providing discounted health care to their members. Such organizations were able to secure group discounts from physicians, which meant their members were able to enjoy affordable medical care. One of the reasons for the decline in and eventual disappearance of the fraternal associations' role in providing medical care and other services that we associate with the modern welfare state is the growth of the welfare state itself. As Beito argues, when the state begins providing services and performing functions that had previously belonged to the care of civil society, it crowds out these private institutions, which tend to atrophy in proportion to the growth of the state.[19]

The year prior to the establishment of Medicaid, poor families had higher hospital admission rates than did those in wealthier brackets. And while higher-income individuals had an average of 5.1 doctor visits a year, low-income individuals had 4.3—hardly a dramatic difference. What Medicaid did result in was a dramatic decline in the reduced-cost or pro bono services that doctors had once provided the poor as a matter of routine. According to historian Allan Matusow, "Most of the government's medical payments on behalf of the poor compensated doctors and hospitals for services once rendered free of charge or at reduced prices....Medicare-Medicaid, then, primarily transferred income from middle-class taxpayers to middle-class health-care professionals."[20]

Author Jacob Hornberger recalls growing up in Laredo, Texas, in the 1950s, at a time when the Census Bureau had labeled that city the poorest in the country on a per-capita income basis. Yet according to Hornberger, "I never knew of one single doctor who turned people away. They treated everyone who came into their office. I never heard of a doctor complaining about having to provide free services to the poor."[21]

And how were doctors doing in those days?

"They were among the wealthiest people in town," Hornberger says. "The money they made from the middle class and the wealthy and the poor who could pay subsidized the patients who couldn't pay." Those who received free care were grateful to receive it, and typically brought the doctor in-kind gifts.

When government got involved, an impossible regulatory thicket invaded and complicated medicine to the point that physicians began retiring early, having come to despise a profession they had once loved. Meanwhile, among patients a sense of entitlement began to supplant the normal human instinct of gratitude. What had once been a harmonious and mutually satisfying relationship became frustrating for everyone.

The very fact that people today, so long accustomed to government-provided medical care, would actually wonder what would happen to the poor under a system without government coercion shows, as Hornberger says, "what America's welfare state has done to people's faith in themselves, in others, and in a free society."

To be sure, there *are* measures that can be taken to rein in health-care costs. Employers should be free to offer their workers a choice between continuing to receive employer-provided medical insurance or instead receiving the tax-free cash equivalent of the present average cost of such insurance (say, $10,000 to $15,000, indexed for inflation). This change would make clear to employees that the money an employer pays for their medical insurance comes out of their own pockets in the form of lower salaries. (Right now, most workers doubtless consider their fringe benefits to be "free.") If the employee chooses the tax-free income, he would then have a much greater incentive to carry only a high-deductible policy. That is, since he can pocket any money he doesn't spend on his policy, he has an incentive to keep that policy inexpensive. High-deductible policies, in turn, make people more cost conscious, since more of their medical expenses come out of their own pockets. And under this arrangement, the typical worker would save more than enough to pay the full deductible on whatever insurance policy he may choose to purchase (should he even need that much medical attention in a year), with money to spare.[22]

If a free market in medical care is not politically feasible as a policy option for the whole country, economist Fred Foldvary of Santa Clara University proposes that individuals be allowed to choose it for themselves. He calls it the Complete Private Medical Option (CPMO). People opting for it would forfeit all forms of government medical assistance, but they would also enjoy exemption from all forms of government medical restriction. Foldvary makes an exception for emergency services, but says that anyone choosing his plan would be ineligible for any other government medical benefit. On the other hand, they would pay no taxes for medical services, including the Medicare portion of payroll taxes and the sales taxes on medical products. They would be exempt from licensing laws and drug restrictions, such that they could purchase medical services from anyone they wished according to their own good judgment, and obtain any drug, dietary supplement, or medical service. They could purchase any kind of medical plan from any willing provider anywhere. That, excepting a few technical details, is Foldvary's plan, which he contends would establish a free market in medicine alongside the government-controlled alternative.

What else can be done? Upon reaching age sixty-five, Americans should be given the option of giving up federal entitlement benefits in exchange for complete exemption from income tax for the rest of their productive lives. Likewise, such individuals should be exempt from taxation of any interest and dividend income that accrues from money they save from their tax-exempt income, and anything they hand on to their heirs from that income should likewise be exempt from estate and gift taxes. The incentives thus created would doubtless make a substantial dent in the Medicare and Social Security crises by dramatically lowering the number of people demanding payments from those programs.[23]

Medical licensure is unlikely to be going anywhere, so deeply entrenched is the public-good justification for this barrier to entry. Short of removing that requirement, some measures might be taken that would painlessly increase the supply of physician services and thereby reduce costs. Every physician might be granted the right to select, say, six individuals whom he might train and supervise, and who would serve as "associate physicians." Thus the physician could extend the benefits of his own license to six individuals of his choosing. Those individuals might be drawn from a pool of candidates consisting of people who have attained some degree of distinction within the medical field. The physician could delegate to them whatever tasks his good judgment and their qualifications justified.[24] Such a liberalization of licensing requirements would mean, in practice, that someone with strep throat, if his pharmacist were an associate physician, could be examined and granted a prescription on the spot, rather than having to make an expensive office visit. A registered nurse or paramedic might set a broken limb and put it in a cast. Obviously, the efficiency and cost gains would be significant. According to some estimates, nurses could provide as much as 80 percent of the medical care that primary physicians currently deliver, and at only 40 percent of the cost.[25]

There seem to be two major perils of health-care reform. One is intensifying the very factors contributing to the increase in medical costs, which is precisely what the Obama plan does. The other is implementing piecemeal reforms in the right direction at a time when nothing short of radical surgery will do. The Medicare crisis, to say nothing of the health-care crisis as a whole, is much too severe to be dealt with by anything short of a complete revolution in our expectations and philosophy of government. It is not an ideological statement, but a practical one, to conclude that the system can be fixed only if we return to individuals, families, doctors, and communities full control over decisions pertaining to their own health and well-being.

Americans hear a great deal about the alleged superiority of "national health care" programs around the world. Critics of those systems, in turn, rightly point to shortages, waiting lists, and declines in medical innovation in countries where government has taken over the health-care sector. In Canada, for example, the average wait in 2009 between a referral and actual treatment by a specialist was more than sixteen weeks, a 73 percent increase from 1993. That year 649,161 people sat on waiting lists for surgery and medically necessary treatments. Since the government took over health care in 1970, Canada has fallen from fourth to twenty-sixth out of thirty countries in number of doctors per thousand people. In 2009 the president of the Canadian Medical Association described the country's health-care system as "sick" and "imploding."[26] In Sweden, where nationalized health care has caused a similar shortage of physicians, Swedish policy analyst Johnny Munkhammar notes that in desperation, some Swedes resort to visiting veterinarians—because "veterinarians are private and there are many."[27] In Britain, the National Health Service announced in mid-2010 that it was preparing to cut millions of surgical procedures in order to save money over the ensuing four years.[28] Existing facilities are notoriously dilapidated. When news anchor David Asman admitted his wife to a London hospital after her stroke, he was shocked at the condition of the equipment. "On occasion," he recalls, "my wife and I would giggle at heart and blood-pressure monitors that were literally taped together and would come apart as they were being moved into place. The nurses and hospital technicians had become expert at jerry-rigging temporary fixes for a lot of the damaged equipment. I pitched in as best as I could with simple things, like fixing the wiring for the one TV in the ward. And I'd make frequent trips to the local pharmacies to buy tissues and cleaning wipes, which were always in short supply."[29]

But these criticisms, serious though they are, are almost beside the point: the government health systems in question—as finance ministers will privately concede—are about to be swamped by the aging of Western populations. The "progressives" who say the problem with the Obama plan is that it doesn't go far enough in extending government control over health care couldn't be more wrong. At a time when governments need to be scaling back their promises in the face of reality, they are maintaining or increasing them. In the demographic tidal wave that is about to hit much of the developed world, these systems will be completely swept away.

So will Obamacare.

For the Economy, Red Bull Is No Substitute for Sleep

Shortly after taking office, President Obama urged the Congress to approve a "stimulus" package amounting to $787 billion—a price tag that later rose to $862 billion—in order to (he said) restore the economy to health. In his first news conference as president, Obama warned that a failure to pass this bill "could turn a crisis into a catastrophe." "I can tell you with complete confidence," he continued, "that a failure to act will only deepen this crisis as well as the pain felt by millions of Americans."[30]

The American people were warned that in the absence of the stimulus package, unemployment would rise to 9 or 10 percent, but assured that with the stimulus it would not get higher than 8 percent. As it turned out, *with* the stimulus, unemployment topped 10 percent. What conclusion did the political class draw? Why, the stimulus must not have been great enough! As usual, the initial premise was never re-examined.

(The reader will not be shocked to learn that, according to the *New York Times*, the corporations most favored by the stimulus package had in fact consulted with Obama's advisers to help shape it to their liking.)[31]

Fashionable superstitions notwithstanding, government spending—that is, draining resources from the productive sector and devoting them to arbitrary projects—cannot improve the economy. It can only make things worse. So blinded are Keynesian economists, from whom Obama takes his inspiration, by the view that prosperity is attributable to "spending" per se that they predicted a return to depression conditions when World War II spending came to an end. (Alvin Hansen, John Maynard Keynes' most prominent American disciple, warned in 1943: "When the war is over, the government cannot just disband the Army, close down munitions factories, stop building ships, and remove all economic controls.")[32] And indeed in 1946, the year after the war ended, the federal budget was cut by two thirds. But instead of reverting to depression, what occurred was the single most robust year the private economy has ever seen.[33]

What the economy really needs, contra Obama, is not government "stimulus" spending to try to revive it as it is. We should not want to "stimulate" what should now be obvious to everyone was an unsustainable economy. What the economy instead needs is to undergo a market-driven *restructuring* without government interference, in which bubble activities shrink, and resources are reallocated into lines of production that conform to what consumers want and can afford.

Much of the debate over the stimulus turned, unfortunately, on how much "pork" was in the bill. This or that spending program was silly or an obvious waste of money, critics said. All too true, of course, but unless we're content to rearrange deck chairs on the Titanic, this misses the point.

The problem with fiscal stimulus is the tooth-fairy economics on which it is based, the very idea that economic health is the product of government spending. After all, such spending must be financed either by borrowing (which leaves private businesses with a smaller share of the pool of savings to borrow from), printing money out of thin air, or direct seizure from the population. All of these courses of action merely impoverish the rest of society, yielding no net benefit. It is like drinking Red Bull instead of sleeping. You merely exhaust yourself further, making the eventual crash all the more intense. The stimulus spending, for its part, exhausts the remaining pockets of profitability in the economy, squeezing them and depriving them of resources in order to fund arbitrary government projects.

And it is not unfair to call these projects arbitrary. Government lacks the measuring stick of profit-and-loss that keeps the private sector from squandering resources and creating things consumers don't want. Government can seize its resources from the people without their consent, and it makes no difference to government whether or not people actually want or wind up using the things it has produced. Meanwhile, the economy loses the goods that would have been produced by the voluntary sector had the government not seized these resources for its own use. "Stimulus" packages, in other words, drain the productive economy of resources in order to subsidize money-losing ventures.

The more sophisticated Keynesians will come back with the argument that while they really do agree with you in cases when the economy is at "full employment," your point doesn't apply when there are "idle resources." In that case, we can "stimulate" those idle resources into action without drawing resources out of alternative employments. These resources are sitting there idle, and currently have no alternative employments.

Nice try. But whatever projects our wise planners dream up to put these "idle resources" to work are unavoidably going to draw complementary resources away from more pressing private needs. Resources will inevitably be diverted from current employments in the private sector. Our "idle" resources in the wake of the recent financial crisis included, for instance, some of our automobile production capacity, some construction capacity, some of our financial services sector, and the like, as well as a wide variety of types of labor. How can a government bridge project put these and only these idle resources to work? "Is it really the case," asks economist Robert Murphy, "that bridges and roads require labor and other inputs in the same proportions as housing construction and finance? Does the construction of a new sewer system require the services of investment bankers and roof layers in such combinations that local government spending can perfectly offset the bursting of the housing bubble?" As a practical matter, therefore, stimulus spending will inevitably bid resources away from current employments. "If the city of Houston wants to build a new bridge," Murphy continues, "is it really the case that every last person even remotely involved with the project will come from the ranks of the unemployed *who are within commuting distance of the Houston bridge site*? Surely the project will draw on engineers, construction foremen, and other skilled workers, who were still gainfully employed even amidst the recession, and who therefore will not be able to work on as many private-sector projects as they otherwise would have."[34]

Moreover, once the bridge project is complete, we will merely have succeeded in giving unemployed people on one side of the bridge a convenient way to get to the jobs they don't have on the other side.

Beyond that, stimulus advocates show remarkably little curiosity about *why* the so-called idle resources are idle in the first place. They are idle because of some previous entrepreneurial miscalculation. What might have caused systemic miscalculation of this kind? Could it be the Federal Reserve's manipulation of interest rates, which interferes with entrepreneurs' assessments of profitability and provokes false economic booms, as the Austrian School argues and F. A. Hayek won the Nobel Prize for showing in 1974? (See chapter 3.)

During an artificial boom, resources wind up deployed in lines of production where, it is discovered during the bust, they did not belong. Left to their own devices, the market economy and its price system will rearrange these resources into the pattern that consumers prefer. During the bust, market actors sort out which projects and business ventures are healthy and sustainable, and which are artificial activities that cannot survive without a constant increase in the money supply, and cannot (and should not) survive now that reality has reasserted itself. Stimulus spending merely disrupts and confuses this necessary process.

But Wait—There's More

Now, to describe the health-care bill and the stimulus spending as the most significant Obama policies from an economic point of view is not to dismiss the importance of other White House initiatives. The restructuring and takeover of General Motors and Chrysler, particularly in such a way as to reward union members disproportionately, added both to the taxpayers' bill and to the uncertainty of entrepreneurs evaluating their next moves. For a man who had made such a big deal about his supposed immunity to the demands of special interests, it seemed a bit rich for the president to claim it was in the public interest for him to stiff senior creditors while handing over major portions of these companies to an institution that had spent $5 million to help elect him.[35] If a century and a half of bankruptcy law could be thrown out the window, investors doubtless wondered, what principles would the regime respect?

The "Cash for Clunkers" program was the usual Washington foolishness—we'll make ourselves wealthier by destroying things. People with old cars whose gas mileage fell below an arbitrary threshold received a government credit toward a new, more fuel-efficient car if they traded in their old one (which would be destroyed). So much for all the cheap used cars people on low incomes wanted to buy. And so much for all the goods produced by other industries that people might have purchased had they not been given the artificial incentive to buy a new car. Why should the automobile industry receive this kind of windfall at the expense of other struggling industries?[36]

That the government was subsidizing the automobile industry would have been more obvious only if the Treasury secretary had dumped a truckload of cash in front of GM's corporate headquarters. The automobile industry understood this well, which is why the National Automobile Dealers Association pushed so hard for the program. Also lobbying for the legislation was Nucor Steel, whose factory in Auburn, New York, recycles scrap steel. Nucor would enjoy quite a bit of subsidized scrap steel if Cash for Clunkers went through.[37] The environmental effects of the program, meanwhile, were so negligible as not to be worth mentioning.

Administration proposals that as of this printing had not become law (such as cap and trade) were not unimportant for not having passed. To the contrary, the very prospect that such measures might pass has increased uncertainty among entrepreneurs about future economic conditions. That kind of uncertainty translates into lower levels of private investment. Economic historian Robert Higgs calls this phenomenon "regime uncertainty." It helps to account for why private investment remained so far below trend during the 1930s, but rebounded after World War II.[38] Investor Lammot du Pont summed up business feeling in 1937: "Uncertainty rules the tax situation, the labor situation, the monetary situation, and practically every legal condition under which industry must operate."[39]

Is this happening again? In 2010, billionaire developer Steve Wynn said: "Washington is unpredictable these days. No one has any idea what's next.... The uncertainty of the business climate in America is frightening, frightening to everybody, and it's delaying recovery."[40] Wynn complained of "wild, uncontrolled spending" and "unbelievable, unsustainable debt." As Robert Higgs wrote in December 2008:

> I do not know that the regime uncertainty that an increasing number of commentators and others have perceived recently is comparable to that of the latter 1930s—by now there's not much real capitalism left for the government to destroy, in any event. However, it is clear that the government's frantic actions of the past several months have created a situation in which investors have little confidence about the character of future property rights in the United States. The takeovers of Fannie, Freddie, and AIG, the massive interventions into financial markets, the huge bailouts of banks and other financial institutions, mixed with letting Lehman Brothers go down and resisting a bailout [*which eventually came*] for the Big Three auto manufacturers (so far, at least)—all these actions, and others, imply that a rational investor would do well to attach a huge risk premium to any money he puts into investments even for the intermediate term, not to mention the long term.[41]

The Obama economic program has perpetuated and intensified the problems that are sinking the U.S. economy. Those parts of it that can be legislatively reversed, like the health-care plan, ought to be promptly repealed. Those parts that cannot, like the "stimulus" packages, ought to be refuted and ridiculed. The nicest thing we can say about the president's economic program is that it is only one in a long line of presidential programs that have wrecked Americans' futures in the name of helping them.

CHAPTER 3

Government and Economic Crisis: Savior or Perpetrator?

Confronted by the financial crisis that gained steam in 2008, President Barack Obama responded the way any fool could have predicted: "What I won't do," he said early in his term, "is return to the failed theories of the last eight years that got us into this fix in the first place, because those theories have been tested and they have failed."[1]

The president did not elaborate on what "theories" he had in mind. George W. Bush had been the biggest-spending U.S. president since Lyndon Johnson, not exactly a sign of laissez-faire.[2] Did Obama's repudiation of his predecessor mean he would *cut* spending? Did he mean deficits and the debt would be reduced? Did he mean he wanted the Federal Reserve to stop tinkering with interest rates?

No president ever means that. Obama took those policies and doubled down on them. Change we can believe in turned out to mean more of the same, except worse.

What Obama was trying to say, of course, is that the supposedly free-market policies of the past eight years had failed. This was the response of the political class. Why, the free-market economy has once again gone haywire, and once again—just for your own good, you understand—we need more power and more of your wealth.

It was not the "free market" that failed us. It was a ginned-up housing market, overheated from political manipulation and artificially low interest rates courtesy of the Federal Reserve. Governments do not "smooth out" or eliminate business cycles. They cause and exacerbate them. Then they cite problems they themselves caused as good reasons for them to expand their authority.

What happened to financial institutions is important, to be sure, but it gets too far ahead of the story to try to figure out why so many of them went bust. The real question is why they went boom, unnaturally, in the first place. Had there been no artificial boom, there could have been no bust.

Part of the story involves government intervention into the housing market. That's a story that has been told elsewhere,[3] but the basic contours are worth revisiting.

Fannie Mae and Freddie Mac were "government-sponsored enterprises" (GSEs) whose mission was to make housing affordable. Although ostensibly "private," Fannie and Freddie enjoyed special tax and regulatory privileges that other institutions did not, and it was generally assumed that if it ever came to that, the GSEs' special line of credit at the Treasury would be transformed into a bailout in whatever amounts were required. These advantages allowed the GSEs to dominate the mortgage market. Fannie and Freddie could buy whole or securitized[4] mortgages from banks (so that from that moment on, the mortgage would be handled by Fannie or Freddie instead of the originating bank).

Fannie and Freddie played an important role in creating a market for risky mortgages, particularly as housing prices were beginning to climb in the late 1990s; from 1998 to 2003 they were the most frequent buyers of mortgage loans.[5] When apologists for Fannie and Freddie try to claim that, after all, private lenders originated most of the mortgage loans that eventually went sour, they are being disingenuous. Had Fannie and Freddie not stood ready to buy those loans from the originators, many of them would never have been made in the first place. Countrywide, for example, sold about 90 percent of its loans to Fannie and Freddie.[6]

Fannie and Freddie did not typically need to be pushed into taking risk. Fannie Mae CEO Daniel Mudd told company employees to "get aggressive on risk taking, or get out of the company."[7] Email correspondence reveals that risk managers objected strenuously to such directives from senior management, and warned that the GSEs would thereby lead the whole market down the road of overpricing risky mortgages.[8]

In the decade leading up to Fannie and Freddie's collapse in 2008, the two mortgage giants spent millions of dollars lobbying congressmen. With "affordable housing" charities dotting the landscape in congressional districts across the country, and with comfortable sinecures thereby available to the relatives of important politicians, the result was an American political class that was all too happy to do Fannie and Freddie's bidding. And when Fannie Mae executives were caught in accounting scandals in 2004, cooking their books to justify larger bonuses for themselves, no one went to jail, as would have happened in the case of a genuinely private firm.[9]

Thanks to their government guarantee, Fannie and Freddie had been able to operate with far more leverage than even the worst of the investment banks would later be criticized for. (In calling Fannie and Freddie highly leveraged, we mean they had far too little capital on hand to make good on their obligations, and that they could continue functioning only by constant borrowing.) Indeed, with only $83 billion in capital covering $5 trillion in liabilities, their leverage ratio was more than 60 to 1. In July 2008, as Fannie and Freddie headed toward collapse, Treasury secretary Hank Paulson calmly observed that "their regulator has made clear that they are adequately capitalized." When confronted with this statement two months later in the wake of the two giants' failure and subsequent takeover by the federal government, Paulson replied: "I never said the company was well capitalized. What I said is the regulator said they are adequately capitalized."[10] (And you thought Paulson had misled us.)

Now it's true that Fannie and Freddie did not enjoy an *explicit* bailout promise from the U.S. government. There was a chance that they would be allowed to go bankrupt. But the markets, which turned out to be correct, evidently did not think that chance was very great. The U.S. government, which is considered the safest of safe investments, can borrow from the public at low interest rates. As late as September 2008, when Fannie and Freddie were at death's door, they were still able to borrow at rates only one percentage point higher than the federal government itself could.[11] Investors obviously believed the federal government would come to the rescue. From 2000 to 2006, in fact, during the height of the housing boom and at a time when Fannie and Freddie's risk grew considerably, their borrowing costs held steady with or even fell relative to those of the U.S. government.[12]

At the time Fannie and Freddie were taken over by the federal government, we were told that a combined cap of $400 billion had been placed on how much assistance those entities could receive. Several months later, that cap was removed. Taxpayer assistance to Fannie and Freddie would now be potentially unlimited. It was probably just a coincidence that the cap was removed on Christmas Eve, a day when no one would have been paying attention.[13]

Defenders of Fannie and Freddie, and of the federal government in general, have tried to hold these entities blameless for the crisis. Economist Paul Krugman stumbled around making up stories in their defense, but each time, astute readers exposed them as false. Each time, Krugman moved on silently to another line of argument, never actually admitting his earlier ones had been wrong. First he claimed that Fannie and Freddie were not allowed to hold subprime mortgages. That was false. Krugman then switched to the claim that Fannie and Freddie's share of residential mortgage securitizations actually fell slightly during the height of the boom. Critics noted that Krugman had failed to mention the whole (non-securitized) loans Fannie and Freddie had purchased during that time, or the private-label mortgage-backed securities it bought. Finally, Krugman argued that if Fannie and Freddie had behaved irresponsibly, they had done so in search of profit, and not out of a policy mandate to increase homeownership. He did not disclose how he managed to intuit the motivations of the companies.[14]

But if Fannie and Freddie had nothing to do with undermining lending standards, and federal programs designed to do the same thing had in fact *not* had any such effect, where was Krugman when the government was *boasting* of everything Fannie and Freddie had done to expand homeownership by watering down lending standards? They *took credit* for the very things their defenders today try to pretend they didn't do. In 2000, the Department of Housing and Urban Development (HUD) declared:

Lower-income and minority families have made major gains in access to the mortgage market in the 1990s. A variety of reasons accounted for these goals, including improved housing affordability, enhanced enforcement of the Community Reinvestment Act, more flexible mortgage underwriting, and stepped-up enforcement of the Fair Housing Act. But most industry observers believe that one factor behind these gains has been the improved performance of Fannie Mae and Freddie Mac under HUD's affordable lending goals. HUD's recent increases in the goals for 2001-03 will encourage the GSEs to further step up their support for affordable lending.

Four years later, HUD added:

Over the past ten years, there has been a "revolution in affordable lending" that has extended homeownership opportunities to histori-cally underserved households. Fannie Mae and Freddie Mac have been a substantial part of this "revolution in affordable lending." During the mid-to-late 1990s, they added flexibility to their under-writing guidelines, introduced new low-downpayment products, and worked to expand the use of automated underwriting in evaluating the creditworthiness of loan applicants. HMDA data suggest that the industry and GSE initiatives are increasing the flow of credit to underserved borrowers.[15]

Andrew Cuomo, Secretary of Housing and Urban Development under Bill Clinton, broadened the scope of the Federal Housing Administration (FHA), whose programs were supposed to help low-income people become homeown-ers. Cuomo nearly doubled the upper limit of FHA loans, to $235,000. He reduced required down payments to a mere 3 percent, and saw to it that home buyers could avoid paying even that.[16] The Bush administration pushed things even further, and as late as 2008 increased the percentage of low-income and very low-income earners (to a goal of 56 percent) whose mortgages Fannie Mae and Freddie Mac were urged to buy.[17] Every federal agency connected with housing leaned on lenders like this, and Fannie and Freddie, particularly in the wake of Fannie's accounting scandals, were strongly pressured to expand their exposure to risky mortgages.

The other culprit the establishment has tried without success to exonerate is the Federal Reserve System, the U.S. central bank that holds government-granted monopoly privileges. Had the Fed not repeatedly intervened to push interest rates down, the market would have stopped the housing bubble in its tracks. Faced with an inordinate demand for mortgage loans, banks would have found their supply of loanable funds rapidly depleted. As a result, interest rates would have shot up, and further speculation in real estate would have been arrested. These high interest rates would also have encouraged people to save, and those increased savings would have provided the genuine wherewithal for any further home lending to take place. The role of the Fed was much more significant than that of the U.S. government itself, since without the wherewithal to finance these home purchases, attempts to manipulate the housing market on the political side would have hit a natural brick wall.

Asset bubbles, which involve goods whose prices are unsustainably high for long periods of time, should always incline us to look for monetary mismanagement. When demand for a particular asset (such as a house) rises, this increased demand pushes its price above the level it would otherwise have reached. Yet in a bubble, people keep buying the asset even though its price goes on rising, without a contraction in other sectors of the economy. Where does all the money come from to make the ever-rising prices of the bubble possible, such that people can continue buying the asset even as its price goes through the roof? That is where the monetary spigot comes in. When money is cheap, the purchase of assets of ever-increasing price becomes possible.[18] Looking back on the dot-com boom of the late 1990s, the *Economist* concluded: "Without easy credit the stock market bubble could not have been sustained for so long, nor would its bursting have had such serious consequences. And unless central bankers learn their lesson, it will happen again."[19]

The artificially high prices in the U.S. housing market fed on themselves. Artificially high home prices made it more and more difficult for the average person to buy a home. In some parts of the country, people earning the median income couldn't afford a median-priced home. The result was the creative financing schemes that would later cause so much grief, with people who were otherwise unable to crack into such an inflated housing market lying about their income or employment status, taking out "no doc" mortgages (in which they did not need to provide any documentation of income), and so on, in order to cope with the high prices.[20] The down payment, which once served to give a buyer a stake in his house, began to disappear. By 2005, 43 percent of first-time buyers made no down payment, and 68 percent were putting less than 10 percent down.[21] This kind of activity drove up prices still further, and the cycle continued.

The "laissez-faire" Alan Greenspan, Federal Reserve Chairman from 1987 to 2005, found nothing wrong with the decline in lending standards. He recalled in his 2008 autobiography: "I was aware that the loosening of mortgage credit terms for subprime borrowers increased financial risk, and that subsidized homeownership initiatives distort market outcomes. But I believed then, as now, that the benefits of broadened homeownership are worth the risk."[22]

The saccharine promises of politically driven increases in homeownership rates were bound to come face to face with reality, and the bust of 2007 was it. Homeownership levels have begun to return to their pre-boom magnitudes— except now, countless Americans have ruined asset portfolios and credit ratings to show for the federal government's grand social experiment.[23]

Meanwhile, with the folly of the housing boom years now obvious to everyone, it was discovered that the Federal Housing Administration (FHA), which is part of the Department of Housing and Urban Development, continued to back risky loans with down payments as low as 3.5 percent. (FHA insurance was established for families that could not afford the traditional 20 percent down payment.) In just a couple years, the FHA had gone from guaranteeing just 2 percent of mortgages to over 20 percent. The number of companies whose mortgages it backed grew from about 1,000 to over 3,300.[24]

And there are problems. One in six FHA borrowers is behind on payments. A recent audit found that only 5 percent of these mortgages included all the necessary documents. And thanks to the Stimulus Act of 2008, the maximum loan the FHA could insure was temporarily doubled, to $729,750. One may well wonder what a "low-income" family is doing taking on a mortgage of three quarters of a million dollars. The following year the temporary maximum was extended. As of this printing, some people were concerned that the limits on loans the FHA could insure would be reduced in 2011, all the way down to— wait for it—a mere $625,000.

This is all part of a strategy to keep home prices inflated. Congressman Barney Frank admitted as much: these mortgages are necessary, he said, to "keep prices from falling too fast." Got that? We need to help low-income people afford expensive houses in order to keep house prices from falling.

Good thing these people are in charge.

So where can people turn for common sense? In the wake of the financial crisis that began to unfold in 2007 and 2008, some Americans began looking for answers in unconventional places—since all the conventional places had been completely blindsided by what occurred. In particular, a tradition of thought known as the Austrian School of economics has enjoyed an explosion in popularity and interest since 2008. A couple million people have watched a YouTube video called "Peter Schiff Was Right," which collected television segments of Euro Pacific Capital president and financial commentator Peter Schiff predicting in 2006 exactly what wound up happening to the U.S. economy, with other commentators dismissing or even laughing at him. Schiff is an Austrian School economist. Another 2 million people watched "Fear the Boom and Bust," a rap video that depicts John Maynard Keynes and Austrian School economist and Nobel Prize winner F. A. Hayek explaining their differing views of what causes economic booms and busts. My own book *Meltdown* (2009), which provided an Austrian account of what had happened to the U.S. economy, became a *New York Times* bestseller.

Normally the debate at a time like this would have taken place between people who thought government needed to borrow lots of money and spend it, and people who thought the Fed needed to print a lot of money and spend it. That would have been the permitted range of the conversation. Anyone who doubted that America's economic problems could be solved by kicking the can down the road with more borrowing, spending, and printing would have been out of luck. But the Austrians, whose writings and speeches have been critical of both fiscal and monetary stimulus, refuse to play by these rules. Neither form of stimulus, in the Austrian view, gets to the heart of what's wrong with the economy, and both promise to prolong the agony. The Austrian School, the oldest continuously existing school of economic thought, and probably still among the smallest, is, as a result, now the fastest growing.

Paul Krugman, the Keynesian economist who has pushed for even greater "stimulus" measures than have been undertaken so far, has been frustrated by how many people are "asking how we got into this mess rather than telling us how to get out of it."[25] For the Austrians, this is the central question. They are asking it not to annoy Paul Krugman, but because only if the genesis of the crisis is understood can alleged recovery measures be properly evaluated.

When the Austrian economist F. A. Hayek won the Nobel Prize in economics in 1974, it was his work in business-cycle theory four decades earlier that was being honored. And it's that theory that has been attracting the most attention from a curious public today. What is it that makes the economy move in a boom-bust pattern? That's what business-cycle theory seeks to explain.

To understand the Austrian theory, consider two scenarios.

Scenario 1. Consider what happens when the public increases its savings. Since banks now have more funds to lend (namely, the saved funds deposited by the public), the rate of interest they charge on loans will fall. These lower interest rates stimulate an expansion in long-term investment projects, which are more interest-rate sensitive than short-term projects. Considerably more money in interest payments is paid over the life of a long-term than a short-term project, thanks to compound interest, so a downward move in interest rates will make such projects seem disproportionately attractive.

(A brief digression: the Austrians speak of a "structure of production." In that structure, lower-order stages of production are those stages closest to finished consumer goods: retail stores, services, and the like. Wholesale and marketing are stages of higher order than these. Mining, construction, and research and development are of still higher order, since they are so remote from the finished good that reaches the consumer.)

The other side of the coin when the public increases its saving is that it is consuming less. When people's consumption spending falls, it is a perfect time for higher-order stages of production to expand: what with people's additional saving, there is relatively less demand for consumer goods, and the resulting contraction of lower-order stages of production will release resources for use in the higher-order stages. In other words, if people are saving more and thus buying fewer hats or decks of playing cards, the hat and playing-card industries will need fewer trucks, less gasoline, fewer employees, and so on. An employee who answered the phones at the playing-card factory, for example, can get a job filing work orders for a contractor as construction increases. The goods and employees released by consumer-goods industries like these are now available to make possible the completion of the higher-order projects that the low interest rates have made more attractive to entrepreneurs. The lower-order stages contract, thereby making possible the expansion of the higher-order stages.

In short, when interest rates are free to fluctuate, they coordinate production across time and ensure that the configuration of the production structure is sustainable. Long-term production is begun only when sufficient savings are available to fund it.

Scenario 2. Government-established central banks have various means at their disposal to force interest rates lower even without any corresponding increase in saving by the public. (For more on this, see Murray N. Rothbard's *The Mystery of Banking*, or his shorter *What Has Government Done to Our Money?*) Just as in the case in which public saving has increased, the lower interest rates spur expansion in higher-order stages of production.

The difference, though, is a critical one, and it guarantees that these *artificially* low interest rates will not yield the happy outcome in Scenario 1. For in this case, people have not decreased their consumption spending. If anything, the low interest rates on loans encourage further consumption. If consumption spending is not constricted, the lower-order stages of production do not contract. And if they do not contract, they do not release resources for use in the higher-order stages of production. Consequently, the economy is inadvertently arranged in an unsustainable configuration. The public does not want this ratio of higher-order to lower-order production. Not enough resources exist to fund both the lower-order production the public wants *and* the wave of higher-order projects the economy has been misled into initiating. Instead of harmonious economic development, there will ensue a tug-of-war for resources between the higher and lower stages. In the process of this tug-of-war, the prices of these resources (labor, trucking services, etc.) will be bid up as the various firms and industries compete for them, thereby threatening the profitability of higher-order projects that were begun without the expectation of this increase in costs.

What all this means is that the economy-wide discoordination that reveals itself in the bust is not caused by the "free market." To the contrary, it is *intervention* into the free market, in the form of distortions of the structure of interest rates—which are crucial coordinating mechanisms—that causes the problem. Production projects that are interest-rate sensitive, housing among them, are given artificial and unhealthy stimulation that eventually reverses itself in losses and bankruptcies.

As the boom turns into bust, the economy tries to readjust itself into a configuration that conforms to consumer preferences. That is why it is so essential for government to stay entirely out of the adjustment process, because arbitrary government behavior can only delay this necessary and healthy process. Wages and prices need to be free to fluctuate, so labor and other resources can be swiftly shifted away from bloated, bubble sectors of the economy and into sustainable sectors of the economy where consumers want them. Bailouts obstruct this process by preventing the reallocation of capital into the hands of firms that genuinely cater to consumer demand, and instead propping up those firms that have deployed resources in ways that do not conform to consumer preferences. Fiscal and monetary stimulus, as we discussed in chapter 2, do nothing to address the imbalances in the economy, and indeed only perpetuate them.

Note that the problem is not a decline in consumer spending that needs to be reversed through various government stimuli to consumption. To the contrary, there is too much consumer spending. It is this relatively high consumer spending that is pulling factors of production back from the higher to the lower-order stages of production. Stimulating consumption only makes the situation worse, by squeezing the already collapsing profitability of the higher-order stages.

There is no improving on Ludwig von Mises' metaphor of the master builder. An economy stimulated by artificially low interest rates is like a master builder engaged in the task of building a house that he lacks the materials to complete. If he discovers his error right away he can limit the damage. Perhaps only a small part of the house will have to be knocked down. Perhaps none of it will: it may suffice to alter his blueprint for the rest of the house in light of the decreased supply of building materials he now knows are available to him. What we do not want to do, in the name of helping him, is to intoxicate him to the point at which he does not notice his depleted supply of building materials until he has laid his very last brick. Now he is in a far worse situation; probably the entire house will have to be torn down, and all the materials and labor hours he expended on the project will have been squandered forever.

The artificially stimulated economy is like the master builder in that it, too, has become too ambitious in the face of the real level of resources at its disposal. Higher-order stages of production are being encouraged to expand at a time when no corresponding contraction has occurred in the lower-order stages, which indeed may actually be expanding. This cannot go on forever.

The story of the master builder also reveals that the real problem occurs during the boom period, not the bust. The artificial boom gives the superficial impression of prosperity—why, the master builder is employed, and he is producing goods for consumer use. But it is during the boom that resources are misallocated—i.e., when the master builder squanders building materials on a house he can never complete. The bust is the moment when his errors come to light, and he realizes he must modify his activities. Likewise, the economy that, as a whole, appears to be prospering during a boom—and some of what occurs during the boom is indeed the generation of real wealth—is in fact engaged in a misdirection of resources. The bust or recession, painful as it is, is the necessary stage whereby resources are redeployed to lines of production that satisfy real consumer demand.

Most observers cheered in the months following 9/11 when it seemed as if Alan Greenspan had successfully navigated the economy through the dot-com bust at the cost of only a relatively mild recession. The man the *New York Times* identified as "the infallible maestro of our financial system" had lived up to expectations. But all Greenspan's interventions did was to hold off the inevitable recession, and make the downturn of 2007 and beyond all the worse. The recession of 2001 was the only one on record in which housing starts did not decline. From 2000 to 2001, home prices actually increased by 8.8 percent. Austrian economists at the time wondered about this. "What could explain a bull market in a non-earning asset in a non-inflationary era?" asked James Grant, editor of the famed *Grant's Interest Rate Observer*. The answer, he believed, involved artificial credit expansion and artificially low interest rates.[26]

So people drew the false conclusion—amplified by the alleged experts, including some Fed economists—that the housing sector is robust through thick and thin, housing prices never fall, a house is the best investment someone can make, and so on. Because Greenspan would not allow the full correction to take place, clearing out entrepreneurial errors caused by his previous fiddling with interest rates, market actors persisted in their errors for years thereafter.

With the economy having continued along this unsustainable trajectory all that time, the bust that inevitably came was that much worse.

Paul Krugman, columnist for the *New York Times* and winner of the 2008 Nobel Prize in economics, called for precisely this policy in 2001: force down interest rates to encourage lending and to stimulate the economy, housing in particular. Krugman told a German interviewer: "During phases of weak growth there are always those who say that lower interest rates will not help. They overlook the fact that low interest rates act through several channels. For instance, more housing is built, which expands the building sector. You must ask the opposite question: why in the world shouldn't you lower interest rates?"[27]

Here is Krugman in October 2001: "Economic policy should encourage other spending to offset the temporary slump in business investment. *Low interest rates, which promote spending on housing and other durable goods, are the main answer.*"[28] Two months later he again spoke of the benefits of keeping housing strong by means of intervention in the economy: "The good news about the U.S. economy is that it fell into recession, but it didn't fall off a cliff. Most of the credit probably goes to the dogged optimism of American consumers, but *the Fed's dramatic interest rate cuts helped keep housing strong* even as business investment plunged."[29]

That, as we've seen, was the problem: by keeping housing "strong" instead of allowing the economy to correct itself, the Fed encouraged people to continue along an unsustainable path, thereby making the eventual and inevitable bust all the more severe when it finally arrived. Writing for the *New York Times* evidently means never having to apologize for being wrong—if you weren't wrong, you wouldn't be writing for the *New York Times* in the first place.

Alan Greenspan once declared his inability to discern any kind of common pattern between the various boom-bust cycles in American history. "There is always something different," Greenspan said, "something that does not look like all the previous ones. There is never anything identical and it is always a puzzlement." In fact, there *is* something identical—namely, artificial credit expansion. It is evident throughout all the nineteenth-century panics, and we likewise find it in the depressions and recessions of the twentieth and twenty-first centuries. Other features of the cycle may vary—there may be a spectacular rise in tech stocks in one case and in real estate in another—but this factor is consistently present. "How many more crises must we endure," wondered economist George Reisman in *Barron's*, "until we realize the common denominator is the creation of money and credit by the Fed? Wall Street bankers and speculators, who try to game the system and make profits during each boom, are mere bit players in these crises. By fostering the booms and triggering the busts, the real villain is the institution of central banking itself."[30]

The Austrian theory of the business cycle strongly implies what should be done once the bust hits. Certainly all inflation of the money supply must come to an end. It was this policy, which brings artificially lower interest rates in its train, that caused the misdirection of resources into unsustainable lines in the first place. Further misdirection, even if we dignify it with the word "stimulus," will not repair the broken economy.

Prices and wages need to be free to fluctuate in accordance with changing conditions. The price system is the outcome of trillions of buying and selling decisions by businesses and the public. Entrepreneurs who are trying to figure out how to combine factors of production in such a way as to produce the goods consumers want at the lowest possible cost to society must refer to it. Any interference with prices and wages during the critical time in which bust evolves into recovery will subvert and thus delay the economy's adjustment process. Only an unhampered system of prices and wages can ensure that the misallocated resources (including labor) of the boom are redirected to sectors of the economy where they conform to, rather than stand in inadvertent defiance of, consumer demand.

During a boom, labor and physical resources are attracted to sectors where, it will later be discovered, they did not belong. During the housing boom some 40 percent of all new jobs were in the housing sector.[31] That could not continue.

Failing firms need to be allowed to go bankrupt. The structure of production undergoes considerable change during the recession period, and the sustainable pattern of consumption and production that results will not permit all firms to continue as before. Bankruptcy permits new owners to take over the assets of failing firms, and either conduct those firms according to a different business model, turn the assets (if possible) toward the production of different goods, or simply sell off the assets and compensate as many of the creditors as can be accommodated.

The government's predation on the economy, in the form of spending and taxation, should be reduced. Resources are thereby released that entrepreneurs can use to realign the capital structure in light of the changed conditions that the bust brought to light.

This strategy was followed in the depression of 1920–21, which saw unemployment shoot up to 12.4 percent and production decline by 17 percent. Wholesale prices fell by 56 percent. The political class today would be screaming for all kinds of "stimulus" to reverse this death spiral. But the federal government at the time cut its budget in half from 1920 to 1922 and cut the national debt by one third over the course of the 1920s. Income tax rates were lowered for all income groups throughout the decade, but these lower taxes took effect after the recovery was already in progress. The Federal Reserve, for its part, did not engage in open-market operations (in which the Fed purchases assets with money it creates in order to increase the amount of money in circulation) to increase the money supply.[32] The economy was allowed to adjust without the so-called countercyclical government policies that we are told are essential. Signs of recovery were evident by the late summer of 1921, which is when the National Bureau of Economic Research says the depression ended.[33] Joseph Schumpeter, one of the eminent economists of the twentieth century, believed that the 1920–21 case "shows better than any theory could how the system pulls itself out of troughs under its own steam."[34]

Since 2007, the market has been trying to move consumers away from personal finance models based on indebtedness and consumption, and toward more saving and a sustainable level of consumption. To accommodate this shift, labor and capital will need to be reallocated out of some sectors and into other ones. As we've seen, "stimulus" spending only disrupts and confuses this purgative process, by misdirecting resources into arbitrary projects and artificially stimulating politically favored industries at the expense of the economy's healthy and productive sector. Obama's program for recovery, such as it is, looks instead to reinflate the bubble, keep the spending spree going, and give still more artificial stimulus to debt while introducing or exacerbating disincentives to save. It refuses to allow the market to correct the unsustainable excesses in the economy.

"No scheme which has ever been devised…has ever made a collapsed boom go up again," said William Graham Sumner in 1896.[35] Nothing in the historical record since then has altered that verdict.

Too Big to Fail?

Throughout the financial crisis, we were told that certain firms—like General Motors, Bear Stearns, and AIG—were "too big to fail" (TBTF). The prevalence of this doctrine helps to account for why, only weeks after the failure of Bear Stearns, Lehman Brothers, which held the same kind of assets as Bear, was still able to raise hundreds of millions of dollars—with even a major money-market fund (Reserve Primary), which is supposed to make only the most conservative investments, getting a piece of the action. Many observers considered it likely that Lehman would be bailed out by the government. That assumption wound up being false, but the episode indicates the extent to which private actors have come to take the TBTF doctrine for granted.[36]

Any firm, whether a financial institution or otherwise, that is deemed too big to fail enjoys artificial advantages at the expense of its competitors. Lenders know these firms enjoy government protection. As a consequence, lenders consider their investments in them to be essentially without risk. The net result is that TBTF firms are able to attract capital with artificial ease, while smaller firms are put at a competitive disadvantage. Thus, when the next crisis comes, the TBTF firms will have grown all the larger, warnings of "systemic risk" will be all the more hysterical, and the cycle of bailouts will begin anew.

Thus we learned in 2009 that in the wake of the bailouts the largest banks were able to borrow from the Fed at considerably lower rates than smaller ones, a factor that gave them a substantial competitive advantage. According to the *Wall Street Journal*, "The handful of banks with more than $10 billion in assets were paying 1.18% to borrow money in the second quarter, the FDIC said in data issued Thursday. By contrast, banks with $100 million and $1 billion in assets were paying 1.97%, a big difference in a business where tenths of a percentage point translate into millions of dollars in profits."[37]

The incentives to which the TBTF gives rise aren't particularly subtle. Writes economist Craig Pirrong:

> Goldman [Sachs] knows it is too big to fail. How does it know this? Well, the government bailed out AIG not so much for AIG's sake, but for the sake of big AIG counterparties—most notably Goldman. Moreover, given the conventional wisdom that the government's

primary error in the financial crisis was its failure to bail out Lehman—a piker compared to Goldman—it doesn't take a rocket scientist to figure out that it won't repeat that mistake in the future, and let Goldman go down. So Goldman knows it can get bigger, and take more risk. It is the classic heads Goldman wins, tails the sucker taxpayer eats the loss gambit.[38]

Fannie Mae and Freddie Mac surely knew they were TBTF. "The thinking was that if something really bad happened to the housing market," recalls Freddie Mac's David Andrukonis, "then the government would need Freddie and Fannie more than ever, and would have to rescue them."[39] A top Freddie Mac executive added, "It basically worked exactly as everyone expected—when things got bad, the government came to the rescue."[40]

The most fundamental reasons to allow companies to fail include the following:

- Without market discipline, large firms will adopt artificially risky (and often heavily debt-based) strategies, in the knowledge that any downside risk will be shared with the public.
- Instead of promptly discontinuing wealth-destroying activities, we keep them alive.
- Genuinely profitable wealth-generating activities are deprived of investment capital and other resources, which are diverted to ongoing wealth destruction in the hands of bailed-out firms.
- The mechanism by which the market puts resources into the hands of the most skilled and deserving is undermined.
- Firms that are marginally below the magical "too-big-to-fail" threshold now have an incentive to take still greater risks, in the hope that they may be thereby thrust into the promised land of government protection.
- Allowing large firms to fail would encourage other market participants to move toward savings-based rather than debt-based finance models—a healthy shift in light of how artificially attractive debt has been made to seem over the years.

In the specific case of Bear Stearns, the official rationale for its bailout was that the company was too "interconnected" to be allowed to fail, since its failure would have triggered a cascade of other failures, ending in general catastrophe. One of the problems with this story is that the Financial Crisis Inquiry Commission's investigation found that Bear's assets exceeded its liabilities—meaning it was legally solvent—at the end of its first fiscal quarter of 2008. This estimate may have been mistaken, to be sure, but Bear was obviously not worthless or a mere shell, and creditors would have been made largely whole in bankruptcy proceedings. Bankruptcy seemed perfectly designed for a situation like this. It allows the ailing firm breathing room to assess its situation, amass what resources it can, and arrange for orderly satisfaction of creditor claims.[41]

When Lehman Brothers failed just six months later, the situation was different. Lehman was likely both illiquid and insolvent. It was allowed to go under. The alleged cascade of failures never materialized, as Peter Wallison explains:

> Even Lehman's credit-default swap [CDS] obligations, and the CDSs written specifically on Lehman by others, did not cause any substantial disruption in the CDS market when Lehman collapsed. Within a month after the bankruptcy, all of the CDSs specifically written on Lehman were settled through the exchange of approximately $6 billion among hundreds of counterparties, and while Lehman had over nine hundred thousand derivatives contracts outstanding at the time it filed for bankruptcy, these did not give rise to any known insolvency among those of its counterparties that were protected by a Lehman CDS. In cases where Lehman's derivatives counterparties suffered losses, the counterparties filed appropriate claims in the Lehman bankruptcy proceeding, which are being adjudicated in the ordinary course. In other words, Lehman— a larger firm than Bear and one that had more "interconnections"—had no significant effect in dragging down its counterparties....If Lehman's interconnections did not drag down its counterparties, Bear's certainly would not have done so.[42]

The shock that hit the markets in the wake of the Lehman collapse was due less to the collapse per se than to what it seemed to suggest about the government's ad hoc approach to the crisis. According to Stanford's John Taylor, the movements of interest-rate spreads do not necessarily indicate that the Lehman collapse is what spooked the markets. Instead, Taylor wrote, the realization by the public "that the government's intervention plan had not been fully thought through, and the official story that the economy was tanking, likely led to the panic seen in the next few weeks. And this was likely amplified by the ad hoc decisions to support some financial institutions and not others and unclear, seemingly fear-based explanations of programs to address the crisis. What was the rationale for intervening with Bear Stearns, then not with Lehman, and then again with AIG? What would guide the operations of the TARP [Troubled Asset Relief Program]?"[43]

What in fact happens during a financial crisis is not that one bankruptcy leads to another, and so on down a road to general catastrophe. The string of failures we observe is caused not by interconnectedness among the firms involved, but rather by a common exposure they all share. In the case of 2008, the firms in question were all exposed to a mortgage market that began to collapse. Financial firms as a rule diversify their assets precisely in order not to expose themselves unduly to the fortunes of any one institution. In Lehman Brothers' bankruptcy filing, the largest creditor turned out to be Tokyo-based Aozora Bank. Aozora was owed $463 million, which was in fact less than one-tenth of one percent of the total sum of the claims adjudicated in the filing. And it was not about to threaten the solvency of Aozora, whose capital base was $7.4 billion.[44]

What happened during the recent financial crisis was that the mortgage-backed securities held by large firms fell dramatically in value, threatening these institutions' solvency. These assets, it turns out, had been wildly overvalued. But bear in mind that recognizing the true values of previously mispriced assets, even if that means their prices fall dramatically, leaves the amount of physical stuff in the economy unchanged. Such a fall in asset values could well lead to the bankruptcy of institutions heavily invested in them, but that would mean only that the distribution of that unchanged amount of wealth would shift from one group of people to another. Bankruptcy courts would establish new ownership titles, and economic activity could then resume on a new and sounder foundation.

Wasn't "Deregulation" the Culprit?

On the campaign trail, then-Senator Barack Obama frequently if imprecisely identified deregulation as the source of the crisis. To his credit, he has largely abandoned this unpromising line of argument since taking office. But it continues to be believed, though specific examples of such deregulation are usually not named.

For some people, the argument seems so natural that no real research is necessary—they just *know* deregulation must have caused our problems, even if they have no idea what deregulation is, what it consisted of, or what exactly our problems are. Countless Americans have permitted themselves to believe that there is no serious problem their wise overlords could not have prevented had they been able to crack a few more skulls. The possibility that our protectors may themselves be the source of the problem is unthinkable.

A review of the key planks of financial regulation over the past several decades reveals little that could account for the severity of the crisis that struck in 2008. First, Regulation Q, which limited the amount of interest banks could pay on savings deposits, was mostly repealed under Jimmy Carter. That move seems unlikely to cause a global financial meltdown thirty years later. Next, the Riegle-Neal Interstate Banking and Branching Efficiency Act of 1994 repealed restrictions on interstate branch banking. Far from destabilizing the banking system, that repeal presumably strengthened it by making portfolio diversification easier. And finally, bank holding companies were allowed to underwrite corporate securities. That in itself is not particularly risky, and Columbia Business School's Charles Calomiris is right to note that we would be in much better shape today had these institutions been doing more corporate underwriting (similar to insurance) and less securitizing of bad mortgages.[45]

There is nothing relevant that the banks did in the years leading up to the crisis that they could not have done in the absence of deregulation. Banks have always been free to hold or securitize mortgages, including the subprime and "no doc" varieties. There is no repealed regulation that would have prevented them from doing these things.

The one specific act of deregulation that is sometimes pointed to as a contributor to the crisis is the partial repeal of the 1933 Glass-Steagall Act by means of the Gramm-Leach-Bliley Act in 1999. We heard less about it once proponents of this theory realized that future vice president Joe Biden had supported it while in the Senate, and Bill Clinton had signed it into law.

The Glass-Steagall Act of 1933 consisted of four basic provisions that combined to erect a wall between commercial and investment banking. First, it prohibited banks from underwriting or dealing in securities, apart from essentially riskless government-issued or government-backed securities. The prohibition on "dealing" in securities meant that banks could not acquire securities for the purpose of selling them, but they could acquire them to hold because they believed them to be good investments; banks could later sell them when they concluded they were no longer good investments or when they simply needed cash. Second, securities firms could not take deposits. The remaining two provisions prevented banks even from being affiliated with firms whose main function was to underwrite or deal in securities.

Gramm-Leach-Bliley repealed only this last part of the earlier legislation, thereby making it possible for a commercial bank and an investment bank to coexist under the umbrella of a common holding company. It did not repeal the provision preventing banks from underwriting or dealing in securities. Commercial banks continue to operate under the same Glass-Steagall restrictions that have existed since 1933.

The financial condition of the banks, and the financial crisis itself, had nothing to do with the "repeal" of Glass-Steagall. The problem occurred because banks made bad loans and investments—in other words, banks did a poor job at traditional banking activities, not some newfangled activity that "deregulation" had made possible.[46] Many commercial banks held large portfolios of mortgage-backed securities, but it wasn't some "repeal" of Glass-Steagall that allowed them to accumulate those portfolios. They were always allowed to do so.

But did the repeal of two provisions of Glass-Steagall allowing affiliation of commercial banks with securities firms through their control by the same holding company contribute to the losses and risk that permeated the system? Certainly not. For one thing, commercial banks bought mortgage-backed securities for their AAA rating, their attractive return, and the minimal capital requirements associated with holding them; they did not acquire these assets because they were connected to investment banks that were trying to unload them.[47] Moreover, severe regulatory firewalls essentially prevent this kind of affiliation from contributing to losses or increased risk on the part of the commercial bank involved. The reverse problem, that affiliation with a commercial bank might bring down an investment bank, is exceedingly unlikely, given the relative magnitudes of assets held by each institution. The commercial banks' assets were only a tiny fraction of those held by the investment banks they were affiliated with. These banks were in no position to cause the investment banks any serious problem, much less their complete downfall.[48]

So what deregulation can critics have in mind? "I would challenge anybody to point to something important that was deregulated during the last eight years," writes Carnegie Mellon's Allan Meltzer. "The last major financial deregulation was the 1999 act that President Clinton signed, removing the Glass-Steagall provisions separating commercial and investment banking. No other country in the world separates commercial and investment banking, and none of them have problems on that account. Nor have we had problems on that account."[49]

"Glass-Steagall is a red herring," concurs economist Bill Woolsey. "I think it is brought up because it is the only bit of deregulation that seems slightly relevant, and some people cannot accept that misregulation, and entrepreneurial error, rather than deregulation, was the key source of the problem."[50]

In fact, during the boom years the Federal Reserve boasted of its unique ability to foresee and prevent financial crises. In January 2007, on the verge of the crisis, Federal Reserve Chairman Ben Bernanke told a gathering of academics:

> Together with the knowledge obtained through its monetary-policy and payments activities, information gained through its supervisory activities gives the Fed an exceptionally broad and deep understanding of developments in financial markets and financial institutions....
>
> In my view, however, the greatest external benefits of the Fed's supervisory activities are those related to the institution's role in preventing and managing financial crises.
>
> In other words, the Fed can prevent most crises and manage the ones that do occur.
>
> Finally, the wide scope of the Fed's activities in financial markets— including not only bank supervision and its roles in the payments

system but also the interaction with primary dealers and the monitoring of capital markets associated with the making of monetary policy—has given the Fed a uniquely broad expertise in evaluating and responding to emerging financial strains.[51]

Later that year, the housing bubble burst.

Of course, the Fed failed to prevent the current crisis—and, as we have argued, itself bears much responsibility for what went wrong. Did that make the political class re-examine the Fed's claims about its wondrous abilities? To the contrary, in the wake of the crisis the Fed was given still more regulatory authority.

It seems to be a general rule: no matter how badly regulators fail, every crisis brings calls to empower them further. There appears to be nothing regulators could do to make the public consider the excluded possibility that mere "regulation" of a flawed system doesn't make the system at root any less flawed. Our talking heads who thoughtlessly call for "more regulation" as a panacea are attributing quasi-magical powers to people who in the real world tend to be unworthy of these exaggerations. As Robert Higgs puts it, "Had they been given even greater powers, budgets, and staffs, what enchantment would have transformed the regulators into smart, dogged champions of the public interest, rather than the time-serving drones and co-conspirators with the regulated firms that they have always been?"[52]

The case of Bernie Madoff comes readily to mind. Madoff ran a scheme in which wealthy if gullible individual and institutional investors wound up losing $50 billion. Madoff, his clients thought, was extraordinarily skilled at beating the market. In fact, all he was doing was taking later clients' money and using it to pay earlier clients, a scheme that required the addition of a greater and greater number of new clients over time—the definition of a Ponzi scheme.

The immediate and predictable response ran as follows: the Madoff fiasco shows what happens when you cut funding and personnel for the Securities and Exchange Commission (SEC), which (critics said) suffered under George W. Bush. Additional regulators and more funding would solve the problem.

Back on planet Earth, George W. Bush hadn't cut funding or personnel for anything at all—SEC funding *increased* at an 11.3 percent annualized rate, as compared to 6.8 percent under Bill Clinton, and its staff grew at 1.0 percent per year, as compared with negative 1.2 percent under Jimmy Carter. So we have to entertain another theory: perhaps for all its employees and wealth, the government had simply failed.[53] The SEC had been warned about Madoff for at least ten years, and perhaps as many as sixteen. Madoff even boasted of his family ties at the SEC. Even though it had the largest budget and largest staff in its history, it still failed to act. By contrast, Harry Markopolos, one of Madoff's competitors, simply examined the options strategy Madoff told his clients he was using and concluded that his alleged results had to be fraudulent. (An alert competitor has a powerful incentive to be a good regulator.)

Well, it may have taken them at least a decade of warnings, but at least the SEC finally wised up and nabbed him, right? Actually, the SEC had nothing to do with it. Madoff's own sons turned him in after he came to them and explained what he had done. And he felt compelled to approach them with the real story in the first place only because his financial situation had begun to deteriorate so badly. Catching him had nothing to do with the SEC at all.

The very existence of the SEC lowers investors' natural alertness—e.g., if such-and-such investment outlet were in fact a criminal Ponzi scheme, people assume the SEC would have done something about it. A private certification agency that made an error of this magnitude would be finished, never to be heard from again. Would you, dear reader, continue to rely on it? Meanwhile, other institutions would quickly gain market share at the incompetent firm's expense. The SEC, on the other hand, is going to get more money.

As it turns out, spending and personnel have increased dramatically, not just on the SEC, but throughout the whole arena of financial regulation: the 12,190 people in Washington, D.C., alone who are charged with overseeing American financial markets would probably have something to say about the "unregulated" American financial system. Adjusted for inflation, spending on the regulatory agencies in charge has tripled since "deregulation" began in 1980.[54] Boston University economist Laurence Kotlikoff came up with a tally of 115 regulatory agencies for financial services; are we supposed to believe things would improve with 116?[55]

But the presence of more regulators doesn't need to translate into more genuine oversight. According to Nobel Laureate George Stigler's capture theory of regulation, firms in a regulated industry tend to "capture" the regulatory body, such that they and their concerns dominate the regulatory agenda, and that agenda becomes an instrument of the further aggrandizement, rather than the genuine supervision, of the industry.* If Stigler is correct, then we have here another reason to consider it simplistic, even childish, to foist major tasks of economic stabilization onto regulatory bodies in the superstitious hope that this race of supermen will identify and act upon problems before anyone else perceives them, and always with an eye to the public interest. At a Federal Reserve conference in 2008, economist Willem Buiter spoke of "cognitive capture," a phenomenon in which regulators eventually become incapable of thinking about the relevant issues except in the way the regulated industry thinks about them.[56] And that is not to mention the revolving door that often exists between the regulatory agencies and the private sector. "SEC Lawyer One Day, Opponent the Next" ran a *Wall Street Journal* headline in 2010.[57] Observing the traditional common-law treatment of fraud and bad dealing would be much more effective than still more layers of rules, which would have results no different from what they have always had. According to Gerald O'Driscoll, a former vice president of the Dallas Fed, "The idea that multiplying rules and statutes can protect consumers and investors is surely one of the great intellectual failures of the 20th century. Any static rule will be circumvented or manipulated to evade its application."[58]

Regulators failed to identify the growing problems in the U.S. economy that culminated in the crash. To the contrary, we were told things were fine and that the economy was robust. For one thing, regulators made the mistake of relying heavily on the risk assessments of a small cartel of government-approved ratings agencies that were not subject to competition.[59] Beyond that, they either grossly misread the condition of the housing market or they simply misled the public. Alan Greenspan said in 2005 that conditions in the housing market were actually "encouraging." Ben Bernanke, who became chairman of the Fed

---

* We might be bolder still and suggest that from the start, public-interest rhetoric notwithstanding, the regulatory agencies are often demanded and shaped by the regulated industry.

the following year, declared that "our examiners tell us that lending standards are generally sound and are not comparable to the standards that contributed to broad problems in the banking industry two decades ago. In particular, real estate appraisal practices have improved." Bernanke admitted that a "slower growth in house prices" may be possible, but then added that he would simply lower interest rates if that were to occur.[60]

But suppose regulators had been able to perceive the problem. Would they know how to fix it, or even have the courage to try? "A regulatory crackdown on loose mortgage underwriting standards in 2004," writes economist Russ Roberts, "would have meant taking away a punch bowl filled with more home ownership—particularly among minorities—as well as expansion and profits in the businesses of home building, real estate brokerage, mortgage origination, and Wall Street financial engineering."[61] Not too likely, in other words.

And to put it bluntly, how many business school or other graduate students aspire to become regulators? The brighter students go on to become successful businessmen and entrepreneurs, and the slower ones wind up in the regulatory agencies. We expect a kid who graduated number 505 out of a class of 508 not to get his clock cleaned by a kid who graduated number 12?

The Dodd-Frank Financial Regulations Act, the financial reform bill passed in 2010, proposes to solve the problem of financial instability, but perhaps financial instability might have been avoided in the present case had the federal government and the central bank not distorted the housing market in the first place. Not a word in the bill mentions the Fed's role in financial bubbles; bubbles, once again, are assumed to be spontaneous events that come from nowhere, and against which we need rafts of regulators to focus their watchful eyes. As I argued in *Meltdown*, in discussions of financial crises, the Federal Reserve is the elephant in the living room everyone pretends not to notice.

No one quite knows what the bill's full impact will be. Its text contains over one hundred references to "The agency shall set," "The agency shall determine," and so on. It will be years before its full significance becomes clear.[62] What we do know is that as of November 2010, financial lobbyists had met with regulators 510 times over the Dodd-Frank Act. The bill's 2,300 pages still leave enormous discretion in the hands of regulatory agencies, and the usual suspects are angling to get things to go their way. "Frank-Dodd has created huge power-centers at these agencies," writes economist Robert Wenzel. "And it is real expensive to get access. Try calling up [Federal Deposit Insurance Corporation chairwoman] Sheila Bair and see if you can get a meeting with her the way [J.P. Morgan's] Jamie Dimon did."[63]

It is interesting to note, though, how the bill addresses admitted regulatory failures. According to Congressman Barney Frank, the Fed "has a terrible record of consumer protection." Consumer protection duties are therefore to be transferred to a new regulator. That'll show 'em! Except no Fed employee previously responsible for consumer protection is actually being fired. They're all being hired by the new regulator, as called for in Section 1064 of the bill: "All employees of the Board of Governors identified…shall be transferred to the Bureau for employment."[64]

The bill abolishes the Office of Thrift Supervision, diverting its responsibilities to the Office of the Comptroller of the Currency. That'll show 'em! Except (need we even say it?) no one is actually being fired. Says Section 322: "All employees of the Office of Thrift Supervision shall be transferred to the Office of the Comptroller of the Currency" or to the FDIC. (By the way, the Office of Thrift Supervision was created as the alleged solution for the economy in the wake of the Savings and Loan collapse in the 1980s.)[65]

What's more, the kind of prudential regulation that we are assured will prevent future crises wound up contributing to the present one. The capital requirements under which banks operated rewarded them for holding mortgage-backed securities by permitting them to hold fewer reserves against them (thereby freeing up more money for loans). For every one hundred dollars it held in standard loans, a bank needed ten dollars in capital. For every hundred dollars in mortgage loans, the amount was five dollars. But for every one hundred dollars of AAA-rated mortgage-backed securities they held, banks were required to have only two dollars in capital. This advantage naturally encouraged an artificial rush into this particular kind of asset. On a free market, institutions are likely to hold a wide variety of assets. But when government regulation artificially fosters one kind of asset over another, as it did in this case, the favored asset will be more widely held than it would otherwise have been, and if it declines in value the economic effects will be that much more severe. "Regulations," say economists

Jeffrey Friedman and Wladimir Kraus, "are like mandatory instructions for herd behavior, *automatically* increasing systemic risk."[66]

To be sure, we encounter much hand-wringing about poor management at major financial institutions. What we do not hear so much about is that the current regulatory environment makes it essentially impossible for professional and institutional investors to do anything about it. Institutions like insurance companies, pension funds, mutual funds, and banks are not permitted to hold more than a very small stake in any particular company. Hedge funds and private equity investors are restricted by regulations that prevent them from acquiring a controlling interest in a bank holding company. But it is these kinds of institutional investors who have a direct stake in the firms in question that are best positioned to keep wayward management in line. Hoping that "regulators" will perceive such problems, when they have none of their own money at stake, and when (as in the present crisis) they have a track record of identifying problems as virtues, holds out much less promise. Because of this government policy, stockholders of these institutions are artificially disorganized and scattered, and cannot discipline bank management properly. Management, meanwhile, enjoys an artificial protection that would not exist on the free market. When bank managers feather their nests under such a system, our commentators then react with surprise.[67]

Investment bank "leverage" was too high, say critics. In other words, these institutions were looking to multiply their gains by using money borrowed at low interest rates to purchase long-term assets they expected to increase in value. These institutions may well have engaged in too much of this, but we should pause to consider why they might have done so. Why would equity ratios be so low in the financial industry, and so much higher everywhere else? (And it is a contagion: once one firm starts borrowing short-term funds to buy longer-term assets, other firms feel compelled to follow suit if they don't want to be left in the dust.) Could it be that the financial industry, unlike the shellfish industry or the publishing industry, has a giant sugar daddy in the form of the Federal Reserve standing in the wings to provide "liquidity" at critical moments, with the federal government, on "too big to fail" grounds, standing ready to assist them in case of an especially serious problem? When Alan Greenspan made sure the Long Term Capital Management hedge fund was bailed out in 1998,

Wall Street firms naturally concluded that if a hedge fund wasn't allowed to fail, then surely no investment bank would be permitted to go under. Even the International Monetary Fund admitted, in an April 2008 report, that big financial institutions were taking excessive risks in the expectation that their central bank would bail them out. They have grown "more complacent about their liquidity risk management systems and 'underinsure[d]' against an adverse liquidity event, depending more heavily on central bank intervention for their liquidity problems."[68] The Fed's interference with short-term interest rates, moreover, and what has been politely called its "overly accommodative" monetary policy, has much to do with the leverage employed by financial intermediaries. New York Fed President William Dudley observed in 2009 that "there is a growing body of economics literature on this issue that links monetary policy to leverage."[69]

It is the system itself, in other words, that is the problem. According to economist Guido Hülsmann:

> The banks must keep certain minimum amounts of equity and reserves, they must observe a great number of rules in granting credit, their executives must have certain qualifications, and so on. Yet these stipulations trim the branches without attacking the root. They seek to curb certain known excesses that spring from moral hazard, but they do not eradicate moral hazard itself. As we have seen, moral hazard is implied in the very existence of paper money. Because a paper-money producer can bail out virtually anybody, the citizens become reckless in their speculations; they count on him to bail them out, especially when many other people do the same thing. To fight such behavior effectively, one must abolish paper money. Regulations merely drive the reckless behavior into new channels.
>
> One might advocate the pragmatic stance of fighting moral hazard on an ad hoc basis wherever it shows up. Thus one would regulate one industry after another, until the entire economy is caught up in a web of micro-regulations. This would of course provide some sort of order, but it would be the order of a cemetery. Nobody could make any (potentially reckless!) investment decisions anymore. Everything

would have to follow rules set up by the legislature. In short, the only way to fight moral hazard without destroying its source, fiat inflation, is to subject the economy to a Soviet-style central plan.

If we want to understand the source of banking instability, we might start there, instead of fooling ourselves into believing that another round of regulations, which as surely as night follows day will be gamed by the major players, will keep things stable.

Fake Deregulation Causes Problems? Blame Them on Capitalism

One of the reasons deregulation is viewed with so much skepticism and even hostility is that disasters of various kinds have been falsely, even laughably, blamed on deregulation. For Americans over a certain age, deregulation recalls the presidency of Ronald Reagan, and in particular the sad story of the Savings and Loan institutions (S&Ls), in which 747 of those institutions failed at a cost of over $160 billion, most of which was paid by means of a federal government bailout. In the days before Reagan and his crazy deregulation spree, the story runs, everything worked fine. Then Reagan was elected, and he repealed all the laws. Society reverted to barbarism. Wolves ran free in the streets.

What actually happened was rather less cartoonish. First, so-called deregulation of the S&Ls began under Jimmy Carter, not Reagan. I say "so-called" because, as with most measures trumpeted as "deregulation," it was not really deregulation: all throughout the process of alleged deregulation, the S&Ls' deposits continued to be covered under government deposit insurance. Deregulation means the removal of government involvement and control. Does this sound like the removal of government involvement and control? To the contrary, it gave us the worst of both worlds—now the government-guaranteed institution was permitted to take greater risks while taxpayers remained on the hook for any losses. Not exactly the free market at work.

Under the government-established rules, the S&Ls could charge 6 percent on 30-year mortgage loans, and could offer depositors 3 percent. Since most depositors had nowhere else to go, they had to content themselves with a mere 3 percent return. But with the advent of the money-market mutual fund, ordinary people suddenly had the chance to earn higher returns than S&Ls could pay, and began pulling their money out of S&Ls in droves. Consequently, the S&Ls wanted permission to offer higher interest returns for depositors, so "deregulation" allowed them to do so. Had the original government requirements remained in place, the S&Ls would have gone under then and there.

A consensus began to form that in order to save the S&Ls, their government-established loan and deposit interest-rate requirements, as well as the kind of loans they could make, had to be modified in light of the impossible conditions under which these institutions were then being forced to operate. The S&Ls needed to be permitted to engage in riskier investments than 30-year mortgages at 6 percent. (Notice: it's the free market's fault when the *government* modifies the *government-established* rules of a *government-established* institution, while deposits continue to be guaranteed by the *government*. Got it?)

Maybe the S&Ls *should* have gone under in 1980. Perhaps they really did have an impossible business model. There is no non-arbitrary basis for deciding one way or the other, since the S&Ls were never genuinely subject to a market test. The government husbanded and cartelized the S&Ls, and stood ready to bail them out after that. Yet the string of failures continues to be blamed on "deregulation" and the market.

More recently, in the financial crisis that first gripped the world in 2007 and 2008, we have seen yet another crisis falsely blamed on the market. We have already discussed the American case, but Iceland, which was particularly hard hit, is supposed to be the classic case of the free market run amok. Before it was over, the country's stock market had fallen 90 percent, all major banks had gone under, and a severe recession and a shortage of consumer goods bore down on the public.

What remedy did our media class propose for Iceland? More regulation—what else?

Without having to know the first thing about that country, readers will already have surmised what a closer look at "free-market" Iceland will turn up: government interventions, guarantees, and moral hazard all over the place, particularly in money and banking. And that is exactly what we find.

Iceland, like the United States, experienced a gigantic housing bubble in the years leading up to the crash.[70] And like the United States, the sources of that bubble were government and the central bank. Iceland's Housing Financing

Fund, whose debt enjoyed an explicit government guarantee (in contrast to the only implicit guarantees enjoyed in the United States by Fannie Mae and Freddie Mac), artificially stimulated home purchases. Its low-interest loans were available to anyone without discrimination, and not just to those who fell below a certain income level. It was against this government-subsidized system that the "private" banks of Iceland had to compete. The predictable result was a race to the bottom in loan quality.

Add to this a very loose monetary policy: the Bank of Iceland, a creature of the Icelandic government rather than the free market, increased the money supply (M1) by between 20 and 30 percent per year from 2002 to 2007. This monetary expansion added fuel to the housing bubble, and gave rise to the structural distortions that Austrian business cycle theory describes. Unsustainable expansions in the aluminum, construction, and financial services industries were only the most obvious of these.

The Bank of Iceland also offered Icelandic banks an explicit guarantee that it stood ready to roll over their short-term debt if a liquidity crisis should arise. With that guarantee in their pockets, banks engaged in what would ordinarily be the risky practice of maturity mismatching, borrowing short term (and consistently rolling over, or renewing, those loans) in order to invest in long-term assets, pocketing the difference in interest rates between the two. Risk was practically removed by the Central Bank of Iceland, and thus the practice grew to levels it would never have reached on a free market.

When liquidity began to dry up in 2008, the Icelandic banks were stuck—and the Bank of Iceland, promise or no, could not help them. It could create additional supplies of the króna, the domestic currency, but it couldn't create yen and other currencies to help the banks pay off their foreign liabilities. And the banks had been piling up liabilities in other currencies, particularly the Japanese yen. Loans denominated in yen must be paid back in yen. The credit-induced mania ended in disaster, which—in spite of the fingerprints of the government and the central bank all over it—was promptly blamed on the free market.

You Need Your Head Examined, Says Harvard

The way the political and media establishments have addressed the claim that the housing bubble and resulting financial crisis might have been caused by something other than "unregulated capitalism" has been by pretending such a point of view does not exist. The academic world has been even worse. In 2009, Harvard University sponsored a conference called "The Free Market Mindset: History, Psychology, and Consequences." Its purpose was to try to figure out why, since *everyone knows* the financial crisis amounted to a failure of the market economy, the stupid rubes continue to believe in it. The promotional literature for the conference opened with Alan Greenspan's testimony before Congress in 2009, when he claimed in the face of all the arguments we have raised here that there was a "flaw" in the free market he hadn't noticed before.

Well, that does it, then. If our Soviet commissar in charge of money and interest rates says the free market doesn't work, who are you to disagree?

The promotional material continued: "If the current state of the U.S. economy makes clear that former Federal Reserve Chairman Alan Greenspan's faith in free markets was misplaced, the question remains: what was it about free markets that proved—and still continues to prove—so alluring to economists, scholars, and policy-makers alike?" Because if there's one guiding principle behind the largest government in history, it's *free markets*.

This conference, we were told, would bring together "leading scholars in law, economics, social psychology, and social cognition to present and discuss their research regarding the historical origins, psychological antecedents, and policy consequences of the free market mindset." So instead of trying to understand the free-market position itself, they prefer instead to study the twisted brains of those who advance it.

In short, the conference was about this: *Why do people still think the interaction of free individuals is a superior economic system to one directed by Harvard Ph.D.s? Why do people cling to the idea that being herded into a collective run by the experts isn't the best way to live? Why won't the proles just shut up and go along with what their betters tell them?*

So by assuming from the outset the very thing that needs to be proven—namely, that the current state of the economy just occurred spontaneously, as the result of wicked market forces—our betters relieve themselves of the need to consider their opponents' case. Their opponents do not have a case. They are deranged.

I wonder if anyone at the conference asked questions like this:

When Alan Greenspan flooded the economy with newly created money and brought interest rates down to destructively low levels, thereby distorting entrepreneurial calculation as well as consumers' home purchasing decisions, was that the fault of the free market? Do you think the Fed's creation of cheap credit out of thin air makes market participants more careful or less careful in how they allocate borrowed funds?

When Long Term Capital Management was bailed out in 1998, and Alan Greenspan made clear that the Fed's assistance would be forthcoming were he unable to lean on his friends in the financial industry, was that a "free market" phenomenon? Do you think the Fed thereby encouraged more or less risk-taking among other major market actors?

The *Financial Times* spoke in 2000, in the wake of the dot-com boom, of an increasing concern that the so-called "Greenspan put" was injecting into the economy "a destructive tendency toward excessively risky investment supported by hopes that the Fed will help if things go bad." "All the insane dot-com investment we've seen, all this destruction of capital, all the crazy excesses of the past few years wouldn't have happened without the easy credit accommodated by the Fed," added financial consultant Michael Belkin.[71] Did the free market cause that?

Do lending standards decline for no particular reason, or could this phenomenon have a teensy bit to do with (a) government regulation aimed at increasing "homeownership" and (b) loose monetary policy by the Fed?

Questions like these could go on and on. Not one, you can be certain, was raised that day at Harvard.

Now if you really wanted to sponsor an event whose purpose was to try to understand why people continue to believe things that have been falsified by reality, you'd do much better to hold a conference on socialism, or on economist John Maynard Keynes and his school. It would be fascinating to learn the psychological motivation behind the persistence of Keynesian economics, whose popular version is a non-falsifiable, ersatz religion. Is Japan's economy still suffering? Why, that's because Japan didn't spend enough—even though it spent so much that it became the most indebted country in the developed world. Have people spent so much that they're now burdened with debt they can't possibly repay? Then we need *more* spending. (But don't worry—we'll repay it when the economy turns around, just as we always have in the past!) Is the economy a distorted mess after an artificial boom? Then instead of letting the economy restructure itself along sustainable lines, let's instead "stimulate" the system just as it is, with the goal of bringing about more "consumption," more "labor" employed, and higher "income," without bothering to disaggregate any of these things and deciding *what kinds* of labor need to go where, *what kinds* of consumption are sustainable and what are figments of the bubble economy, or how the capital structure needs to be reassembled in order to cater to genuine consumer demand.

People who believe in the market economy support a social order in which free individuals make voluntary contracts with each other, and no one can initiate physical force against anyone else. Is that vision so obviously unattractive that we have to refer its supporters for psychological evaluation? We might instead wonder about the psychological condition of those who would denounce such a system: might they be motivated, for all their noble talk, by nothing but base envy of those with more material wealth than they, or by a pathological desire to dominate other people? Maybe that will be covered at next year's conference.

CHAPTER 4

Elephant in the Living Room: The Real Story of the Federal Reserve

s recently as 2006, the Federal Reserve System (or the "Fed") was exactly where it prefers to be: quietly engaged in its policy decisions regarding interest rates and money creation, and off the table for political discussion. Most Americans had no idea what it did or even what it was, and politicians never said a word about it. Anyone who did mention it was probably a crank, who really ought to have more confidence in the wise management of the experts.

Most Americans still have no idea what the Fed is, but popular awareness of, and opposition to, the Fed is now at its highest level in American history. Thanks to the financial crisis, the work of Congressman Ron Paul, and the ability of the Internet to circumvent the gatekeepers of approved opinion, a small but determined anti-Fed constituency has developed among people who understand that the Fed, supposedly the source of economic stability, is giving us instability. This alleged guardian of the dollar has actually been lowering the dollar's value. And this institution, supposedly a great bulwark of capitalism, is in fact a central-planning agency at odds with the basic principles of a free market.

Commentators with high media profiles have helped to pour fuel on this growing anti-Fed fire. Peter Schiff, the president of Euro Pacific Capital we noted in chapter 3, may be the best known of these. Schiff foretold the crisis, including the bankruptcy of Fannie Mae and Freddie Mac. His books *Crash Proof, The Little Book of Bull Moves in Bear Markets*, and *How an Economy Grows and Why It Crashes*, all of which have sold well, take an Austrian approach to current conditions.

Schiff is far from alone. James Grant, editor of the influential *Grant's Interest Rate Observer*, is another Austrian analyst prominent in the print media and television. Famed investor Jim Rogers calls for the abolition of the Fed when he's a guest on business networks, and has in fact predicted the Fed's demise sometime in the next ten years. Rogers, incidentally, co-founded the Quantum Fund in 1970, which saw its portfolio gain 4,200 percent over the following ten years; he is also the founder of the Rogers International Commodity Index. There are more such critics. Their number is growing.

The Federal Reserve System, the American central bank, enjoys a government-granted monopoly on the creation of legal-tender money. It has been given the task of manipulating the money supply in such a way as to maximize employment and output and minimize price inflation. It is designed to give the United States a "flexible" currency, which in practice means a currency that can be inflated in order to suit the needs of government and financial institutions. Fed chairmen have boasted of their institution's ability to foresee and prevent economic crises, and to mitigate those that do occur. For a long time, people accepted claims like these.

These days, more and more people are less and less sure about them.

Since the Fed opened its doors in 1914 following the passage of the Federal Reserve Act in December 1913, the dollar has lost more than 95 percent of its value, after having held its value intact from the beginning of the republic until the creation of the Fed. Most of this debasement of the dollar has taken place since 1971, when the last vestiges of the gold standard were removed and the central bank could inflate the money supply with much greater abandon.

When people raise questions about the utility of the Fed, they are usually lectured about how volatile the economy used to be and how much better it is now, thanks to the wise oversight of our central bank. Recent research has thrown cold water on this claim. Christina Romer finds that the numbers and dating used by the National Bureau of Economic Research (NBER, the largest economics research organization in the United States, founded in 1920) exaggerate both the number and the length of economic downturns prior to the creation of the Fed. In so doing, the NBER likewise overestimates the Fed's contribution to economic stability. Recessions were in fact not more frequent in the pre-Fed than the post-Fed period.[1]

But let's be real sports about it, and compare only the post-World War II period to the pre-Fed period, thereby excluding the Great Depression from the Fed's record. (The Great Depression, we all know, was just *practice*.)[2] In that case, we do find economic contractions to be somewhat more frequent in the period before the Fed, but as economist George Selgin explains, "They were also almost three months *shorter* on average, and no more severe."[3] Recoveries were also faster in the pre-Fed period, with the average time peak to bottom taking only 7.7 months as opposed to the 10.6 months of the post-World War II period. Extending our pre-Fed period to include 1796 to 1915, economist Joseph Davis finds no appreciable difference between the length and duration of recessions as compared to the period of the Fed.[4]

But perhaps the Fed has helped to stabilize real output (the total amount of goods and services an economy produces in a given period of time, adjusted to remove the effects of inflation), thereby decreasing economic volatility. Not so. Some recent research finds the two periods (pre- and post-Fed) to be approximately equal in volatility, and some finds the post-Fed period in fact to be *more* volatile, once faulty data are corrected for. The ups and downs in output that did exist before the creation of the Fed were not attributable to the lack of a central bank. Output volatility before the Fed was caused almost entirely by supply shocks that tend to affect an agricultural society (harvest failures and such), while output volatility after the Fed is to a much greater extent the fault of the monetary system.[5]

When we look back at the nineteenth century, we discover that the monetary and banking instability that existed then were not caused by the absence of a government-established agency issuing unbacked paper money. According to Richard Timberlake, a well-known economist and historian of American monetary and banking history, "As monetary histories confirm...most of the monetary turbulence—bank panics and suspensions in the nineteenth century—resulted from excessive issues of legal-tender paper money, and they were abated by the working gold standards of the times."[6] In a nutshell, we are faced once again with the faults of interventionism being blamed on the free market. Here we'll look at just two illustrative examples.

The Panic of 1819 was the result of years of artificial credit creation by the banks, including the newly chartered Second Bank of the United States, established in 1817.[7] That is to say, the banks issued far more paper money than they had gold to back it in their vaults. As often happens when the country is flooded with money created out of thin air, speculation of all kinds grew intense, as eyewitness testimony abundantly records. The country was on a sugar high, based not on real savings but on mere paper.

During the years when the United States had no central bank (the period from 1811, when the charter of the first Bank of the United States expired, and 1817), government had granted private banks the privilege of expanding credit while refusing to pay depositors demanding their funds. In other words, when people came to demand their money from the banks, the banks were allowed to tell them they didn't have the money, that depositors would simply have to wait a couple years—and at the same time, the bank was allowed to continue in operation. By early 1817 the Madison administration finally required the banks to meet depositor demands, but at the same time chartered the Second Bank of the United States, which would itself be inflationary. The Bank subsequently presided over an inflationary boom, which came to grief in 1819.[8]

The lesson of that sorry episode—namely, that the economy gets taken on a wild and unhealthy ride when the money supply is dramatically and artificially increased and then suddenly reduced—was so obvious that even the political class managed to figure it out. Numerous American statesmen were confirmed in their hard-money views by the Panic. Thomas Jefferson asked a friend in the Virginia legislature to introduce his "Plan for Reducing the Circulating Medium," which the Sage of Monticello had drawn up in response to the Panic. The plan sought to withdraw all paper money in excess of specie over a five-year period, then redeem the rest in specie and have precious-metal coins circulate exclusively from that moment on. Jefferson and John Adams were especially fond of Destutt de Tracy's hard-money

Treatise on the Will (1815), with Adams calling it the best book on economics ever written (its chapter on money, said Adams, defends "the sentiments that I have entertained all my lifetime") and Jefferson writing the preface to the English-language edition.[9]

While the Panic of 1819 confirmed some political figures in the hard-money views they already held, it also converted others to that position. Condy Raguet had been an outspoken inflationist until 1819. After observing the distortions and instability caused by paper-money inflation, he promptly embraced hard money, and went on to write *A Treatise on Currency and Banking* (1839), one of the great money and banking treatises of the nineteenth century. Davy Crockett, future president William Henry Harrison, and John Quincy Adams (at least at that time) were likewise opposed to inflationist banks; in contrast to the inflationary Second Bank of the United States, Adams cited the hard-money Bank of Amsterdam as a model to emulate. Daniel Raymond, disciple of Alexander Hamilton and author of the first treatise on economics published in America (*Thoughts on Political Economy*, 1820), expressly broke with Hamilton in advocating a hard-money, 100 percent specie-backed currency.[10]

For a long time, the Panic of 1873 was said to have inaugurated the so-called Long Depression, which lasted until 1879 in the more sober accounts, and until 1896 in the more outlandish ones. However, the modern consensus is that there was in fact no "Long Depression" after all. Even the *New York Times*, which admits nothing, admits this:

> Recent detailed reconstructions of nineteenth-century data by economic historians show that there was no 1870s depression: aside from a short recession in 1873, in fact, the decade saw possibly the fastest sustained growth in American history. Employment grew strongly, faster than the rate of immigration; consumption of food and other goods rose across the board. On a per capita basis, almost all output measures were up spectacularly. By the end of the decade, people were better housed, better clothed and lived on bigger farms. Department stores were popping up even in medium-sized cities. America was transforming into the world's first mass consumer society.

Farmers, moreover, who panicked at falling prices for agricultural com-modities, at first failed to note that other prices were falling still faster. The terms of trade for American farmers improved considerably during the 1870s.[11]

As for historians, they seem to have been fooled by the statistics on consumer prices, which fell an average of 3.8 percent per year. And since the conventional wisdom says that consistently falling prices will cause the earth to break free of its axis and go tumbling toward the sun, they concluded that this must have been a time of terrible depression. With the gold standard restored in 1879 after being abandoned during the Civil War, the 1880s were likewise a period of great prosperity, with real wages rising by 20 percent.

The argument that the U.S. economy was susceptible to panics without the wise custodianship of a central bank can also be dismantled another way. In the nineteenth century, nearly all American states instituted a regulation known as unit banking, which limited all banks to a single office. No branch banking was allowed, whether intrastate or interstate. The obvious result was a very fragile and undiversified banking system in which banks could be brought to ruin if local conditions turned sour.

The banking panics that struck the United States between the Civil War and World War I occurred either during the spring planting season or the fall harvest, and were closely connected to the cycle of cotton production. That is no coincidence. Those are the times when bank lending (and leverage) is at its peak, and thus the banks are most vulnerable to shifts in depositor confidence and the likelihood of withdrawals by risk-averse depositors.[12] In other words, with bank capital constant but the amount of loans increasing, bank leverage by definition grows, and those depositors most concerned about the riskiness of their bank's activities are at that moment most likely to take their money out, thereby making the bank's condition more fragile. The Fed supplied banks with a source of liquidity during moments of temporary but intense depositor pres-sure like these.

So is the Fed therefore the great savior? Only if we forget two things. First, other countries, which had not crippled their banking systems with unit banking laws, had been safe from these panics all along. Canada, which had fractional-reserve banking like the United States but no unit banking laws, avoided all the financial turmoil of American bank panics, and without the help of a central bank—the Bank of Canada was not established until 1934.

As Milton Friedman was fond of pointing out, although the Great Depression claimed over 9,000 American banks, the number of banks that failed in Canada at that time was *zero*. American bank panics, it turns out, were in large part the result of government intervention—in the form of unit banking—in the first place.

Imagine that: less regulation, more stability.

Second, it is by no means clear that the Fed was particularly successful in stopping bank panics, a phenomenon that came to an end only with the advent of deposit insurance in 1934. Andrew Jalil of the University of California, Berkeley, concluded in a 2009 study that "contrary to the conventional wisdom, there is no evidence of a decline in the frequency of panics during the first fifteen years of the existence of the Federal Reserve."[13] Elmus Wicker, in *Banking Panics of the Gilded Age* (2000), observes that "there were no more than three major banking panics between 1873 and 1907 [inclusive], and two incipient banking panics in 1884 and 1890. Twelve years elapsed between the panic of 1861 and the panic of 1873, twenty years between the panics of 1873 and 1893, and fourteen years between 1893 and 1907: three banking panics in half a century! And in only one of the three, 1893, did the number of bank suspensions match those of the Great Depression." By contrast, there were five separate bank panics in the first three years of the Great Depression alone.[14]

Even during these pre-Fed panics the bank failure rate was small, as were the losses depositors suffered. Depositor losses amounted to only 0.1 percent of GDP during the Panic of 1893, which was the worst of them all with respect to bank failures and depositor losses. By contrast, in just the past thirty years of the central bank era, the world has seen twenty banking crises that led to depositor losses in excess of 10 percent of GDP. Half of those saw losses in excess of 20 percent of GDP.[15]

Contrary to popular belief, the age of central banking has not in fact given us a world with fewer banking crises, if we define a crisis as a wave of bank failures associated with large losses. Between 1874 and 1913, we count four such crises: Argentina (1890), Australia (1893), Italy (1893), and Norway (1900). (Interestingly enough, each of these countries experienced a boom and bust in real estate, which had been subsidized by these governments in ways meant to evade market discipline.) Between 1978 and 2008, on the other hand, there were 140 banking crises, twenty of which were worse than the two worst (Argentina and Australia) from the earlier period.[16]

Our Enemy, Inflation

Just as important as revising the history of the Fed in light of sounder data and research is increased scrutiny of what the Fed is doing in the present. The Federal Reserve has been criticized for bringing about ever-higher prices, for instance. (Inflation is the increase in the supply of money; higher prices, which are themselves sometimes called inflation, are merely the effects of inflation.) An artificial increase in the supply of money tends to push prices higher than they would have moved otherwise. When we read criticisms of inflation, they're usually confined to the problems faced by people on fixed incomes when prices rise. If someone's income consists of an invariable one thousand dollars per month and the prices of the goods he buys double, the purchasing power of his income is cut in half.

But the problems of inflation go much deeper than this. For one thing, inflation has unjust redistribution (or Cantillon) effects. The process whereby government or its privileged central bank creates money inevitably enriches politically well-connected groups at the expense of everyone else. When the Fed creates new money out of thin air, that new money is not distributed in equal proportions to all Americans. A helicopter does not fly over the country, evenly distributing the new money among the people. To the contrary, the new money enters the economy at discrete points. Whoever receives it first gets to spend it before it has circulated throughout the economy and raised prices. The windfall the privileged enjoy comes at the direct expense of average people, who lack the political connections to be among the first in line to receive the newly created money. Those people pay the higher prices that the new money brings about before that new money reaches them. And who gets the new money first? Banks, businesses with government contracts, investment banks that sell government bonds to the Federal Reserve, and the like. The reader will detect a pattern here.

All known cases of hyperinflation, which is sometimes defined as a 50 percent or higher rise in the price level per month, have occurred under a system of paper money. The devastating consequences of hyperinflation are not just economic, as the frugal and provident watch the value of their savings vanish into thin air. Its consequences are social, political, cultural, and even spiritual.

Inflation at any level has these kinds of effects. Saving and thrift seem less desirable when money is going to lose value over time; it makes more sense to spend right now while its value is at its height. Old-fashioned moral advice about thrift and provision for the future seems stupid and backward to an inflationary generation.

Governments that hold a monopoly on the issuance of money have had a bad habit of debasing and destroying that money, a habit whose ill effects have been all the greater as governments have moved away from precious-metal money and into paper money whose value they can more readily manipulate. From 1066 to the early seventeenth century, the English silver pound was debased by one third, for a depreciation factor of 0.3. Over the next 200 years, with the rise of modern banking, the supply increased by a factor of sixteen. In just the thirty years from 1973 to 2003, the U.S. money supply (M1) increased by a factor of five. Naturally, with a record like this, prices have fluctuated considerably, especially compared with the relative stability of prices under the gold standard of the nineteenth century. "A study of about 30 currencies," writes Swiss economist Peter Bernholz, "shows that there has not been a single case of a currency freely manipulated by its government or central bank since 1700 that enjoyed price stability for at least 30 years running."[17]

As we saw in chapter 3, the very existence of a monopoly producer of legal-tender paper money fosters moral hazard. There is no physical limitation on the creation of additional paper money, as there would be on the creation of additional gold. Virtually no scarce resources are necessary. For that reason, major market actors know there is no physical constraint on bailing them out in emergencies. The only obstacle—easily conquered, as we know all too well—is one of political will.

Fiat money likewise bestows on government far more power than it would otherwise enjoy. Government can now raise money for itself in the inconspicuous way of creating it out of thin air. It can get away with siphoning resources from the citizenry without having to raise taxes or borrow so much that it drives up interest rates for private borrowers. Both of these means of raising revenue attract public ire. In political calculations, it appears far better to tax the people by the surreptitious means of not allowing prices to fall, as they would naturally, and in fact causing them to rise, thereby reducing the people's standard of living. Hardly anyone will understand this process, and most people can be made to believe that greedy businessmen and price gougers are the source of their woes.

Fiat money artificially and unjustly increases the wealth and economic power of the banking system, well beyond what would occur in the free market. Ordinary individuals earn money by providing some good or service, and then take that money into the market to acquire the goods and services they themselves wish to have. Creating money out of thin air, on the other hand, allows the money creator to enter the market and seize the goods or services he wants *without* having supplied anything himself. As one monetary economist has written,

> The market economy can be understood as a great organism that caters to the needs of consumers as expressed in money payments. When the economy is flooded with legal-tender fractional-reserve notes, the whole economic body of society begins to cater excessively to the needs of those who control the banking industry. The American economist Frank Fetter once observed that the unhampered market economy resembled a grassroots democratic process: one penny, one market vote. From this point of view the imposition of fractional-reserve notes through legal-tender laws creates market votes out of nothing. The bankers and their clients (usually the government in the first place) have many more votes than they would have had in a free society.[18]

While others are enriched, the average person has to struggle to save. With his money losing value every year, he would be ruined if he saved for the future by piling up paper dollars. Under a precious-metal money, people could save for the future by simply acquiring gold and silver coins. (Investing that money could yield them still higher returns, but they always retained this more conservative option.) Back when they circulated as money, they held or increased their value over time. Today, on the other hand, just to hold on to the purchasing power of their savings, to say nothing of increasing it, people have to become speculators, navigating their way through the financial markets as best they can. If the stock market should tumble, there goes their retirement.

Even this does not exhaust the arguments against irredeemable paper money. Artificial money creation by a central bank can also influence the business cycle, which we discussed in chapter 3. Business calculation is undermined when what looks like profits can turn out to be nothing more than a general rise in prices. Then there is the moral argument that no system of fiat money has ever emerged voluntarily; it is always imposed by means of the state's apparatus of compulsion.

Still, supporters of government fiat money insist on the beneficial aspects of inflation. We need inflation, we're told, because a growing economy can function only if the supply of money increases along with it. This is a fallacy. Any supply of money can facilitate any number of transactions. If the supply of goods and services should double, we do not need—and it would be positively disruptive—to double the supply of money along with it. Prices simply fall by half, and the same supply of money can purchase the entire supply of goods.

Until the early twentieth century, in fact, peacetime prices fell consistently throughout American history. This will come as a surprise to most Americans, who, having grown accustomed to seeing consumer prices rise over time, have thoughtlessly if understandably assumed that this must be how the economy works. But it isn't. Under hard money the supply of money grows relatively slowly, and the supply of other goods and services increases more rapidly. With these goods and services more abundant with respect to money, their prices fall.

Today we're told that this would be a terrible situation. Just terrible. Because if consumer prices fell, and were expected to continue falling, no one would ever buy anything. We'd all be sitting back waiting for prices to fall even more. Only on our deathbeds, presumably, as we were taking in our last breaths, would we frantically grasp an iPod, a paperback, and a new leather jacket.

We wouldn't need to spend any time refuting this crazy theory if it weren't constantly repeated by our talking heads, whose job it is to warn us of the unthinkable scenarios that would arise were we not carefully supervised by our self-sacrificing public servants. It is true that people prefer lower prices to higher ones, but it is also true that they value goods in the present more highly than they do the same goods in the future. This factor offsets the desire to wait indefinitely for a lower price. A candy bar today is more serviceable to a consumer than is a candy bar available only two, ten, or four hundred years from now, even if the candy bar will be cheaper then. Sane people do not refuse to purchase a one-dollar cup of coffee just because they expect the price to fall to 95 cents three years from now. The prices of personal computers have steadily fallen while their quality has steadily risen. Have we all stoically awaited still further declines in price, or have a few of us broken down and actually purchased a computer?

Then we're told that falling prices must threaten business profitability and even lead to mass bankruptcies. How can business firms survive if the selling prices of their goods suddenly fall?[19]

If the deflation is anticipated, there is no problem. Businesses remain just as profitable as they would have been had prices risen or remained constant (as long as they had anticipated those outcomes as well). If business firms expect prices to fall by the time they bring their goods to market, they will be willing to pay less in the present for all the inputs, or factors of production (resources employed to produce goods and services), they need to produce their goods. If a general fall in prices is expected, suppliers of these factors of production will have no choice but to accept these lower bids for their goods and services, since no one will be able to afford to continue buying inputs from them at the old, higher price level while remaining profitable. In this way, an expected fall in consumer prices *is factored in* to the prices business firms pay for the goods they use as inputs, thereby maintaining profitability for these firms even in the face of falling prices.

Thus a widget company may pay $10 in inputs for every widget it produces, and be able to sell each of these widgets to the public at $15. Suppose prices begin to fall, and widgets are expected to sell at only $9 (instead of $15) by the time they are ready to be brought to market next year. The widget manufacturer can now afford to continue producing widgets if he can acquire his inputs for, say, $6 instead of the previous $10. If he can do so, then he will still make a profit even in this deflationary environment. There will still be a positive spread between his sales revenues and his costs. But if, as is the case in a general deflation, all prices are falling, suppliers will have no choice but to cut prices (which they can

indeed do, since their own costs will be falling given the general fall in prices).*
Production will continue profitably as before.

What if the deflation is unanticipated? In that case, some firms will find
themselves unable to sell their product at a price that will bring them an adequate return, and they may even suffer losses (because the prices they can fetch
for their products, thanks to the deflation, are lower than they expected them
to be). In effect, they find that they had paid too much for the factors of production to leave them with a profit, in light of the lower prices they can now
charge for their products. For that reason, the result of unanticipated deflation
for a given firm could very well be bankruptcy. The firm would then wind up
in bankruptcy court, where reorganization of the firm or the sale and distribution of its assets to its creditors in order of seniority takes place.

Now if the assets are sold off, they are merely shifted from one production
process to another but continue in use. If the firm continues in operation but
under new ownership, as the firm's creditors take the reins, its previous production process likewise continues as before. So while bankruptcy is most unfortunate for a particular firm, it is of no significance to the economy in the
aggregate. It does not matter to economic activity who the particular owners of
firms happen to be. If ownership changes hands from one group of people to
another as the result of bankruptcy proceedings, this does not matter from the
point of view of the economy as a whole. From the economy's perspective,
nothing has changed. Production continues as before.

As we saw in chapter 3, central bank inflation that pumps money into the
banking system and pushes interest rates down gives rise to an artificial economic
boom that distorts the structure of production and encourages the creation or
expansion of sectors of the economy that will have to contract or close down when
the inevitable bust comes along. These kinds of inflation-fueled distortions do not
occur in a deflationary environment. The worst that could happen from the point
of view of production is a series of hiccups, minor and temporary interruptions,
while bankruptcy courts sort out questions of ownership and compensation.

---

* If suppliers of factors of production will not lower their prices, that means they have profitable
opportunities elsewhere to sell their goods. This is not deflation but the common, indispensable process of the free market whereby factors of production get bid away from less urgent
to more urgent uses, thereby rearranging the structure of production to conform to consumer
demand.

Critics will reply that deflation is indeed a terrible fate to be avoided because firms loaded with debt will find those debts harder to pay back—a $1 million loan contracted five years ago is more difficult to repay today if the dollar has increased in value (and is thus now harder to come by) in the meantime, just as a debt is easier to pay if the dollar has lost value during the period of the loan. For one thing, banks could simply renegotiate the debt in light of the money's increased purchasing power. But even if banks insisted on payment of the debt in the agreed-upon number of nominal dollars, we are faced merely with the problem of bankruptcy—again, a problem for an individual firm, but not a problem for the economy at large. Once again, new owners take over, and production continues as before.

And who says heavy debt and high leverage are the best means for financing a business firm? Why should these means be artificially encouraged? Perhaps it would be better, especially in light of the staggering private debt levels of recent years, to have a system that encourages firms to finance themselves with equity rather than more and more debt.

Finally, we might note that deflation, contrary to what we often hear, has not in fact been associated with economic depression in history. According to a 2004 study in the *American Economic Review*, which examined data from around the world, "The data suggest that deflation is not closely related to depressions. A broad historical look finds more periods of deflation with reasonable growth than with depression, and many more periods of depression with inflation than with deflation. *Overall, the data show virtually no link between deflation and depression.*"[20]

To be sure, there is much more that both sides can say about deflation, but this simple analysis should be enough to make the reader suspect that a fall in prices may not be the end of the world after all. But if that's true, then why all the hysteria about deflation, hysteria we never hear with respect to *in*flation?

Think about who suffers most during deflation. One victim is the government—which, always deeply in debt in the modern era, has a much harder time servicing that debt when it has to repay debt-holders with more valuable dollars than it borrowed. Another is the array of financial firms on Wall Street that have arranged their debt-based investment strategies in the Fed-inspired expectation of ongoing price inflation. When these firms suddenly find they need to repay short-term debt in more valuable dollars than they borrowed, their debt-fueled house of cards comes crashing down.

Note that some of the most powerful and influential forces in society—those that benefit most from cheap money, and who get the newly created money before anyone else—are the ones most hurt by deflation. Everyone else benefits from falling prices and therefore higher real incomes. More to the point, those people who suffered from the inflation—not just those on fixed incomes but also the general run of the population—and who wound up paying higher prices for everything they bought, now benefit from the increase in the dollar's value and the fall in prices. (Economist Joseph Salerno suggests the term *rabbatage* to refer to this reversal of fortunes that occurs during deflation.)[21]

Thus it is little wonder that we hear nothing but hysteria about deflation, which hurts the political and economic establishment the most, and only the mildest concern about inflation, which hurts everyone else. If I were the head of a highly leveraged firm and worried about my firm's ability to service its debt, or if I headed the Federal Reserve System, which consistently inflates away the dollar's purchasing power and gives the country higher prices than we would otherwise have faced, I too would want to portray deflation as an unthinkable disaster from which ongoing doses of inflation are meant to protect you. But deflation is not an economic problem, as we have seen. It is a political problem, in that those parties that expect to be hurt by it seek to use the machinery of government and central banking to prevent it or at least mitigate its effects.

Now it's true that a massive unanticipated deflation would cause widespread and undesirable disruption for a lot of business owners, though as we've seen it need not interfere with overall production to any significant extent. But if this is your concern, then hard money becomes all the more desirable. Because the process of gold and silver mining is so time consuming, and thus increases in gold and silver coming on to the market are telegraphed well into the future, it is far easier to anticipate the future movement of the money supply under gold or silver than it is to anticipate how much money a central bank chairman might choose to create or destroy. More importantly, the supply of gold and silver isn't going anywhere. It is not subject to sudden drops the way paper money is. All the gold and silver that have ever been mined are still available somewhere on the earth's surface. The supply of paper money, precisely because it can be created at will and in any amount out of thin air, fluctuates wildly in supply when compared to the relatively stable supply of gold and silver. Sudden crashes involving massive drops in the supply of money do not occur in a hard-money system.

Fashionable opinion is of course horrified at and dismissive of the gold standard. It's stupid, it's backward, it's not sophisticated like our money-printing system of today, etc. If figures of prominence ridicule it enough, average people will assume it must be a foolish idea and think no more about it. Economist Ludwig von Mises cut through the propaganda to explain the virtues of the gold standard, virtues which account for why supporters of power oppose it with such vigor:

> The eminence of the gold standard consists in the fact that it makes the determination of the monetary unit's purchasing power independent of the measures of governments. It wrests from the hands of the "economic tsars" their most redoubtable instrument. It makes it impossible for them to inflate. This is why the gold standard is furiously attacked by all those who expect that they will be benefited by bounties from the seemingly inexhaustible government purse.
>
> What is needed first of all is to force the rulers to spend only what, by virtue of duly promulgated laws, they have collected as taxes....No backdoor must be left open where inflation can slip in. No emergency can justify a return to inflation. Inflation can provide neither the weapons a nation needs to defend its independence nor the capital goods required for any project. It does not cure unsatisfactory conditions. It merely helps the rulers whose policies brought about the catastrophe to exculpate themselves.
>
> One of the goals of the reform suggested [a return to sound money, a system in which governments cannot create money at will] is to explode and to kill forever the superstitious belief that governments and banks have the power to make the nation or individual citizens richer, out of nothing and without making anybody poorer. The shortsighted observer sees only the things the government has accomplished by spending the newly created money. He does not see the things the nonperformance of which provided the means for the government's success. He fails to realize that inflation does not create additional goods but merely shifts wealth and income from some groups of people to others.[22]

This is not a side issue that we can safely neglect, that we might focus instead on matters that might be considered more fashionable or politically viable. Economist F. A. Hayek warned about this excessive concern with political feasibility. If this is a group's overriding concern, it will never influence public opinion. It will simply be steamrolled by events.

> What we lack is…a program which seems neither a mere defense of things as they are nor a diluted kind of socialism, but a truly liberal radicalism which does not spare the susceptibilities of the mighty… which is not too severely practical, and which does not confine itself to what appears today as politically possible. We need intellectual leaders who are willing to work for an ideal, however small may be the prospects of its early realization. They must be men who are willing to stick to principles and to fight for their full realization, however remote.
>
> Those who have concerned themselves exclusively with what seemed practicable in the existing state of opinion have constantly found that even this had rapidly become politically impossible as the result of changes in a public opinion which they have done nothing to guide.[23]

Issues become politically viable precisely because they are discussed rather than evaded. That is the proper reply to those timid "free-market" economists who supported various aspects of the Wall Street bailouts on the grounds that a particular measure was the best of the "politically viable" options. Perhaps other options would have been politically viable if cowardly economists had helped to *shape* the debate by telling the truth, defending the free market, and letting the chips fall where they may, instead of meekly acquiescing in mainstream opinion.

To his credit, Rush Limbaugh tried to devote one of his programs to the critical subjects of money and credit, subjects Americans need to understand cold if we are to have any hope of reversing the terrific mess our government and central bank have caused. Rush doesn't have the right answers, but at least he was asking the right questions, which is more than can be said for most radio hosts. Unfortunately, he was promptly flooded with listener emails urging him to drop that subject and talk instead about Caroline Kennedy's intentions to run for U.S. Senate, an issue of zero importance.[24]

The government and its privileged central bank are not the indispensable supports of our monetary system. They are, as Mises said, interlopers. They give us discoordination and chaos. They enrich the favored few at the expense of the many. They make possible an expansion of government power that would have been unthinkable in earlier times. The Federal Reserve is truly the elephant in the living room. We are supposed to pretend it isn't there. Fewer and fewer people are playing this game any longer. They have pulled back the curtain and taken a good, hard look at the Fed and its central planning mandate. No wonder Thomas Cooley urged the Fed in May 2009 that it needed to become "boring" again: all its unprecedented activities were attracting attention to it.[25] The peons are not to worry their pretty little heads about what goes on at the Fed.

It is not just that the Fed has been a failure according to the unreasonably exacting standards of its incorrigible critics, as its supporters allege. As we have seen in this chapter, the Fed has been a failure *on its own terms*. It has not in fact delivered what it promised. Old data that its supporters once pointed to in triumph have been shown in recent years to be hopelessly flawed. People who claim the Fed has been a fantastic success are bluffing, or do not know what they are talking about. The emperor truly has no clothes.

We need neither a monopolistic, government-issued paper money, nor indeed a government-imposed gold standard (although that would be a significant improvement). If ever there were anything government cannot be trusted to monopolize, it is money, as Hayek concluded four years after winning the Nobel Prize in economics.[26] As I wrote in *Meltdown*, we either believe in the free market or we do not. The market has no need of, and is positively harmed by, an anomalous planning agency in the realm of money and interest rates. Contracts, private property, and voluntary human relations are as capable of providing money as they are any other economic good.

The ray of hope in all this is that for the first time in nearly a century, the Fed is routinely subjected to close scrutiny, with more and more Americans informing themselves about its history and its activities. More Americans than ever are reading the work of economists like Murray Rothbard (1926–1995), whose books *The Case Against the Fed* and *What Has Government Done to Our Money?* are available to read online for free. People are worried about the condition of the dollar, and it is increasingly difficult to persuade them that the Fed is the hero rather than the villain in that story. Until the Internet increased the average person's access to information, those who highlighted objections to the Fed could be ignored or derided as cranks. But as people have begun to listen to and read the economists of the Austrian School, they have found thinkers who are not cranks. They have found just about the only people who make any sense. It is the alleged experts who have begun to sound like the cranks.

This newfound interest in the Fed couldn't have come at a better time. All the otherwise welcome talk about rolling back government power and spending will come to naught unless the Fed, the elephant in the living room, is confronted squarely. Tea Partiers and other critics of the federal government say we should just get back to the Constitution. Yet waving a piece of paper in Washington's face will do nothing as long as the money creation machine established in 1913 continues to churn away.

CHAPTER 5

Less Bang for the Buck: Pentagon Spending, the Military, and the U.S. Economy

Three words guarantee the coming federal bankruptcy: "Off the table." Everyone has something he considers off the table. For most Americans, in fact, everything is off the table.

In 2010 *The Economist* polled Americans about what category of government spending they were willing to cut. The only area a majority (71 percent) would cut was foreign aid, which is about one percent of the government budget. The numbers on the other spending categories broke down like this: Social Security (7 percent of Americans would cut), national defense (22 percent), Medicare (7 percent), aid to the poor (17 percent), Medicaid (11 percent), veterans' benefits (6 percent), health research (13 percent), education (12 percent), highways (12 percent), mass transit (27 percent), unemployment benefits (19 percent), science and technology (22 percent), agriculture (27 percent), housing (27 percent), and the environment (29 percent).[1]

Well, that's pretty much all the government spends money on. And it's all off the table, according to Americans. That means the only thing *on* the table is default.

For many conservatives, military spending in particular is off the table. That needs to be revisited, to put it delicately. It is unreasonable to expect a crisis of this magnitude to be resolved only by asking other people to rethink *their* cherished assumptions. We need to take a frank and unprejudiced second look at our true situation—even if it means asking hard questions not just about Barney Frank, but about ourselves.

The Unseen

To get a sense of the impact the U.S. military has on the American economy, we must remember the most important lesson in all of economics: to consider not merely the immediate effects of a proposed government intervention on certain earmarked groups, but also its long-term effects on society as a whole. That's what economist Frédéric Bastiat (1801–50) insisted on in his famous essay, "What Is Seen and What Is Not Seen." It's not enough to point to a farm program and say that it grants short-run assistance to the farmers. We can see its effects on farmers. But what does it do to everyone else in the long run?

The example from that essay that most people remember involves a boy who breaks a businessman's window. Some people, Bastiat says, are inclined to think of the unfortunate incident as a concealed boon, for the money spent to repair the window will "create jobs" by employing the glazier. Yet that analysis is juvenile since it confines itself only to *what is seen*—namely, the enrichment of the glazier. What is not seen is what the shopkeeper would have purchased with his money had he not needed to replace the window. Perhaps he might have bought a new pair of shoes. In that case, the shoemaker rather than the glazier would have been enriched. But since the repair to the window *is seen*, while the shoes that might have been purchased had there been no window to fix in the first place *are not seen*, careless observers neglect the foregone purchase of shoes and conclude that destruction can actually confer economic benefit, or stimulus. From the point of view of the shopkeeper himself, of course, the incident amounts to a total loss: whereas he might have had a window and a new pair of shoes, now he has only a window. So it is with government spending, which is accomplished through destruction in the form of taxation. Less wealth exists, and society is worse off than it otherwise would have been. Instead of potentially expanding our capital stock (the value of the nation's plants, equipment, and infrastructure), we must devote resources to merely breaking even.

Often overlooked is the military example Bastiat uses in the essay. He discusses the demobilization of one hundred thousand soldiers from the French army—a prospect many entertain with dread, for what will these men do for a living? And what about the foregone stimulus to French businesses previously provided by the military's expenditures on wine, clothes, and weapons for these men? Of course, Bastiat points out, such critics are focusing once again only on what is seen. They fail to consider that the money that had previously been confiscated from the taxpayers in order to support the soldiers, once returned to the taxpayers, will now be available for other purposes, including expenditures on goods that these demobilized soldiers can help produce. Likewise, the money the military once spent on wine, clothes, and weapons can now be spent by the general public on other things, so here again economic activity is none the worse for the soldiers' demobilization.

Seymour Melman (1917–2004), a professor of industrial engineering and operations research at Columbia University, focused much of his energy on the economics of the warfare and military-oriented state. Melman's work amounted to an extended analysis, in light of Bastiat's insight, of the true costs not only of war but also of the military establishment itself. As he observed,

> Industrial productivity, the foundation of every nation's economic growth, is eroded by the relentlessly predatory effects of the military economy.... Traditional economic competence of every sort is being eroded by the state capitalist directorate that elevates inefficiency into a national purpose, that disables the market system, that destroys the value of the currency, and that diminishes the decision power of all institutions other than its own.[2]

Throughout the Cold War, politicians and intellectuals all over the political spectrum could be heard warning of the catastrophic economic consequences of substantial reductions in military spending. The radical left in particular, as part of its critique of American state capitalism (which it sometimes conflated with pure laissez-faire, an altogether different system), lent important support to that position. As Marxists Paul Baran and Paul Sweezy warned: "If military spending were reduced once again to pre-Second World War proportions, the nation's economy would return to a state of profound depression, characterized by unemployment rates of 15 per cent and up, such as prevailed during the 1930s."[3] Yet this was the same fallacy Bastiat had refuted over a century earlier when he wrote about the French military. These politicians and intellectuals were focusing on the direct effects of discontinuing a particular spending stream without considering the *indirect* effects—all the business ventures, jobs, and wealth creation that those funds would create when steered away from military use and toward the service of the public as expressed in their voluntary spending patterns.[4] The full cost of the military establishment, as with all other forms of government spending, includes all the consumer goods, services, and techno-logical discoveries that never came into existence because the resources to provide them had been diverted by government.

Measurements of "economic growth" can be misleading if they do not dif-ferentiate between productive growth and parasitic growth. Productive growth improves people's standard of living and/or contributes to future production. Parasitic growth merely depletes manpower and existing stocks of goods without accomplishing either of these ends.[5] In Melman's view, productive growth involves both the production of consumer goods as well as the production of capital goods that increase the economy's capacity to produce consumer goods in the future. Both are aimed at satisfying human needs.

Beyond a certain limit, military spending constitutes the classic example of parasitic growth. Not himself a pacifist, Melman believed that since the nation's security demanded some kind of military establishment, military spending, up to a point, could be not only legitimate but also economically valuable. But astronomical military budgets, surpassing the combined military spending of the rest of the world, and exceeding many times over the amount of destructive power needed to annihilate every enemy city, were clearly parasitic. Melman used the term "overkill" to describe that portion of the military budget that constituted this kind of excess, observing facetiously that it was not possible to annihilate the same city more than once. By the 1960s the U.S. government, in its strategic aircraft and missiles alone, was capable of unleashing in explosive power the equivalent of six tons of TNT for every person on Earth. "Now that we have 6 tons of TNT per person in our strategic missiles and aircraft alone,"

Melman wondered, "have we become more secure than when we had only 1 ton of TNT per human being on earth?"[6] The labor, time, and other resources that were used to produce this overkill material were taxed away from the productive population and diverted from the creation of civilian goods.[7]

GDP calculations do not draw this distinction between the parasitic and the productive. All government spending is simply added—as if it were something positive—to the sum of all final goods and services sold in a given year. Parasitic growth is thus a component of a figure whose magnitude is supposed to indicate a country's economic well-being. For that reason alone, GDP can obscure as much as it reveals.[8]

The scale of the resources siphoned off from the civilian sector becomes more vivid in light of specific examples of military programs, equipment, and personnel. To train a single combat pilot, for instance, costs between $5 million and $7 million.[9] Over a period of two years, the average U.S. motorist uses about as much fuel as does a single F-16 training jet in less than an hour. The Abrams tank uses up 3.8 gallons of fuel in traveling one mile. Between 2 and 11 percent of the world's use of fourteen important minerals, from copper to aluminum to zinc, is consumed by the military, as is about 6 percent of the world's consumption of petroleum.[10] The Pentagon's energy use in a single year could power all U.S. mass transit systems for nearly fourteen years.[11]

Still other statistics illuminate the scope of the resources consumed by the military. According to the U.S. Department of Defense, during the period from 1947 through 1987 it used (in 1982 dollars) $7.62 trillion in capital resources. In 1985, the Department of Commerce estimated the value of the nation's plants, equipment, and infrastructure (capital stock), at just over $7.29 trillion. In other words, the amount spent over that period could have doubled the American capital stock or modernized and replaced its existing stock.[12]

That is a startling statistic, to be sure, but the economic costs of these expenditures extend well beyond the dollar amounts spent on the materials, the machinery, the physical plant, and the manpower involved in weapons construction. Any portion of this money that might otherwise have been devoted to investment for civilian purposes would have brought returns *in excess* of the amount invested, since the machinery it purchased would have increased the country's productive capacity and thus, in perpetuity, its capability for future production.[13]

Then there are the damaging effects on the private sector. Since World War II, between one-third and two-thirds of all technical researchers in the United States have been working for the military at any given time. The result has been "a short supply of comparable talent to serve civilian industry and civilian activities of every sort."[14]

> When research and development is not properly done on behalf of civilian industry, results like poor product design or poor production methods can have disastrous effects on the economic position of the industry. When as little as one and a half percent of U.S. national product is diverted to military research it seems little enough, but that accounts for more than half of the national research and development effort and has left many U.S. civilian-products industries at a competitive disadvantage due to faltering product designs and insufficient improvement in industrial-production efficiency.[15]

Government jobs, whose funding source—taxation—is unavailable to private firms, have been able to offer substantially higher salaries than those in the private sector. By the 1960s major companies were already complaining of being unable to meet their hiring targets for new researchers. *The Wall Street Journal* warned in 1963:

> Top research men in industry reason this way: Frantic bidding, by space and military contractors, for scientists and engineers is creating a big shortage for industry. This scarcity, along with the skyrocketing salaries it is provoking, is bringing almost to a halt the hitherto rapid growth of company-supported research. This development hampers efforts to develop new products and processes for the civilian economy.

"Government research programs serve as a brake on research in the private sector," added Du Pont Company vice president Samuel Lenher.[16]

This was not just a case of special pleading on the part of private firms. A study in the *American Economic Review* argued that the growth of military and space research and development (R&D) "has significantly retarded the growth of civilian R&D." The consensus among R&D directors, according to the study, was that "the growth of defense R&D, by bidding up salaries and by taking the cream of the new science and engineering graduates, has tended to reduce significantly the quantity and quality of R&D undertaken in civilian-created laboratories."[17]

Such arguments reached the general public only infrequently, as when President John Kennedy acknowledged in 1963 that the United States had "paid a price by sharply limiting the scarce scientific and engineering resources available to the civilian sectors of the American economy."[18] At a Senate committee meeting the year before, Senator Hubert Humphrey had wondered aloud,

> What is happening to our civilian economy as we plow more and more of our scientific personnel, our brains, into the military and into space and into atomic energy for military purposes? Where are we going to end up in this trade competition with these Belgians and these Dutch, who are clever, and the Germans who are very clever, who are spending more money for civilian aspects and will develop products cheaper, better, and more serviceable?[19]

Now one may object, as a mitigating factor, that military research at times has civilian uses, and that the research being done in the defense industry is therefore not altogether mislaid from the point of view of consumer welfare. In fact, though, the number and utility of such crossover applications, and whether they would not have occurred anyway in the absence of military research, is a matter of serious dispute.[20] In the middle of the Cold War, the Engineers' Joint Council concluded that such spillovers occurred only infrequently, and that "the military program must be recognized as utilizing a large fraction of the most talented individuals in research and development in the country and of denying to the civilian economy the services of these individuals."[21]

Researchers Stephen Broadberry and Mark Harrison are skeptical of grandiose claims on behalf of military technology with civilian applications, speaking in 2005 of "how difficult it is to show that any of these wider changes were actually the result of the war and would not have occurred anyway in its absence."[22] Herbert Holloman and Alan Harger, in a 1971 study, cited spinoff estimates ranging from 5 percent to as much as 33 percent.[23] Melman himself was inclined toward the lower end of that range, having been given the estimate of 5 percent spillover from specialists in the Commerce Department.[24]

Even on those occasions when a legitimate advance in civilian well-being can be shown to have derived from military research, such research is not thereby vindicated. We always have to remember opportunity cost—in this case, what Americans would have spent their money on had it not been diverted to government research projects. There is no non-arbitrary way to determine that funds diverted from civilian use to military research, whatever its value in civilian spinoff, yield greater social utility than the purposes to which people would have directed those funds themselves. When two parties engage in a voluntary exchange, we know they are both better off *ex ante*, for they would not otherwise have taken part in the exchange. One party prefers what the other party has to what he himself has, and vice versa, and thus the exchange improves each party's well-being. But if a thief, after robbing his victim, gave that victim in a moment of remorse an item he (the thief) considered valuable, we cannot say the same thing. The thief is undoubtedly better off, but since the exchange in question did not take place voluntarily, we must presume that the victim's well-being has been harmed rather than improved (otherwise, he would have entered into the exchange of his own free will). Much less can we say that something called "social utility" has been increased by this incident, since no matter how much happier we may think the thief is, or how satisfied the victim should be with the item the thief chose to give him, utility is necessarily subjective and incommensurable. In short, in the absence of voluntary action on the victim's part, we have no way of determining what exchanges would yield an individual additional utility.[25]

Therefore, given that the necessary funds were seized from them by force, it is impossible to say with certainty, as those who trumpet military crossovers typically do, that people were truly better off by being deprived of their resources in order to contribute involuntarily to new technology. Imagine the social resources that would have been necessary to bring about the production of the automobile in, say, 1800. The unspeakable sacrifice that would have been involved in order to mobilize that level of technological research at a time when the vast majority of the component parts, much less the technology and overall design, of the automobile had neither been discovered nor conceived of, would surely not have been compensated for by the premature introduction of that important invention. It would have come at a staggering cost that no people would voluntarily have borne. The same kinds of costs, albeit to a greater or lesser degree, are necessarily at work in any involuntarily supported technological research. Any military innovation with civilian applications may serve to mitigate the harm done to consumer welfare by the existence of a vast military apparatus, but claims that such applications prove the merit of such an apparatus, or show that the apparatus is actually necessary to consumer welfare, are unfounded.[26]

Catering to the Pentagon also distorts a firm's business sense and makes it less mindful of controlling costs than it would be if its customers resided exclusively in the private sector. Since the Pentagon's funds come from involuntary taxation rather than through profits reaped by offering a useful good or service on a competitive market, it can afford to be less concerned with cost than could a private firm. As well, firms servicing Pentagon needs have grown almost indifferent to cost.[27] They operate outside the market framework and the price system: the prices of the goods they produce are not determined by the voluntary buying and selling by property owners that comprise the market, but through a negotiation process with the Pentagon in isolation from market exchange.

Beginning in the 1960s, the Department of Defense required the military-oriented firms with which it did business to engage in "historical costing," a method by which past prices are employed in order to estimate future costs. Superficially plausible, this approach builds into the procurement process a bias in favor of ever-higher prices, since it does not scrutinize these past prices or the firm's previously incurred costs, or make provision for the possibility that work done in the future might be carried out at a lower cost than related work done in the past. This is not nit-picking: advancing technology has often made it possible to carry out important tasks at ever-lower costs, yet rising costs are a built-in assumption of the historical cost method. Moreover, if some piece of military equipment—a helicopter, plane, or tank, for example—winds up costing much more than initial estimates indicated, that inflated price then becomes the baseline for the cost estimates for new projects belonging to the same genus.[28] The Pentagon, in turn, uses the resulting cost hikes to justify higher budget proposals submitted to Congress.

Cost-minimizing incentives that exist for civilian firms are often absent with the military-industry firm. The largest contracts are negotiated with a single supplier, and cost is not the major factor in the Pentagon's reckoning. Much more important is the Pentagon's confidence that the firm in question can actually deliver the product, interact successfully with the military community, and adapt to ongoing and sometimes quite frequent changes to the initial design. As for cost, even if the resulting military hardware exceeds the negotiated price by three or four times, the Pentagon will generally find a way to come up with the money.[29] Melman also found administrative overhead ratios in the defense industry to be double those for civilian firms, where such a crushing burden simply could not be absorbed. He concluded:

> From the personal accounts of "refugees" from military-industry firms, from former Pentagon staffers, from informants still engaged in military-industrial work, from the Pentagon's publications, and from data disclosed in Congressional hearings, I have found consistent evidence pointing to the inference that the primary, internal, economic dynamics of military industry are cost- and subsidy-maximization.[30]

These incentives also supply little reason to exert the intellectual and physical effort necessary not only to control costs but also to make complex systems simpler and more user-friendly, as truly competitive firms and industries must try to do when catering to the public. "In one major enterprise," Melman reported, "the product-development staffs engaged in contests for designing the most complex, Rube Goldberg-types of devices. Why bother putting brakes on such professional games as long as they can be labeled 'research,' charged to 'cost growth' and billed to the Pentagon?"[31]

The efforts of Boeing Vertol, Rohr, and Grumman to enter the field of mass transit are revealing. In each case, their products were simply too complex and unreliable.[32] Boeing Vertol's trolley cars, introduced on Boston's Green Line in the 1970s, broke down regularly, and were largely replaced by cars built by Japan's Kinki Sharyo. Rohr Industries' subway cars, introduced in San Francisco's Bay Area Rapid Transit (BART) system and in the nation's capital, were enormously costly and for years suffered from chronic malfunctions. Grumman buses in New York City were so unreliable that the city ended up suing the company.

The once-vigorous American machine-tool industry can tell a sorry tale of its own. Once highly competitive and committed to cost-containment and innovation, the machine-tool industry suffered a sustained decline in the decades following World War II.[33] During the wartime period, from 1939 to 1947, machine-tool prices increased by only 39 percent at a time when the average hourly earnings of American industrial workers rose by 95 percent. Since machine tools increase an economy's productivity, making it possible to produce a greater quantity of output with a smaller input, the industry's conscientious cost-cutting had a disproportionately positive effect on the American industrial system as a whole.

But between 1971 and 1978, machine-tool prices rose 85 percent while U.S. industrial workers' average hourly earnings increased only 72 percent. The corresponding figures in Japan were 51 percent and 177 percent, respectively.

These problems can be accounted for at least in part by the American machine-tool industry's relationship with the Defense Department. Once the Pentagon became the American machine-tool industry's largest customer, the industry felt far less pressure to hold prices down than it had in the past.[34] That decreased pressure undoubtedly contributed to the negligible investment by the machine-tool industry in modern production techniques of a kind used routinely in Europe. No longer under traditional market pressure to innovate and lower costs, the machine-tool industry saw a considerable drop in productivity.

Prior to the 1960s, the prices of machinery typically rose more slowly than did the wages of American industrial workers. (This occurred because productivity improvements occurred regularly within the machine-tool industry itself.) As a result, firms had an incentive to purchase more and better machinery to incorporate into their production processes.[35] The results for the American economy were all good: worker productivity increased, more wealth was produced, wages rose, and any labor displaced by machines could now produce other goods for which the necessary labor had not previously been available. When machine-tool prices began to outpace wages, it suddenly made less economic sense for firms in the United States to invest in those tools. They became content to shift into additional labor at the current rate of productivity rather than invest in equipment that could have increased that rate.

In the short run, therefore, the American machine-tool industry's woes affected U.S. productivity at large. Firms were now much more likely to maintain their existing stock of machines rather than to purchase additional equipment or even to upgrade what they already possessed. By 1968, nearly two-thirds of all metalworking machinery in American factories was at least ten years old. The aging stock of production equipment contributed to a decline in manufacturing productivity growth after 1965.[36]

Why Americans couldn't have switched to lower-cost imported machine tools as soon as prices began to rise involves the reluctance of machinery buyers to change their suppliers—particularly to suppliers who are not close by. Not only do they prefer to deal with established firms with good reputations, but they also want to avoid unnecessary and costly downtime, so they patronize suppliers who can perform repairs and supply spare parts on short notice. In the long run, American firms did indeed begin to shift into imported machine tools, and by 1967 the United States for the first time imported more machine tools than it exported.[37]

The military-induced distortion of the American machine-tool industry, and the industry's correspondingly decreased global competitiveness, is not confined to the perverse incentives created by the Pentagon's cost-maximization approach to procurement. Another factor is at work as well: the more an industry caters to the Pentagon, the less it makes production decisions with the civilian economy in mind. Thus in the late 1950s the Air Force teamed up with the machine-tool industry to produce numerical-control machine-tool technology, a technique for the programmable automation of machine tools that yields fast, efficient, and accurate results. The resulting technology was so costly that private metalworking firms could not even consider using it. The machine-tool firms involved in this research thereby placed themselves in a situation in which their only real customer was the aerospace industry. Some twenty years later, only 2 percent of all American machine tools belonged to the numerical-control line. It was Western European and Japanese firms, which operated without these incentives, that finally managed to produce numerical-control machine tools at affordable prices for smaller businesses.

The distortion of business decisions and strategy that contributed to the decreasing competitiveness of the machine-tool industry is at work in thousands of American firms in rough proportion to their reliance on Pentagon contracts.

It may be objected that this "cost maximization" model is not inherent to the weapons procurement process, and that with the firm application of political pressure these abuses might be minimized. But political pressure *has* been brought to bear on the matter. We might cite the 1971 Fitzhugh Commission, the 1977 Steadman Review, the 1981 Carlucci Acquisition Initiatives, the 1986 Packard Commission, the 1986 Goldwater-Nichols Department of Defense Reorganization Act, the 1989 Defense Management Review, the Defense Science Board's 1990 "Streamlining Review," the 1993–94 report of the Acquisitions Streamlining Task Force and the Defense Science Board, or the Air Force's Total System Performance Responsibility initiative. These and other initiatives were supposed to look into the procurement process and recommend reforms. In October 2000, Bill Clinton signed legislation "to set up a 12-member commission with the aim of recommending improvements to the sometimes troubled relationship between the federal government and the nation's aerospace and defense companies."[38]

So unsuccessful was each of these major commissions in bringing about reform that each time a new one was established, the previous ones may as well never have occurred—the same abuses and the same proposed solutions were raised again and again. Thomas Christie, who spent half a century with the Pentagon and was the Defense Department's most senior official for testing weapons, concluded in 2006, "After all these years of repeated reform efforts, major defense programs are taking 20 to 30 years to deliver less capability than planned, very often at two to three times the costs and schedules planned." Another expert, Ernest Fitzgerald, was only saying what many others were thinking when he declared, "Government officials, from the majestic office of the president to the lowest, sleaziest procurement office, lie routinely and with impunity in defense of the system....The combination of loose procurement rules and government acquiescence in rip-offs leaves many a crook untouched."[39] And finally, the Center for Defense Information's Winslow Wheeler: "Despite decades of acquisition reform from Washington's best minds in Congress, the Pentagon and the think tanks, cost overruns in weapon systems are higher today, in inflation-adjusted dollars, than any time ever before. Not a single major weapon system has been delivered on time, on cost and as promised for performance."[40]

Despite reform efforts, military suppliers have two strategies for helping maximize the loot seized from the public: front-loading and political engineering. Front-loading refers to the practice of understating the monetary costs and (often) overstating the technical capabilities of a proposed project. Then, when costs rise higher—sometimes much, much higher—than initially planned, or technical problems and failures slow down the production process, political engineering is employed to keep the program running anyway. Political engineering seeks to spread the jobs and the money associated with a particular program among a wide array of important congressional districts in order to get as many influential congressmen politically invested in the program as possible. Thus once front-loading gets the money flowing, political engineering makes it all but impossible to stop. Neither of these strategies, says a former CIA analyst, is pursued by accident or without malicious intent. They both involve "criminal intent to turn on the spigot of taxpayer money and then to jam it so that it cannot be turned off."[41] Thus when a coalition developed in July 1989 to cancel the $60 billion B-2 bomber, chief contractor Northrop Corporation wasn't exactly subtle in responding, releasing previously classified information showing tens of thousands of jobs and hundreds of millions in profits at stake in nearly 400 congressional districts and all but a few states.[42]

Front-loading also encourages complex, technologically demanding systems over simpler and more straightforward ones. The more complex a system is, the more difficult it is at the outset to anticipate difficulties, and thus the easier to front-load. Also, complex weapons are typically composed of numerous subsystems, which in turn require subcontracts, each of which can be spread around important congressional districts.[43]

According to former Pentagon military analyst Chuck Spinney,

> front-loading and political engineering encourage immoral behavior at all levels within the Defense Department. We exaggerate the threat to justify larger budgets. We use deceitful if not illegal accounting tricks to hide the true costs of programs. We reduce the chances of weapons being terminated for poor performance by designing success-oriented operational tests and by rushing weapons into production before they are fully tested. We obscure future costs behind the cloak of excessive secrecy. We tolerate cost overruns and bad management practices, some of which are spilling over into the civilian economy and damaging our international competitiveness.[44]

This is how we wind up with cases like the C130J prop plane, which was so poorly designed that none of the fifty the Air Force purchased have ever been able to be put into service. The propeller system malfunctions so badly during bad weather that the planes can be used only for training. Yet the Lockheed Corporation was paid 99 percent of the contract price for what turned out to be nearly useless planes.[45]

The F-22 Raptor, also produced by Lockheed, puts the C130J in the dust in terms of impracticality. It was originally designed in the 1980s for use against the Soviet Union. Today it appears to serve no purpose at all, although with so much money and employment at stake, the reader will not be shocked to learn that production continued for decades anyway. A Senate aide put it this way: "It's showy, unimaginably expensive, fragile and utterly useless. But there's no stopping it."[46]

The F-22 was sold as a stealth fighter. But it keeps showing up on radar systems—and even if it didn't, the thing is huge, some five times the size of an F-16. "The only way to make the F-22 stealthy," says retired Air Force Colonel Everest Riccioni, "is to tear the eyes out of enemy pilots' heads."[47] It wasn't until 2010 that the program was finally scrapped. Over the life of the program some $65.3 billion was spent, which translates into over $356 million per plane. (Even if R&D is written off as a sunk cost, the figure is still likely to be about $216.3 million per plane.)[48]

Meanwhile, the plane was not suited for use in Iraq and Afghanistan, so it never saw action there. It can play no role at all against non-state actors like al Qaeda, which has no air force and no intention of acquiring one.[49]

In spite of all this, the program persisted for years and years. The political engineering was obvious. More than one thousand subcontractors in forty-four states had a stake in the program. Naturally, U.S. congressmen spoke of the economic consequences for their districts if the program were terminated.[50]

How did the whole problem get started in the first place? When President Franklin Roosevelt decided to increase and improve U.S. military capabilities beginning in 1940, he found himself faced with a major difficulty. Having spent the previous seven years punishing and demonizing business—even some in the president's own inner circle thought his attacks on business went much too far and were hampering recovery from the Depression—FDR faced a business sector too suspicious of Washington to cooperate with him without wide-ranging guarantees and concessions.

Those guarantees and concessions were quickly forthcoming. Procurement by solicitation and sealed bids began to be replaced by cost-plus-fixed-fee contracts. Tax breaks, government loan guarantees and other financing assistance, and direct government funding were just the thing to persuade the private sector to accept government contracts, even if issued by their erstwhile adversary. The standard procedure for what would later become the military-industrial complex—a term immortalized by Republican Dwight Eisenhower—were coming into place.[51]

The changes that took root were obvious, even glaring. Before 1940, there was no incentive for businessmen to try to woo congressmen by means of poker, prostitutes, or cash bribes. If a company did not make the lowest, sealed-bid offer on a particular project, it would not be awarded the contract. But once price was set aside as the chief consideration, to be replaced by less precise criteria like the ones we have seen in this chapter (e.g., reputation, technical capabilities, ability to work with the military community—as Higgs puts it, "vaguer attributes that are easier to fudge for one's friends"), the wining and dining began in earnest.[52]

Military contractor Brent Wilkes threw poker parties at the Watergate and Westin Grand hotels for legislators and lobbyists for fifteen years, beginning in 1990. Wilkes was a high-school friend of Kyle (Dusty) Foggo, the third-ranking figure at the CIA. According to allegations, Wilkes provided prostitutes, limousines, and hotel suites to those who attended, though Foggo says he went "just for poker." Then-CIA Director Porter Goss was sacked in the scandal, though he denies having attended the parties as CIA director (leaving open whether he attended as a Republican congressman who headed the House Intelligence Committee). Also in attendance was Congressman Randall "Duke" Cunningham, who is currently in federal prison.

For a brief moment the general public got to see a small sliver of daily life in Washington, D.C., in general and the military-industrial complex in particular. "Evidently," notes Robert Higgs, "the daily routine there is not all wailing and gnashing of teeth over how to defend the country against Osama bin Laden and his horde of murderous maniacs—our country's leaders require frequent periods of rest and recreation. If this sort of fun and games at taxpayer expense is your idea of responsible government, then you ought to answer 'yes' when the pollster calls to ask whether you favor an increase in the defense budget. Our government is clearly at work—at work making chumps out of its loyal subjects and laughing at these rubes all the way to the bank."[53]

Congressman Cunningham, by the way, the future jailbird who attended the parties, wound up in prison for taking $2.4 million in bribes. Mitchell Wade, CEO of MZM, Inc., reportedly intimidated employees into donating to Cunningham's campaign, and his company's political action committee donated still more. Cunningham was even invited to live in Wade's yacht rent free, paying only nominal dock fees (in order to evade the law that prohibits congressmen from living rent free on someone else's property). Wade was fairly blunt about his relationship to certain influential congressmen. According to a former MZM employee, Wade said: "The only people I want to work with are the people I give checks to. I own them." Cunningham, in turn, steered lucrative contracts MZM's way, such that the once-struggling firm found itself flooded with cash by 2004.[54]

One reporter described Cunningham's demise this way:

It's fine to live on the dole of a defense company; just don't press the point by reposing for free on their yacht. That's the kind of exposure that might spoil the game for everyone. The profligacy of an individual member of Congress must not be permitted to interfere with the grander profligacy of the munitions makers. In the end, [Cunningham] was told that he should fall on his sword, like a true Praetorian, to protect the business of the Empire. In mid-July the congressman suddenly announced his retirement, saying he had decided to "conclude the public chapter of my life" and not seek reelection to a ninth term.[55]

Scholars have also uncovered a pattern of implicit bailouts, whereby particular firms are awarded contracts because they are experiencing economic difficulties and need to make a sale, as when Lockheed got the contract for the C-4 (Trident I) missile.[56] A more notorious case was the no-risk $30 billion contract awarded to Boeing, at a time when the company was encountering financial difficulties, to lease refurbished 767 passenger jets to the Air Force. These jets were supposed to serve as refueling tankers, even though 767s weren't the best choice for that purpose and even though the Air Force said it didn't need any more tankers. On top of that, it would have been cheaper had the Air Force purchased the planes outright rather than leasing them from Boeing.[57]

The idea for the tanker deal materialized at a meeting in September 2001 with Boeing executives and Darlene Druyun, who was then Deputy Assistant Secretary of the Air Force, and Major General Paul Essex, who headed the Air Force's Global Reach Program. Soon enough, Air Force Secretary James Roche was pushing the deal vigorously. According to Winslow Wheeler, the idea actually originated with Senator Ted Stevens of Alaska, who for years had been a loyal water carrier for Boeing.

Druyun came to personify the revolving door between government and private industry when it was announced at the beginning of 2003 that she would direct the company's missile defense division. She had been negotiating the new job while still in government, helping to finalize the tanker deal. She went to jail for that (which is why we know about this particular incident), even though such things go on all the time. She became the fall guy, and investigations stopped there.

Is Military Spending Too Low?

We sometimes hear it said that the military budget is too low. As of this printing the Pentagon absorbs the equivalent of 3.3 percent of GDP; some say this figure should be increased to at least 4 percent. That figure sounds moderate and reasonable, especially since it has reached more than twice that level at various times in the past. But the problem with determining the adequacy of the military budget by measuring it as a share of GDP is that the two figures have no logical connection to each other. One would think, instead, that a reasonable metric for determining the military budget would involve some calculation of what expenditures were necessary to defend the United States from potential aggressors. Whatever that figure turns out to be, its ratio to GDP is of no relevance at all.

A better way to measure the U.S. government's military spending would be to compare it to that of other countries around the world. As of this writing, the U.S. government's military expenditures *equals* the sum of what all the other countries in the world spend. *This* percentage is, presumably, rather more revealing than the percentage-of-GDP figure. Economist Robert Higgs correctly wonders: "Why can't the Department of Defense today defend the country for a smaller annual amount than it needed to defend the country during the Cold War, when we faced an enemy with large, modern armed forces and thousands of accurate, nuclear-armed intercontinental ballistic missiles?"[58]

In fact, a great many military experts have begun to conclude that the enormously expensive and complicated equipment and programs that the Pentagon has been calling for would be of limited help even in fighting the Second Generation Warfare with which the American military seems most comfortable, and a positive detriment to waging the kind of Fourth Generation Warfare of which the War on Terror consists. William Lind, a key theorist of Fourth Generation Warfare, says the U.S. Navy in the twenty-first century is "still structured to fight the Imperial Japanese Navy." As Lind puts it, the Navy's aircraft-carrier battle groups "have cruised on mindlessly for more than half a century, waiting for those Japanese carriers to turn up. They are still cruising today, into, if not beyond, irrelevance."[59]

On top of this, the Department of Defense is the only federal agency not subject to audit. The seriousness of problems with the Department's books has been emphasized and acknowledged for decades. In the 1990s the Defense Department actually secured from Congress a special exemption from the general audit requirement that exists for other federal agencies. So it is not that the Department has failed an audit—meaning accountants tracked its expenditures and found its money misspent. With the Department of Defense, accountants cannot track the money in the first place.[60] It is not uncommon for the Pentagon not to know whether contractors have been paid twice, or not at all. It does not even know how many contractors it has.[61] Meanwhile, so-called fiscal conservatives, who know nothing of this, continue to think the problem is excessively low military budgets. This, no doubt, is just the way the establishment likes it: exploit the people's patriotism in order to keep the gravy train rolling.

In order to tabulate the full amount of government expenditure on defense, it is not enough to glance at the budget for the Department of Defense. That number was $518.3 billion in 2009 and excludes hundreds of billions of dollars in additional defense-related expenditure. Economist Robert Higgs suggests that the real defense budget is closer to $1 trillion. Winslow Wheeler reaches a comparable figure. To the $518.3 billion, he adds the military-related activities assigned to the Department of Energy ($17.1 billion), the security component of the State Department budget ($38.4 billion), the Department of Veterans Affairs ($91.3 billion), non-Department of Defense military retirement ($28.3 billion), miscellaneous defense activities spread around various agencies ($5.7 billion), and the share of the interest payments on the national debt attributable to military expenditure ($54.5 billion).[62] When we add the roughly $155 billion for the wars in Iraq and Afghanistan to Wheeler's tabulation, we arrive at a grand total of $948.7 billion for 2009.

The two major wars of the early twenty-first century have likewise been enormously expensive. At one time, Columbia University's Joseph Stiglitz estimated the wars' full cost, including such typically neglected factors as the price of long-term care for maimed servicemen, at $3 trillion—hence his book *The $3 Trillion War*, co-authored with Harvard's Linda Bilmes. He now says that number understates the actual figure. "It's much more like five trillion."[63]

And we're worried about trivialities like "earmarks," which comprise such a small portion of spending that they barely amount to a rounding error in the federal budget?

Yet after all this spending, the end result has actually been a smaller military with older equipment. Since the attacks of September 11, 2001, more than $2 trillion has been added to the 1999 baseline Pentagon budget. Roughly half went to the wars in Iraq and Afghanistan, while the other trillion went to nonwar military spending. What did Americans get for that trillion bucks? A *smaller* Navy and Air Force, and a trivial increase in the size of the Army.[64]

Hard to believe, even by government standards, but true. At a time when the Air Force saw its budget increase by 43 percent, the combat air fleet shrank by 51 percent. In 1998, the Navy had 333 battleforce ships. In 2010, the Navy had 287 such ships. In the Army, a 55 percent funding increase yielded three more brigade combat team equivalents—in other words, an increase of a mere 7 percent. It has been, in the words of one expert, "the most relentless squandering of resources the federal government has perpetrated since the end of World War II....Having failed to reform a system that requires an increasing amount of money to shrink, age, and blunt the armed forces, each of the military services can only suggest one solution: more of the same. The military services have put themselves and the nation on a treadmill of squandered resources with no positive result."[65] Thomas Christie, the half-century veteran of the Pentagon and related fields we introduced earlier, wrote in 2009 that "despite the largest defense budgets in real terms in more than 60 years, we have a smaller military force structure than at any time during that period, one that is equipped to a great extent with worn-out, aging equipment."[66]

But the Republican Party, which won a major victory in the off-year election of 2010, has already refused to consider the Pentagon when looking for spending cuts. And so the gravy train will continue on its way, as it always does.

Meanwhile, $250 billion is spent every year maintaining a global military presence that includes 865 facilities in more than 40 countries, and 190,000 troops stationed in 46 countries and territories.[67] Let's clarify that. Every year $250 billion is borrowed from China so the U.S. government can play superpower. (Paul Craig Roberts, assistant secretary of the Treasury under Ronald Reagan, was more blunt: "A country whose financial affairs are in the hands of foreigners is not a superpower.")[68] It is not "liberal" to find something wrong with this. Most liberals, in fact, find nothing wrong with it. Who was the last Democratic presidential candidate to call for a reduced military presence abroad? The policy is bipartisan.

President Obama is being portrayed in some circles as a radical who wants to gut the U.S. military. This is a crude and misleading assessment. Obama is a center-left variant of the bipartisan foreign-policy consensus whose basic premises are shared by John McCain, Hillary Clinton, Madeleine Albright, Newt Gingrich, and the *Washington Post*. He has no intention of withdrawing American troops from where they are stationed around the world, and in fact he is increasing military spending to levels beyond those of Ronald Reagan. Between 2010 and 2013 Obama plans to spend $2.47 trillion on the Pentagon. Were he to be re-elected, he intends to spend another $2.58 trillion. The combined total of $5.05 trillion is a whopping $840 billion in inflation-adjusted dollars more than was spent by the Gipper himself.[69]

It is impossible to be concerned about budgets, deficits, and debt while refusing even to consider an overhaul in the way the country thinks about foreign affairs. Afghanistan must be central to such an overhaul. As of the end of 2009 there were about 100 members of al Qaeda in Afghanistan. A report in late 2007 found only about 3,000 Taliban to be full-time insurgents.[70] The war is costing $1 million per soldier per year, not to mention the horrific loss of life.[71] It involves waging what is perceived as a colonial war against a country that has ground some of the world's most powerful empires into dust. With the U.S. government's Afghan forces drawn from the hated Tajik and Uzbek minorities and therefore anathema to the majority Pashtun, the task becomes more hopeless still. Even Tony Blankley, former chief of staff to Newt Gingrich, has reached "the lamentable conclusion that a continued, substantial U.S. military presence in Afghanistan will do no good for the United States or the long-suffering people of Afghanistan....Only self-deception can justify the continued sacrifice of our finest young men and women in uniform."[72]

The dispute between Russia and Georgia over South Ossetia in 2008 had nothing to do with, and was in no non-hysterical sense a threat to, the United States, but our political class makes its living in such situations trying to persuade us otherwise. Bruce Fein, who served in the Justice Department during the Reagan administration, was a rare voice of sanity: "The United States' hyper-alarm at the Russia-South Ossetia-Georgia jousting illustrated the American Empire's psychology in full blossom. It viscerally exaggerates danger from abroad to frighten the people into saluting a global military footprint, yielding their civil liberties, indulging secret over transparent government and conferring on the President omnipotent military and economic power."[73]

There need be no American concern about a Russia (1) that can barely cope with ramshackle Islamic resistance movements within its own borders, (2) whose navy didn't even challenge American ships as they supplied aid to Georgia during the South Ossetia dispute, and (3) whose population and life expectancy are both on the decline. China is beset by even greater internal troubles, and its government grows less legitimate in the minds of its people all the time.[74]

Supporters of the bipartisan foreign-policy consensus, says Fein, are "blind to the obvious: that indiscriminately seeking to suppress or eliminate every conceivable potential danger creates new enemies, squanders military resources that should be exclusively devoted to defending Americans at home, and cripples the rule of law."[75] With the accuracy of predator drone attacks estimated at two percent, it can scarcely be doubted that potential antagonists are being created faster than other ones are being killed.[76]

This is "isolationism," the propagandists will say. But is it really "isolationism" to think there's something odd about borrowing from Europe to protect Europe, borrowing from Japan to keep cheap oil flowing to Japan, and borrowing from Arab regimes to install democracy in Iraq?[77] "Isolationism" is a propaganda term the media and political establishments use to shout down sensible alternatives to the bipartisan foreign-policy consensus. George Orwell should have demanded royalties on it.

Phil Giraldi, a conservative former counter-terrorist specialist for the CIA, suggests that the whole War on Terror needs to be re-evaluated, and that it is not "liberal" to be skeptical of the official government line. "Most Americans would be surprised to learn that no U.S. citizen has been killed in the United States since 9/11 by an actual member of any of the groups that the State Department defines as 'terrorist,'" Giraldi observes. "Recent attacks were carried out by 'loners,' individuals who wanted to get even for U.S. attacks on Muslim civilians worldwide....Underwear, SUV, and letter bombs have all failed to explode and experts are divided on whether they can work at all given the limitations of the technology. If I were a terrorist wannabe, I would be laughing all the way to the bank as the U.S. and Europe prepare to pour more money into preventive measures in response to chemical bombs that are often mixed together in somebody's kitchen." Osama bin Laden said in 2004, "We are continuing in the same policy to make America bleed profusely to the point of bankruptcy."[78] We shouldn't let our political class give him the satisfaction.

Meanwhile, another fiefdom has been established, this one in "homeland security." In 1999, nine companies contracted with the federal government for "homeland security" purposes. By 2006, that number was 33,890. That is not to mention what Robert Higgs describes as "a multi-billion-dollar industry selling security-related goods and services [that] has emerged complete with specialized newsletters, magazines, websites, consultants, trade shows, job-placement services, and a veritable army of lobbyists working around the clock to widen the river of money that flows to these opportunists."[79] Michael Chertoff, who once headed the Department of Homeland Security, has spent a great deal of time on television calling for ever more elaborate machinery to be installed at airports, without disclosing that he is currently a partner in a company that sells such machinery.[80] As usual, the "public interest" rationale for government action is making plenty of people rich.

■   ■   ■   ■

Out with the phony conservatives, the Tea Party movement says. We want the real thing. But the real thing, far from endorsing global military intervention, recoils from it. The conservative cannot endorse a policy that is at once utopian, destructive, impoverishing, counterproductive, propaganda-driven, contrary to republican values, and sure to increase the power of government, especially the executive branch.[81] George Nash, whose book *The Conservative Intellectual Movement in America Since 1945* has long been a standard reference work on American conservatism, identifies Russell Kirk, Richard Weaver, and Robert Nisbet as the three most significant figures in the branch of conservatism he describes as "traditionalist"; all three were wary of militarism and the warfare state.[82]

Kirk, whose seminal book *The Conservative Mind* became one of the most important texts of the postwar conservative movement, was a withering critic of the Persian Gulf War, and called for "prudence and restraint in the conduct of foreign affairs." Writing of Senator Robert Taft, known in his day as "Mr. Republican," Kirk noted his subject's aversion to war.

> War, Taft perceived, was the enemy of constitution, liberty, economic security, and the cake of custom....Though he was no theoretical pacifist, he insisted that every other possibility must be exhausted before resort to military action. War would make the American President a virtual dictator, diminish the constitutional powers of Congress, contract civil liberties, injure the habitual self-reliance and self-government of the American people, distort the economy, sink the federal government in debt, break in upon private and public morality.[83]

Weaver, perhaps best known for his book *Ideas Have Consequences*, penned a devastating indictment of total war in his book *Visions of Order*. In reflecting on the change in American foreign policy that took place with the

Spanish-American War in 1898, Weaver composed a lament that too many modern conservatives, unfamiliar with their own history, might (incorrectly) confuse with left-liberalism:

> One cannot feign surprise, therefore, that thirty years after the great struggle to consolidate and unionize American power [i.e., the Civil War], the nation embarked on its career of imperialism. The new nationalism enabled Theodore Roosevelt, than whom there was no more staunch advocate of union, to strut and bluster and intimidate our weaker neighbors. Ultimately it launched America upon its career of world imperialism, whose results are now being seen in indefinite military conscription, mountainous debt, restriction of dissent, and other abridgments of classical liberty.[84]

Of all the misapplications of the word "conservative" in recent memory, said Columbia University sociologist Robert Nisbet, the "most amusing, in an historical light, is surely the application of 'conservative' to…great increases in military expenditures.…For in America throughout the twentieth century, and including four substantial wars abroad, conservatives had been steadfastly the voices of non-inflationary military budgets, and of an emphasis on trade in the world instead of American nationalism."[85] War, Nisbet reminded readers, is about the least conservative enterprise one can imagine. "Nothing has proved more destructive of kinship, religion, and local patriotisms than has war and the accompanying military mind."[86]

"National greatness conservatism," as the alternative presented to conservatives is at times clumsily known, bears no resemblance to the central tradition of American conservative thought as embodied in Kirk, Weaver, and Nisbet. It has far more in common with leftism than with conservatism, for it was the Left that was always unsatisfied with the prosaic pursuit of bourgeois life. A conservative is an abiding skeptic of saccharine promises about remaking the world or putting "an end to evil" (to quote two exceptionally unfortunate neoconservatives). Such delusions are the polar opposite of conservatism, or at least they used to be.

The conservative temperament shuns utopian schemes, and seeks instead those finite but noble (and attainable) virtues we associate with hearth and home. These are the things the conservative is supposed to delight in and defend. Nathaniel Hawthorne once observed that a state was about as large an area as the human heart could be expected to love, and G. K. Chesterton reminded us that the genuine patriot boasts not of how large his country is, but of how small it is. As Patrick Henry said, "Those nations who have gone in search of grandeur, power and splendor, have always fallen a sacrifice and been the victims of their own folly. While they acquired those visionary blessings, they lost their freedom."

Now this is all very mundane and uninteresting to those who would urge "greatness" upon us. But ever more glory to the state is only the tyrant's definition of greatness. If traditional conservatism is less exciting than ideological crusades waged from now until eternity, it is also more realistic and sensible, and less likely to hurry us down the path to ruin.

CHAPTER 6

The Myth of "Good Government"

One of the many reasons it has been so difficult to limit government's growth is that the public has been conditioned to believe that despite whatever occasional corruption they may observe in politics, the government by and large has their well-being at heart. Schoolchildren are taught a version of history worthy of *Pravda*. Governments, they are convinced, abolished child labor, gave people good wages and decent working conditions; protect them from bad food, drugs, airplanes, and consumer products; have cleaned their air and water; and have done countless other things to improve their well-being. They truly cannot imagine how anyone who isn't a stooge for industry could think differently, or how free people acting in the absence of compulsion and threats of violence—which is what government activity amounts to—might have figured out a way to solve these problems. The history of regulation is, in this fact-free version of events, a tale of righteous crusaders winning victories for the public against grasping and selfish private interests who care nothing for the common good.

A distorted view of history will affect how we think about current events. If we are misled into believing that the free market has historically enriched the few at the expense of the many, the latter of whom are condemned to lives of miserable and unrelenting toil, we will recoil from the unhampered free market in the present.

The truth is exactly the opposite of this junior-high caricature that's drummed into students' heads. All government can do is impoverish and slow down or even reverse the free market's natural trend toward higher living standards for the population. It is purely parasitic on the productive efforts of the people.

That's why it matters when practically everyone is misled into thinking that the Industrial Revolution led to the impoverishment of workers, even though historians who specialize in this area generally believe no such thing. In the middle of the twentieth century there emerged a historical controversy that became known as the "standard-of-living debate," which sought to determine whether the average person had been helped or harmed by industrialization. That debate was won by the "optimists," who held that the Industrial Revolution had been a net benefit. Even a Marxist like E. P. Thompson was forced to concede that no one any longer believed that everything had gotten worse.[1]

By any objective measure, from life expectancy to caloric intake and living space per capita, the situation of the British worker improved. (The standard of living would have improved still more if England hadn't been at war with revolutionary France during many of these years.) Britain was able to support a dramatically rising population precisely because of the wealth and opportunities created by the Industrial Revolution. There was no way to integrate all these people into the stagnant, almost exclusively agricultural economy that preceded the Industrial Revolution. T. S. Ashton, one of the great historians of the period, pointed out that if one cared to observe a country that experienced a population explosion without an industrial revolution, he might look at eighteenth-century India and the starvation and poverty that was to be seen everywhere.

Now it's true: living conditions for workers during the early Industrial Revolution were dreadful by modern standards. Only a fool would want to exchange places with those workers today. But (1) however undesirable from a modern standpoint, these conditions were considerably better than people had been accustomed to in the past, either in England or anywhere else; and (2) the continual improvements in people's standard of living, such that today we can look upon these workers' plight with pity and disgust, came about—as we shall see below—precisely by the operation of the free market itself.

In the twentieth and twenty-first centuries, at the very time market reforms began to take root in parts of the developing world, those areas also experienced enormous advances in living standards and dramatic declines in poverty. What economists call "absolute poverty" afflicted 85 percent of the world's population in 1820. That figure had fallen to 50 percent by 1950, and to 33 percent by the early 1980s. According to the World Bank, absolute poverty in the developing countries fell from 40 to 21 percent, and thus the global rate from 33 to 18 percent from 1981 to 2001. Not only the percentage but also the absolute number of people living in absolute poverty fell. This had never happened in any other twenty-year period in history. Indeed, poverty has been reduced more in the past fifty years than in the previous five hundred. In 1960, the life expectancy of the poorer countries was only 60 percent of that of the richer countries. That figure is now 80 percent. Caloric intake in the Third World has grown by one-third since the 1960s.[2] In late-nineteenth-century England, rich and poor were separated by seventeen years in life expectancy and five inches in height; that difference has narrowed to two years and less than one inch in England today.[3]

In the United States, the poverty rate (a higher standard of material comfort than the "absolute poverty" metric just referred to) fell from about 95 percent of the population at the beginning of the twentieth century to about 12 to 14 percent by the end. The bottom quintile of the population saw its real incomes rise by 1,900 percent, a much greater jump than occurred in the higher quintiles of the income distribution. The average household below the poverty line around the year 2000 would have ranked among the richest 5 to 10 percent of households in real incomes in 1900.[4]

The poor likewise have found themselves able to obtain goods that no one in history, no matter how wealthy or powerful, could have been able to imagine, much less possess: electricity, climate control, automobiles, air transportation, refrigeration, microwave ovens, personal computers, cell phones, and a great deal else. Even the Hapsburgs lacked indoor plumbing in their summer palace on the eve of World War I, but practically all poor households had it by the close of the twentieth century.[5]

Now couldn't it just be a coincidence that this explosion in poverty reduction and wealth occurred in the wake of the adoption of market reforms in so many places around the world? Or is there a clear connection between the one and the other?

We can answer that question with the aid of a thought experiment. Imagine a primitive economy, in which practically all consumer goods are produced by hand rather than with the aid of machinery. That society would be extremely poor. But its poverty would not be the result of wicked exploiters. It would be the result of the relatively few goods people could produce with their bare hands. An economy like this can produce only a tiny fraction of the supply of goods we today take for granted, and would be unable to produce certain classes of goods (personal computers, say) altogether. With so few goods available for purchase, they would be quite expensive in terms of the time it would take to earn enough money to buy them.

Passing a law demanding that everyone in this economy should enjoy the standard of living of the average person in 2011 would accomplish nothing. Reality is not so easily defied.

How, then, does this economy break free of its poverty?[6] It would help if more goods could be produced, so there would be more to go around for everyone. That means this economy needs capital equipment, which makes each person's labor able to produce a greater supply of goods. Saving and investment, in turn, make possible the production and acquisition of this equipment. When individuals save, the saved resources are available to entrepreneurs, who use the savings to acquire the capital resources necessary to make their production processes more productive and efficient. As a result, they can produce more output with less input. Instead of needing 200 people to produce 1,000 widgets, they may now need only 50 people to produce 5,000 widgets. That means 150 people are now available to contribute to the production of the countless other goods this society desperately needs, but could not previously have enjoyed because the necessary labor had been tied up in widget production.[7]

In a market economy, in short, producers are allowed to earn and keep profits, which they use to purchase capital equipment that will make it possible for them to produce in much greater quantities at lower cost. (Firms that do not reinvest their profits like this will be wiped out by those who do, so they have little choice.) People's real incomes rise because the economy becomes physically capable of producing in greater and greater abundance and at ever lower costs, and competition spreads around the benefits of this greater abundance in the form of lower prices.* That is precisely what happened during the nineteenth and twentieth centuries. People at the end of the century had to work far less than those at the beginning in order to earn the necessary purchasing power to buy a wide range of important consumer goods.[8]

So it is the market economy itself that makes possible our rising standard of living. Taxing this process, which is what government does, discourages capital investment and thereby slows down the process by which greater abundance yields higher real incomes. If we genuinely care about the welfare of mankind, therefore, we should want peaceful and honest business activity to be entirely unhampered. Taxing it is the very last thing we should want to do.

But people worked in horrendous conditions in the past, didn't they? By modern standards, they certainly did. No one in his right mind would switch places with a nineteenth-century factory worker. But we tend to forget, when we see photographs of factory workers in the early Industrial Revolution, just how punishing and backbreaking was the agricultural work from which these factory workers had made the deliberate decision to flee. No one could force them to take a factory job. They took such jobs because they represented an improvement in these workers' standard of living at a time when society was still so poor that the ability to meet one's basic needs was just about all most people could hope to aspire to.[9]

Still, we tend to assume that improvements in workplace conditions can come about only through state edict. That is absolutely not true.

Even critics of capitalism will admit that profit-seeking businesses will adopt workplace improvements that pay for themselves by increasing the firm's bottom line because the improvement means less disruption of the production process, less work missed, less litigation, or whatever. But not all such improvements

---

* Before the creation of the Federal Reserve System in 1913, Americans did indeed see lower prices every year thanks to this process. Since that time, a fairly consistent increase in the money supply has pushed up prices and wages in nominal terms, thereby obscuring what would otherwise be a consistent fall in prices that contributes to our standard of living. But this process is still at work when, in a world of rising nominal prices and wages, prices rise more slowly than wages.

have a noticeable direct impact on that bottom line, or at least not great enough to justify the expense of implementing it. What then?

Some occupations, either because of the risks or other undesirable features inherent in the work itself, carry a wage premium in order to attract labor away from more pleasant and desirable employment. Economists call these wage differences "compensating differentials." Suppose we have two factories that are otherwise identical, except one has air conditioning and the other does not. Air conditioning in and of itself may not make workers more productive in proportion to the expense involved in installing and running an air conditioning system. But the factory without air conditioning will have to pay its workers a higher wage to attract them away from the more comfortable work environment of the air-conditioned factory. If this wage differential becomes great enough, the second factory will simply install air conditioning rather than go on paying the wage differential.[10]

Now what if, as soon as air conditioning was invented (and at a time when it was far more expensive than it is now), government had required all facilities to be air conditioned? The result would have been a significant spike in unemployment because factories that couldn't afford it would go out of business while those that could would do so at the expense of wages or (job creating) expansion of their business. Workers would have realized that at that stage of technological progress, their choice was not between a job without air conditioning and a job with air conditioning. Their choice was between a job without air conditioning and no job at all. To this day, air conditioning is still far less prevalent in relatively poorer Europe than it is in the United States. We would not be doing European workers any favors by imposing it as a mandate on all employers.

We cannot reflexively demand that every comfort with which we might wish to endow workers be introduced immediately. Workers value other goods, including the prospect of employment itself, more than air conditioning. The wage differential mechanism ensures that amenities are introduced at a pace that makes sense from the point of view of society as a whole. Insisting on them arbitrarily and prematurely will simply push many workers into less desirable circumstances overall than if the market had been allowed to indicate when it made sense for these improvements to be adopted.

There is, after all, no limit to the amenities we would prefer to enjoy at work. Most of us would doubtless enjoy being transported to work by hovercraft, having free prime rib for lunch, and (as the United Auto Workers famously demanded) receiving massages during the working day. We cannot have these things. Society is not yet wealthy enough to provide them for everyone who wants them. Unless we are prepared to remain indefinitely unemployed, we have to reconcile ourselves to a particular level of workplace amenities. That is the situation workers have always faced. Although the level of amenities enjoyed today is much higher than it was in the past, the principle remains the same.

Employers are prepared to pay a particular sum for labor services. They do not care what form that payment takes. If the government demands that workers receive some fringe benefit, employers are happy to offer it, while correspondingly reducing the money wages they pay. The same thing holds for mandated improvements in working conditions. Because employers are prepared to pay only a particular amount for labor, these mandated improvements will come at the expense of the workers' take-home pay or in the reduction of some other benefit. By forcing a particular payment configuration on all workers, we do not necessarily improve their condition. We simply deprive them of the opportunity to choose a different configuration that suits them better. In other words, we do not improve the condition of the poorest by looking through the options available to them and taking away the one they actually chose.[11]

Now how about children? We all remember what we were taught in eighth grade. Under the free market, children were condemned to lives of hard labor. Before the rise of industrial capitalism, children spent their days picking flowers and skipping through meadows. Then capitalism appeared and whisked the children away into lives of miserable toil. Only our wise public servants could have rescued them from this cruel fate.

Economist Ludwig von Mises threw cold water on this junior-camper rendition of history as early as the late 1940s. "It is a distortion of facts," he wrote, "to say that the factories carried off the housewives from the nurseries and the children from their play. These women had nothing to cook with and to feed their children. These children were destitute and starving. Their only refuge was the factory. It saved them, in the strict sense of the term, from death by starvation."[12]

Child labor is not a unique feature of wicked capitalism. It has existed since the beginning of time. Until very recently, hardly anyone imagined that its abolition was even conceivable. Before the rise of the market economy, societies were far too poor for families to survive at all unless every member contributed to the household's income. That remains the issue today. It is not that whole countries just happen to be filled with bad parents; it would be rather an extraordinary coincidence if all the bad parents just happened to live in Bangladesh. It is that these families cannot survive without income generated by their children.

Economist Anna Krueger, while concerned about "legitimate issues of intolerable working conditions," finds that "employment of children may provide food that prevents a family from starving. In some instances, also, it may provide girls with an alternative to forced early marriages."[13] The International Labor Organization, not known for a bias against government intervention, admitted in a 1997 report: "Poverty, however, emerges as the most compelling reason why children work. Poor households need the money, and children commonly contribute around 20 to 25 percent of family income. Since by definition poor households spend the bulk of their income on food, it is clear that the income provided by working children is critical to their survival."[14]

If reality could be wished or legislated away, there would be no poverty or misfortune anywhere in the world. According to Oxfam, the British charity, when Westerners cajoled the government of Bangladesh into outlawing child labor, the children by and large went into prostitution instead, or simply starved to death. UNICEF reports that a boycott of the Nepalese carpet industry forced five thousand desperate young girls into prostitution.[15] We can assume the children thus liberated took little consolation in knowing that at least they weren't working in factories anymore. Still less would they have cared about the good intentions that supposedly motivated the crusaders, who could not pencil in to their schedule of moral outrage the five minutes it would have taken to study the likely consequences of what they were demanding.

The increase in an economy's productive capacity, and therefore in its overall standard of living, is what puts an end to child labor without these horrific consequences. Over the past half century, the proportion of child workers in India has fallen from 35 percent to 12 percent. The poorest developing countries have seen the proportion of child laborers in their economies fall from 32 to 19 percent over the past forty years; in the medium income group the figure has fallen from 28 to 7 percent.[16]

In light of all this, we can now understand the fallacies involved in the uncomprehending refrain: why, of course we need this or that government protection—surely you don't want to return to the conditions of the Industrial Revolution!

But Don't We Need Wealth Redistribution Programs?

As far back as the Civil War pension system, the official rationale of helping the needy became the cover for politicians to build their fiefdoms by rewarding friends and buying votes. Initially, these pensions were available only to (1) people who could prove they had service-related disabilities, and (2) their dependent survivors. In no time, eligibility requirements were liberalized to the point of absurdity: one could receive a pension without having a disability, and even without having engaged in combat. Being old and a veteran were sufficient; even deserters were known to receive pensions that had originally been intended for men who had been injured in war.[17]

Since the 1960s we have seen another wave of liberalizations in programs designed to help the needy. To put it delicately, these changes were not followed by the restoration of family and community life and a flourishing of self-respect and a sense of responsibility. But suppose they had been. What if poverty, crime, and social dysfunction had been very high before the Great Society programs were instituted and then were dramatically reduced? Can we doubt that its advocates would have attributed the decline in these features of inner-city life to the government's wise new programs? Yet when things work the other way, and the inner cities become almost unlivable after these programs are introduced, we're hastily assured that the one has absolutely nothing to do with the other.

In *Losing Ground: American Social Policy 1950-1980*, one of the most influential social-science studies of the past several decades, Charles Murray famously argued that poverty persisted in the United States not in spite of anti-poverty programs, but because of them. He wanted to know why it should be that "the number of people living in poverty stopped declining just as the public-assistance program budgets and the rate of increase in those budgets were highest."[18] He went on to explain why, counterintuitive as it may be, we should in fact *expect* this result.

Murray challenged his readers to devise a social program that would not cause net harm.[19] He gave the example of a government program aimed at discouraging smoking. We won't reproduce his whole argument, which is lengthy, but his point is that the reward the government offers for people who quit smoking has to be substantial enough to persuade them to go to the trouble of quitting, but not so substantial as to encourage nonsmokers to start smoking in pursuit of the reward. Just as Murray says, this task turns out to be next to impossible.

To start with, we have to identify a target group to which the program will apply, and an appropriate monetary reward for quitting. Someone who has been smoking for three days cannot be eligible for such a reward. Likewise for someone who smokes only one cigarette a day. We have to draw some line, arbitrary though it be, to determine eligibility, so we say the program will apply to people who have been smoking at least a pack of cigarettes a day for five years. And (writing in 1984) Murray proposed a reward of ten thousand dollars.

Now the problems begin. Anyone who has been smoking for four years and eleven months has an incentive to continue smoking for at least another month. A correspondingly weaker, but nevertheless significant incentive exists for someone who has been smoking for four years, to continue for another year. And so on. Likewise for those who smoke less than a pack a day: someone who smokes, say, eighteen cigarettes a day has an incentive to smoke two extra cigarettes per day in order to qualify for the reward. For people on the fence about whether to begin smoking, teenagers in particular, the reward may be the deciding factor. Anyone who has been smoking for fewer than five years (or not at all), or less than a pack a day, has an incentive to begin smoking, to continue, or even to increase his smoking.

The ten thousand-dollar reward of Murray's hypothetical program may seem like adequate inducement to quit once someone begins smoking, but once they become addicted they may find the reward is not so powerful after all. For a similar reason it is very difficult to devise a welfare program that does not produce net harm. Given man's inclination to acquire wealth with the least possible exertion, programs like these threaten to drag additional people into a cycle of dependency that mankind's inclination to sloth will only reinforce over time.

And this is the fallacy in the common refrain that "it would cost only $X billion to give every American who needs it" this or that benefit. Once people realize the government is giving out a benefit for free, more and more people will place themselves in the condition that entitles them to the benefit, thereby making the program ever more expensive, society poorer, and the system more fragile, as a narrower and narrower base of productive individuals is forced to support an ever-growing population demanding benefits. The very philosophy of "welfare rights," which gained traction in the 1960s, poisons and corrupts civil society by suggesting that recipients of government largesse are *entitled* to live off the efforts of others. Infantilism is thereby rewarded and productive work punished.

Critics reply that for all the documented problems with the welfare state, private charity is surely inadequate. They sometimes point to the wretched conditions in which many people lived 100 years ago and congratulate themselves for relieving that misery. This is a fallacy. The entire society was far poorer then. As we have seen, this is a common error: if working conditions, or product quality, or sanitary practices, were lower 100 years ago than they are today, that is assumed to be the product of a lack of government regulation. Never considered is that to a much poorer society, standards we have come to expect would have been considered luxury goods, whose adoption had to be considered in light of having to forego other things people desired.

One way to blunt this objection is to recall the true history of American charitable work, which involves the voluntary organizations that Americans once formed to provide for the poor or to provide for their own needs during unforeseen emergencies. This part of American history is almost completely unknown. Not just private charity but also fraternal organizations performed roles we today associate exclusively with government. Historians David Beito and Marvin Olasky have done excellent work in this area.[20]

Another way to approach it is to recall that at least two-thirds of the money assigned to government welfare budgets is eaten up by bureaucracy. Taken by itself, this would mean it would take three dollars in taxes for one dollar to reach the poor. But we must add to this the well-founded estimate of James Payne that the combined public and private costs of taxation amount to 65 cents of every dollar taxed. When we include this factor, we find the cost of government delivery of one dollar to the poor to be five dollars.[21] So a private system would not *need* to duplicate the entire government welfare budget out of private funds.

And private charities are far better stewards of the money entrusted to them. They have donors to answer to who do not want to hear that only twenty cents of their dollar is actually reaching someone, or that the people who use their facilities are not finding work or turning their lives around at all. They want results. They are much less likely to countenance a condition of dependency for years on end. Government agencies operate under exactly the opposite kind of incentive. And private institutions can tailor unique approaches for particular individuals, as opposed to the bureaucratic uniformity of the welfare state.

During the question period after a lecture I'd given at a church on Long Island in 2005, a critic demanded that the crowd consider the consequences of abolishing a $250 Social Security death benefit. (For whatever reason, this particular feature of the welfare state was of special concern to him.) He could not imagine a society getting by without it, even though all of human civilization had done exactly that since the beginning of time. I replied along these lines: here you are sitting in the middle of a flourishing parish, filled with people, and you honestly have no idea what someone would do if he needed $250 for death-related expenses? In a normal society, helping people in need is precisely what parishes and other voluntary organizations do. They donate their money and time. They hold benefits to help defray large expenses. They provide in-kind services. Handymen help with simple repairs. People are cared for. No one watches anyone starve.

The man's question reflected precisely the kind of relationship it is in government's interest to foster between itself and its citizens: helpless dependence, amplified by a fairy-tale historical narrative that urges them to believe that all improvements in their condition come from the benevolent hand of their wise rulers. When Otto von Bismarck introduced wide-ranging social insurance in Germany in the 1870s, he did so for the express purpose of buying the people's loyalty to his regime. An enervated, spiritless people is far less likely to rise up against parasites who live off their labor, even when that regime is exploiting and robbing them blind, if they have been conditioned to believe they cannot live any other way.

A genuinely humane approach to the misfortunes of our fellow men, as opposed to a coldly bureaucratic one, does not occur to a nation of zombies. Just as a muscle atrophies from lack of use, civil society's ability to manage its affairs withers away when all its functions are usurped by an outside force. The man's objection to eliminating the $250 Social Security benefit only proved my point. We have been rendered so helpless and dehumanized that we can scarcely imagine how the voluntary institutions of civil society might lend assistance to people in need without the government gun in the ribs.

If I may be permitted another anecdotal note: not long ago a volunteer firefighter in Virginia shoveling snow in his driveway was approached by two cross-country skiers. "They should pay to have someone shovel the driveways of volunteer firefighters," the skiers said. The firefighter thought of two responses:

(1) I *am* "they."

(2) Why don't you two grab a shovel?

He thought better of it and simply thanked them for their concern.[22]

Alexis de Tocqueville, the Frenchman whose visits to the young United States yielded the classic two-volume study *Democracy in America*, was struck by how readily Americans came together, without the threat of government violence hanging over them, to solve their problems. "The political associations which exist in the United States are only a single feature in the midst of the immense assemblage of associations in that country," he wrote. "Whenever, at the head of some new undertaking, you see the Government in France, or a man of rank in England, in the United States you will be sure to find an association." De Tocqueville was impressed by "the extreme skill with which the inhabitants of the United States succeed in proposing a common object to the exertions of a great many men, and in getting them voluntarily to pursue it."[23]

Even now that spirit is not entirely dead. It's true (and hardly unexpected) that charitable giving fell substantially during the late 1960s, at a time when the federal government was announcing its intention to tackle the problem of poverty. But it grew just as substantially during the 1980s, when people were told that government was cutting back.[24] (In fact, the federal budget doubled during the 1980s, and welfare payments, contrary to a belief so widespread that it is apparently impossible ever to overturn, were not cut.)

Still, skeptics will assure us that nonviolent approaches to poor relief cannot work. Those skeptics should be confronted with this scenario: if the entire federal welfare state were suddenly done away with, and for some reason state and local governments made no effort to fill the breach, wouldn't these critics themselves be more likely to volunteer their time on behalf of a charitable cause, or put their talents or professional services at the service of the poor for free or at a reduced rate? Of course, comes the reply. Then why aren't these critics doing these things right now? What answer can they give, apart from undermining their position by admitting that the reason they don't help their fellow man as much (or at all) now is that somebody else is doing it for them?[25]

Some call federal welfare initiatives failed government programs—after all, poverty has stagnated while they have been in effect, and the stagnation has occurred over a period of time in which the amount of money spent per poor person has quadrupled (as indeed happened between 1967 and 1994).[26] That's a failure by anyone's definition. And poor people who do not receive government welfare are two and a half times more likely to escape poverty within a year than those who do receive it.[27] But these programs have not been failures for the bureaucracies and interest groups that have been enriched by them. James Payne, author of *Overcoming Welfare*, gives a sense of the dynamics:

> Welfare today is an enormous industry, much larger than the defense establishment, or the tobacco industry, or chemical companies. It supports over 700,000 social workers, 420 schools of social work, thousands of special-interest groups, nonprofit organizations, and commercial firms, and some 43 million beneficiaries. Day in and day out, welfare leaders work to expand their industry.[28]

Payne cites a candid description of the system by a Social Security official in a Midwest field office:

> In the field—I was a supervisor out there for years and years—your staffing, your budget for supplies, and your awards money for the employees was based on work units. Now, work units were assigned based on the number of claims you took. So we would sit around and figure out how we could get more people on the SSI rolls, because it would benefit us. The more applications we took, the more work units, the bigger the staff: we could build up an empire.[29]

"Affordable housing" programs have fared little better than these more direct forms of wealth redistribution. But as with so many federal programs, people think back to earlier and much poorer periods in the country's history, observe that people lived in much less desirable housing than they do today, and casually assume that government intervention is what separates our fortunate situation now from the terrible conditions then. In fact, though, even at a time when the country possessed far less wealth than it does today, a genuinely free market in housing did a much better job providing housing for a largely immigrant population whose sheer numbers and sudden appearance would have overwhelmed any system. An enormous quantity of housing for working-class people was built in American cities beginning in the late nineteenth century. In Philadelphia, 300,000 brick row homes, many of which still stand today, were constructed. These results were fairly typical throughout the United States. Many people who lived in poor neighborhoods were not in fact confined to the overcrowded tenements we associate with housing during that time, but owned small homes or rented space made available by homeowners.[30]

The substandard housing we recall from Jacob Riis's book *How the Other Half Lives* (1891), while of course deplorable by modern standards, were a temporary phase for those who dwelled in them. Lillian Wald (1867–1940), the settlement-house pioneer whose Henry Street Settlement and Visiting Nurse Service of New York continue in operation over a century after their founding, noted that by 1930 she found the houses where Riis had once decried overcrowding to be practically empty. The families who had once lived there had since moved to more comfortable accommodations in Brooklyn and the Bronx.[31] Writes Howard Husock:

> From the end of the Civil War until the New Deal and the National Housing Act of 1937, which gave public housing its first push, the private housing market generated a cornucopia of housing forms to accommodate those of modest means as they gradually improved their condition. In those years Chicago saw the construction of 211,000 low-cost two-family homes—or 21 percent of its residences. In Brooklyn 120,000 two-family structures with ground-floor stores sprang up. In Boston some 40 percent of the population of 770,000 lived in the 65,376 units of the city's three-decker frame houses.
>
> These areas of low-cost, unsubsidized housing were home to the striving poor. In Boston, as pioneer sociologists Robert Woods and Albert Kennedy describe it in their brilliant 1914 work, *The Zone of Emergence*, those neighborhoods teemed with clerks and skilled and semi-skilled workmen.

Some 65 percent of those clerks and workmen owned their own homes.[32]

It is difficult to survey the history of government housing programs and conclude they have been a net good. Public housing has been such a clear disaster that hardly anyone can be found to defend it any longer. When the poor working families for which public housing had originally been intended made their way to the suburbs, they left behind a demographic consisting almost entirely of nonworking families headed by single women. As so often happens, this confluence of factors culminated in gang activity that terrorized residents and passersby. Soon enough it had become all but uninhabitable, with crime, property damage, and pathological behavior the drearily predictable norm. The successful and entrepreneurial stayed away from such neighborhoods and their surrounding areas. Many of them have had to be demolished entirely.

With public housing such a persistent failure, its advocates began to call for housing vouchers instead. The poor could apply a voucher (a "Section 8" benefit) toward rent in a private building of their choosing. Section 8 rent is capped at 30 percent of income; should someone pursue more remunerative work that might benefit him in the long run, he is hit immediately with a significant rent increase. There is no time limit for Section 8 housing, so it has yielded the same dependency problems of all traditional welfare programs.[33]

Public-housing subsidies and rental vouchers are based on the false idea that the private sector cannot make low-income housing available, when in fact the market economy over time has consistently led to less and less expensive goods (in terms of the number of hours necessary to earn the purchasing power to buy them), and naturally leads to a lowering of costs and a greater abundance of the goods people need.[34] The typical way we have been encouraged to improve housing for low-income families is to require all houses to have a certain number of closets, so much counter space, and so on. This is, once again, a case of scanning the options of the poor and eliminating the choice they actually selected. It is hardly surprising that many developers have decided to stay away from low-income housing entirely. In short, government makes housing more expensive by its regulations and zoning laws—not to mention all the other housing policies we've discussed—and then pretends to be shocked at rising housing prices.

But What about Federal Education Programs?

We know all about the easy-money policies that lured people into crushing amounts of mortgage debt, but we hear less about how those same policies have encouraged impossible amounts of debt related to higher education, for under-graduates and graduate students alike—especially in the wake of the financial crisis, when the job picture for these students is so bleak.

In early 2009, *Forbes* magazine told the story of Joel Kellum and Jennifer Coultas, who met at the California Western School of Law and were later mar-ried. When they graduated in 1995, their combined debt was $194,000. Each got a six-figure job. But even with one of them moonlighting, they managed to come up with only $145,000 in loan payments. With interest accruing at 12 percent a year, their payments reduced the principal of the loan by $21,000. Just $173,000 to go.[35]

When they divorced last year, the couple cited the crushing burden of law school debt as a key factor in ruining their marriage. "Two people this much in debt just shouldn't be together," said Kellum.

Or there's Mindy Babbitt, who enrolled at Davenport University in her mid-twenties to get a degree in accounting. She borrowed $35,000 at 9 percent interest and assumed the income she could command with her degree would make it all work. Instead, the entry-level job she found upon graduating barely kept her above water. She deferred her loan payments, and for a while was out of work. At age forty-one, she told *Forbes* she despaired of ever paying off her loan. She earns $41,000 per year—$10,000 more than the average high school graduate. But by now her student loan balance has risen to $87,000.[36]

In May 2010 the *New York Times* reported on the case of Cortney Munna, who graduated from New York University with $100,000 in debt. Of course, the *Times* could have chosen a great many individuals to profile for such a story; the number of people leaving college with over $40,000 in debt had increased ninefold over the previous decade. Munna and her mother bought into the propaganda: forget about the money you're spending on college, since the rewards you'll reap will far surpass them. In fact, she barely scrapes by, working for a photographer. That plus her degree in religious and women's studies is what her $100,000 investment yielded her.[37]

But perhaps we are being too cynical: what about the extra $1 million that college graduates are supposed to earn over their lifetimes compared to their high-school graduate counterparts? *Forbes* tackled that one, too. The $1 million figure is arrived at by taking the difference in annual income between college graduates and high school graduates, and multiplying it by the forty years of the average working life. Where this claim falls short is that it assumes that the additional income earned by college graduates is caused by the college education, when it more likely reflects the fact that smarter, more motivated people are more likely to go to college in the first place.

Meanwhile, the combination of compound interest and low salaries is leaving wreckage everywhere. The four-year cost of undergraduate tuition, room, board, books, and fees at a public university is $46,700, and $99,900 at a private one, even after financial aid and scholarships are included. That also doesn't include four years' worth of foregone income—in other words, another $125,000. Bankruptcy won't save these poor souls: college debt is one category of loans that cannot be written off in bankruptcy proceedings. They'll follow you forever.

Of course, it is the subsidies themselves that push tuition costs ever higher. Here's the obvious point everyone pretends not to realize: *colleges know the students have access to low-interest loans courtesy of government.*[38] Aware that prospective students enjoy artificially increased purchasing power, college administrations raise tuition (and cut back their own aid programs) accordingly. When tuition thus continues to rise, as any fool could predict, we hear huzzahs for the government—for how could students pay this high tuition without government assistance? It is the classic case, as Harry Browne said, of the government breaking your leg, handing you a crutch, and saying, "See? Without me you couldn't walk."

This, incidentally, is how the government defines *affordable*. As with housing, government programs artificially increase prices. What makes those inflated prices "affordable," in the government's version of things, is that you can get a government-subsidized loan to pay them. Letting prices fall in the first place, so people might be able to pay college tuition or buy a house without enslaving themselves to debt for the rest of their lives, is not even on the table. (Incidentally, Fannie Mae, which was created in order to foster affordable housing, makes loans in excess of $938,000.[39] Hooray for "affordable housing" programs!)

Just about any professor, left, right, or center, can tell you how few college students today show the slightest intellectual curiosity about anything. Give me my B-minus and let me out of here. Even with all the grade inflation and the dumbing down of curricula, the National Center for Higher Education Management Systems found in 2006 that the six-year—*six-year*—graduation rate for students seeking bachelor's degrees was a mere 56.4 percent.[40]

For those students who actually belong in college, a combination of falling tuition and increased private aid—along with more part-time work, in place of full-time drunkenness—will keep college within reach. One form of private assistance that would no longer be crowded out by government involvement should subsidized college loans be phased out is Milton Friedman's proposed human capital contract, by which students would pledge a percentage of future earnings for a fixed period of time in exchange for tuition assistance in the present. Such a proposal has the added benefit of not making every single American into a debt slave the moment he enters the workforce. Students would not have to live in terror that their future salaries might be insufficient to repay their student loans. Repayment according to the terms of these contracts would be based on the student's earnings and thus his ability to pay. Investment funds could spread out the risk of default by purchasing these contracts in large quantities. Shares in the funds would be traded analogously to how shares in real estate investment trusts are purchased today.[41]

Most people seem to be under the impression that education funding at the elementary and secondary level has been "cut" over the years, and that test scores would be higher if more money were spent. But spending on education (which is mostly local), even adjusting for inflation, has skyrocketed. The $5,064 spent per student during the 1970–71 school year had already more than doubled by 2002–03, when $10,464 was spent.[42] And in 2003, the federal government found only 13 percent of Americans at or above age sixteen to be "proficient" in reading prose, following written directions, and carrying out quantitative tasks.[43] Had the free market produced such an outcome, we would never hear the end of it. But when a government monopoly is responsible for the kind of result no one would tolerate from any other institution, it will not admit failure. Why, it just needs more resources.

When a federal Department of Education was being considered by Congress in 1979, even some on the Left were skeptical of the merits of a centralized education bureaucracy. Senator Daniel Patrick Moynihan (D-NY) warned that "we risk the politicization of education itself." The president of the American Federation of Teachers complained that the problems of American education "won't be solved by a new bureaucracy in Washington." Editorials in the *Washington Post* and the *New York Times* came out against the idea.[44] In our day, on the other hand, abolishing the Department of Education is considered "extreme," the left-wing blogger's most cherished word. George W. Bush, in fact, managed to get the 2000 Republican platform to exclude the plank calling for the Department's abolition, and later said that "change will not come by disdaining or dismantling the federal role in education."[45] The Department of Education, which we managed to do without for more than 85 percent of our history, is premised on the idea that Americans are too dumb to administer their own schools without handing over tens of billions to the federal government for the privilege of being supervised and pushed around by their betters. Presumably the sun would continue to rise and set if the Department were abolished, but even in the midst of the worst debt crisis the United States has ever faced, the respectables wag their fingers at any such suggestion.

Is there really no fat to be cut here? The Brookings Institution's John Chubb once inquired as to how many bureaucrats were employed by the central administrative offices of the New York City public schools. After a dozen phone calls, he finally reached someone who both knew the answer and was authorized to disclose it. The answer: *six thousand*. He then called the Archdiocese of New York, to find out how many bureaucrats were employed in the Catholic school system, which educated one-sixth as many children. The telephone was answered by someone who replied, "Wait a minute; let me count." The answer? Twenty-six.[46]

But when budget cuts appear on the horizon, it is rarely the army of bureaucrats that gets cut. Governments typically move to cut their most popular services first, in order to provoke a public outcry in favor of reversing the cuts. This tactic is known as the "Washington Monument Syndrome," so named for the National Park Service's threat to close the Washington Monument, one of the District of Columbia's most popular tourist attractions, when the Park Service's budget was about to be reduced. City and town governments pull the same trick all the time—why, without higher taxes, they'll have no choice but to cancel garbage collection, put fifty students in a class, and cut back on police! The budget is just that lean.[47]

Doesn't Sweden Show Us the Way?

Supporters of the welfare state often reply to arguments like these by pointing to the alleged counter-example of the Scandinavian countries, Sweden in particular, where a cradle-to-grave welfare state exists alongside robust economic growth and vigorous employment figures. We really can have it all.

Can we?

In 2008, Swedish Prime Minister Fredrik Reinfeldt urged his countrymen to face facts: Swedish prosperity had been built up by the free market, and the much-vaunted Swedish welfare state merely drew parasitically upon that wealth until the country was forced to begin returning to the market economy once again. Wealth that "took a hundred years to build was almost dismantled in twenty-five years," he said.[48]

He was telling the truth. Thanks to a largely free-market economy and its avoidance of war, Sweden could boast the world's highest rate of per-capita income growth between 1870 and 1950. That growth rate had fallen to about average by international standards after a quarter century of expansions in the size of government. The economic interventions accelerated under the hard-left Olof Palme, whose increases in taxation and the regulatory apparatus seriously undermined the country's international competitiveness.

After years of instability and currency devaluations, Sweden began a program of deregulation and selling off state-owned companies. Cuts in spending and tax rates also contributed to improving Sweden's relative performance compared to other European countries, after having fallen so far behind by 1990. Tax reductions have continued into the twenty-first century, with income and corporate tax rates coming down and gift and inheritance taxes being abolished altogether. Sweden is now ranked as the world's second-most competitive economy in the world, according to the World Economic Forum. When the *Wall Street Journal* and the Heritage Foundation compiled the 2010 Index of Economic Freedom, they found Sweden offered "greater business freedom, trade freedom, monetary freedom, investment freedom, financial freedom, freedom from corruption, and property-rights protection than does the United States."[49] (What this really means is that the rest of the world is so unfree that even the still-bloated welfare state of Sweden could in some sense still qualify as one of the world's freest economies.)[50]

To be sure, the Swedish welfare state is still very extensive, and the top marginal income tax rate is 57 percent. On the other hand, corporations get much better tax treatment in Sweden than in the United States. And for all the attention lavished on the welfare state, it turns out that most of the wealth redistribution involves transfers from each income group back to itself rather than from the rich to the poor. Lund University economist Andreas Bergh notes that "the majority of the taxes you pay are given back to you during your life cycle," and thus "if you pay more when you work, you will also get more when you retire." That's why even wealthy Swedes receive a hefty amount of government funds.[51]

Sweden's condition has improved thanks to recent market reforms, but the situation is still not as good as the statistics can lead us to believe. Swedish economist Stefan Karlsson explains that the official numbers hide significant patches of unemployment by simply not classifying them as unemployment. Many unemployed are assigned to "labor market political activities," which exist for the sole purpose of pushing the official unemployment rate down. When people living on "sickness benefits" are included, unemployment (as of 2006, when Karlsson wrote) was as high as 25 percent. Non-Western immigrants have an unemployment rate in excess of 50 percent.[52]

Per Bylund, a Swedish-born doctoral candidate studying economics in the United States, sums it up this way: "Sweden would have been like Romania without the extensive reforms of the past 20 years—Sweden is much 'freer' now. But Sweden is also not as good as it seems—the numbers cannot be trusted."[53]

Won't Monopolies Swallow Us Up?

The cartoon version of American history we all learned in seventh grade is largely responsible for why people are convinced that if government shrinks, predatory big business will take its place and enslave us all. Isn't that what the so-called robber barons did in the nineteenth century? Well, not really. It's true that some people enriched themselves at the public's expense thanks to special privileges they received from government, but those privileges are the opposite of the free market. In fact, supply increased and prices fell dramatically during the period we're told was dominated by "monopolies." Andrew Carnegie, for instance, almost single-handedly managed to reduce the price of steel rails from $160 per ton in the mid-1870s to $17 per ton in the late 1890s. Given the importance of steel to a modern economy, that massive price reduction yielded greater wealth and a higher standard of living for everyone. Carnegie was so efficient, in fact, that the 4,000 people who worked at his Homestead plant in Pittsburgh produced three times more steel than the 15,000 workers at Germany's Krupps steelworks, Europe's most modern and renowned facility.[54]

We might also mention James J. Hill, who grew up in poverty but whose entrepreneurial skill helped make the Great Northern Railroad, which extended from St. Paul to Seattle. It was a major success without any government subsidies at all. In 1893, when the government-subsidized railroads went bankrupt, Hill's line was able both to cut rates and turn a substantial profit.

Still another of the alleged robber barons was Cornelius Vanderbilt. In 1798 the government of New York granted Robert Livingston and Robert Fulton a monopoly on steamboat traffic for thirty years. Vanderbilt was hired to run a steamboat between New Jersey and Manhattan in defiance of that monopoly. Vanderbilt evaded capture while at the same time charging only one-quarter of the monopolists' fare.

After *Gibbons* v. *Ogden* (1824) overturned New York's steamboat monopoly, the fare for a trip from New York City to Albany dropped from seven dollars to three. The trip from New York to Philadelphia, which had been three dollars, fell to one dollar. Travelers going from New Brunswick to Manhattan now paid only six cents, and ate for free. When he moved his steamboat operation to the Hudson River, Vanderbilt charged a fare of ten cents, as opposed to the previous three dollars. Later he dropped the fare entirely, running his operation on the proceeds from concessions aboard the ship.

Even when his competitors had unfair advantages, Vanderbilt came out on top. Edward Collins received a government subsidy for his steamship business to provide mail delivery across the Atlantic—to the tune of $858,000 a year by the 1850s. When Vanderbilt entered the field in 1855, he outperformed Collins in passenger travel and mail delivery with no subsidy at all. Congress did away with Collins' subsidy in 1858, and before long he went bankrupt.

Meanwhile, Vanderbilt was also outperforming two subsidized steamship lines that brought passengers and mail to California. They charged $600 per passenger per trip. The unsubsidized Vanderbilt charged $150 per passenger, and nothing to deliver the mail.

This was nothing unusual. When economics professor Thomas DiLorenzo actually examined the data, something economic historians had not actually bothered to do, he found that the industries that were accused in the late nineteenth century of being dominated by "monopolies" were in fact lowering prices and increasing output—the opposite of what the textbooks tell us monopolies are supposed to do. In the 1880s, output in the alleged "monopolized" industries grew seven times faster than the rest of the economy. Prices in these industries were falling much faster than they were in the rest of the economy.[55]

Forgive me, but I am supposed to fear and despise these benefactors of mankind why, exactly?

The Vanderbilts and Carnegies were able to acquire such substantial portions of their industries because they consistently produced goods and services people wanted at low prices. When they stopped innovating, they lost market share. The cartoon version of events notwithstanding, competition was vigorous. It was only after voluntary efforts—pools, secret agreements, mergers, and the like—failed to stabilize this highly competitive environment that some firms began to look to the federal government and its regulatory apparatus as a way to reduce competition coercively. "Ironically, contrary to the consensus of historians," writes historian Gabriel Kolko, "it was not the existence of monopoly that caused the federal government to intervene in the economy, but the lack of it." Speaking of the situation that faced the mighty Standard Oil (which had reduced the price of kerosene from one dollar to ten cents), Kolko writes:

> In 1899 there were sixty-seven petroleum refiners in the United States, only one of whom was of any consequence. Over the next decade the number increased steadily to 147 refiners. Until 1900 the only significant competitor to Standard was the Pure Oil Company, formed

in 1895 by Pennsylvania producers with $10 million capital....By 1906 it was challenging Standard's control over pipelines by constructing its own. And in 1901 Associated Oil of California was formed with $40 million capital stock, in 1902 the Texas Company was formed with $30 million capital, and in 1907 Gulf Oil was established with $60 million capital. In 1911 the total investment of the Texas Company, Gulf Oil, Tide Water-Associated Oil, Union Oil of California, and Pure Oil was $221 million. From 1911 to 1926 the investment of the Texas Company grew 572 percent, Gulf Oil 1,022 percent, Tide Water-Associated 205 percent, Union Oil 159 percent and Pure Oil 1,534 percent.

Standard Oil's decline preceded the antitrust ruling against it in 1911, and was "primarily of its own doing—the responsibility of its conservative management and lack of initiative."[56] (Kolko, by the way, is a New Left historian, not a supporter of the free market.)

As a matter of fact, it was very difficult for top firms to maintain their positions in a great many industries in the United States in the late nineteenth century. This was true of industries as diverse as oil, steel, iron, automobiles, agricultural machinery, copper, meat packing, and telephone services. Competition was extremely vigorous.[57] The so-called whiskey trust failed to monopolize the market for whiskey, and was unable to keep competitors from entering the market and whittling away its market share. The sugar trust tried one kind of cartel after another, only to find prices—and their own market share—continuing to fall. J.P. Morgan's attempts to monopolize the market for agricultural machinery were systematically eroded by competition.[58] When the great merger movement took place at the very end of the nineteenth century and the beginning of the twentieth, the final result was that most mergers turned out to be complete failures. Bigness in business did not guarantee success, as people tend to assume.

The National Biscuit Company (Nabisco) tried for four years to monopolize biscuit production, buying out all competitors. The strategy, as should have been obvious, would end up nearly bringing the company to ruin. In 1901, the company issued a memo acknowledging its disastrous strategy and deciding from then on to compete on the basis of the efficiency of its production and the quality of its product:

> In the past, the managers of large merchandising corporations have thought it necessary, for success, to control or limit competition. So when this Company started, it was believed that we must control competition, and that to do this we must either fight competition or buy it. The first meant a ruinous war of prices and a great loss of profits; the second, constantly increasing capitalization. Experience soon proved to us that, instead of bringing success, either of those courses, if persevered in, must bring disaster. This led us to reflect whether it was necessary to control competition.... We soon satisfied ourselves that within the Company itself we must look for itself.
>
> We turned our attention and bent our energies to improving the internal management of our business, to getting full benefit from purchasing our raw materials in large quantities, to economizing the expenses of manufacture, to systematizing and rendering more effective our selling department, and above all things and before all things to improving the quality of our goods and the condition in which they should reach the customer.
>
> It became the settled policy of this Company to buy out no competition.[59]

Business firms have in fact been eager in many cases to employ government power on their behalf because coercion solidifies their positions far more effectively than does the free market, the system through which consumers keep them on their toes every single day. On the free market, these firms must serve the consumer effectively or close their doors. Even the mightiest corporations have learned this lesson. It is government, with its subsidies, special privileges, and restrictions on competition that promotes monopoly and grants truly unfair advantages to some at the expense of everyone else. Albert Jay Nock put it with his usual bluntness: "The simple truth is that our businessmen do not want a government that will let business alone. They want a government they can use. Offer them one made on [Herbert] Spencer's [free-market] model, and they would see the country blow up before they would accept it."[60] That may be an overstatement, but it is much closer to the truth than the simplistic version of history taught to nearly all American schoolchildren.

That's why, by the 1920s, the decade many people associate most with the free market, many business firms were begging for government protection from competition. One businessman, for instance, noted in horror that "our profits are absolutely unprotected." A trade association executive condemned any private actor who operated his business "in entire disregard of the effects on his competitor and the rest of the industry." A pledge by members of the American Bottlers of Carbonated Beverages declared: "My desire shall not be to undersell my fellow bottlers, but to contend with them for first place in the quality of my products and the service I render my patrons." Appeals like this were all over the business magazines. It became especially fashionable during the 1920s to suggest that laissez-faire was a thing of the past, a foolish, discredited system that needed to give way to rules of "fair competition" to be established in each industry.[61] If capitalism allows the private sector to grow fat on the backs of the oppressed masses, with private firms able to maintain their position without constant cost-cutting and innovation, someone apparently forgot to tell this to the private firms themselves.

But isn't it the case that without government intervention we would suffer under predatory pricing, the strategy by which a large firm temporarily takes losses in order to drive all its competitors out of business and then raises prices for hapless consumers? This widely believed scenario is actually a phantom. Economist George Stigler declared that "today it would be embarrassing to encounter this argument in professional discourse."[62] For one thing, the firm attempting it loses disproportionately, for it must take losses on its large market share. Consumers, meanwhile, stock up on items at these fire-sale prices, making it all the longer before the firm can expect to make up those losses. If the firm does manage to drive everyone else out of business, its problems are only beginning. Any one of these firms can start up again at any time as soon as the "predatory" firm begins charging the high prices it has been craving. If those firms literally went bankrupt as a result of the predatory pricing scheme of their competitor, then other entrepreneurs would have been able to acquire their assets for low prices at auction, making these firms much fiercer competitors as a result. And finally, scholars have found it all but impossible to find a real-world example. Sure, firms lower prices, but where are the alleged monopoly prices that are supposed to follow?[63]

Wouldn't We Be Helpless, and Probably Dead, Without the Regulatory Apparatus?

Regulation in the real world is not a simple matter of selfless, disinterested public servants innocently seeking to provide for the common good in areas where private markets are supposedly incompetent. The actual operation of regulation tends to be far less benign than abstract models suggest. And there are plenty of voluntary solutions that for both moral and practical reasons are to be preferred to the coercive, bureaucratic kind. But the longer a government intervention exists, the less capable people become of imagining how life could be lived without it, and the more convinced they are that anyone proposing an alternative is an enemy of society.

A key problem in the debate over regulation is that the term "deregulation" has been carelessly applied to cases in which deregulation did not actually take place. Then, when terrible results are evident for all to see, we are solemnly informed that deregulation has failed once again, and that next time we ought to shut our mouths and do as our overlords say.

For example, the alleged deregulation of the California energy industry was blamed for the rolling blackouts that hit that state in the latter half of the 1990s. But where was the deregulation? Wholesale prices of electricity (purchased by the state's electric power distributors) could fluctuate, but the state enforced price controls on retail prices, and additional regulations gratuitously sabotaging the industry were introduced. Demand for electricity grew dramatically during the 1990s, driven by population growth and the voracious power demands of the state's flourishing computer industry. At the same time, no additional power facilities were allowed to be built, and the environmental lobby even managed to close down several existing plants. Thus with demand rising, supply not allowed to expand, and providers unable to price electricity in accordance with these conditions, the result was rolling blackouts.[64] This is surprising?

Time after time the environmental lobby intervened to prevent the alleviation of the power shortages by the production of additional facilities. And time after time the shortages were blamed, nonsensically, on "deregulation"—which is more easily made into a bogeyman than the politically fashionable environmental movement.

Airline deregulation, which has been closer to the real thing, has been an unmitigated boon, uninformed complaints to the contrary notwithstanding. Fares are 25 to 44.9 percent lower in real terms than they were before deregulation. Service has expanded dramatically, in terms of both flights and destinations. Flying is safer.[65]

Even here, deregulation did not occur across the board, and so problems remain. Obstacles to further progress can be found in the sectors of air travel that remain under government control, namely airports and air-traffic control. Airports might otherwise use market prices to cope with congestion and encourage more off-hour flights, using the proceeds to finance expansion and technology upgrades. Europe has moved well past the United States in air-traffic control technology, with this crucial function carried out by nonprofit corporations under the airline industry's control. The United States, meanwhile, uses clumsy technology from the 1950s, and is only belatedly introducing NextGen systems (that won't be fully ready until 2025).[66]

Prior to deregulation, airlines operated under the authority of the Civil Aeronautics Board (CAB). The CAB clearly operated in the interests of the airline industry, and particularly the large airlines. Even though demand increased by 4,000 percent between 1938 and 1956, the CAB did not approve a single new trunkline carrier, and thereby artificially boosted the position of the established airlines.[67] It encouraged another form of monopoly by limiting competition among the airlines in the routes they could serve. If the CAB told an airline it could not fly on a particular route, then it could not do so.

For a long time these large airlines offered only very expensive seats. There was no coach seating; the entire passenger cabin was the equivalent of today's first class. Smaller airlines, sensing an opportunity for profit, began to compete with the larger airlines on the basis of price, by offering cheap, no-frills travel. The established airlines were appalled, though the competition eventually forced them to offer lower-priced seating as well. It was the smaller companies that revolutionized air travel in America for precisely this reason—forcing prices lower, they dramatically increased the market for air travel.

But the CAB continuously made life difficult for the smaller companies, or "nonskeds." They were called nonskeds, first of all, because the CAB did not allow them to schedule their flights by hour. They could announce that they were flying to Los Angeles on Thursday, but could not say at what time. They had to make do with waiting for their planes to fill up and then departing. In the early 1950s, the CAB declared that the nonskeds could not fly more than eight times per month between the same two points. Aircoach Transport Association President Amos E. Heacock said the order was part of "a calculated campaign by the scheduled airlines to gouge millions of extra…dollars from the public."[68] *Time* magazine understood the motivation: "With air traffic heavy, the non-skeds' competition doesn't matter. But in a slump they would cut deeply into the scheduled airlines' business."[69] These restrictions were gradually eased, but not until many of the nonskeds had been driven out of business.

Financial regulation and its relevance (or otherwise) to economic ups and downs has already been discussed, but we might note here that under the George W. Bush administration, which is condemned by the progressive Left for its allegedly laissez-faire stance, the expansion of federal regulations increased by some 78,000 pages a year, faster than at any time in American history. Bill Clinton actually reduced the number of federal bureaucrats by 969, while Bush *increased* the total by 91,196. And while Clinton slightly reduced the cost of financial regulation, it grew under Bush by 29 percent.[70]

Then, in 2002, the president signed into law a new layer of regulation called the Public Company Accounting Reform and Investor Protection Act in the Senate and Corporate and Auditing Accountability and Responsibility Act in the House—known popularly as the Sarbanes-Oxley Act of 2002. This would put a stop to the kind of corporate accounting scandals that had been all over the news.

But existing statutes sufficed to indict executives from firms like Enron. The SEC already possessed all the authority it needed to handle accounting fraud. Additional regulations often had nothing to do with what caused the problems at Enron, but they did give the public the impression that their public servants were "doing something." For instance, Sarbanes-Oxley required that every corporate board's audit committee be composed of independent directors who had no history with the company, along with a financial expert. Enron's board, chaired by a Stanford accounting professor, was in fact 86 percent independent, and *Chief Executive* magazine rated it among America's five best. As for the merits of "independence" in corporate governance, watchdogs gave Warren Buffett's Berkshire Hathaway a "D" in independence at a time when the horrendously run Fannie Mae received an "A."[71]

And in fact it was investors who figured out the real condition of Enron and WorldCom well before federal regulators discovered any problems. World-Com stock plummeted below a dollar even before the accounting scandals came to light, and Enron stock had fallen 61 percent by the time that notorious story became public. The *Wall Street Journal* noted in 2006 that of the 700 prosecutions of corporate crimes prosecuted over the previous four years, not one conviction resulted from Sarbanes-Oxley. Meanwhile, the cost of being a public company in the United States has more than tripled, and the percentage of new stock offerings executed on U.S. exchanges was down to 8 percent in 2006, from 48 percent in the 1990s. Sarbanes-Oxley "helped to create an environment that destroyed far more wealth than was ever destroyed through the prior corporate scandals put together."[72]

In sum, Sarbanes-Oxley has served no good purpose. The SEC already possessed the authority to carry out everything it demands with regard to accounting and the composition of corporate boards. It neglects the ways (including the 1968 Williams Act, which put restrictions on corporate takeovers) in which government itself has made it difficult for badly managed companies to be taken over by more competent managers. It has made doing business as a U.S. corporation needlessly costly and risky.[73]

As this book went to press, a scandal was developing in which it was alleged that in many cases banks lacked proper documentation, or even arranged for the forgery of important documentation, for mortgages on which they attempted to foreclose. Was this problem uncovered by politicians, in their never-ending search for justice? In fact, the politicians were busy passing the Interstate Recognition of Notarizations Act, pocket-vetoed by Obama, that would have made it more difficult for judges from other states to call fraudulent documents into question. The real whistleblowers were the title insurers, who stopped being willing to insure titles whose validity they could not determine for certain.

But what would we do without government *safety* regulation? Surely the corpses would be piling up from cars without seatbelts, exploding cell phones, and poison everything.

Critics of the market pretend, or perhaps really believe, that the choice is between government regulation on the one hand and everyone watching out for botulism on his own on the other. They look back in history at times when society was far poorer than it is now, note that (for example) its sanitary standards were lower, and conclude that any progress we have made since then must be attributable to the wise regulatory stewardship on the part of our vigilant public sector. The voluntary sector may have managed one miracle after another over the past century, from high technology to communications, transportation, and industrial organization, but we are supposed to believe that in the absence of the regulatory apparatus we would all be completely stumped when it came to finding a non-lethal sandwich.

We often thoughtlessly assume certain things to be true because they seem so obvious as to make data collection on the subject appear unnecessary. Yet so much of what we assume is true about safety regulations is in fact the opposite of the truth. The University of Chicago's Sam Peltzman found that seatbelt regulations did not in fact decrease traffic fatalities: people drove more recklessly, and more pedestrians were killed. This became known as the "Peltzman effect."[74] A recent study discovered that bicycle helmets increase the likelihood that a cyclist will be hit by a car. The reason, it turns out, is that drivers drive closer to cyclists wearing helmets.[75]

We are told that workplace injuries have declined since the Occupational Safety and Health Administration (OSHA) was established in 1970. We are not told that such injuries were already on the decline before 1970, and that they have not fallen any faster with the opening of this federal agency. To the contrary, in roughly the quarter century before the creation of OSHA, the decline in the frequency of workplace fatalities was 70 percent larger than in the quarter century that followed.[76]

An evaluation of OSHA's performance a quarter century after its creation discovered, after a survey of the existing literature, that its effects on workplace safety had been negligible, and that the costs it imposed on the private sector far outweighed the alleged benefits. "The most optimistic figures," wrote Professors Thomas Kniesner and John Leeth, "show OSHA currently creating three times more costs than it generates in benefits." Increasing its funding seems unlikely to make much difference; Quebec spends over four times as much per worker and has had no more success than OSHA.[77]

The study also found that 40 percent of recent workplace deaths had been transportation related, with half of those being highway fatalities. Another

20 percent involved assaults and violence at work. There isn't much OSHA can do about any of this. That means only about two-fifths of workplace fatalities are in fact the kind of incidents most people associate with "workplace fatalities" in the first place.

Firms spend about 1,600 times as much on compensating wage differentials (i.e., higher wages they must pay to compensate for potentially dangerous work) and workers' compensation as they do on all of OSHA's annual fines combined, so their incentives to improve workplace safety come overwhelmingly from these other sources rather than from OSHA's trivial influence.[78]

OSHA regulators, moreover, who know more about bureaucratic procedure than they do about industry, are often in over their heads when trying to carry out proper safety inspections. Not surprisingly, then, the most cited violations by OSHA are paperwork related. OSHA inspectors often wouldn't know an actual safety problem if it landed on their heads. In testimony before a subcommittee of the U.S. House of Representatives, the safety services manager at R.R. Donnelly, the world's largest commercial printer, described what actually happens during an OSHA inspection:

> Any time an OSHA inspector comes into one of our facilities, it is probably the first time they [sic] have ever seen a large commercial printing press. In our plants, where the presses are 100 feet long and three stories high, the OSHA inspector doesn't know where to start. In every case the inspector will invariably find a guard off, or some other minor, readily apparent violation, but will pass by process equipment which, if it failed, could blow up our facility. Because they are not experts in the industry they cannot know the critical issues we deal with on a daily basis....Our informal conferences end up being training sessions on safety in the printing industry to the local OSHA offices. They do not know our industry, yet try to cite us as if they do.[79]

When we turn to automobile safety, we find that between 1925 and 1960 automobile fatalities decreased by 3.5 percent per mile driven per year, at a time when safety regulations were essentially nil. The decline in fatalities reflects the simple principle that as society grows wealthier, it begins to demand quality improvements and safety measures that would have been prohibitive luxuries in poorer times, in the same way that a wealthier society demands (and can afford) greater protection against bad food and many other potential hazards. No one today would buy a car with safety features from 1930.[80]

And incidentally, take a wild guess as to the rate of decrease in fatalities per mile in the post-regulation, National Highway Traffic Safety Administration era. Would you believe 3.5 percent per year?[81]

Critics seem to think that in the absence of federal regulations (of airlines, for example), individuals would be forced to research the safety records, hiring practices, and fleet condition of each carrier, if indeed they dared to fly at all. But suppose an airline, as part of its efforts to assure people of its safety, offered to pay damages in the amount of $1,000,000 in the event of a passenger death aboard one of its aircrafts. It would, in turn, need to take out insurance against crashes in order to be able to make any necessary payouts. Is the insurance company going to grant this policy without the most detailed inquiry, employing expert consultants in aviation, into the condition of its fleet, the qualifications of its pilots, and the adequacy of its safety measures? The question answers itself. So *they* would monitor the airlines, since they would have a direct financial stake in doing so. And since the airlines want to keep their premiums down, they will want to ensure that they comply with insurance company demands. The insurance companies, on the other hand, prefer to see no crashes at all, and thus have an incentive to verify the soundness of the airlines they insure. This kind of system ensures that the socially optimal level of regulation is enacted. Unreasonably costly levels of regulation will make an insurance company uncompetitive. Too little regulation and the company will be wiped out by passenger claims.[82]

Now only a hopeless ideologue could dispute the need for a government agency to assure us of the safety of the drugs we are prescribed, right? Most people are unaware that scholars who specialize in this area tend to be critical of the existing regulatory apparatus, principally the Food and Drug Administration (FDA). "The policy experts who have evaluated the costs and benefits of drug regulation," reports economist Randall Holcombe, "have almost uniformly concluded that the costs of the regulations are not worth their benefits."[83]

Examples could be multiplied, but Peltzman echoes a very common refrain when he observes that the FDA's drug approval process, particularly its proof-of-efficacy requirement, is clearly a net negative for consumers and health:

> My reading of the available evidence [he wrote in 2005] was that this latter cost far outweighs any benefit. Indeed, the death toll from this regulatory delay can easily number in the thousands per year. By contrast, the benefits were small.
>
> I found that the unregulated market was very quickly weeding out ineffective drugs prior to 1962 [when the FDA's authority was substantially increased]. Their sales declined rapidly within a few months of introduction, and there was thus little room for the regulation to improve on market forces....Most of the subsequent academic research reached conclusions similar to mine....
>
> The carnage of this regulation, I regret to assure you, will continue for a long time....The deaths I speak of are counterfactual deaths, not deaths that can be directly connected to any regulatory malfeasance....The actual victims of the regulation did not swallow a bad FDA-approved pill. They merely failed to swallow a good one in time and never knew what they had missed.
>
> I concluded that the proof-of-efficacy requirement was a public health disaster, promoting much more sickness and death than it prevented. Nothing I have seen since has moved me to change that conclusion—the disaster is ongoing.

Is there any way a free society could look after the safety of drugs? Underwriters Laboratories is a private firm that certifies electrical equipment. Companies pay a premium to be able to display the UL seal of approval on their products, which tells consumers (and, just as important, retailers) that the product in question has been found to be safe. Similar institutions for drugs and medical devices have been slower to develop, largely because their function has already been usurped by a government monopoly against which it makes no sense to compete—if a particular drug is going to be forbidden, there is no point in devoting resources to defending it. Even so, "knower" organizations do exist in medicine, and would obviously grow more numerous and expand their role in the absence of official government certification. Anything from reference works like the *AMA Drug Evaluations, American Hospital Formulary Service Drug Information,* and *U.S. Pharmacopoeia's Drug Information for Healthcare Providers* to newsletters like *Clinica, Health Devices Alert,* and the *Medical Letter*—not to mention academic journals, Internet resources, and other outlets—can alert physicians and the public to the safety and efficacy of various drugs.[84]

Middlemen, like drug stores and pharmacists, have a vested interest in ensuring the safety of the products they dispense (for the sake of maintaining their reputation and avoiding lawsuits), and can likewise be expected to play an important role in how a free society ensures drug safety. Speaking of the pharmacist in the age before the federal government extended its authority over drugs, Glenn Sonnedecker wrote: "The pharmacist exercised a scientific sense of responsibility as the last link in a chain of medicopharmacal services and the guarantor that the patient would receive exactly what was intended, in the form and quality intended. [A] pharmacist whose living depended on his knowledge of drugs, and upon his reputation for providing unwavering quality in pharmaceutical service, could best appreciate the significance of reliable and impartial standards."[85]

In short, a free people would not stand around scratching their heads regarding what to do about drug safety. The institutions of civil society are as capable of handling drug safety as they are electrical safety.

Still another overlooked aspect of regulation involves how private firms have actually embraced it as an anti-competitive device. In California, for example, a company called Unocal secured a U.S. patent for its method of reducing harmful emissions from gasoline-powered vehicles. Several months after getting the patent, Unocal received more good news: the California Air Resources Board (CARB) had released its final clean gasoline rules, and it turns out that in order to comply with California law you had to use the very method of emissions reduction for which Unocal had just received a patent.

Oh, and the CARB knew that was the right method to use because…Unocal told them so. Unocal helped to draft California's clean-air rules at the very moment it had a patent pending on the method it was proposing for universal adoption. And that, in turn, meant that Unocal could demand licensing fees from anyone who was legally selling oil in California. A lawsuit by Exxon, Mobil, Chevron, Texaco, Shell, and other refiners came to naught as Unocal successfully counter-sued for patent infringement.

On top of all this, Unocal also benefited from the new regulations because they disproportionately harmed its smaller competitors, despite the longer period of time they had been granted in order to comply with the rules. (Unocal had lobbied against even this minor allowance, by the way.)[86]

Such examples could be multiplied almost endlessly. Every major innovation in retailing was fought tooth and nail by established firms that attempted to employ state violence against the upstarts. Certain firms were horrified by the advent of the traveling salesman, for example, who was a means by which a wholesaler in one city or state could compete directly with one elsewhere. A traveling salesman could bring samples of the wholesalers' products to all the retailers in a given city. Naturally, the angry firms turned to state violence to solve their problem. Impossibly high license fees to operate in each of the towns they visited had nothing to do with promoting the common good, as government activity is normally described to us, and everything to do with crushing a pesky source of competition. The reason people once told jokes about traveling salesmen was that these poor souls lived a precarious and in effect illegal existence. They couldn't pay the fees that were imposed on them, so they tried to do their work quickly and leave town. For many years these special fees persisted for the purpose of regulating the traveling salesman business, entirely in order to suppress competition.[87]

Department stores were also attacked as unfair competition (why, they sell numerous products, and on more than one floor!) as soon as they came into existence in the late nineteenth century, and special taxes were imposed on them, failing all efforts to outlaw them completely. Mail order met a similar fate—this is grossly unfair, said competitors, since mail-order companies can function with so much less overhead. Sears-Roebuck catalogs were burned in ritual bonfires, organized by retailers around the country. Then it was the chain stores. We need regulation! A&P must be crushed! But A&P was quickly enough displaced by the market, losing substantial market share and nearly going bankrupt with the advent of self-service supermarkets.

Then the villain was the discount houses. Retailers had managed to get government to support resale price maintenance laws that made it illegal for any retailer to sell a product for an amount less than the officially announced retail price given by the manufacturer. This was obviously an attempt by retailers to keep prices up, though of course this kind of activity is always camouflaged by solemn appeals to the public good that the perpetrators hope a gullible public will accept. (We must regulate the market in order to prevent "cutthroat competition," etc.) But discount houses began popping up that simply defied the law and offered lower prices. One of the ways these houses were able to cut costs was their no-frills salesmanship, with salesmen prepared to answer basic questions but primarily serving the function of getting the product that the consumer arrives knowing he wants. The Sunbeam Corporation complained vigorously about Masters, the biggest New York discount house, for selling below the "fair-trade" price for its small appliances, like shavers, coffee makers, and toasters. Masters had to pay $16,530 in legal fees and court costs—not an insignificant sum more than half a century ago. Masters had been thus enjoined nearly one hundred times by then. Undeterred, they began selling fair-trade products at discount prices through the mail from Washington, D.C., where there were no fair-trade laws.[88]

Life magazine took a fairly conventional, establishment view in a 1954 article surveying the phenomenon. These stores, said *Life*, echoing the retailers' critique, sold their merchandise in "cramped, ill-lit, unswept aisles"; their goods were arranged in a "glorified pushcart display," which is "customarily presided over by a group of hoarse, misanthropic clerks."[89] Yet even *Life* had to admit that the discounters played an important role in forcing traditional retailers to become more competitive, and that regulations imposed on discounters were obviously meant as a form of protection for existing stores, rather than the protection of the public. It mentioned, for example, the case of William Lavell, sales and promotion manager for the Ashburn Furniture Company near Los Angeles. Having studied the local discount houses, Lavell cut all his prices to meet or beat theirs. "Throw away those phony discount cards!" his advertisements read. In three weeks Lavell had tripled his store's appliance sales.[90]

Life observed that most states did indeed have laws forbidding anyone to sell below the "fair-trade" price set by the manufacturer. Manufacturers typically didn't care at what price the stores sold their products as long as they sold. They went along with fair-trade pricing laws (or "resale price maintenance") laws out of fear of retailer boycotts if they didn't. But as long as the discounters kept quiet and didn't do anything too flagrant that might cause them problems with their retailers, manufacturers tended to look the other way. Meanwhile, discounters still had to operate on the edges, until by the 1960s the regulations imposed on them were overturned. The regulations had become difficult to enforce anyway. William E. Phillips was the biggest discounter on the West Coast. When the Sunbeam Corporation enjoined him from selling its products below the fair-trade price, Phillips went on doing it, except he took the difference between his price and the fair-trade price and donated it to whatever charity the customer named. Soon afterward, having made his point, he dropped Sunbeam products entirely.[91]

Big business has also opposed tax cuts or supported tax increases, again contrary to the portrayals of those who imagine businessmen as implacable foes of government intervention. For example, Bill Gates and Warren Buffett have been portrayed in the media as selfless benefactors for opposing the elimination of the estate tax. As men of wealth themselves, the media line goes, these men ought to favor the abolition of the tax, but instead they have publicly campaigned for its retention. What men of the people these are!

But there may be more to the Gates/Buffett stance than meets the eye.[92] For one thing, the estate tax will never hit Microsoft, since, as a publicly held corporation, its owner will never die. Moreover, if repeal of the estate tax were to be made revenue-neutral, additional taxes to make up the shortfall would very likely fall on corporations. So if you head a large corporation, you might not want to see the estate tax repealed.

A family-owned business, on the other hand, is liable to be devastated by the estate tax. A son inheriting the family business—whose plant and equipment are worth, say, $2 million—from his father and who has been running the business for five years could be hit with a tax bill of $500,000, an amount he couldn't possibly pay out of the company's annual profits. He has to sell, and fast.

It so happens that an avid buyer of businesses desperate to sell in the face of a massive estate-tax bill is—surprise!—Warren Buffett. In addition to the *Buffalo News*, reports investigative journalist Tim Carney, "other motivated sellers facing the estate tax who have found a willing buyer in Warren Buffett [include] Dairy Queen, a Utah furniture store, and a Nebraska jeweler."

Now it could be that Buffett's support for the estate tax has nothing at all to do with self-interest and instead derives from a pristine devotion to egalitarian ideology. But shouldn't some of these facts at least be mentioned in media coverage of Buffett and his pro-tax crusade?

Finally, regulation can be not merely ineffective or redundant, but actually counterproductive, as in the case of the celebrated Americans with Disabilities Act (ADA) of 1990. This regulation was supposed to increase employment opportunities for disabled Americans. Yet employment of such Americans fell noticeably in the wake of its passage. What's going on here?

For one thing, note that before the regulation was introduced, employment opportunities for the disabled had already been increasing. "The gradual shift of economic activity from brawn power to brain power, from producing goods to producing services, virtually guarantees that employment opportunities for the disabled were increasing over time," writes an expert on the economics of regulation. "The ADA reject[s] the adequacy of this sort of gradual improvement."[93]

A close look at the regulation makes clear why it caused so much additional suffering for the disabled. Before the ADA, an employer might hire a disabled person and then see if his productivity outweighed whatever special accommodation his disability required. After the ADA, federal regulators will decide what constitutes a fair wage, how much should be spent on accommodation, and so on, and if things don't work out, the employer is subject to a discrimination suit. Employers will therefore be less likely to hire the disabled in the first place, or to hire the least disabled among the officially protected disabled class (e.g., someone with a cleft palate as opposed to a paraplegic in a wheelchair). True, their failure to hire a disabled person also puts them at risk of discrimination suits, but if they are clever about how they advertise the job, the disabled will never learn about it in the first place.

Why don't the disabled fight to repeal a regulation that clearly harms them? Because some of them do benefit from it—in particular, those already safely employed. Their employers made the decision to hire them before the regulation was enacted and invite all kinds of trouble if they fire a disabled worker.

The Endangered Species Act (ESA) of 1973 further illustrates how regulations alter people's behavior in ways that defy or offset the aims of the regulations themselves. Peltzman gives the example of the red-cockaded woodpecker. If one of these should be discovered on your property, you will not be allowed to chop down any of your trees for lumber. They are part of the woodpecker's habitat. But since woodpeckers do fly around, after all, what incentive does this regulation give landowners who get word of the woodpecker's presence on neighboring land? Chop down their trees right away, before the woodpecker settles in and your rights to your lumber are stripped from you. Writes Peltzman, "Change 'woodpecker' to 'owl' and 'preemptively cutting down trees in the forests of North Carolina' to 'preemptively developing land in the suburbs of Tucson'" and you begin to have a sense of the wide-ranging (and presumably unanticipated) effects of the law.[94]

Oh, and how have endangered species been doing since 1973? There has been a net recovery rate of 6 out of over 1,300 listed species.[95] That's less than one-half of one percent.[96]

Without Government Science Funding, Everyone Would Be an Idiot

Surely we can't favor cutting government science funding.

Yes, we can.

The history of government science funding is the opposite of what it should be if the propaganda in favor of such funding were correct. Britain provided essentially no government funding for science during the nineteenth century, and yet it became the world's richest and most industrialized country and home to many of its most accomplished scientists—at a time when France and Germany, where government involvement in science was far more extensive, lagged behind. Had the results been reversed, and France and Germany had vastly outperformed Britain, this would be cited as evidence of the urgency of government science funding. Since the reality is just the opposite, we hear complete silence. Today, Japan's civil research and development is funded almost entirely by the private sector, and Japan's academic science is the most privatized in the world. Japan engages in an enormous amount of basic science, but in industrial laboratories rather than in tax-funded universities.[97]

In *The Economic Laws of Scientific Research*, Terence Kealey discusses the funding of basic science in Britain: "Britain funded pure science because, as the Industrial Revolution developed, industrialists increasingly perceived that they were exhausting technological development, and they needed to explore science more profoundly. Since the Government refused to do it, and since the industrialists were not anxious to pay any extra taxes to enable the Government to do it, they invested their own money in science."[98] Kealey also gives good reason to believe that government funding of science not only displaces private funding, but that government funding will wind up being lower than the private funding it displaces.[99]

A key notion behind government science funding is that scientific progress begins with basic science, in a laboratory, which gives rise to discoveries, which in turn are adopted by private industry and employed in the service of human welfare. A plausible theory, to be sure. But wrong. That is not how science has in fact progressed. The steam engine, for instance, emerged not from scientists in lab coats but from the minds of practical men adapting pre-existing technology to the service of modern problems. The scientists, in turn, had to adapt to the technology: Carnot's work on thermodynamics was inspired by the steam engine, which was more efficient than existing science said it could be. So the science had to change. When Mendel described the laws of genetics, he was merely codifying what practical men had known for centuries from their own work in breeding. More recently, when the Department of Defense commissioned Project Hindsight to uncover how many of the 700 research breakthroughs that had made possible a score of weapons systems were attributable to basic science, the answer that came back was *two*. Applied science builds on applied science, the report concluded, not on basic science. Edwin Mansfield found that 90 percent of new technology comes from the further development of existing technology, and only 10 percent derives from academic research.

According to the usual argument, the market will fund "basic research"— that is, research not aimed at any immediate practical result, but whose findings will presumably assist scientists in various practical endeavors at some point in the future—below a level that is socially optimal. Private industry would have no incentive to engage in basic science because (1) it is not geared toward immediate results; and (2) any research breakthroughs will certainly become widely known and freely available to competitors, thereby undermining the firm's own ability to profit from its research.

This argument is false.

First, the very idea of a "socially optimal" amount of basic research is itself arbitrary. No such figure exists. If we devoted all our resources to basic research and none to agriculture, that would presumably be too much. In other words, as wonderful as basic research is, it too is subject to the constraints imposed by scarcity. It too must compete for resources with other ends people also value.

Second, the knowledge derived from scientific research is far from "free." One needs substantial, laboriously acquired scientific knowledge even to be able to read an article published in a professional scientific journal. Science is "free" in the sense that law is "free." One could try to defend himself in court on the basis of what he read in a law book somewhere, but he would be at a very great disadvantage against real masters of the law, who not only know the material with a thoroughness he can never have, but who also know the ins and outs of courtroom procedure.

Finally, what private firms are interested in is keeping abreast of what is going on in scientific research around the world, in order that they might take advantage of advances in knowledge. The only people who can monitor these developments and read and understand the scholarly literature for them are scientists. But scientists do not enjoy spending all their time in libraries. They enjoy being in laboratories, doing work of their own. What happens, therefore, is that firms give their scientists the laboratories they want, in exchange for having the scientists keep up with important conferences and ongoing break-throughs reported in the scientific literature. Basic science thereby takes place in defiance of what abstract models may predict.

Basic or "pure" science has consistently been funded by the private sector, whether by foundations, private university endowments, or private industry itself. Charitable giving for the endowment of laboratories and scientific facilities of all kinds was common in an age when estate taxes did not decimate fortunes. "Science will attract generous patrons—if taxation spares them," writes Kealey. "Almost everyone in a wealthy country believes that pure science should be funded. Under *dirigisme* [statism] this sentiment is transmitted to the politicians (who, being human beings, will share the general values) but under laissez-faire people, especially rich people, keep their money....As a percentage of GDP...the empirical evidence shows that private donors are actually more generous to pure science than is the State."[100]

Government funding also distorts the course of scientific research. Real science must be carried out in an intellectual environment in which competing theories freely circulate. Government funding yields the opposite. It would be hard to justify to the public the practice of funding mutually exclusive theories; this would seem aimless, and much funding would, in the long run, prove to have been wasted because devoted to the pursuit of an erroneous theory. Politicians are happier to follow the consensus of the experts and let government funding be allocated so as to favor researchers who follow the dominant theory. Thus government-funded science inevitably privileges one theory at the expense of others.

That's the opposite of how private-sector research and development is carried out—an array of approaches are tried at once, in pursuit of one that will bear fruit. But "when all research eggs are in one basket," warns science writer Tom Bethell, "it's a different world. Competition may stagnate, or be eliminated entirely, if that is what the government decrees (as happened under Communism). When any single source of funding dominates, science will almost certainly become the handmaiden of politics. There is no recognition in our leading journals that this is a problem. *Science* magazine, for example, keeps a vigilant watch on government science funding, unhesitatingly equating 'more' with better." Government funding, Bethell says, has "promoted the idea that a theory can be regarded as true if it enjoys enough support....Consensus discourages dissent, however. It is the enemy of science, just as it is the triumph of politics. A theory accepted by 99 percent of scientists may be wrong. Committees at the National Institutes of Health that decide which projects shall be funded are inevitably run by scientists who are at peace with the dominant theory."[101]

Don't We Need the War on Drugs?

The war on drugs and the hundreds of billions of dollars that have been devoted to it are taken for granted across the political spectrum as the very epitome of wise and necessary government policy. That tends to be a sign of a bad policy. Although conservatives in particular have tended to favor the drug war, several prominent ones have publicly questioned its utility in recent years, including Thomas Sowell, George Shultz, and the late William F. Buckley, Jr. Sowell argues that there is nothing "conservative" in the proper sense about the War on Drugs. According to Sowell, conservatives are not so utopian as to expect to stamp out foolish and destructive behavior. They seek to minimize the damage caused by that behavior, not to pretend that it can be abolished, or that human frailty can be legislated away. That is what conservatives accuse liberals of doing.

More than a dozen years ago, I myself came to the conclusion that the federal drug war, which I had supported for quite a long time, was based on the usual tissue of government falsehoods and propaganda I should have known to expect, and that almost everything I thought I knew about illegal drugs, health, violence, and crime was close to the opposite of the truth.[102] After $1 trillion spent, even the United States drug czar, Gil Kerlikowske, concedes that "in the grand scheme, it has not been successful. Forty years later, the concern about drugs and drug problems is, if anything, magnified, intensified."[103] Meanwhile, with 5 percent of the world's population, the United States now has 25 percent of the world's prison population.

In a recent report, the Associated Press assembled some pretty grim statistics. Here are just a few. The federal government has evidently spent $33 billion in various antidrug messages and prevention programs. But high school students continue to use illegal drugs at the same rate as in 1970, and drug overdoses have risen steadily since then. Some 37 million nonviolent drug offenders—about 10 million of them for marijuana—have been arrested, at a cost of $121 billion; jail time, research shows, tends to increase drug abuse. Another $450 billion has been spent on locking these people up in federal prisons alone.[104]

The problems are legion, beginning with law enforcement's relatively decreased attention to crimes against person and property in order to focus on crimes that do not involve the use of physical aggression. Thus in the 1980s, when the country saw the first major crackdown on drugs since Richard Nixon, at least half of the ensuing increase in property crime was attributable to the shift of public resources out of property crime and into drug prohibition enforcement.[105]

The thirteen years of alcohol prohibition saw property crimes climb by 13.2 percent, homicide by 16.1 percent, and robbery 83.3 percent.[106] According to Mark Thornton, author of *The Economics of Prohibition*, although numerous factors likely contributed to these outcomes, Prohibition itself "appears to be the significant explanatory variable for changes in the crime rate." The federal murder rate, which rose consistently during Prohibition, fell for eleven consecutive years following its repeal.[107]

This is hardly a coincidence. The policy of prohibition naturally drives from the field anyone who might have supplied a forbidden product in the open and in a professional and peaceful way. Such a vendor would be promptly reported to the authorities and shut down. That leaves only those who operate in the shadows, and who use violence and intimidation to maintain their market position.

After returning from a two-week vacation in the late 1990s, Judge James P. Gray, a trial judge in Orange County, California, asked his court reporter what had occupied her time during his absence. She had reported twenty-five felony preliminary hearings, twenty-one of which were drug related. One involved a homeless man, who pushed his belongings through the city in a shopping cart, and who was arrested for selling ten dollars worth of cocaine. "A courtroom, judge, clerk, court reporter, and two bailiffs were taken up by this hearing for half a day," the judge noted, "which did not include all of the preparation, reports, and efforts of a prosecutor, public defender, and four police witnesses." Time and resources that might have been devoted to rather more urgent cases are routinely wasted in pointless exercises like this. Television cop and court dramas notwithstanding, the system wastes "scarce resources churning low-level, nonviolent drug offenders like the homeless man through the system, to no effective purpose. If the same resources were used to investigate and prosecute homicides, rapes, robberies, and automobile and home burglaries, crime rates would drop dramatically, both because the perpetrators could be removed from society and because the higher prosecution rate really would have a deterrent effect."[108]

A major problem with outlawing what are sometimes called victimless crimes is that the lack of a victim in the traditional sense of someone whose person or property has been physically aggressed against means there is no one to report the incident.[109] For the police to find out about the transaction at all, therefore, they must employ the search power aggressively, which in turn gives rise to nearly irresistible tendencies toward abuse. With 1.4 million drug arrests every year, it seems unlikely that every case involves the voluntary disclosure of possession by a user, or an officer seeing some quantity of a drug lying in plain sight. Numerous surveys have found that judges believe false testimony regarding the legitimacy of searches is a common occurrence.[110]

The power to seize assets from people accused of drug crimes is likewise prone to abuse. Former Reagan administration official Paul Craig Roberts points out that drug-war supporters who wanted to use the seizure power against drug offenders discovered what they really should have known all along, had they been observing the behavior of government: these penalties are inevitably applied to the innocent. The "routine confiscation of the assets of the innocent" was, according to Roberts, the "main result of their efforts."[111] Americans can be stripped of their property without a warrant, on the basis of mere "probable cause." We have reached a point at which people can have their property taken away even without a criminal conviction, and in fact an estimated 80 percent of people who lose their property in this way are never charged with a criminal offense. Worse still, they must sue the government in order to get it back. They must file a petition very shortly after the seizure and post 10 percent bond, in a procedure the government is not even obliged to explain to them. If they can afford to do that, they find themselves up against still another obstacle: the substitution of a "preponderance of the evidence" for the more demanding "beyond a reasonable doubt." Meanwhile, the burden of proof is on them to prove their innocence, by showing that the seized property had no connection to drug money.[112] Think that power might be liable to abuse?

And then there's the simple bribery and corruption that the prohibition policy obviously invites. "The illicit drug market," say economists David Rasmussen and Bruce Benson, "is probably the most lucrative source of police corruption that has ever existed in the United States."[113] Why should that be? The police are in a position to protect certain drug gangs and their turf, while driving out competitors. The resulting monopoly profits for the protected gang are a lucrative privilege for which members are prepared to pay a hefty sum in bribes.

And all for what? In the late 1990s, Judge Volney Brown recalled a revealing incident early in the drug war under Richard Nixon, involving the short-lived Office for Drug Abuse Law Enforcement (ODALE), in which Judge Brown had served as a staff attorney. His regional division of ODALE decided to try to arrest all known drug providers in a given city at the same time. In San Diego, law enforcement acting under the auspices of ODALE managed to arrest all thirty-nine members of the drug gang responsible for providing nearly all the heroin sold there. For a full week, heroin was impossible to find in the city. By the second week, new suppliers began to appear. Within a month things were back to the way they were before the successful bust. And now, instead of knowing who the thirty-nine suppliers were, law enforcement had no idea where the heroin was coming from. Meanwhile, the availability and price of heroin were unaffected, after an extraordinarily difficult law enforcement effort.

Judge Brown observed that even though his ODALE region enjoyed more success than any other, it had no lasting effect. "It was not more difficult or more expensive to obtain illegal drugs than it was in the beginning. We had failed to solve, or even affect, the 'drug problem' with law enforcement. If we had been given 10 or 20 times the resources, we still would have failed. I have learned from experience that there is no practical level of law enforcement that will prevent people from using the narcotics and dangerous drugs they wish to use."[114]

Once in a while we hear statistics about drug seizures that can sound as if real progress is being made on the supply side. But "seizure statistics can be especially misleading because they are often reported without context and in terms of street prices, which far overstate actual costs to traffickers," according to the General Accounting Office. "Arrests and seizures are significant only when they help raise costs and risks enough to deter traffickers, and there is no indication they are approaching that point."[115] It has been said that in order to achieve such a goal, it would be necessary to interdict 75 percent of all drugs, a figure that has never remotely been approached.[116]

Even if drug interdiction should suddenly and against the expectations of everyone become truly effective and substantially cut off the flow of illegal drugs—an impossibility, needless to say—would-be users would turn to ordinary household products like paint, glue, gasoline, and cleaning agents of various kinds as inhalants. The war on glue is a nonstarter. At some point, it becomes impossible to pretend any longer that government and its law enforcement arm can solve a problem of this nature. This is a job for families and local institutions, not a paramilitary police state. Particularly since the major cause of drug overdose is not cocaine or heroin—prescription drugs are responsible for more deaths than those two combined.[117]

Since demand is so great for these products, it is also fruitless and absurd for the U.S. government to travel the globe offering incentive packages—e.g., subsidies coupled with threats—for poor peasants to stop making their most lucrative products. Programs involving burning and destroying crops have done little either for the cause of international goodwill or for staunching the flow of these goods.

The U.S. government has poured enormous sums into helping the Colombian government fight drug production in their country. The situation simply gets worse. Left-wing guerrillas and right-wing paramilitary groups, both funded by drug money, terrorize the country. Law enforcement admits it solves at most 5 percent of all crimes, and most murders are not even investigated. Between 1997 and 1999, thirty-four Colombian mayors had been murdered and over one hundred more assassinated; by November 1999 half the country's mayors threatened resignation because the situation had become completely impossible. Meanwhile, the production of coca plants in Colombia continued to set all-time records, with producers able to create new supplies faster than military helicopters could destroy them.[118]

Since 1976, Holland has pursued a marijuana decriminalization policy in which law enforcement will not harass people in possession of small quantities of the drug. Harder drugs are treated in a similar fashion: as long as the quantities remain within certain limits and the individuals involved commit no other criminal behavior, the laws will not be enforced. Two decades later, teenage marijuana use in Holland is half the level in the United States. Hard drug use decreased among the same group from 15 percent to 2.5 percent, and the average age of the users of such drugs increased by more than seven years. Even among adults, drug use is moderate.[119]

Portugal recently introduced an even more sweeping policy, abolishing criminal penalties for possession of previously illegal drugs. Again, the results that critics predicted have not come to pass. Portugal was not overrun by so-called drug tourists, and its drug problem has not been exacerbated. To the contrary, five years after the implementation policy, drug use was down considerably among young people, deaths related to heroin and drugs of similar caliber had been cut in half, and the number of people seeking drug treatment had more than doubled. Had drug use and deaths increased, critics would have pointed to them as evidence of the failure of the policy.[120]

Meanwhile, in the United States it has been full steam ahead with the imprisonment strategy. The number of drug prisoners has increased twelvefold since 1980, at a time when the number of people behind bars has only quadrupled.[121] If we add up the number of people incarcerated for *all crimes* in England, France, Germany, and Japan, we would not reach the number incarcerated in the United States for drug crimes alone.[122] A key watershed was reached in 1994, when the number of people incarcerated for drug crimes alone reached the level of U.S. imprisonment for *all* crimes in 1970.[123]

In order to seem tough on drugs, the Democrats pushed hard for mandatory minimum sentences for drug offenses in 1986, without calling relevant witnesses or engaging in sensible deliberation.[124] Even nonviolent drug offenders are required to serve their entire sentences, even when that means violent offenders have to be released to make room for them. No such requirement exists for bank robbers, kidnappers, and other violent offenders.[125]

The Rockefeller drug laws in New York required prison time for any adult caught in possession of illegal drugs. Predictably enough, drug dealers turned more and more to adolescents to assist in the drug trade. These teenagers found themselves with more money than they could have imagined. And just as predictably, they turned to other young people their age—their peers—when looking for new customers.[126]

When twenty teenagers died of drug overdoses in one year in the town of Plano, Texas, the community discovered that the victims' friends, afraid of potential prosecution for using illegal drugs, pursued medical assistance for them only after it was too late. Asked why the town had not simply declared sometime during that year that people reporting drug overdoses could do so without risk of criminal penalty, authorities replied that such a statement would "send the wrong message"—the right message, apparently, being that you should let your fear of the police prevent you from bringing your dying friend to a hospital.[127]

A similar incident occurred in 1986, involving the death of basketball star Len Bias. Excited about being the Boston Celtics' first-round draft pick, he tried cocaine for the first time. An allergic reaction to the drug killed him. By the time his friends got him medical attention, though, he was already in his third convulsion. No one wanted to get Bias or himself arrested. He might be alive today were it not for the prohibition policy.[128]

Finally, the use of ever more potent drugs is itself encouraged by the prohibition policy. In order to get the greatest bang for their buck while doing their best to avoid detection, dealers prefer to smuggle small quantities of potent substances rather than large quantities of less potent substances.[129] During the period of Prohibition itself, the same phenomenon was at work: since hard liquor packed a much greater punch than beer, that's where illegal suppliers focused their activities.

As with any government program, though, the bureaucracies to which the drug war has given rise and those who work on its behalf become addicted to the ongoing spending stream and fight with all their organizational strength to keep it going. It is yet another of the fiefdoms that grows in power and wealth beneath a public-interest façade. Within a generation of the beginning of the War on Drugs under Nixon, some 19,000 state and local police officers were pursuing the drug war full time, with another 11,000 engaged in it part time.[130] Two California congressmen confided to a U.S. judge that every federal agency he could think of was getting extra funding in the name of the war on drugs—not just the Drug Enforcement Administration, the military, and the State Department, but also agencies one would never think of, like the Department of Agriculture or the Department of Land Management. These agencies, he was told, are "addicted to the funding provided by the War on Drugs, and they do not want to give up that money."[131]

The war on drugs, in short, has been counterproductive and vain. An "Open Letter from Lawyers and Judges," sponsored by the Voluntary Committee of Lawyers, summed up the case against it:

> Though we differ in political orientation and career experience, we unanimously observe that neither drugs nor drug abuse has been eliminated nor appreciably reduced, despite massive spending on interdiction and harsh punishments. Attempts at enforcement have clogged the courts, filled the prisons with non-predatory offenders, corrupted officials at home and abroad, bred disrespect for the law in important communities, imperiled the liberties of the people, burdened the taxpayers, impeded public health efforts to stem the spread of HIV and other infectious diseases, and brought the nation no closer to abstinence. As Congress and state legislatures enact more punitive and costly drug control measures, we conclude with alarm that the war on drugs now causes more harm than drug abuse itself.[132]

The author of a recent book on the drug war adds:

If I were to be scandalized by anything, it'd be a policy that exacerbates crime, especially in communities often the least able to bear it; that produces so much corruption in the ranks of those charged with enforcing it; that empowers terrorists and insurgents with easy money; that squanders immense resources trying to interdict drug shipments; that requires the erosion of property and privacy rights to sufficiently enforce it; that encourages the outright looting of the American people to pad drug-war budgets; that militarizes police and threatens innocent citizens' lives; and that unjustly imprisons so many people for either a preference of their own taste or a crime problem created by the government in the first place.[133]

The 2008 National Survey on Drug Use and Health found that 43.7 percent of American adults—over 98 million people—admitted to marijuana usage at some point in their lives, with 10 percent having used it in the past year. That's 22.5 million people. At that time the entire incarcerated population of the United States amounted to about 2.3 million. Since it is impossible, and obviously not desirable, to incarcerate tens of millions more, what on earth are we doing?[134]

■　　　■　　　■　　　■

It is in part because we are so convinced of how indispensable government is, and how intractable some problems would be without its intervention, that even now so many people chafe at the idea of serious reductions in government revenue and power. They cannot abandon the thought that at some level it really does have the people's interests at heart, and that things would be so much worse were its social footprint reduced or eliminated.

Imagine a world in which Walmart supplied people with the various services we today associate with government. Then suppose children in Walmart schools learned all about the wonders of Walmart, how it alone guarantees their safety, protects them from their own foolish decisions, guards them against the exploitation of non-Walmart corporations, and so on. Would we believe it? Or wouldn't we know, Walmart's propaganda notwithstanding, that in the absence of Walmart we probably wouldn't be the heap of helpless boobs it says we'd be, and that we'd probably figure out some way to take care of the problems Walmart says only it can handle?

CHAPTER 7

Rollback

W e have reached the part of the book in which the reader expects the five-part plan that will set everything right. There *are* five-part plans that would set everything right, but none of them would have a chance in Washington. What we *can* do is propose some ideas—most of which are off the table right now, but which may gather steam as the crisis approaches. Crises have a way of opening minds. What would once have been unthinkable is suddenly taken seriously, since all the conventional approaches by that time have failed.

Before proposing these ideas, I have to throw cold water on hopes that the Republican off-year victory in 2010 is likely to bring about major changes in Washington. I am not by nature a pessimist. But I'm also not a fool.

Let's review the record. We've already seen that George W. Bush was the biggest domestic spender since Lyndon Johnson. Among other things, he signed a bill adding a "prescription drug benefit" to Medicare, even though doing so added another $20 trillion to Medicare's unfunded liabilities. He increased farm subsidies, expanded Bill Clinton's national service program, added thousands of pages of new regulatory requirements, and a great deal else. The federal government's control over neighborhood schools was expanded thanks to the No Child Left Behind Act (a federal intervention also supported by 2008 presidential hopefuls Mitt Romney, Mike Huckabee, and John McCain), while federal spending on education increased by over 60 percent. (Romney and Gingrich also support giving a "free" laptop to every American child.)[1]

Speaking of children, Republicans widely considered (rightly or wrongly) to be among the most conservative have called on the federal government to hand every child a pile of cash at birth. Former U.S. senator Rick Santorum called for a grant of $2,000 per child. Republican Senator Jeff Sessions of Alabama has called for $1,000. David Brooks, the *New York Times'* house conservative, has written sympathetically about the idea, and major "conservative" think tanks have come out in support.[2] (Brooks once noted disdainfully that "wishing to be left alone isn't a governing doctrine."[3] We know—that's what we like about it.)

Former House Speaker Newt Gingrich has a reputation for being a right-wing ideologue. But it is surely a strange right-wing ideologue who credits Franklin Roosevelt with lifting the country out of the Great Depression, joins with John Kerry on "climate change," and supports (among many other things) the Medicare prescription drug benefit, federal programs to pay for more teachers, Internet access for every American, and rewards to students who choose to take challenging math and science courses—not to mention his sympathy for federal energy policy and Hillary Clinton's proposed national health-care database, among other things.[4]

And as of this printing, which candidate is leading among polls of self-identified Tea Party voters? Yes, Newt Gingrich.

In light of the entitlements crisis the country faces, it's worth remembering that it was Republican Richard Nixon who suddenly announced his support, in 1972, for a 20 percent hike in Social Security benefits. The bigger new benefit checks reached seniors just days before the November election. The message wasn't particularly subtle: the envelopes contained little American flags, which by that time had become a Nixon symbol. Not a word from Nixon about the long-term cost of this little stunt.[5]

Republicans will fight against the deeply unpopular health-care bill, right? Senator John Cornyn, who chaired the committee seeking to get Republicans elected to the Senate in the fall, initially proposed running on a repeal-and-replace platform. That lasted about ten seconds. Then the caveats came: surely we do not want to repeal the "non-controversial stuff" like the provision relating to pre-existing conditions, even though it is precisely those features that are said to make the more obviously objectionable features of the bill necessary. With the passage of time, Cornyn began tiptoeing away from his initial idea even more: we'll see what our candidates think, he said, about focusing on the health-care bill. Just before the passage of the health-care bill, Congressman Mark Kirk, who was running to fill Barack Obama's old Senate seat, promised to "lead the effort" to repeal the bill. After the bill passed, Kirk told a local paper: "Well, we lost." Predictably enough, we were then treated to a discussion of the "sliver of good things in the bill which Republicans agreed with."[6] Jim Antle wondered in the *American Spectator*: "If Republicans cannot repeal an unpopular bill where many of the costs are front-loaded, many of the benefits are yet to come, and where the creation of another entitlement is as detrimental to their own partisan self-interest as it is to the nation's finances, then conservatives cannot count on Republicans to undo very much of what they routinely denounce and campaign against."[7]

When we recall what happened in the wake of the massive off-year Republican victory of 1994, we are reminded that this kind of preemptive surrender is nothing new. The GOP leadership made the contest into a referendum on its "Contract with America," a series of proposals the party pledged to champion if elected. Democrats and Republicans alike pretended it was a radical assault on government spending and activity—Democrats in order to frighten their base, and Republicans in order to energize theirs. The Contract, was, in fact, a hodgepodge of trivial changes that both kept the basic structure of the American Leviathan intact and neutralized the more ambitious plans and proposals of freshman congressmen who may actually have wanted to change something. The center-left Brookings Institution had it right: "Viewed historically, the Contract represents the final consolidation of the bedrock domestic policies and programs of the New Deal, the Great Society, the post-Second World War defense establishment, and, most importantly, the deeply rooted national political culture that has grown up around them."[8]

One plank from the Contract was a balanced-budget amendment to the U.S. Constitution. Balanced-budget amendments are a waste of time. There is no way they could be worded that the federal government could not find some way to evade. Faced with a balanced-budget requirement, the federal government will simply take more and more expenditures off budget. On top of that, any such amendment inevitably allows for exceptions. And the Contract's Fiscal Responsibility Act allowed for an unbalanced budget as long as three-fifths of Congress approved it. *There's* a hurdle they'd never clear.

The National Security Restoration Act, another plank in the Contract, sought to prevent U.S. troops from being placed under United Nations or foreign command—unless the president believed that doing so was "vital to U.S. national security interests." Is this how stupid they think Americans are? That law would have applied to the staggering number of cases in which U.S. presidents said, "I am placing Americans under UN command just for fun, and for reasons that have nothing to do with U.S. national security interests."

Despite the timidity of the GOP leadership's proposals after the 1994 elections, the media stuck to the script: Republicans are poised to abolish the entire federal government. Naturally, the people believed what they were told. A *Time*/CNN poll taken in December 1995 found that 47 percent of Americans believed that "the cuts in federal spending proposed by the Republicans in Congress" had "gone too far." An interesting follow-up question would have been: "How drastic have you been led to believe those cuts are?" The battle over Medicare in the 1990s was in fact so trivial as almost to defy belief: Bill Clinton wanted the rate of the program's spending growth set at 7.5 percent a year, while the Republicans advocated an allegedly draconian 6 percent growth. (Six percent spending *growth*, by the way, is what the media meant at the time by "budget cuts.") By 2002, the difference in an individual's monthly premiums authorized by Administration and Republican proposals would have amounted to *five dollars*.

The overall budget debate that year was also much ado about nothing. The difference between Clinton's seven-year budget proposal and that of the Republicans was that the former called for an increase of $500 billion in the annual budget for the year 2002, while the latter sought a $350 billion increase. (A glorious thing, this two-party system.) Since Republicans will apparently take the heat in the press whether their proposed reforms are trivial or substantive, why *not* make the spending cuts the people need? How could the public relations get any worse? The whole country, after all, was under the impression that this was what the Republicans were already doing, so why not just go ahead and do it?

There is no simple political solution to the crisis we face. There may well be no political solution at all. But here are some possible approaches.

Social Security and Medicare opt-outs. In chapter 2 we suggested that upon reaching age sixty-five, people should be given the choice of (1) participating in Social Security and Medicare or (2) for the rest of their lives, be completely exempt from income, gift, and estate taxes. This is a free country, we're told in school, so what's the problem?

Across-the-board cuts. One way to start the slash-and-burn process is to go through every line in the federal budget, and the individual budgets of the various cabinet departments, arguing the merits of cutting this or that particular thing. I do not recommend this approach.[9] It will only bog us down in endless policy debates: why, Program X has been a wonderful success! Surely you don't want to cut it! Why, yes, I do, because Program X has had undesirable consequences A, B, and C. Not so, comes the reply! If the program got more money, those things wouldn't happen! And on and on, with every program in the budget.

That's why it's much better to cut everything across the board by the highest percentage possible. Set a fixed percentage by which every federal agency has to cut its budget, and let each one come up with how they're going to do it. If *everything* is cut, any of the fiefdoms that protest the cuts will immediately expose themselves as special-interest groups seeking special privileges.[10] Why should they and they alone be spared?

Currency competition. If in the coming years our wise public servants destroy the dollar in their frantic efforts to make good on their impossible promises, holders of dollars—that is, practically all Americans—will be ruined. Americans need alternatives to the dollar.

As usual, Congressman Ron Paul—ridiculed by the intellectual pygmies who sowed the seeds of our economic crisis—has the right idea. If people prefer to transact in precious metals rather than the depreciating dollar, they should be allowed to do so without having to cope with the artificial disabilities the government imposes on them. Legal-tender laws, a monopolistic intrusion into the free market, should be abolished. Taxes on gold and silver should be repealed. Contracts calling for payment in something other than the dollar should once again be made enforceable in the courts. Private mints should be allowed to issue coins as money.

Nobel Laureate F. A. Hayek laughed at the public-interest rationales behind the government monopoly on money. Money emerged spontaneously on the free market. It was not instituted by government. Only later did governments interfere with it, and not out of a commitment to the public good. Governments wanted to monopolize money creation so they could hand newly created money to favored constituencies. As Hayek said, there is no reason to expect governments to give us good money. Ludwig von Mises, for his part, described the history of money as the history of government efforts to destroy money. No more making exceptions when it comes to money: if monopolies are dangerous and invite abuse and poor quality in every other case, they do likewise when it comes to money. Money, because it is the heart of a modern economy, is the very worst commodity for government to monopolize.

State nullification. In 2010, I released a book called *Nullification: How to Resist Federal Tyranny in the 21st Century*. According to Thomas Jefferson, the "rightful remedy" when the federal government reaches beyond its constitutional powers is state nullification, whereby the states refuse to enforce unconstitutional measures. It is foolish and vain to wait for the federal government to restrain itself. If the federal government is allowed to hold a monopoly on determining the extent of its own powers, Jefferson warned, we have no right to be surprised when it keeps discovering new ones.

Nullification was first proposed by James Madison and Thomas Jefferson in the Virginia and Kentucky Resolutions of 1798, respectively, though the idea is traceable at least to the Virginia ratifying convention at which that state debated the U.S. Constitution ten years earlier. The New England states, as I show in *Nullification*, had repeated recourse to these principles throughout the nineteenth century, particularly with reference to the 1807–1809 embargo, military conscription, and fugitive-slave laws (aspects of which some northern states considered constitutionally dubious). In 1820, the Ohio legislature declared that the principle of nullification had been accepted by a majority of the American people. In the mid-1850s the Wisconsin Supreme Court declared the Fugitive Slave Act of 1850 unconstitutional, and in 1859 the Wisconsin legislature cited the Kentucky Resolutions of 1798 in defending its obstruction of that Act.

No one learns about any of this. They should. I've assembled the details—including replies to common if misplaced criticisms—at StateNullification.com.

The point of nullification is that the federal government, if it can be limited at all—a question on which by now we ought to be skeptical—cannot be expected to limit itself. The limiting must come from a force outside the federal government. For Thomas Jefferson, the states—and ultimately the people themselves—were the logical candidates for the task. The states created the federal government as their agent in the first place. The agent cannot presume to dictate to the principals what their Constitution means and how power is to be apportioned between them.[11]

By 2010, nullification was being proposed for issues as diverse as health care, gun rights, marriage, medical marijuana, the Transportation Security Administration (TSA), and federal interference in education, to name a few. Department of Homeland Security Secretary Janet Napolitano complained that the Real ID Act of 2005 had failed because the states refused to comply. Who wants to be the first governor to stand up and say *not in my state*? Every state, red or blue, can find some unconstitutional federal outrage to oppose. What if they all opposed them at once? Would everyone's highway money be taken away, or might the states' resistance at last bring about a new *modus vivendi* between themselves and the federal government, as Jefferson would have wanted?

Repeal Amendment. Alongside the robust use of nullification, the principle that the limiting of the federal government has to be carried out by parties other than the federal government should be emphasized wherever possible. In tandem with constitutional scholars like Georgetown University Law Center's Randy Barnett, I have previously endorsed a constitutional amendment by which a federal law is actually *repealed* if two-thirds of the states register their official disapproval.[12] Such an amendment would partially restore the balance between the federal government and the states that was undermined by the Seventeenth Amendment to the Constitution.

Almost immediately after endorsing that proposal, though, I reproached myself for how timid it was. Instead, the rule could be that if even a simple majority—i.e., twenty-six states—disapprove of a federal law, it is repealed. Whether this determination is made by their state attorney general, their state legislature, or popular referendum is immaterial and can be left up to each state.[13] As long as this Amendment could work in tandem with, rather than in opposition to, the much-needed Jeffersonian remedy of state nullification, it could have some good effect.

Self-education. As Albert Jay Nock said, the one person in the world whom you can certainly improve is yourself. No matter how much we learn, we should always think of ourselves as students.

The past several years have seen a completely unanticipated revival of the free-market Austrian School of economics. Investors and academics are giving it a second—or a first—look. Average Americans, who never expected to find themselves interested in economics, have found themselves hooked forever after reading just one book. Young people in particular are devouring Austrian materials. Now they understand how things work, and where their professors have gone so dreadfully wrong.

You can find a complete program of self-education in Austrian economics, most of whose recommended readings and lectures you can download for free, at www.LearnAustrianEconomics.com. At Mises.org, the website of the Ludwig von Mises Institute, you will find more free resources on more topics of interest than you can imagine. I myself teach online courses in American history, to students ranging from homeschoolers to professionals to retirees, via the revolutionary Mises Academy interface. You can join at www.StudyWithTomWoods.com.

Imagine living in a country filled with people who see through the arguments for "stimulus," bailouts, and the other forms of government direction of the economy, and respond with intelligent and compelling arguments of their own. We can populate such a country, one person at a time.

Crack through the media monopoly—for free. Thanks to the Internet, schools of thought that have previously been excluded from public debate can now circumvent the guardians of approved opinion.

Here's one clever example of how to spread important ideas even if the establishment shuts you out. In the fall of 2010, economist Robert P. Murphy, who holds a Ph.D. from New York University, challenged *New York Times* columnist and 2008 Nobel Prize winner Paul Krugman to a public debate on Austrian versus Keynesian business cycle theory. Krugman refuses debate invitations as a rule. This one is different. Murphy is using a website called The Point to invite people to make pledges. If Krugman agrees to debate, *all this pledged money is donated to a New York food bank.*

As of this printing, Murphy had already garnered $60,000 in pledges, thanks to some funny YouTube videos and a few articles that made the rounds on the Internet. That figure is going to rise. Murphy wants it to reach at least $100,000, but it will surely get much higher. If Krugman doesn't debate, he must explain to his supporters that one hour of his time isn't worth seeing $100,000 get distributed to hungry people. If he does debate, the Austrian School garners more attention, and Krugman himself comes out second best. If Krugman debates, says one critic, "he runs into a buzz saw. He will get his head handed to him by Murphy. His Nobel Prize will not do him any good."

And as long as Krugman refuses to debate, Murphy keeps putting on the pressure—more YouTube videos, more press coverage (CNBC and the FOX Business Network, among other financial outlets, have already reported on Murphy's challenge), and more Internet buzz. Murphy never relents. His videos get funnier. The pledge figure rises. The pressure on Krugman grows. The strategy is brilliant, and Murphy and his ideas win no matter what the outcome.

So far, all of this has cost Murphy exactly $7—the amount he spent registering the domain www.KrugmanDebate.com. Lesson: be like Robert Murphy.

Jury nullification. Most of the Founding Fathers took jury nullification for granted as an essential instrument of a free people.[14] It is the doctrine that a jury judges not just the facts of a case but also the law itself. The enforcement of an otherwise good law may in particular cases yield a travesty of justice. Jury nullification is meant to prevent this. But it may also be used when a jury believes a particular law to be unjust in and of itself. Although our civics textbooks tell us that laws are passed for the common good and with public consent, most of us are more cynical. Legislators and lawmaking are generally beyond the reach of the people. Jury nullification is the ultimate tool by which the people may deliver a verdict on the laws that govern them.

Theophilus Parsons supported the Constitution in Massachusetts' ratification convention in 1788 and turned down John Adams' offer to serve as U.S. attorney general in order to become Chief Justice of Massachusetts. Parsons penned my favorite quotation in support of jury nullification: "An Act of usurpation is *not obligatory—it is not law.* Any man may be justified in his resistance to it. Let him be considered as a criminal by the General Government—yet his own *fellow citizens alone* can convict him. They are *his jury*—and if they pronounce him innocent, *not all the powers of congress can hurt him*—and innocent they certainly will pronounce him, if the *supposed* law which he resisted was an act of usurpation."[15]

The regime will grow more and more desperate as conditions worsen and the crisis grows nearer. It will reach for whatever it can get its hands on. It will impose capital controls, it will crack down further on barter exchanges, and it will offer ever-larger rewards for ratting out people who evade its myriad restrictions, taxes, and regulations. We must not cooperate. We must remain silent. We must refuse to convict our fellow countrymen of peaceful activities that only the predatory state calls crimes.

On jury nullification, visit the Fully Informed Jury Association at www.fija.org.

Free State Project. The Free State Project was established in 2001 with the goal of identifying a low-population state where supporters of freedom would pledge to move, with an eye to influencing its political life in the direction of liberty. In 2003, when 5,000 people had committed to settle in whatever state was chosen, a majority of participants voted for New Hampshire as the destination. In this way, some Americans might be spared at least some portion of the total package of government predation. See www.FreeStateProject.org.

Agorism. Agorism (www.agorism.info) rejects political activity altogether, not merely because it achieves no good purpose—if evidence is necessary, say its proponents, look at the continued expansion of federal power over the past century—but also because participating in it involves consenting to an immoral system. *Agorism* comes from the Greek *agora*—marketplace—and seeks a society in which the peaceful interaction of the market replaces the violence of the state.

Agorism begins with the libertarian premise that individuals have the right to interact with each other peacefully without the intervention of aggressive force by the state. More precisely, it involves the moral principle that no one may initiate aggression against any innocent party. That principle sounds simple enough, but most shrink in practice from its full implications. It means taxation is morally illicit, since it involves seizing the property of a peaceful individual, with violent repercussions should he resist. It means all forms of state-granted or state-held monopoly are likewise unacceptable, and for the same reason: they are maintained by the use of physical force to keep out competitors. If it is true, as we see in case after case, that monopoly leads to rising prices and poorer service, then every service provided monopolistically by the state could be provided better by the entrepreneurial efforts of a free people. Civilized people do not initiate physical force against each other. The agorist, like any consistent libertarian, refuses to make an exception for the behavior of the state. A single moral code must govern all of mankind. If stealing is wrong for individuals, then groups of individuals operating under the banner of the state are likewise forbidden from stealing, even if they choose to call it taxation. Individuals are not allowed to kidnap other people and force them to pursue particular ends; the state, likewise, may not do such a thing and call it conscription. The state, in short, far from making civilization possible, is instead a parasite on the productive activity of civilized people.

But agorism proceeds beyond libertarianism, which is a political philosophy only, into the realm of strategy. That strategy involves ignoring the state where feasible, and building a counter-economy that to the greatest extent possible evades state supervision, taxation, and regulation. Samuel Edward Konkin III outlined the idea in his *New Libertarian Manifesto* and *An Agorist Primer*. "Nearly every action," Konkin wrote, "is regulated, taxed, prohibited, or subsidized," and for that reason "everyone is a resister to the extent that he survives in a society where laws control everything and give contradictory orders. *All (non-coercive) human action committed in defiance of the State constitutes the Counter-Economy.*" As the state's reach grows more extensive, more people join the counter-economy in one form or another. "The more controls and taxation a State imposes on its people, the more they will evade and defy them. Since the United States is one of the *less* (officially) controlled countries, and the Counter-Economy here is fairly large, the global Counter-Economy should be expected to be even larger—and it is."[16] Konkin hoped to see not just a series of disconnected black markets, but an entire parallel economy.

As the political and economic situation in the United States has worsened and the chances of positive change via official channels have grown less and less likely, Konkin's ideas have attracted more attention. But it was Konkin's view that one could be an agorist to some degree even if he pursued his counter-economic activities without a fully elaborated philosophical grounding. Anyone who uses a radar detector, or has ever had a yard sale and not reported the proceeds to the IRS, or has ever worked or paid someone under the table, is to that extent an agorist. When agorist activities are small, government does not know about them. When they are large and extensive, they become impractical to shut down. Homeschooling, for instance, the practice of withdrawing from officially approved educational outlets, grew so large that it became essentially impossible for the state to suppress it.

By the end of 2009, the press was beginning to pick up on the increasing size of the underground economy in the United States. Even concentrating only on the production of legal goods and services, economics professor Friedrich Schneider estimates its size at $1 trillion per year. Not surprisingly, experts say underground economic activity increases when people begin to doubt the honesty and legitimacy of the regime that governs them.[17]

For agorists, the present system cannot be reformed even if we should be inclined to reform it. Instead, deprive it of income, strain its resources, and undermine its legitimacy in the minds of the people. If the agorists are correct, the proper approach against the state is not direct confrontation, but death by a million cuts.

Debt repudiation? Doug Casey's *Crisis Investing* is the largest-selling financial book of all time. Recently, Casey has been arguing that some kind of default on the national debt is inevitable. It can never and will never be paid. The default will either occur out in the open or will be concealed through inflation, with the government reducing its debt burden by debasing the currency in which the payments are made. The latter course is more likely, but Casey suggests open default is in fact more desirable. In a 2010 interview with *The Gold Report*, Casey explained:

> The debt will be defaulted on one way or another. The trouble is they're almost certainly going to default on it through inflation, by destroying the currency, which is much worse than defaulting on it overtly. That's because inflation will wipe out the relatively few people who are prudent in this country, those who are actually saving money. Because they generally save in the form of dollars, they're going to wipe them out financially.
>
> It's just horrible. Runaway inflation will reward the profligates who are in debt—people who've been living above their means. And punish the producers who've been saving and trying to build capital. That's in addition to the fact it will destroy millions of productive enterprises. A runaway inflation is the worst thing that can happen to

a society, short of a major war. They just should default on it honestly, as it were.

Should the government openly default on its debt, Casey argues, people will hesitate to lend to it in the future—and that can only be a good thing. (Thomas Jefferson favored a constitutional amendment prohibiting government borrowing.) Furthermore, there is no good moral reason to saddle generations not yet born with an impossible debt burden. And finally, Casey suggests a default would serve a useful moral purpose in that it would directly punish those who have lent to the government and thus allowed it to carry out its various forms of exploitation of the American public.[18]

Short of repudiation, it has been suggested that the federal government should do what is required of any other bankrupt entity: sell off its assets in order to pay its creditors to the extent possible. The federal government owns plenty of assets, including a great deal of land, whose sale would relieve the staggering burden that hangs over the heads of a population that has been impoverished enough already.[19]

These ideas are unthinkable, the guardians of approved opinion will say. Not unthinkable, evidently, are (1) trusting the same people who caused the problems to solve them, (2) doing nothing as the political class intensifies the coming crisis at every turn, and (3) ruining the lives of the rising generation. The solutions we consider have to be commensurate with the seriousness and nature of the problem. The writing-policy-studies strategy, the voting-for-the-guy-who-gives-a-good-speech strategy, the waiting-for-the-Supreme-Court-to-declare-anything-at-all-unconstitutional strategy—what have these achieved? Why should we expect any more success with them in the future than we've had in the past? And why should we confine our response to the officially approved forms of resistance vetted for us by the *New York Times*?

The one approach sure to fail is the one routinely urged upon the Tea Party movement: vote for Newt Gingrich or other hand-picked establishment candidates, and all will be well. If only our problems were so trivial that replacing one wing of the establishment by the other could put things right. Gingrich and his allies are part of the problem.

■　　　■　　　■　　　■

In the end, though, this is not primarily about money, balanced budgets, or debt. It is about right and wrong.

In *Anarchy, State, and Utopia* (1974), Harvard philosopher Robert Nozick recounts what he calls the Tale of the Slave, and invites the reader to consider himself as the slave in the story. The story moves through nine stages.[20]

First: You are a slave at the mercy of a brutal master, who forces you to work for his purposes and beats you arbitrarily.

Second: The master decides to beat you only for breaking the rules, and even grants you some free time.

Third: You are part of a group of slaves subject to this master. He decides, on grounds acceptable to everyone, how goods should be allocated among you all.

Fourth: The master requires his slaves to work only three days per week, granting them the other four days off. They can do as they wish during their free time.

Fifth: The master now allows the slaves to work wherever they wish. His main caveat is that they must send him three-sevenths of their wages, corresponding to the three days' worth of work they once had to do on his land every week. In an emergency he can force them to do his bidding once again, and he retains the power to alter the fraction of their wages to which he lays claim.

Sixth: The master grants all 10,000 of his slaves, except you, the right to vote. They can decide among themselves how much of their (and your) earnings to take and what outlets to fund with the money. They can decide what you are and are not allowed to do. We can suppose for the sake of argument that the master irrevocably grants this right to the 10,000 slaves. You now have 10,000 masters, or a single 10,000-headed master.

Seventh: You are granted the freedom to try to persuade the 10,000 to exercise their vast powers in a particular way. You still do not have the right to vote, but you can try to influence those who do.

Eighth: The 10,000 grant you the right to vote, but only to break a tie. You write down your vote, and if a tie should occur, they open it and record it. No tie has ever occurred.

Ninth: You are granted the right to vote. But functionally, it simply means, as in the eighth stage, that in case of a tie, which has never occurred, your vote carries the issue.

Nozick's question is this: at what stage between 1 and 9 did this become something other than the tale of a slave?

It is an unexamined premise of the American political spectrum that society cannot function without a single coercive institution with the power to dispose of the lives and fortunes of over 300 million individuals. While throwing the poor a few scraps, in a thousand and one open and covert ways this institution enriches various elites at the expense of the productive population. The more it grows the worse it gets. More and more sectors of society conclude that they, too, must enrich themselves by means of government-granted privilege. Everyone begins to clamor for subsidies, just in order to break even vis-à-vis the already subsidized. The industrialists take, the farmers take, the scientists take, the military establishment takes, the social workers take, the education bureaucracy takes—*everybody* takes.

All of this looting under cover of law is what Frédéric Bastiat, the nineteenth-century French economic thinker, memorably called "legal plunder." No one considers it legitimate to stick a gun in his neighbor's ribs and take his things. Yet we are taught to believe a dramatic moral difference separates that kind of direct stealing with the indirect kind—e.g., when the government sticks a gun in your neighbor's ribs and hands the proceeds to you.

Nozick put it like this: when you tax away from someone the fruits of five months of his labor, you are in effect taking away five months from him. You are taking away *part of his life*. Dance around the issue all you like, but this is forced labor by any reasonable definition of the term.

Is this really the most humane way human beings can interact with each other? Is it so unthinkable to imagine a society in which we finally put the guns down and deal with each other on the basis of reason and compassion rather than force?

Bastiat once described the state as "the great *fictitious entity* by which everyone seeks to live at the expense of everyone else." This arrangement is coming to an end. Something will eventually have to give. We are facing fiscal collapse; we may also confront a currency collapse, in which the dollar's purchasing power will fall precipitously over a very short period of time. At that point there won't be anything left for the poor, for the pressure groups, or for anyone else, except a bunch of worthless promises. And with every year the crisis is not addressed, the ensuing pain becomes all the greater.

Oh, but *our intentions were good*, the architects of ruin will pointlessly assure us. That'll feed a lot of people.

It is impossible to time precisely when the crisis will hit. At any moment a particular news item could send confidence in the dollar plunging and interest rates skyrocketing (as investors demand higher bond yields to compensate for their lack of faith in the viability of U.S. government promises). Then it becomes all the more difficult to finance all the borrowing and spending. According to Harvard's Niall Ferguson:

> One day, a seemingly random piece of bad news—perhaps a negative report by a rating agency—will make the headlines during an otherwise quiet news cycle. Suddenly, it will be not just a few policy wonks who worry about the sustainability of U.S. fiscal policy but the public at large, not to mention investors abroad. It is this shift that is crucial: A complex adaptive system is in big trouble when its component parts lose faith in its viability.
>
> Over the last three years, the complex system of the global economy flipped from boom to bust—all because a bunch of Americans started to default on their subprime mortgages, thereby blowing huge holes in the business models of thousands of highly leveraged financial institutions. The next phase of the current crisis may begin when the public begins to reassess the credibility of the radical monetary and fiscal steps that were taken in response.
>
> Neither interest rates at zero nor fiscal stimulus can achieve a sustainable recovery if people in the United States and abroad collectively decide, overnight, that such measures will ultimately lead to much higher inflation rates or outright default. Bond yields can shoot up if expectations change about future government solvency, intensifying an already bad fiscal crisis by driving up the cost of interest payments on new debt. Just ask Greece.[21]

Suppose the crisis hit tomorrow. What would we do? Exactly what the circumstances called for: care for our families, help friends and neighbors in need, volunteer with charitable institutions to help those who fall through the cracks, and establish online clearinghouses to share our professional skills and talents with those who need them, perhaps in exchange for the skills and talents of others. The institutions of civil society, long dormant, would quickly be resurrected.

We ought to begin doing these things now.

Americans in their twenties and thirties (and I myself belong to the latter group) confront an especially grim future unless a radical change in direction occurs very soon. Many have college debts to repay, at a time when jobs—especially well-paying ones—are scarce. For now, at least, housing prices are still out of reach for people with low incomes. Taxes are certain to be increased—especially if we include inflation as a tax—throughout our lives. After all this, the amount of money this age group will have left to save for the future will be pitifully small. And it will be a long future, with many of us living into our eighties and nineties. Leaving aside the risible prospect of government pensions and Social Security half a century from now, we can safely say that most of us will never be able to retire. A world in which people's productive lives ended around age sixty or even earlier will seem like something out of science fiction. The price for the political decisions of previous generations, who enjoyed rather a nice ride while it lasted, had to be paid by someone. It will be paid by us.[22]

It will be paid by us if we choose to pay it, that is. The federal government may have ruined the job market and made the lives of young people difficult to impossible, but this need not be a permanent feature of American life. The sooner that younger generation liberates itself from the philosophy of plunder and intervention that has led us to this point, the better its prospects will be.

Kevin Dowd, who recently retired as a professor of economics at England's University of Nottingham, told a largely young audience in Paris in 2009:

> You can play by the rules your elders would impose on you. You can expect to pay higher and higher taxes, work harder and harder to stand still, and get less and less back in return for yourselves—a life little different from slavery—and then the system will collapse anyway.
>
> Or, alternatively, you can fight back. There is no law of nature that says you have to honor checks that other people write at your expense. You are not slaves—you are slaves only if you choose to submit to slavery. You can repudiate those checks....

[Dowd continued]

Let's be blunt about what I am suggesting. I am suggesting that if default is inevitable, and if default is more damaging the longer it is delayed, then it would be a good idea to consider embracing it. We should lance the boil, as it were, and kill off the scam—sooner rather than later.

Do you want a life of toil and slavery, followed by ultimate destitution, or do you want to stand up for yourself and fight for the chance of a decent life? It's your choice.

It is the choice facing America.

Acknowledgments

I owe a debt of gratitude to Regnery's executive editor, Harry Crocker, for helping me come up with the idea for this book during a brainstorming session in late 2009. I'm also grateful to Regnery for permitting me to put this project on hold for a short while in order to write an additional book that occurred to me while I was working on it: *Nullification: How to Resist Federal Tyranny in the 21st Century* (June 2010).

Once again, Anneke Green, who was my editor for *Nullification*, made crucial suggestions regarding the book's organization and helped me clarify many of my points. The text is cleaner, smoother, and an easier read thanks to her conscientious work.

For helping answer some last-minute questions I am indebted to Peter J. Wallison, William S. Lind, Gary North, Anthony Gregory, Mark Thornton, Phil Giraldi, Robert Murphy, David Howden, Per Bylund, and Zach Bibeault. Thanks to Professor Joseph Salerno of Pace University for introducing me to the work of Seymour Melman several years ago. Members of my Facebook fan page—facebook.com/ThomasEWoods—helped me get a better handle on agorism.

Thanks to *Taki's Magazine* for letting me use a portion of my article "Don't Know Much About Capitalism."

Thanks to the Ludwig von Mises Institute for allowing me the use of portions of my article "The Neglected Costs of the Warfare State: An Austrian Tribute to Seymour Melman" from the *Journal of Libertarian Studies*, as well as parts of "When to Cheer" from *The Free Market*. More importantly, I am grateful to the Institute for the time I spent on this book while a resident scholar there. President Doug French and Chairman Lew Rockwell have been great benefactors to me over the years, and I cannot thank them enough for their generosity and support.

Of course, it is my wife, Heather, to whom I owe my greatest debt. This was a rough one: we were in the middle of a move when crunch time for this book hit, and we both had some pretty exhausting days. She was extremely helpful and understanding during the crucial final weeks before the manuscript was due. To borrow a line from one of the masters, she is truly my indispensable framework.

Notes

CHAPTER 1

1. Joanne Allen, "Majority of Americans Distrust the Government," Reuters.com, April 19, 2010, available at http://www.reuters.com/article/idUSTRE-63I0FB20100419

2. Lila Rajiva, "Green Shoots and White Lies: The Verbal Pandemic that Saved the Experts," LewRockwell.com, September 11, 2009, available at http://www.lewrockwell.com/rajiva/rajiva27.1.html

3. Nouriel Roubini, "Brown Manure, Not Green Shoots," Forbes.com, July 9, 2009, available at http://www.forbes.com/2009/07/08/jobs-report-mortgages-unemployment-recession-opinions-columnists-nouriel-roubini.html

4. The figures are regularly updated at http://www.usdebtclock.com. These are not unusually high or inflated figures. As of 2008, Federal Reserve Bank of Dallas president Richard Fisher came up with a combined total of $99.2 trillion

in unfunded liabilities, a figure that has only risen in the years since. See Charles Goyette, *The Dollar Meltdown* (New York: Portfolio, 2009), 34–35.

5. Peter G. Peterson, *Running on Empty* (New York: Farrar, Straus, and Giroux, 2004), 33.

6. Ibid., 34.

7. Robert Murphy, "Spending Will Confine Americans to Debtors' Prison," *Buffalo News*, May 8, 2010; see also Edmund L. Andrews, "Wave of Debt Payments Facing U.S. Government," *New York Times*, November 23, 2009.

8. Peterson, *Running on Empty*, 34.

9. Laurence Kotlikoff, "The U.S. Is Bankrupt and We Don't Even Know It," Bloomberg.com, August 10, 2010, available at http://www.bloomberg.com/news/2010-08-11/u-s-is-bankrupt-and-we-don-t-even-know-commentary-by-laurence-kotlikoff.html

10. Gary North, "Confirmation from High Places: You're Not Crazy After All. The Federal Government Really Is Busted," August 12, 2010, available at http://*www.garynorth.com/members/6812.cfm*

11. David Stockman, "Beware the Light at the End of the Tunnel," MarketWatch.com, August 11, 2010, available at http://www.marketwatch.com/story/story/print?guid=FC60311E-9958-4B34-9F22-84B0B786E9CD; Gary North, "No V-Shaped Recovery, but a V-Shaped Deficit: The Point of No Return," August 12, 2010, available at http://www.garynorth.com/members/6814.cfm

12. David Stockman, "Our Failed National Economy," Minyanville, November 4, 2010, available at http://www.minyanville.com/articles/print.php?a=30936.

13. Peter G. Peterson, *Gray Dawn: How the Coming Age Wave Will Transform America—And the World* (New York: Three Rivers Press, 2000), 5.

14. Ibid., 13, 42–43.

15. Ibid., 33.

16. Peterson, *Running on Empty*, 58–59.

17. Ibid., 38, 45.

18. Ibid., 58.

19. Ibid., 62.

20. Ibid., 75.

21. Ibid., 76. Emphasis in original.

22. Peterson, *Gray Dawn*, 34.

23. Peterson, *Running on Empty*, xxx.

24. Ibid., xxxiv.

25. Pamela Villarreal, "Social Security and Medicare Projections: 2009," National Center for Policy Analysis Brief Analysis No. 662, June 11, 2009, available at http://www.ncpa.org/pub/ba662

26. Steve Forbes and Elizabeth Ames, *How Capitalism Will Save Us* (New York: Crown Business, 2009), 138–39.

27. Jeffrey Rogers Hummel, "Why Default on U.S. Treasuries Is Likely," August 3, 2009, available at http://www.econlib.org/library/Columns/y2009/Hummeltbills.html

28. Peterson, *Running on Empty*, 39–40.

29. Ibid., 123–24.

30. Peterson, *Gray Dawn*, 8.

31. Mac Slavo, "Broke and Jobless: 85% of College Grads Moving Home," SHTF Plan, October 17, 2010, available at http://www.shtfplan.com/headline-news/broke-and-jobless-85-of-college-grads-moving-home_10172010

32. Mac Slavo, "This Recession Tops the Great Depression," SHTF Plan, October 25, 2010, available at http://www.shtfplan.com/headline-news/this-recession-tops-the-great-depression_10252010

33. Mike Shedlock, "Missouri Budget Overstates Revenues By Up To $1 Billion; Indiana Revenue Falls Short; Budget Battles in Washington; Budget Gaps In Kansas," Mish's Global Economic Trend Analysis, March 6, 2010, available at http://globaleconomicanalysis.blogspot.com/2010/03/missouri-budget-over-states-revenues-by.html

34. Jordan Schrader, "Republicans Eye State Workers' Pay," *The Olympian*, March 5, 2010.

35. Eric Bradner, "Indiana Receipts Again Fall Short of Projections," *Evansville Courier & Press*, March 2, 2010.

36. Danny Hakim, "State Plan Makes Fund Both Borrower and Lender," *New York Times*, June 11, 2010.

37. Joe Mysak, "State Pension Plans Go Broke as Payrolls Expand," Bloomberg. com, June 10, 2010, available at http://www.bloomberg.com/news/2010-06-11/pension-plans-go-broke-as-public-payrolls-expand-joe-mysak.html

38. Mike Shedlock, "Miami Commissioner Says Bankruptcy Is City's Best Hope; Chris Christie Says New Jersey Careens Towards Becoming Greece," Mish's Global Economic Trend Analysis, May 27, 2010, available at http://

globaleconomicanalysis.blogspot.com/2010/05/miami-commissioner-says-bankruptcy-is.html

39. Simone Baribeau, "Miami Imposes Pay, Health, Pension Cuts to Ease Pressure on Budget Deficit," Bloomberg.com, August 31, 2010, available at http://www.bloomberg.com/news/2010-08-31/miami-to-consider-cutting-salaries-after-budget-gap-leads-to-lower-ratings.html

40. Benjamin Wachs and Joe Eskenazi, "The Worst-Run Big City in the U.S.," *SF Weekly*, December 16, 2009, available at http://www.sfweekly.com/2009-12-16/news/the-worst-run-big-city-in-the-u-s/

41. Gary North, "Health Care and Detroit: Killed by Government," LewRockwell.com, March 24, 2010, available at http://www.lewrockwell.com/north/north828.html

42. John Gittelsohn, "Washington Beats U.S. Housing Slump on Obama Budget," Bloomberg.com, November 2, 2009, available at http://www.bloomberg.com/apps/news?pid=newsarchive&sid=aQelOG6kQtj8

43. Dennis Cauchon, "For Feds, More Get 6-Figure Salaries," *USA Today*, December 10, 2009.

CHAPTER 2

1. Sally C. Pipes, *The Truth About Obamacare* (Washington, D.C.: Regnery, 2010), 16–17.

2. Ibid., 17–18.

3. George Reisman, "The Real Right to Medical Care Versus Socialized Medicine," *Mises Daily*, August 6, 2009, available at http://mises.org/daily/3613

4. Thomas E. Woods, Jr., *33 Questions About American History You're Not Supposed to Ask* (New York: Crown Forum, 2007), ch. 30.

5. Vijay Boyapati, "What's Really Wrong with the Healthcare Industry," *Mises Daily*, May 26, 2010, available at http://mises.org/daily/4434.

6. Ibid.

7. Ibid.

8. Steve Forbes and Elizabeth Ames, *How Capitalism Will Save Us: Why Free People and Free Markets Are the Best Answer in Today's Economy* (New York: Crown Business, 2009), 243.

9. Pipes, *The Truth About Obamacare*, 103, 102.

10.   Ibid., 160, 162–63.

11.   Ibid., 92–97.

12.   Hans Bader, "Obamacare Results in 47 Percent Premium Hike," OpenMarket.
      org, October 17, 2010, available at http://www.openmarket.org/2010/10/17/
      obamacare-results-in-47-percent-premium-hike/; Pipes, *The Truth About
      Obamacare*, 186–87.

13.   Pipes, *The Truth About Obamacare*, 183–84.

14.   Gene Epstein, "Obamacare and Small Firms," *Barron's*, March 29, 2010, avail-
      able at http://online.barrons.com/article/SB126964431272068337.html

15.   Pipes, *The Truth About Obamacare*, ch. 20; Douglas Holtz-Eakin, "The Real
      Arithmetic of Health Care Reform," *New York Times*, March 21, 2010.

16.   Forbes and Ames, *How Capitalism Will Save Us*, 251.

17.   Peter G. Peterson, *Running on Empty* (New York: Farrar, Straus, and Giroux,
      2004), 126. As an aside, we might note the question that is completely over-
      looked in the health-care debate: might American seniors and indeed Ameri-
      cans in general be overmedicated? This is the elephant in the living room. Is it
      normal and good for 40 percent of seniors to be consuming at least five pre-
      scription drugs every week, with 12 percent taking at least ten? A study in the
      Journal of the American Medical Association in 2003 estimated 200,000 cases
      every year of seniors who suffer life-threatening or even fatal problems related
      to prescription drugs. Ibid., 126–27.

18.   Peterson, *Running on Empty*, 128.

19.   David T. Beito, *From Mutual Aid to the Welfare State: Fraternal Societies and Social
      Services, 1890-1967* (Chapel Hill: University of North Carolina Press, 2000).

20.   Allen J. Matusow, *The Unraveling of America: A History of Liberalism in the
      1960s* (Athens, GA: University of Georgia Press, 2009 [1984]), 230, 231–
      32.

21.   This section relies on Jacob Hornberger, "Free-Market Health Care and the
      Poor," May 31, 2010, available at http://www.campaignforliberty.com/article.
      php?view=899

22.   Reisman, "Real Right to Medical Care."

23.   Ibid.

24.   Ibid.

25.   Howard Wolinsky and Tom Brune, *The Serpent on the Staff: The Unhealthy Politics
      of the American Medical Association* (New York: Tarcher Putnam, 1994), 142.

26. Pipes, *The Truth About Obamacare*, 20.

27. Forbes and Ames, *How Capitalism Will Save Us*, 246.

28. "The Doctor Will See You Later," *Investor's Business Daily*, June 8, 2010, A10.

29. David Asman, "There's No Place Like Home," *Wall Street Journal*, June 8, 2005.

30. Associated Press, "Obama: 'Stimulus' Needed to Avoid Catastrophe," February 10, 2009, available at http://www.msnbc.msn.com/id/29107790/

31. Charlie Savage and David D. Kirkpatrick, "Technology's Fingerprints on the Stimulus Package," *New York Times*, February 10, 2009; cited in Timothy P. Carney, *Obamanomics* (Washington, D.C.: Regnery, 2009), 34.

32. Richard K. Vedder and Lowell Gallaway, "The Great Depression of 1946," *Review of Austrian Economics* 5, 2 (1991): 14. The title of Vedder and Gallaway's article is, of course, not intended to suggest that there really was a depression in 1946, but that some commentators predicted one and some flawed statistics can even seem to indicate that one occurred.

33. Robert Higgs, "From Central Planning to the Market: The American Transition, 1945-1947," *Journal of Economic History* 59 (September 1999): 600–23.

34. Robert P. Murphy, "Does 'Depression Economics' Change the Rules?" *Mises Daily*, January 12, 2009, available at http://mises.org/daily/3290

35. Carney, *Obamanomics*, 138.

36. John Stossel, "The Economic Illiteracy Behind Cash for Clunkers," available at http://reason.com/archives/2009/09/03/clunker-legislation

37. Carney, *Obamanomics*, 147, 149.

38. Robert Higgs, "Regime Uncertainty: Why the Great Depression Lasted So Long and Why Prosperity Resumed After the War," *Independent Review* 1 (Spring 1997): 561–90.

39. Robert Higgs, "Billionaire Entrepreneur Complains of Regime Uncertainty," May 31, 2010, available at http://hnn.us/blogs/entries/127341.html

40. Ibid.

41. Robert Higgs, "Regime Uncertainty in 1937 and 2008," December 6, 2010, available at http://www.independent.org/blog/index.php?p=635

CHAPTER 3

1. Christi Parsons and Peter Nicholas, "Obama Hits the Stimulus Campaign Trail," *Los Angeles Times*, February 10, 2009.

2. Chris Edwards, "George W. Bush: Biggest Spender Since LBJ," CNSNews.com, December 22, 2009, available at http://www.cnsnews.com/commentary/article/58908

3. Thomas E. Woods, Jr., *Meltdown: A Free-Market Look at Why the Stock Market Collapsed, the Economy Tanked, and Government Bailouts Will Make Things Worse* (Washington, DC: Regnery, 2009), ch. 2.

4. Mortgage-backed securities (MBS) were instruments in which a pool of mortgages were grouped into a financial product for sale to investors. Each MBS consisted of tiny fractions of a number of mortgages. Strictly speaking, the holder of the MBS was entitled to a tiny portion of the income stream from the various mortgage payments that came in for the mortgages bundled in the instrument.

5. Russell Roberts, "Gambling with Other People's Money: How Perverted Incentives Caused the Financial Crisis," Mercatus Center, George Mason University, May 2010, 21, 25.

6. Mark A. Calabria, "Financial 'Reform' Bill Won't Stop the Next Crisis," National Review Online, June 25, 2010, available at http://article.nationalreview.com/437139/financial-reform-bill-wont-stop-the-next-crisis/mark-a-calabria

7. Johan Norberg, *Financial Fiasco* (Washington, D.C.: Cato Institute, 2009), 40.

8. Charles W. Calomiris, "Financial Innovation, Regulation, and Reform," *Cato Journal* 29 (Winter 2009): 69.

9. Steve Forbes and Elizabeth Ames, *How Capitalism Will Save Us* (New York: Crown Business, 2009), 115.

10. Norberg, *Financial Fiasco*, 78.

11. Roberts, "Gambling with Other People's Money," 13.

12. Even the minuscule premium on GSE bonds may not have been due to any serious expectation that the federal government might allow Fannie and Freddie to go bankrupt. Instead, according to Sam Eddins of IronBridge Capital Management, the premium was attributable to the differential tax status between Treasuries and GSE bonds; interest income on the former was tax deductible, while interest income on the latter was not. Ibid., 30, 31n73.

13. Patrice Hill, "Taxpayers to Pay for Fannie, Freddie Aid," *Washington Times*, January 13, 2010.

14. Raghuram Rajan, "Many Are the Errors," *The American*, September 19, 2010, available at http://www.american.com/archive/2010/september/many-are-the-errors

15. Ibid.

16. Norberg, *Financial Fiasco*, 35.

17. Ibid., 37.

18. For a study of three of the best-known speculative bubbles in earlier centuries, see Douglas E. French, *Early Speculative Bubbles and Increases in the Supply of Money* (Auburn, AL: Ludwig von Mises Institute, 2009).

19. Jerry H. Tempelman, "Austrian Business Cycle Theory and the Global Financial Crisis: Confessions of a Mainstream Economist," *Quarterly Journal of Austrian Economics* 13 (Spring 2010): 4–5. The *Economist* further acknowledged that "the recent business cycles in both America and Japan displayed many 'Austrian' features." Ibid., 5.

20. Gerald P. O'Driscoll Jr., "Signs of Life in the Housing Market," *Wall Street Journal*, July 30, 2009.

21. Roberts, "Gambling with Other People's Money," 20.

22. Alan Greenspan, *The Age of Turbulence: Adventures in a New World* (New York: Penguin, 2008), 233.

23. Norberg, *Financial Fiasco*, 25.

24. For the information in this paragraph and the two that follow, see John Carney, "The FHA Is a Looming Disaster," *Business Insider*, October 17, 2009, available at http://www.businessinsider.com/the-fha-is-a-looming-disaster-2009-10; David Streitfeld, "With F.H.A. Help, Easy Loans in Expensive Areas," *New York Times*, November 19, 2009; Froma Harrop, "What Does the FHA Think It Is Doing?" *Richmond Register*, November 5, 2009; Mike Shedlock, "FHA Bailout by Taxpayers on the Way," Mish's Global Economic Trend Analysis, November 13, 2009, available at http://globaleconomicanalysis.blogspot.com/2009/11/fha-bailout-by-taxpayers-on-way.html

25. Rajan, "Many Are the Errors."

26. Norberg, *Financial Fiasco*, 6.

27. See http://www.pkarchive.org/global/welt.html. Thanks to Benjamin Lee and Mark Thornton for the Krugman quotations.

28. Lou Dobbs Moneyline, July 18, 2001, available at http://www.pkarchive.org/economy/ML071801.html (emphasis added).

29. *New York Times*, December 28, 2001, available at http://www.pkarchive.org/column/122801.html (emphasis added).

30. Robert Klein and George Reisman, "Central Problem: The Central Bank," *Barron's*, December 28, 2009.

31. Norberg, *Financial Fiasco*, 7.

32. The Fed's discount rate did come down by mid-1921, but there the Fed was following the market. With prices falling so dramatically (consumer prices plunged 38 percent in a single year), the Fisher premium in the interest rate, which reflects inflation expectations, would have come down economy-wide. Historians have described the Fed as "largely passive" during the crisis.

33. For the full details of the depression of 1920, see Thomas E. Woods, Jr., "Warren Harding and the Forgotten Depression of 1920," *Intercollegiate Review* 44 (Fall 2009): 22–29.

34. Joseph A. Schumpeter, *Business Cycles: A Theoretical, Historical, and Statistical Analysis of the Capitalist Process*, vol. II (New York: McGraw Hill, 1939), 786–87. Thanks to Gregory Bresiger for this quotation.

35. William Graham Sumner, "The Delusion of the Debtors," in *The Forgotten Man and Other Essays*, ed. Albert Galloway Keller (New Haven: Yale University Press, 1918), 170.

36. Roberts, "Gambling with Other People's Money," 12.

37. Cari Tuna, Liz Rappaport, and Julie Jargon, "Halting Recovery Divides America in Two," *Wall Street Journal*, August 29, 2009.

38. Craig Pirrong, "Moral Hazard, Goldman Edition," July 14, 2009, available at http://streetwiseprofessor.com/?p=2139

39. Norberg, *Financial Fiasco*, 77.

40. Ibid., 78.

41. Peter J. Wallison, "Ideas Have Consequences: The Importance of a Narrative," AEI Financial Services Outlook, May 2010, 2, available at http://www.aei.org/docLib/04-May-FSO-g.pdf

42. Ibid., 3–4.

43. John B. Taylor, "How Government Created the Financial Crisis," *Wall Street Journal*, February 9, 2009.

44. Jean Helwege, "Financial Firm Bankruptcy and Systemic Risk," *Regulation*, Summer 2009, 27, 29.

45. "Calomiris on the Financial Crisis," EconTalk (with Russ Roberts), October 26, 2009, available at http://www.econtalk.org/archives/2009/10/calomiris_on_th.html

46. Peter J. Wallison, "Did the 'Repeal' of Glass-Steagall Have Any Role in the Financial Crisis? Not Guilty. Not Even Close," Networks Financial Institute at Indiana State University, Policy Brief, November 2009, 11, online at http://

papers.ssrn.com/sol3/Delivery.cfm/SSRN_ID1507803_code545810.pdf?a
bstractid= 1507803&mirid=2.

47. Bill Woolsey, "The Crisis and Glass Steagall," October 2, 2009, available at
     http://monetaryfreedom-billwoolsey.blogspot.com/2009/10/crisis-and-glass-
     steagall.html

48. Wallison, "Did the 'Repeal' of Glass Steagall Have Any Role in the Financial
     Crisis?" 11–17.

49. Allan H. Meltzer, "Reflections on the Financial Crisis," *Cato Journal* 29 (Win-
     ter 2009): 27.

50. Woolsey, "The Crisis and Glass Steagall."

51. Ben S. Bernanke, "Central Banking and Bank Supervision in the United States,"
     address to the Allied Social Science Association Annual Meeting, Chicago,
     Illinois, January 7, 2009, available at http://www.federalreserve.gov/newsevents/
     speech/bernanke20070105a.htm; cited in Mark Thornton, "Bernanke's Solu-
     tions Are the Problem," *Mises Daily*, November 5, 2010, available at http://
     mises.org/daily/4798

52. Robert Higgs, "Small Government Caused Our Current Problems?" LewRock-
     well.com, August 12, 2009, available at http://www.lewrockwell.com/higgs/
     higgs127.html

53. Robert P. Murphy, "The SEC Makes Wall Street More Fraudulent," *Mises Daily*,
     January 5, 2009, available at http://mises.org/daily/3273

54. Norberg, *Financial Fiasco*, 132.

55. Laurence Kotlikoff, *Jimmy Stewart Is Dead: Ending the World's Ongoing Finan-
     cial Plague with Limited Purpose Banking* (Hoboken, NJ: Wiley, 2010), 82.

56. Willem Buiter, "Lessons from the North Atlantic Financial Crisis," paper pre-
     sented at "The Role of Money Markets" conference of Columbia Business
     School and the Federal Reserve Bank of New York, May 28, 2008, available at
     http://www.nber.org/~wbuiter/NAcrisis.pdf.

57. Tom McGinty, "SEC Lawyer One Day, Opponent the Next," April 5, 2010.

58. Gerald P. O'Driscoll Jr., "An Economy of Liars," *Wall Street Journal*, April 20,
     2010.

59. Mark Thornton, "The Economics of Housing Bubbles," in *Housing America:
     Building Out of a Crisis*, eds. Randall G. Holcombe and Benjamin Powell (New
     Brunswick, NJ: Transaction, 2009), 240.

60. Arnold Kling, "Not What They Had in Mind: A History of Policies that Produced the Financial Crisis of 2008," Mercatus Center, George Mason University, September 2009, 19.

61. Thanks to Robert Wenzel of EconomicPolicyJournal.com for this point.

62. Robert Wenzel, "Financial Lobbyists Have Met at Least 510 Times with Regulators over the New Financial Regulation Act," EconomicPolicyJournal.com, November 15, 2010, available at http://www.economicpolicyjournal.com/2010/11/financial-lobbyists-have-met-at-least.html

63. Mark A. Calabria, "Why Can't We Fire Failed Regulators?" *Investor's Business Daily*, July 8, 2010.

64. Ibid.; Mark A. Calabria, "Chris Dodd's Do-Nothing Financial Reform," *New York Post*, May 20, 2010.

65. Jeffrey Friedman and Wladimir Kraus, "A Silver Lining to the Financial Crisis: A More Realistic View of Capitalism," *Regulation Outlook*, American Enterprise Institute for Public Policy Research, January 2010, 6.

66. Calomiris, "Financial Innovation, Regulation, and Reform," 70–71.

67. International Monetary Fund, *Global Financial Stability Report: Containing Systemic Risks and Restoring Financial Soundness* (Washington, D.C.: International Monetary Fund, April 2008), xi.

68. Tempelman, "Austrian Business Cycle Theory and the Global Financial Crisis," 8.

69. On Iceland, see Philipp Bagus and David Howden, "Iceland's Banking Crisis: The Meltdown of an Interventionist Financial System," *Mises Daily*, June 9, 2009, available at http://mises.org/daily/3499

70. "'Greenspan Put' May Be Encouraging Complacency," *Financial Times*, December 8, 2000.

CHAPTER 4

1. George Selgin, William D. Lastrapes, and Lawrence H. White, "Has the Fed Been a Failure?" Cato Institute Working Paper, November 9, 2010, 18ff., available at http://www.cato.org/pubs/researchnotes/WorkingPaper-2.pdf

2. Thanks to economist George Selgin for that line.

3. Selgin, Lastrapes, and White, "Has the Fed Been a Failure?" 17.

4.   Ibid., 20.

5.   See the extensive citations in ibid., 9–15.

6.   Richard H. Timberlake Jr., "Gold Standards and the Real Bills Doctrine in U.S. Monetary Policy," *Independent Review* 11 (Winter 2007): 349.

7.   The classic study of the Panic is Murray N. Rothbard, *The Panic of 1819: Reactions and Policies* (New York: Columbia University Press, 1962).

8.   Murray N. Rothbard, *An Austrian Perspective on the History of Economic Thought*, vol. 2, *Classical Economics* (Brookfield, VT.: Edward Elgar, 1995), 212.

9.   Ibid., 212–13; Murray N. Rothbard, *The Panic of 1819: Reactions and Policies* (Auburn, AL: Ludwig von Mises Institute, 2002 [1962]), 249; see also Clifton B. Luttrell, "Thomas Jefferson on Money and Banking: Disciple of David Hume and Forerunner of Some Modern Monetary Views," *History of Political Economy* 7 (Spring 1975): 156–73. Rothbard's book on the Panic was originally published by Columbia University Press.

10.   Rothbard, *Classical Economics*, 213–16.

11.   Charles R. Morris, "Freakoutonomics," *New York Times*, June 2, 2006.

12.   Again, 100 percent reserve banking would have prevented crises of this nature.

13.   Andrew Jalil, "A New History of Banking Panics in the United States, 1825-1929: Construction and Implications," unpublished working paper, November 1, 2009, available at http://www.ocf.berkeley.edu/~ajalil/Home_files/A%20- New%20 History%20of%20Banking%-20Panics%20in%20the%20United%20 States,%201825-1929.pdf; cited in Selgin, Lastrapes, and White, "Has the Fed Been a Failure?"

14.   Elmus Wicker, *Banking Panics of the Gilded Age* (Cambridge: Cambridge University Press, 2000), xii; Selgin, Lastrapes, and White, "Has the Fed Been a Failure?" 22–23.

15.   Charles W. Calomiris, "Banking Crises and the Rules of the Game," NBER Working Paper 15403, October 2009, 11, 36.

16.   Ibid., 35–38.

17.   Jörg Guido Hülsmann, *The Ethics of Money Production* (Auburn, AL: Ludwig von Mises Institute, 2008), 91; Johan Norberg, *Financial Fiasco* (Washington, D.C.: Cato Institute, 2009), 143–44. The reference is to Michael Parkin and Robin Bade, "Central Bank Laws and Monetary Policy: A Preliminary Investigation," in *The Australian Monetary System in the 1970s*, ed. M. A. Porter (Melbourne: Monash University, 1978), 24–39.

18. Hülsmann, *The Ethics of Money Production*, 153.

19. This discussion of deflation is indebted to the work of Jörg Guido Hülsmann, in particular *The Ethics of Money Production* and *Deflation and Liberty* (Auburn, AL.: Ludwig von Mises Institute, 2008).

20. Andrew Atkeson and Patrick J. Kehoe, "Deflation and Depression: Is There an Empirical Link?" *American Economic Review* Papers and Proceedings 94 (May 2004): 99–103; quotation on 102.

21. Joseph T. Salerno, "An Austrian Taxonomy of Deflation—With Applications to the U.S.," *Quarterly Journal of Austrian Economics* 6 (Winter 2003): 93–96.

22. Ludwig von Mises, *The Theory of Money and Credit*, new ed. (New Haven: Yale University Press, 1953 [1912]), 438–39.

23. F. A. Hayek, "The Intellectuals and Socialism," *University of Chicago Law Review* (Spring 1949).

24. William Baker, *Endless Money: The Moral Hazards of Socialism* (Hoboken, NJ: Wiley, 2009), 160.

25. Thomas F. Cooley, "The Federal Reserve Needs to be Boring Again," Forbes.com, May 13, 2009, available at http://www.forbes.com/2009/05/12/federal-reserve-bernie-sanders-ron-paul-opinions-columnists-talf.html

26. On money in a free society, see Hülsmann, *Ethics of Money Production, passim*.

CHAPTER 5

1. The poll results can be found online at http://www.economist.com/blogs/democracyinamerica/2010/04/economistyougov_polling

2. Seymour Melman, *The Permanent War Economy* (New York: Simon & Schuster, 1974), 11.

3. Paul Baran and Paul Sweezy, *Monopoly Capital* (New York: Monthly Review Press, 1966), 53.

4. Seymour Melman, "Consequences of a Permanent War Economy, and Strategies for a Conversion to a Demilitarized Society," lecture delivered at Oregon State University, October 13, 1986.

5. Seymour Melman, *Our Depleted Society* (New York: Dell, 1965), 5.

6. Ibid., 7.

7. Melman, *Our Depleted Society*, 42–43. Likewise, Murray Weidenbaum wrote that to convey the true costs of the military establishment in a meaningful way

it was necessary to go beyond billions of dollars spent and consider also the "thousands of men and women pulled away (voluntarily or otherwise) from civilian pursuits, millions of man-years of industrial effort, millions of barrels of oil pumped from the earth, and thousands of square yards of planet space filled with equipment and debris. In short, the real cost of military activities should be measured in human and natural resources and in the stocks of productive capital absorbed in producing, transporting, and maintaining weapons and other military equipment. It is in the sense of alternative opportunities lost that military spending should be considered—the numbers of people employed by the military, the goods and services it purchases from the private sector, the real estate it ties up, and the technology devoted to it. Not only do we lose the opportunity for civilian use of goods and services, but we also lose the potential economic growth that these resources might have brought about." Murray L. Weidenbaum, *The Economics of Peacetime Defense* (New York: Praeger, 1974), 28–29. Arthur Burns, an economic adviser to President Dwight Eisenhower and Federal Reserve Chairman in the 1970s, concurred: "The real cost of the defense sector consists not only of the civilian goods and services that are currently foregone as its account; it includes also an element of growth that could have been achieved through larger capital investment in human and business capital." John Tirman, "Conclusions and Countercurrents," in *The Militarization of High Technology*, ed. John Tirman (Pensacola, FL: Ballinger Publishing, 1984), 13.

8.   Murray N. Rothbard made a similar point when suggested that GNP be replaced by Private Product Remaining, which excludes government expenditures altogether and measures only the size of the private economy. Murray N. Rothbard, *America's Great Depression*, 4th ed. (New York: Richardson & Snyder, 1983), 296–97.

9.   James F. Dunnigan, *How to Make War*, 4th ed. (New York: HarperCollins, 2003), 164.

10.   Asit K. Biswas, "Scientific Assessment of the Long-Term Environmental Consequences of War," in *The Environmental Consequences of War: Legal, Economic, and Scientific Perspectives*, eds. Jay E. Austin and Carl E. Bruch (Cambridge: Cambridge University Press, 2000), 306.

11.   Victor W. Sidel, "The Impact of Military Preparedness and Militarism on War and the Environment," in Austin and Bruch, eds., *The Environmental Consequences of War*, 441.

12.   Seymour Melman, "Economic Consequences of the Arms Race: The Second-Rate Economy," *American Economic Review* 78 (May 1988): 55–59.

13.   Bruce M. Russett, *What Price Vigilance? The Burdens of National Defense* (New Haven: Yale University Press, 1970), 144; Seymour Melman, *The Permanent War Economy: American Capitalism in Decline*, rev. ed. (New York: Simon & Schuster, 1985), 66.

14.   Melman, *Our Depleted Society*, 4, 7.

15.   Melman, *Permanent War Economy*, rev. ed., 64.

16.   Melman, *Our Depleted Society*, 72-73. Another factor is that military research can be more intellectually stimulating than civilian work. Writes Lester Thurow: "Would the typical engineer rather work on designing a new missile with a laser guidance system or on designing a new toaster? To ask the question is to answer it. Military research and development are more interesting since they are usually closer to the frontiers of scientific knowledge and are not limited by economic considerations such as whether a product can be sold in the market. The military is willing to pay almost any premium to have a superior product. The civilian economy is not. As a result the most skilled technicians and scientists move into defense. But suppose you own a civilian computer firm in Boston and many of your best people leave to work in Boston's higher paying and more exciting aerospace firms. How do you compete with Japanese computer firms that will not be losing their most brilliant employees? The Japanese engineer might also like to work on missiles but he does not have the opportunity to do so." John Tirman, "The Defense-Economy Debate," in Tirman, ed., *The Militarization of High Technology*, 20.

17.   Richard N. Nelson, "The Impact of Arms Reduction on Research and Development," *American Economic Review* 53 (May 1963): 445.

18.   "Industry: Aiming at the Market Instead of the Moon," *Time*, June 21, 1963.

19.   Melman, *Our Depleted Society*, 72.

20.   John Tirman writes: "One cannot say with complete confidence that the military's impact on, say, the history of aviation has been positive, because we don't

know what would have happened to aviation if the military had not played such a significant part." Tirman, ed., *The Militarization of High Technology*, xiii.

21. Melman, *Our Depleted Society*, 93.

22. Stephen Broadberry and Mark Harrison, "The Economics of World War I: An Overview," in *The Economics of World War I*, eds. Stephen Broadberry and Mark Harrison (Cambridge: Cambridge University Press, 2005), 29.

23. Herbert J. Holloman and Alan Harger, "America's Technological Dilemma," *Technology Review*, July–August 1971, 38.

24. Melman, *Permanent War Economy*, rev. ed., 134.

25. The essential text here is Murray N. Rothbard, "Toward a Reconstruction of Utility and Welfare Economics," in *On Freedom and Free Enterprise: Essays in Honor of Ludwig von Mises*, ed. Mary Sennholz (Princeton, NJ: D. Van Nostrand, 1956), 224–62. For an excellent case against state-funded science, one of the great sacred cows of public expenditure, see Terence Kealey, *The Economic Laws of Scientific Research* (New York: Palgrave Macmillan, 1997); see also Tibor R. Machan, ed., *Liberty and Research and Development: Science Funding in a Free Society* (Stanford, CA: Hoover Institution Press, 2002) and Joseph P. Martino, *Science Funding: Politics and Porkbarrel* (New Brunswick, NJ: Transaction, 1992).

26. Along these lines, John Clark suggests that "the artificial allocation of funds to this type of research could actually hamper economic progress. It concentrates on programs of special military concern, but the allotment of resources to particular segments of the industrial system so as to support these specialized projects may unduly deprive other vital sectors (housing, local transportation, and so forth) of the capital assets essential for balanced economic growth." It is "not balanced growth nor advancement in speculative knowledge that the God of War seeds; it is merely the accelerated application of the already known for immediate purposes." John J. Clark, "The New Economics of National Defense," in *The Economic Impact of the Cold War: Sources and Readings*, ed. James L. Clayton (New York: Harcourt, Brace & World, 1970), 23, 25. A recent book claiming that military research has a positive effect on economic growth, and that the diminution of such research would harm growth, is Vernon W. Ruttan, *Is War Necessary for Economic Growth? Military Procurement and Technology Development* (New York: Oxford University Press, 2006).

27. Melman, "Economic Consequences of the Arms Race," 57.

28. Melman, *Permanent War Economy*, rev. ed., 28, 30, 31.

29. Ibid., 34.

30. Ibid., 29.

31. Ibid., 39.

32. Robert DeGrasse, "The Military and Semiconductors," in Tirman, ed., *The Militarization of High Technology*, 85.

33. On the machine-tool industry, see Anthony DiFilippo, *Military Spending and Industrial Decline: A Study of the American Machine Tool Industry* (Westport, CT: Greenwood, 1986) and Melman, *The Permanent War Economy*, rev. ed.

34. Melman, *Our Depleted Society*, 53.

35. Melman, *Permanent War Economy*, rev. ed., 81–82.

36. Melman, *Profits Without Production*, 6.

37. Seymour Melman, "From Private to State Capitalism: How the Permanent War Economy Transformed the Institutions of American Capitalism," *Journal of Economic Issues* 31 (June 1997): 311–30.

38. Chalmers Johnson, *Dismantling the Empire: America's Last Best Hope* (New York: Metropolitan, 2010), 167; Robert Higgs, "The Cold War Is Over, But U.S. Preparation for It Continues," *Independent Review* 6 (Fall 2001): 292; William E. Kovacic, "Blue Ribbon Defense Commissions: The Acquisition of Major Weapon Systems," in *Arms, Politics, and the Economy: Historical and Contemporary Perspectives*, ed. Robert Higgs (New York: Holmes & Meier, 1990).

39. Robert Higgs, "Military-Economic Fascism: How Business Corrupts Government, and Vice Versa."

40. Winslow T. Wheeler, "Preface," in *America's Defense Meltdown: Pentagon Reform for President Obama and the New Congress*, ed. Winslow T. Wheeler (Stanford: Stanford University Press, 2009), x.

41. Johnson, *Dismantling the Empire*, 170.

42. Ibid., 172.

43. Chuck Spinney, "Defense Power Games," Fund for Constitutional Government report, October 1990, available at http://pogoarchives.org/m/dni/fcs/def_power_games_98.htm.

44. Ibid.

45. Jeffrey St. Clair, *Grand Theft Pentagon: Tales of Corruption and Profiteering in the War on Terror* (Monroe, ME: Common Courage Press, 2005), 152.

46. Ibid., 209.

47. Ibid., 211.

48. Christopher A. Preble, *The Power Problem: Tallying the Costs of Our Military Power* (Ithaca: Cornell University Press, 2009), 46.

49. Ibid., 48.

50. Ibid., 46–47.

51. Higgs, "Military-Economic Fascism."

52. Ibid.

53. Ibid.

54. St. Clair, *Grand Theft Pentagon*, 18.

55. Ibid., 21.

56. Higgs, "Military-Economic Fascism."

57. St. Clair, *Grand Theft Pentagon*, 187.

58. Robert Higgs, "Military Spending/Gross Domestic Product = Nonsense for Budget Policymaking," *Independent Review* 13 (Summer 2008): 149.

59. William S. Lind, "The Navy," in Wheeler, ed., *America's Defense Meltdown*, 122.

60. Winslow T. Wheeler, "Understand, Then Contain America's Out-of-Control Defense Budget," in Wheeler, ed., *America's Defense Meltdown*, 235.

61. Winslow Wheeler, "How Many More Trillions for Defense?" Center for Defense Information, October 25, 2010, available at http://www.cdi.org/program/document.cfm?documentid=4627

62. Wheeler, "Understand, Then Contain America's Out-of-Control Defense Budget," 219–21.

63. Vivien Lou Chen and Thomas Keene, "Economist Stiglitz Says Iraq War Costs May Reach $5 Trillion," Bloomberg, March 1, 2008, available at http://www.bloomberg.com/apps/news?pid=newsarchive&sid=acXcm.yk56Ko

64. Winslow T. Wheeler, "What Did the Rumsfeld/Gates Pentagon Do with $1 Trillion?" Center for Defense Information, August 30, 2010, available at http://www.cdi.org/program/document.cfm?DocumentID=4623

65. Ibid.; Wheeler, "Understand, Then Contain America's Out-of-Control Defense Budget," 236.

66. Thomas Christie, "Long in Coming: The Acquisitions Train Wreck Is Here," in Wheeler, ed., *America's Defense Meltdown*, 195.

67. Johnson, *Dismantling the Empire*, 183–84.

68. Paul Craig Roberts, "The U.S. Is No Superpower," Newsmax.com, April 26, 2006, available at http://archive.newsmax.com/archives/articles/2006/4/26/95748.shtml

69. Winslow Wheeler, "Actually, the Spigot Is Wide Open," DefenseNews, June 15, 2009, available at http://www.defensenews.com/story.php?i=4138512

70. Bruce Fein, *American Empire: Before the Fall* (Springfield, VA: Campaign for Liberty, 2010), 73.

71. Christopher Drew, "High Costs Weigh on Troop Debate for Afghan War," *New York Times*, November 14, 2009.

72. Tony Blankley, "Afghan War Becoming a Bloody Farce," *Huffington Post*, June 16, 2010, avaialble at http://www.huffingtonpost.com/tony-blankley/afghan-war-becoming-a-blo_b_615196.html

73. Fein, *American Empire: Before the Fall*, 16.

74. Ibid., 15, 16.

75. Ibid., 18.

76. Ibid., 149.

77. Ron Paul, *The Revolution: A Manifesto* (New York: Grand Central, 2008), ix–x.

78. Osama bin Laden, "Address to the American People," October 29, 2004, in *Jihad: Bin Laden in His Own Words*, ed. Brad K. Berner (New Delhi: Peacock Books, 2007), 256.

79. Robert Higgs, "The Song That Is Irresistible: How the State Leads People to Their Own Destruction," *Mises Daily*, October 16, 2007, available at http://mises.org/mobile/daily.aspx?Id=2749

80. Philip Giraldi, "Zero Based Terrorism," Campaign for Liberty, November 9, 2010, available at http://www.campaignforliberty.com/article.php?view=1190

81. A good if provocative place to start is Bill Kauffman, *Ain't My America: The Long, Noble History of Antiwar Conservatism and Middle-American Anti-Imperialism* (New York: Henry Holt, 2008); see also Justin Raimondo, *Reclaiming the American Right: The Lost Legacy of the Conservative Movement* (Burlingame, CA: Center for Libertarian Studies, 1993).

82. George H. Nash, *The Conservative Intellectual Movement in America Since 1945* (New York: Basic Books, 1976); Thomas E. Woods, Jr., "American Conservatism and the Old Republic," *Modern Age* 49 (Fall 2007): 434–42.

83. Russell Kirk and James McClellan, *The Political Principles of Robert A. Taft* (New York: Fleet Press, 1967), 163.

84. Richard M. Weaver, "The South and the American Union," in *The Southern Essays of Richard M. Weaver*, eds. George M. Curtis III and James J. Thompson, Jr. (Indianapolis: Liberty Press, 1987), 247.

85. Robert Nisbet, *Conservatism: Dream and Reality* (Minneapolis: University of Minnesota Press, 1986), 103.

86. Robert Nisbet, *Twilight of Authority* (Indianapolis: Liberty Press, 2000 [1975]), 174. On Nisbet, militarism, and conservatism, see Thomas E. Woods, Jr., "Twilight of Conservatism," *The American Conservative*, December 5, 2005, available at http://www.amconmag.com/article/2005/dec/05/00017/

CHAPTER 6

1. R. M. Hartwell, "The Standard of Living Controversy: A Summary," in *The Industrial Revolution*, ed. R. M. Hartwell (New York: Barnes & Noble, 1970), 178.

2. Johan Norberg, *In Defense of Global Capitalism* (Washington, D.C.: Cato Institute, 2003), 26, 29, 31.

3. John Larrivee, "It's Not the Markets, It's the Morals: How Excessively Blaming Markets Undermines Civil Society," in *Back on the Road to Serfdom: The Resurgence of Statism*, ed. Thomas E. Woods, Jr. (Wilmington, DE: Intercollegiate Studies Institute, 2010).

4. Ibid.

5. Ibid.

6. What follows is indebted to George Reisman, *Capitalism* (Ottawa, IL: Jameson Books, 1996), ch. 14.

7. Of course, if the public demands only 3,000 or even the original 1,000 widgets, then still less labor will be necessary in this line of production, and more will be released for the production of other goods.

8. See W. Michael Cox and Richard Alm, *Myths of Rich and Poor: Why We're Better Off Than We Think* (New York: Basic Books, 1999).

9. Some have tried to argue that the decision to take a factory job was not in fact a free one, and that the enclosure movement had actually forced people into factory work. This claim is false. See Walter Block, Marcus Epstein, and Thomas E. Woods, Jr., "Chesterton and Belloc: A Critique," *Independent Review* 11 (Spring 2007): 579–94.

10. Reisman, *Capitalism*, 662–63; idem, "The Free Market and Job Safety," *Mises Daily*, January 20, 2003, available at http://mises.org/daily/1143

11. I owe this formulation to economist David R. Henderson.

12. Ludwig von Mises, *Human Action: A Treatise on Economics* (Auburn, AL: Ludwig von Mises Institute, 1998 [1949]), 615.

13. Cited in Jim Rose, "Child Labor, Family Income, and the Uruguay Round," *Quarterly Journal of Austrian Economics* 1 (Winter 1998): 78.

14. Ibid.

15. Norberg, *In Defense of Global Capitalism*, 199.

16. Ibid., 200.

17. Theda Skocpol, "America's First Social Security System: The Expansion of Benefits for Civil War Veterans," in Theda Skocpol, *Social Policy in the United States: Future Possibilities in Historical Perspective* (Princeton: Princeton University Press, 1995), 63; cited in Robert Higgs, "The Welfare State and the Promise of Protection," Mises Daily, August 24, 2009, available at http://mises.org/daily/3634

18. Charles Murray, *Losing Ground: American Social Policy 1950-1980*, 10th anniversary ed. (New York: Basic Books, 1994), 58.

19. Ibid., 205–11.

20. David T. Beito, *From Mutual Aid to the Welfare State: Fraternal Societies and Social Services, 1890-1967* (Chapel Hill: University of North Carolina Press, 2000); Marvin Olasky, *The Tragedy of American Compassion* (Washington, D.C.: Regnery Gateway, 1992).

21. James Rolph Edwards, "The Costs of Public Income Redistribution and Private Charity," *Journal of Libertarian Studies* 21 (Summer 2007): 8–9.

22. Thanks to Professor Anthony Carilli of Hampden-Sydney College for relating this incident.

23. Alexis de Tocqueville, *Democracy in America*, vol. II, trans. Henry Reeve (New York: Colonial Press, 1900 [1840]), 114–15.

24. Charles Murray, *In Pursuit: Of Happiness and Good Government* (New York: Simon & Schuster, 1989).

25. Ibid.

26. Edwards, "Costs of Public Income Redistribution," 13.

27. Sheldon Richman, *Tethered Citizens: Time to Repeal the Welfare State* (Fairfax, VA: Future of Freedom Foundation, 2001), 94.

28. Quoted in ibid., 38.

29. James L. Payne, *Overcoming Welfare* (New York: Basic Books, 1998), 72–73.

30. Howard Husock, *America's Trillion-Dollar Housing Mistake: The Failure of American Housing Policy* (Chicago: Ivan R. Dee, 2003), 15–17, 99.

31. Ibid., 17–18.

32. Ibid., 15–16.

33. On the problems and fallacies of Section 8, see ibid., ch. 3.

34. Chris Edwards and Tad DeHaven, "Department of Housing and Urban Development: Proposed Spending Cuts," available at http://www.downsizinggovernment.org/hud/spending-cuts

35. This and the anecdotes and statistics that follow are drawn, unless otherwise indicated, from Kathy Kristof, "The Great College Hoax," *Forbes*, February 2, 2009.

36. Ibid.

37. Ron Lieber, "Placing the Blame as Students Are Buried in Debt," *New York Times*, May 28, 2010.

38. See Gary Wolfram, "Making College More Expensive: The Unintended Consequences of Federal Tuition Aid," Cato Institute *Policy Analysis*, January 25, 2005.

39. "A Remarkable Comparison: Affordable Student Loans vs. Affordable Housing," Mish's Global Economic Trend Analysis, October 29, 2009, available at http://globaleconomicanalysis.blogspot.com/2009/10/remarkable-comparison-affordable.html

40. Neal McCluskey, "Higher Education Policy," in *Cato Handbook for Policymakers*, 7th ed. (Washington, D.C.: Cato Institute, 2008), 238.

41. Miguel Palacios, "Human Capital Contracts: 'Equity-Like' Instruments for Financing Higher Education," Cato Institute *Policy Analysis*, December 16, 2002, available at http://www.cato.org/pubs/pas/pa462.pdf

42. Neal P. McCluskey, *Feds in the Classroom* (Lanham, MD: Rowman & Littlefield, 2007), 116.

43. McCluskey, "Higher Education Policy," 238.

44. McCluskey, *Feds in the Classroom*, 52.

45. Ibid., 84.

46. Ron Paul, *The Revolution: A Manifesto* (New York: Grand Central, 2008), 76–77.

47. William C. Mitchell and Randy T. Simmons, *Beyond Politics: Markets, Welfare, and the Failure of Bureaucracy* (Boulder, CO.: Westview Press, 1994), 62.

48. Fredrik Reinfeldt, "The New Swedish Model: A Reform Agenda for Growth and the Environment," speech delivered at the London School of Economics, February 26, 2008.

49. Duncan Currie, "Sweden's Quiet Revolution," National Review Online, September 30, 2010, available at http://www.nationalreview.com/articles/248263/sweden%E2%80%99s-quiet-revolution-duncan-currie. The quotation is Currie's.

50. Markus Bergstrom, "The Scandinavian Welfare Myth Revisited," *Mises Daily*, March 9, 2010, available at http://mises.org/daily/4146

51. Ibid.

52. Stefan Karlsson, "The Sweden Myth," *Mises Daily*, August 7, 2006, available at http://mises.org/daily/2259

53. Per Bylund, correspondence with the author, November 8, 2010.

54. This discussion of these entrepreneurs is indebted to Larry Schweikart, *The Entrepreneurial Adventure: A History of Business in the United States* (Fort Worth: Harcourt College Publishers, 1999); and Burton W. Folsom, *The Myth of the Robber Barons: A New Look at the Rise of Big Business in America* (Herndon, VA: Young America's Foundation, 1991).

55. Thomas J. DiLorenzo, "The Origins of Antitrust: An Interest-Group Perspective," *International Review of Law and Economics* 5 (June 1985): 73–90.

56. Gabriel Kolko, *The Triumph of Conservatism: A Reinterpretation of American History, 1900-1916* (New York: Free Press, 1963), 5, 40–41.

57. Ibid., 26-56.

58. Murray N. Rothbard, "The Rise of Big Business: The Failure of Trusts and Cartels," available at http://mises.org/media/4463

59. Alfred D. Chandler, Jr., *Strategy and Structure: Chapters in the History of the American Industrial Enterprise* (Cambridge: Massachusetts Institute of Technology, 1962), 32–33.

60. Murray N. Rothbard, *The Betrayal of the American Right*, ed. Thomas E. Woods, Jr. (Auburn, AL: Ludwig von Mises Institute, 2007), 22.

61. Butler Shaffer's important study *In Restraint of Trade: The Business Campaign Against Competition, 1918–1938* (Lewisburg, PA: Bucknell University Press, 1997) provides all the details.

62. DiLorenzo, "The Origins of Antitrust," 82.

63. Reisman, *Capitalism*, 399–408.

64. Thomas J. DiLorenzo, *How Capitalism Saved America* (New York: Crown Forum, 2004), 220–22.

65. Steve Forbes and Elizabeth Ames, *How Capitalism Will Save Us* (New York: Crown Business, 2009), 200.

66. Ibid.

67. Walter Adams, "The Role of Competition in the Regulated Industries," in *Antitrust, the Market, and the State: The Contributions of Walter Adams*, eds. James W. Brock and Kenneth G. Elzinga (Armonk, NY: M.E. Sharpe, 1991), 96.

68. On the nonskeds, see Mary Bennett Peterson, *The Regulated Consumer* (Ottawa, IL: Green Hill, 1971), 136–37; Murray N. Rothbard, "Monopoly and Competition," lecture delivered at Brooklyn Polytechnic University, 1986; lecture series available at http://mises.org/media.aspx?action=category&ID=218

69. "Aviation: Death Edict?" *Time*, April 9, 1951.

70. Johan Norberg, *Financial Fiasco* (Washington, D.C.: Cato Institute, 2009), 133.

71. Alan Reynolds, "The Sarbanes-Oxley Tax," *Investor's Business Daily*, March 14, 2005.

72. Forbes and Ames, *How Capitalism Will Save Us*, 182–84.

73. Reynolds, "Sarbanes-Oxley Tax."

74. Sam Peltzman, "The Effects of Automobile Safety Regulation," *Journal of Political Economy* 83 (August 1975): 677–726. Peltzman wrote in 2004, summarizing the work of Alma Cohen and Liran Einav, that "the actual effect of the safety regulation on the death rate is substantially less than it would be if real people behaved like crash dummies....The real-world effect of these laws on highway mortality is substantially less than it should be if there was no offsetting behavior. They conclude that the increased belt usage occasioned by these laws should, in the absence of any behavioral response, have saved more than three times as many lives as were in fact saved." Sam Peltzman, *Regulation and the Natural Progress of Opulence* (Washington, D.C.: AEI-Brookings Joint Center for Regulatory Studies, 2005), 7.

75. Clive Thompson, "Bicycle Helmets Put You at Risk," *New York Times*, December 10, 2006.

76. Thomas J. Kniesner and John D. Leeth, "Abolishing OSHA," *Regulation*, no. 4, 1995, 49.

77. Ibid., 51, 52.

78. Ibid., 55. Worker's comp programs are enforced by government, to be sure, though here again we are simply faced with the common government practice of reducing people's take-home pay and imposing on them a particular configuration of pay and benefits instead of allowing them to decide for themselves.

79. Raymond J. Keating, "Warning: OSHA Can Be Hazardous to Your Health," *The Freeman*, March 1996.

80. Peltzman, *Regulation and the Natural Progress of Opulence*, 4.

81. Ibid., 12–13.

82. Robert P. Murphy, *Chaos Theory* (New York: RJ Communications, 2002), 26–27.

83. Randall G. Holcombe, *Public Policy and the Quality of Life: Market Incentives Versus Government Planning* (Westport, CT: Greenwood, 1995), 116.

84. See "The Sensible Alternative: The Voluntary Provision of Assurance," FDAReview.org, available at http://www.fdareview.org/voluntary_assurance.shtml

85. Glenn Sonnedecker, "Contribution of the Pharmaceutical Profession toward Controlling the Quality of Drugs in the Nineteenth Century," in *Safeguarding the Public: Historical Aspects of Medicinal Drug Control*, ed. J. B. Blake (Baltimore: Johns Hopkins University Press, 1970), 97–111; cited at FDAReview. org, http://www.fdareview.org/voluntary_assurance.shtml

86. On Unocal, see Timothy P. Carney, *The Big Ripoff: How Big Business and Big Government Steal Your Money* (Hoboken, NJ: Wiley, 2006), 177–80.

87. This and the discussion that follows are covered in detail in Murray N. Rothbard, "Government Cartels," lecture delivered at Brooklyn Polytechnic University, 1986; the lecture series is available at http://mises.org/media. aspx?action=category&ID=218

88. Herbert Brean, "Discount Houses Stir Up a $5 Billion Fuss," *Life*, August 9, 1954, 58.

89. Ibid., 53.

90. Ibid., 56.

91. Ibid., 57.

92. I am indebted for this discussion of the estate tax to Carney, *The Big Ripoff*, 164–68.

93. Peltzman, *Regulation and the Natural Progress of Opulence*, 8. This discussion is indebted to the Peltzman treatment of the subject.

94. Ibid., 11.

95. Ibid., 10.

96. For how pollution and other environmental issues would be addressed in a free society, see Murray N. Rothbard, "Law, Property Rights, and Air Pollution," *Cato Journal* 2 (Spring 1982): 55–99, available at http://mises.org/daily/2120

97. This discussion of science is derived from Terence Kealey, *The Economic Laws of Scientific Research* (New York: St. Martin's, 1996). On the displacement of private funding by government funding, see 240ff. On this general subject, see also William N. Butos and Thomas J. McQuade, "Government and Science: A Dangerous Liaison?" *Independent Review* 11 (Fall 2006): 177–208.

98. Kealey, *The Economic Laws of Scientific Research*, 80.

99. Ibid., 240ff. The remainder of this discussion draws on the Kealey text.

100. Ibid., 265.

101. Tom Bethell, *The Politically Incorrect Guide to Science* (Washington, D.C.: Regnery, 2006).

102. People worry about the confluence of drug use and violence, but alcohol use leads to millions of acts of violence every year, and is a major contributing factor to domestic abuse, sexual assault, and murder. A recent study finds alcohol to be the most lethal drug overall. See Associated Press, "Study: Alcohol More Lethal than Heroin, Cocaine," November 1, 2010, available at http://www.rawstory.com/rs/2010/11/study-alcohol-lethal-heroin-cocaine/; Steve Fox, Paul Armentano, and Mason Tvert, *Marijuana Is Safer: So Why Are We Driving People to Drink?* (White River Junction, VT: Chelsea Green, 2009), x. Thanks to Mark Thornton for this latter reference.

103. Associated Press, "AP IMPACT: After 40 years, $1 Trillion, US War on Drugs Has Failed to Meet Any of Its Goals," FoxNews.com, May 13, 2010, available at http://www.foxnews.com/world/2010/05/13/ap-impact-years-trillion-war-drugs-failed-meet-goals/

104. Ibid.

105. This is the contention of economist Bruce L. Benson. Joel Miller, *Bad Trip* (Nashville, Tenn.: WND Books, 2004), 20–21.

106. Ibid., 22.

107. Judge James P. Gray, *Why Our Drug Laws Have Failed and What We Can Do About It: A Judicial Indictment of the War on Drugs* (Philadelphia: Temple University Press, 2001), 25.

108. Ibid., 71.

109. Miller, *Bad Trip*, 88–89; Gray, *Drug Laws*, 95–96.

110. Miller, *Bad Trip*, 37–38.

111. Ibid., 124.

112. Ibid., 126–27; Gray, *Drug Laws*, 118.

113. Miller, *Bad Trip*, 28–29.

114. Gray, *Drug Laws*, 51–52.

115. General Accounting Office, "Drug Control: Heavy Investment in Military Surveillance Is Not Paying Off," September 1993, 18.

116. Miller, *Bad Trip*, 85.

117. Liz Szabo, "Prescriptions Now Biggest Cause of Fatal Drug Overdoses," *USA Today*, September 30, 2010; Katherine Harmon, "Prescription Drug Deaths Increase Dramatically," *Scientific American*, April 6, 2010; see also Marrecca Fiore, "CDC: Prescription Drug Deaths Increase Sharply," AOL Health, June 17, 2010, available at http://www.aolhealth.com/2010/06/17/cdc-prescription-drugs-send-as-many-to-er-as-illegal-drugs/. According to the federal government, "6.9 million individuals aged 12 or older were current (past month) nonmedical users of prescription-type psychotherapeutic drugs (opioid pain relievers, tranquilizers, sedatives, or stimulants) during 2007." National Drug Intelligence Center, National Prescription Drug Threat Assessment 2009, April 2009, available at http://www.justice.gov/ndic/pubs33/33775/execsum.htm. Internal footnote omitted.

118. Gray, *Drug Laws*, 157–58.

119. Ibid., 220–21.

120. Maia Szalavitz, "Drugs in Portugal: Did Decriminalization Work?" *Time*, April 26, 2009.

121. "Incarcerated America," Human Rights Watch Backgrounder, April 2003, available at http://www.hrw.org/legacy/backgrounder/usa/incarceration/

122. Gray, *Drug Laws*, 29–30.

123. Ibid., 45.

124. Miller, *Bad Trip*, 166–67.

125. Gray, *Drug Laws*, 36.

126. Ibid., 52–53.

127. Ibid., 128.

128. Ibid.

129. Ibid., 54.

130. Ibid., 42.

131. Ibid.

132. For the full letter, see http://www.vcl.org/openLetter.html

133. Miller, *Bad Trip*, 179–80.

134. Ibid., 31.

CHAPTER 7

1. Michael D. Tanner, *Leviathan on the Right: How Big Government Conservatism Brought Down the Republican Revolution* (Washington, D.C.: Cato Institute, 2007), 167.

2. Ibid., 93.

3. David Brooks, "How to Reinvent the GOP," *New York Times Magazine*, August 29, 2004.

4. Tanner, *Leviathan on the Right*, 56–57; Dana Milbank, "Kerry and Gingrich Hugging Trees—and (Almost) Each Other," *Washington Post*, April 11, 2007.

5. Peter G. Peterson, *Running on Empty* (New York: Farrar, Straus and Giroux, 2004), 108.

6. W. James Antle, III, "Republicans Against Repeal," *American Spectator*, April 8, 2010.

7. Ibid.

8. John J. DiIulio and Donald F. Kettl, *Fine Print: The Contract with America, Devolution, and the Administrative Realities of American Federalism* (Washington, D.C.: Brookings Institution, 1995), 60.

9. That is not to say that analyses of particular programs in order to justify their elimination are unwelcome; many of them have much to teach us. In this genre I like Martin L. Buchanan, *To Save America: How to Prevent Our Coming Federal Bankruptcy* (BookSurge, 2007).

10. Gary North, "How to Run a Federal Budget Surplus," LewRockwell.com, May 8, 2010, available at http://www.lewrockwell.com/north/north841.html

11. An occasional critic has tried to claim that although the original 13 states may indeed have created the federal government, the later 37 were themselves created by the federal government. This is a misconception. An American state is created by the people, not the federal government. Jefferson himself amplified this point in the controversy over the admission of Missouri. The people of Missouri had drafted a constitution and were applying for admission to the Union. Were they not admitted, Jefferson told them, they would be an independent state. In other words, *their statehood derived from their sovereign people and its drafting of a constitution, not the approval of the federal government.*

12. Professor Barnett initially proposed a vote of three-fourths of the states, but accepted two-thirds as a friendly amendment in a roundtable discussion on the Mike Church Show (Sirius/XM) in early 2010.

13. I believe it was Professor Marshall DeRosa of Florida Atlantic University who first proposed a constitutional amendment whereby a federal law would be repealed if a simple majority of the state attorneys general found it unconstitutional.

14. See Thomas E. Woods, Jr., *33 Questions About American History You're Not Supposed to Ask* (New York: Crown Forum, 2007), ch. 28; Clay S. Conrad, *Jury Nullification: The Evolution of a Doctrine* (Durham, NC: Carolina Academic Press, 1998).

15. Hampden (pseud.), *The Genuine Book of Nullification* (Charleston, SC: E.J. Van Brunt, 1831), 1. Emphasis added.

16. Jeff Riggenbach, "Samuel Edward Konkin III," *Mises Daily*, July 29, 2010, available at http://mises.org/daily/4597. Emphasis in original.

17. Taylor Barnes, "America's 'Shadow Economy' Is Bigger than You Think—And Growing," *Christian Science Monitor*, November 12, 2009, available at http://www.csmonitor.com/Business/2009/1112/americas-shadow-economy-is-bigger-than-you-think-and-growing; Richard W. Rahn, "New Underground Economy," *Washington Times*, December 9, 2009.

18. "Doug Casey: Exception Among Equities," *Gold Report*, August 19, 2010, available at http://www.kitco.com/ind/GoldReport/aug192010.html

19. Murray N. Rothbard, "Repudiate the National Debt," *Mises Daily*, January 16, 2004, available at http://mises.org/article.aspx?Id=1423

20. Robert Nozick, *Anarchy, State, and Utopia* (New York: Basic Books, 1974), 290–92.

21. Niall Ferguson, "America, the Fragile Empire," *Dallas Morning News*, March 19, 2010.

22. Kevin Dowd, "The Real Financial Crisis—and After," *Mises Daily*, April 9, 2010, available at http://mises.org/daily/4218

Index

About the Author

THOMAS E. WOODS, JR. (B.A., Harvard; M.A., M.Phil., Ph.D., Columbia) is a senior fellow of the Ludwig von Mises Institute in Auburn, Alabama. He is the author of eleven books, including two *New York Times* bestsellers: *The Politically Incorrect Guide to American History* and *Meltdown: A Free-Market Look at Why the Stock Market Collapsed, the Economy Tanked, and Government Bailouts Will Make Things Worse.* His other titles include *Nullification: How to Resist Federal Tyranny in the 21st Century*, *Who Killed the Constitution?: The Fate of American Liberty from World War I to George W. Bush* (with Kevin R. C. Gutzman), and *33 Questions About American History You're Not Supposed to Ask.* Woods's books have been translated into Italian, Spanish, Polish, German, Portuguese, French, Croatian, Slovak, Czech, Russian, Korean, Japanese, and Chinese.

Woods won the $50,000 first prize in the 2006 Templeton Enterprise Awards for his book *The Church and the Market: A Catholic Defense of the Free Economy.* An earlier title, *The Church Confronts Modernity* (Columbia University Press, 2004; paperback 2007), earned praise from the *American Historical*

Review, the *Journal of American History*, and the *Journal of American Studies*, among other prominent historical and theological journals.

Woods served as editor and wrote the introduction for five additional books, including *Back on the Road to Serfdom: The Resurgence of Statism*, *We Who Dared to Say No to War: American Antiwar Writing from 1812 to Now* (with Murray Polner), and Orestes Brownson's 1875 classic *The American Republic*. He co-edited an 11-volume encyclopedia, *Exploring American History: From Colonial Times to 1877*. He is also a contributing editor of *The American Conservative* magazine.

Woods has appeared on FOX News Channel, MSNBC, CNBC, Bloomberg Television, FOX Business Network, and C-SPAN, among other outlets. He has been a guest on hundreds of radio programs, including *The Dennis Miller Show*, *The Michael Reagan Show*, *The Michael Medved Show*, and National Public Radio's *Morning Edition* and *On Point*.

Woods lives in Topeka, Kansas, with his wife and four daughters, and maintains a website at TomWoods.com.

THE MAKING OF A
CATHOLIC PRESIDENT

THE MAKING OF A CATHOLIC PRESIDENT

....

KENNEDY vs. NIXON 1960

Shaun A. Casey

OXFORD
UNIVERSITY PRESS
2009

OXFORD
UNIVERSITY PRESS

Oxford University Press, Inc., publishes works that further
Oxford University's objective of excellence
in research, scholarship, and education.

Oxford   New York
Auckland   Cape Town   Dar es Salaam   Hong Kong   Karachi
Kuala Lumpur   Madrid   Melbourne   Mexico City   Nairobi
New Delhi   Shanghai   Taipei   Toronto

With offices in
Argentina   Austria   Brazil   Chile   Czech Republic   France   Greece
Guatemala   Hungary   Italy   Japan   Poland   Portugal   Singapore
South Korea   Switzerland   Thailand   Turkey   Ukraine   Vietnam

Published by Oxford University Press, Inc.
198 Madison Avenue, New York, New York 10016

www.oup.com

Oxford is a registered trademark of Oxford University Press

Library of Congress Cataloging-in-Publication Data
Casey, Shaun.
The making of a Catholic president : Kennedy vs. Nixon 1960 / Shaun A. Casey.
    p.   cm.
Includes index.
ISBN 978-0-19-537448-3
1. Presidents—United States—Election—1960.   2. Kennedy, John F. (John Fitzgerald),
1917–1963.   3. Nixon, Richard M. (Richard Milhous), 1913–1994.   4. United States—
Politics and government—1961–1963.   5. Catholics—United States—Political
activity—History—20th century.   6. Religion and politics—United States—
History—20th century.   7. Anti-Catholicism—United States—History—20th century.
8. Kennedy, John F. (John Fitzgerald), 1917–1963—Religion.   I. Title.
E837.7.C38 2009
322'.10973—dc22   2008030375

9 8 7 6 5 4 3 2 1
Printed in the United States of America
on acid-free paper

To my beloved Ann

Acknowledgments

....

I would never have completed this book without the support of three remarkable institutions. First and foremost, Wesley Theological Seminary, where I teach, has been supportive in research funding, sabbatical leave, and moral support. I am most appreciative of the support of President David McAllister Wilson and Dean Bruce Birch. Second, the Center for American Progress (CAP), under the leadership of John Podesta, is the rare Washington-based progressive think tank that takes religion seriously as a powerful force in American democracy. I thank John, Melody Barnes, and Sally Steenland for providing me with a home away from home as a Visiting Fellow at CAP. Third, the Wabash Center for Teaching and Learning in Theology and Religion at Wabash College provided me with the initial research funding to launch this project. My thanks are due to Lucinda Huffaker, Ted Hiebert, and Elizabeth Bounds for their early encouragement.

Over the years I have been the beneficiary of so many rich conversation partners on matters political and theological. I would like to thank my siblings—Karen Casey, Michael Casey, Neil Casey, and Rita Casey—and my parents, Melba and Paul Casey, for a lively household growing up and for their ongoing love, friendship, and debate. Many of my teachers, friends, and colleagues deserve special mention: Malaika Amon, Mark Bennington, Sathi Clarke, Brent Coffin, Harvey Cox, John Crossan, Eric Crump, Missy Daniel, E. J. Dionne, Mark Elrod, Francis Fiorenza, Mark Hamilton, Don Haymes, Bryan Hehir, Craig Hill, Stanley Hoffmann, Jan and Richard Hughes, William Stacy Johnson, John Kerry, Helmut Koester, Michael Koppel, Kim Lawton,

Lemoine Lewis, Bill Martin, Charles Mattewes, Mike McCurry, Ivan Mills, Beverly Mitchell, Mary Moschella, Richard Neustadt, Amy Oden, Stacy Patty, Ralph Potter, Robert Randolph, Ann Riggs, Maureen Shea, Yonce Shelton, Kendall Soulen, Peggy Steinfels, Peter Steinfels, Krister Stendahl, Ronald Thiemann, Sondra Wheeler, and Preston Williams.

I owe a special debt of gratitude to my editor, Theo Calderara, whose wisdom, skill, and patience shepherded me throughout the writing of this book.

Last, but not least, I thank my two children, Paul and Sarah, for their patience and understanding, and my wife, Ann, who has endured all manner of nonsense and whose love continues to sustain me.

CONTENTS

THE MAKING OF A
CATHOLIC PRESIDENT

1

THE GHOST OF
AL SMITH

....

Sargent Shriver was in a tough spot. It was the middle of July 1956, just days before the Democratic National Convention, and Shriver was on a mission on behalf of his father-in-law, Joseph P. Kennedy. Shriver had the unenviable task of convincing a recalcitrant Adlai Stevenson that John F. Kennedy should be his running mate in the upcoming presidential election. Shriver had hoped to have the full three-hour flight from Boston to Chicago to work on Stevenson, but Stevenson was making him wait in the back of the plane. Now, he had 10 minutes to make his pitch. He made the most of it.[1]

His assignment was to take Stevenson's temperature on JFK's potential candidacy. Kennedy had launched a public relations campaign to be named as Stevenson's running mate. But Stevenson was also in a difficult position. He was not eager to be beholden to Joseph Kennedy, yet could not risk alienating him and losing his financial support.[2] Joseph Kennedy was a man no one wanted to offend. Indeed, immediately after the flight, Shriver wrote a long letter, not to John Kennedy, but to his father. It was clear who was in charge.

Shriver made his case, and Stevenson expressed three concerns: rumors of John's poor health, Joseph Kennedy's public objections to his son's candidacy, and Kennedy's Catholicism. Shriver assured Stevenson that Kennedy had been cleared by his doctors and that he had the support of his entire family. The religion issue was much more difficult. This cycle of politicking had been set off by a small but telling encounter between Kennedy aide Ted Sorensen and journalist Theodore White, who would

3

later become famous as the author of *The Making of the President 1960*. While on assignment for *Collier's* magazine before the 1956 Democratic convention, White visited Sorensen and passed along the gossip that Stevenson was thinking about choosing a Catholic running mate and that Kennedy and Robert Wagner were under consideration.[3] Sorensen leaped into action and produced an eight-page memorandum on how choosing a Catholic would help the Democrats to defeat Eisenhower. It was released through John Bailey, the chair of the Connecticut Democratic Party, in order to disguise its origins in the Kennedy brain trust. Stevenson received a copy of the Bailey Memo from his aide Newton Minow. The memorandum, entitled "The Catholic Vote in 1952 and 1956," was a brilliant piece of political strategy, mixing objective analysis with bold assertions of Kennedy's assets.[4] Sorensen argued that the Catholic vote was large and powerful because of the concentration of Catholics in 14 states with 261 electoral votes and because Catholics turned out to vote in greater proportion than did non-Catholics. In 1940, 13 of these states went Democratic. Without them, Roosevelt would have lost. But in the next two presidential elections, fewer of these states went Democratic, and in 1952 Eisenhower carried them all for the first Republican victory in 24 years. In 1952, Catholic voters made up roughly a quarter of the electorate, and they had split evenly between the two parties. Stopping this slide, Sorensen argued, was a crucial part of any Democratic strategy to regain the White House.

The way to do it was for Democrats to run Catholic candidates. An array of examples from the 1952 election showed that Catholic Democrats running for governor and Congress in these 14 states had significantly outperformed the national ticket. Sorensen then turned his attention to the question of how a Catholic vice presidential nominee might help or hurt the ticket:

> On June 24, 1956 the Gallup Poll Feature was headlined "Qualified Catholic Could Be President." Nearly three out of four respondents said they would vote for a well-qualified Catholic nominated by their party for *the Presidency itself*. Of those who thought they would be opposed, a large share lived in the South—and if one of three Democrats stayed home (or even voted Republican) in the South due to a nominee's religious affiliation, few if any Southern electoral votes would be lost, even though Democratic margins in several states might be diminished. A large share of the remainder appeared to be Republicans who would not support the Democratic ticket under any circumstances, and northern "liberal intellectuals" who will certainly vote Democratic without regard to the Vice-President's religion.

In short, even a Catholic nominee for President would be judged by most people on his qualifications for the office—and it is that a Democratic Catholic Vice-Presidential nominee, though admittedly prejudices would be stirred, would lose no electoral votes for the ticket simply because a handful of Southerners or Republicans would not support him. Particularly in the key states and cities where he might be expected to concentrate his campaigning, his religion would be irrelevant to most.[5]

But this confident conclusion hardly emerged flawlessly from the data. And a larger question still loomed in the person of Al Smith.

In 1928, Smith had become the first Catholic to run for president on a major party ticket. He was trounced in the general election, and the loss was widely attributed to his religion. The memo addressed the Smith question directly. Marshalling voting data and historical analysis, Sorensen concluded that it was a myth that Smith lost simply because he was a Catholic. But the myth remained potent in the popular political analysis of the day.

The memo ended with questions: Has the Democratic era ended? Has the party permanently lost its political base among Catholics and immigrants in large northern cities? The conclusion was that a Democratic vice presidential candidate could recover the losses in these constituencies and begin a new era of Democratic victories.

In addition to having John Bailey release this memo to the public, the Kennedy camp circulated it widely among journalists, including David Broder, then with *Congressional Quarterly*, and Fletcher Knebel, who two years later would write a flattering article on Kennedy for *Look* magazine.[6] In 1960, *U.S. News and World Report* would print the memo virtually unedited.[7] The height of this stealth campaign for the second slot on the Democratic ticket was an anonymous article in the popular glossy Catholic magazine *Jubilee*. In April 1956, its editor, Robert L. Reynolds, wrote to Kennedy and asked him to contribute an article on the Catholic vote.[8] Kennedy replied that the only way he could fulfill this request would be for Sorensen to write it and for the magazine to print it under a pseudonym.[9] Reynolds agreed and the July–August issue of *Jubilee* ran a version of the Bailey Memo as "The Catholic Vote" signed by "Potomacus."

The JFK camp shrewdly used the media to address Kennedy's Catholicism and to create political leverage to enhance his chances of securing the nomination. The idea was to create public pressure on Stevenson to name Kennedy to the ticket. They also signaled their impulse to address the controversy over his Catholicism rationally with empirical arguments anchored in polling and past election data. Kennedy's advisors sought to debunk the idea that Al Smith's Catholicism was his undoing and thus undermine the conventional wisdom that a Catholic could not be elected to national office. The Bailey Memo did not directly address the arguments that would soon emerge among Protestant intellectuals and leaders that the very nature of the Catholic church and its doctrines made Catholics unfit for national office. But in 1956, these arguments were not fully formed. For now, they just needed to persuade Adlai Stevenson.

Shriver reported that Stevenson was cagey when the conversation turned to the Catholic question. Stevenson believed that Al Smith's loss had been misinterpreted. He felt that it was not Smith's Catholicism, but the combination of his Tammany Hall connections and his cigar-smoking, derby-hat-wearing, big-city, anti-Prohibition orientations that led to his defeat. Shriver then discreetly asked if Stevenson had seen the recent study on the "Catholic issue," meaning the Bailey Memo. Stevenson had seen it and expressed great interest in its contents. "He observed that the statistics in such a report were never complete and so many other factors were always present in political campaigns," Shriver wrote. Such things could never be more than educated guesses.

Stevenson then outlined the various roles that he wanted the vice president to play, without making any suggestion that Kennedy was his choice. Shriver mentioned that, while in Boston, Stevenson had suggested that "the convention would give serious attention and great deliberation to the choice of the V-P." Shriver pressed the issue. Didn't Stevenson believe that the nominee, not the convention, should pick the vice presidential candidate? Stevenson agreed, but having opened up the possibility of throwing the choice to the convention, he would let his staff work something out. Shriver wasn't sure precisely what Stevenson had in mind.

Shriver suggested on the spot that John Kennedy would be capable of generating a basic campaign strategy for Stevenson's staff to evaluate his political skills. Stevenson remarked that Kennedy would make a powerful contrast with Vice President Richard M. Nixon on the campaign trail. The country would have to wait four years before this contest would emerge, but Stevenson's assessment proved to be prophetic.

Shriver concluded his long play-by-play epistle to his father-in-law by saying that it was quite a 10-minute conversation, but he was not able to burrow for facts. In the end, his mission was neither an absolute failure nor an absolute success. On the one hand, Stevenson had held him at arm's length, and he did not fully embrace the thesis of the

Bailey Memo. On the other hand, Stevenson did not reject Kennedy outright, and he did signal what in fact would be his method of selection of his running mate.[10]

The Shriver-Stevenson episode is revealing in several ways. First of all, Joseph Kennedy had a vital stake in promoting his son as the vice presidential candidate in 1956. Regardless of the outcome of the election, John Kennedy would be well positioned for the presidency in the future. After writing to his father-in-law, Shriver called Ted Sorensen and told him the details of the conversation. Four days later, Shriver would write to his brother-in-law John Kennedy and tell him that Joseph Kennedy had replied to his initial missive, and thus Shriver was sending John a copy of the original letter.[11] All parties were reporting to Joseph Kennedy.

But most important, the episode foreshadowed the role that religion would play four years later. By producing and releasing the Bailey Memo, the Kennedy camp showed that it saw overcoming the legacy of Al Smith as the central political issue he faced. And by sending Sargent Shriver on this errand straight to the nominee, it showed that it would engage it directly.

Three weeks after this conversation, Stevenson shocked convention delegates by throwing open the selection of his running mate to the convention itself. While Kennedy had been given a hint that this was a possibility, it seems that his camp was surprised by this move. It is certainly plausible that Stevenson felt that throwing the vice presidential selection to the convention would give him a way to avoid naming Kennedy to the ticket without offending Joseph Kennedy. He could have the Kennedy money with fewer strings attached.

With only one day's notice, Kennedy launched a campaign to secure the second spot on the ballot. Tennessee senator Estes Kefauver, who had been Stevenson's principal rival in the Democratic primaries, narrowly emerged as the winner on the third ballot. In the long run, this proved to be a very good outcome for Kennedy. By narrating the film that opened the convention, giving the main nominating speech for Stevenson, and almost defeating Kefauver in the race for the vice presidential nomination, Kennedy was well placed for a run in 1960 without carrying any negative political baggage that could come with being on the losing ticket in 1956. As he told his aide David Powers shortly after the November election, "with only 48 hours work and a handful of supporters I came within 20 and a half votes of winning the vice presidential nomination. If I work hard for four years I can pick up all the marbles."[12]

From the outset, Kennedy's Catholicism was the largest roadblock on his path to the Oval Office. In the period from 1956 through the end of 1959, as he sought to become the first Roman Catholic president in America's history, Kennedy pursued a variety of strategies to address his faith. Soon after the 1956 convention, many parties within American Christianity began a boisterous debate about the role of the Catholic church in American public life and about the prospects for a Catholic president. The intersection of Kennedy's early strategy on religion and the cacophony of religious voices in this period produced powerful reactions that would reverberate four years later. Three story lines—Kennedy's religion, Nixon's response, and the debates among Protestants—formed a combustible mix.

Both Robert Kennedy and John Kennedy were active in the 1956 election. Robert traveled with Stevenson throughout the fall campaign, observing later that it was a disastrous operation. John stumped tirelessly for Stevenson, visiting 24 states and giving over 150 speeches.[13] After his tantalizingly close encounter with the second slot on the national ticket, Kennedy and his staff embarked on an ambitious plan to lay the groundwork for the 1960 presidential nomination. Sorensen compiled another memo, analyzing the 1956 results in light of the hypothesis of the Bailey Memo, testing the thesis that local Catholic Democratic candidates would outpoll a national ticket without a Catholic, and setting out an initial strategy for 1960. Kennedy was clearly running, and addressing the religious issue, as they called it, was central to this strategy.

Sorensen's analysis of the 1956 returns confirmed the Bailey Memo's argument. Dwight D. Eisenhower continued to win alarming numbers of New Deal Catholics, yet state and local Catholic Democratic candidates outpolled the top of the ticket.[14] After quoting several national political pundits, the memo asked, "What assets does JFK have to distinguish himself?" There were three answers. First, he was the only politician who had worked every state delegation extensively. Second, he had unusual advantages, such as a Pulitzer Prize, being a war hero, a 14-year congressional record, and a 75% share of the vote in his last election. Finally, while other candidates might be able to win either the nomination or the election, he was the only one who could win both.

Then, Sorensen discussed JFK's handicaps and hurdles. Fourth among the six numbered issues was religion. It would hurt him some in the South, among Republicans, and also with some liberals, but Sorensen, showing more than a little naïveté, felt that liberal suspicions had been answered. But the last line under religion in the memo was simply "get it out"—deal with it and deal with it directly.[15]

This emerging strategy tracked with several tactics that Kennedy had employed earlier in his political career. Kennedy had made a modest number of speeches dealing with religion in the two years prior to the 1956 convention. In a speech at St. Michael's College in Vermont, Kennedy outlined the role that Christianity played in the West's struggle to contain the spread of Communism. While it was a thoroughly pedestrian treatment of the issue, he did highlight the role of the moral struggle against totalitarianism that the church played, invoking John Cardinal Newman's prediction of a stern encounter between the forces of good—and the church—against its opponents:

> But in matters of fundamental moral principles, our experience in Indo-China should conclusively demonstrate to us that in the long run our cause will be stronger if we adhere to those basic principles which have guided this nation since its inception. We cannot overlook the moral and ideological basis of our own policies and of the struggles taking place in the world today, in our own emphasis upon the military and physical side of war. If this nation ignores those inner human problems which lie at the root of the great world issues of today, then we cannot succeed in the maintenance of an effective foreign policy no matter how many new weapons of annihilation our modern science can assemble, no matter how many men we pour into the jungles and beachheads all over the world. Unless the United States bases its foreign policy upon a recognition of moral principles and the ideological struggle, we cannot hope to win the hearts and minds of those people of the world whose support is essential to our success.[16]

A year later, Kennedy gave the commencement address at Assumption College in Worcester, Massachusetts, in which he lauded the religious school's function in public life. Citing Catholic sources such as Pope Pius XI, Jacques Maritain, and Cardinal Newman, he again highlighted the church's role in fighting Communism and solving the world's problems. While he did not directly address the barriers to public life that many Catholics like himself faced, he did presuppose that Catholics have a right and a competence to enter into the public debates of the day.[17]

In November 1955, he addressed a Protestant dinner gathering at the North Shore United Church Canvass in which he challenged the notion that the separation of church and state meant that religiously motivated people must shun the public realm. He noted the crucial role that religion played in the work of the founders and concluded that their religious beliefs clearly affected their attitudes toward government.

He then proceeded to laud the Massachusetts Puritans for their role in shaping Massachusetts politics and institutions. He deftly praised John Quincy Adams as an heir to this political tradition in a manner that suggested that Kennedy had his own political future in mind. He told the story of how, in 1803, Senator Adams was appointed as the chair of the select committee to consider a bill to embargo British goods as retaliation for the British seizure of American ships and sailors to serve in the British navy. Passage of the bill would have crippled Massachusetts, home of much of the country's merchant fleet.

Adams brought the bill to the Senate floor and fought for its passage, thus supporting the political enemies of his father and earning scorn in his home state. Kennedy cited Adams as an example of the Puritan conscience for putting principle and the public good above private interest. Kennedy concluded his remarks:

> The example of John Quincy Adams and the Puritan spirit which he represented is worth remembering tonight, as we recall the contributions to our democratic way of life which were made by the religions handed down to us by our forefathers which we—with the help of such efforts as that which brings us together tonight—will hand down to our children. We should do well in our political life to remember the spirit of young Senator Adams, and to remember the principle of Puritan statesmanship which his father had laid down many years before: "The magistrate is the servant not of his own desires, not even of the people, but of his God."[18]

Here, Kennedy advanced an argument that would serve him well in the next five years against many of his Protestant opponents: A commitment to a specific faith tradition empowered a politician to pursue the common good of a society and not simply the private interests of that specific tradition. In fact, he argued, adherence to the high principles of a tradition make it possible for a politician to transcend parochial interests. The irony of the specific example of Adams was that it showed how a Protestant Calvinist resisted the local demands of Massachusetts citizens, including its clergy, and voted for legislation that was in the national interest. This was precisely what many Protestants doubted that Kennedy, as a Roman Catholic, would be capable of doing.

In February 1956, Kennedy accepted an award from the National Conference of Christians and Jews. In his speech, Kennedy chose to highlight a series of politicians who publicly opposed bigotry at some personal and political risk:

Tonight we stand on the threshold of another political campaign—and all of us here tonight share the hope, and pledge our efforts toward its fulfillment, that no racial, religious or other ethnic differences will play any part in this year's campaign. And if they do, I suggest that we take inspiration from the courage displayed by others before us who refused to bow to the passions of prejudice and bigotry.

One such example was a Protestant Senator from the State of Nebraska, George W. Norris. In 1928, as many of you will vividly recall, the Democratic nominee for President, Al Smith, was subjected to a variety of vicious attacks because of his Catholic faith. Governor Smith made it clear that his personal religious views did not affect his belief in the First Amendment, in freedom of religion for all, in the enforcement of our laws and Constitution and in the American public school system; he stated flatly that he recognized no power in the Church which could interfere with any of these matters.[19]

Kennedy went on to chronicle how Norris spoke out forcefully to repudiate the bigotry that Smith encountered. Here, we find the first glimpse of a powerful argument that Kennedy would employ against Richard Nixon. Kennedy attempted to transform the issue of his Catholicism into an issue of religious bigotry. He did not apply it directly to himself in 1956, but at that point the story of Al Smith had led many people to conclude that America was not ready to elect a Catholic. What he did do was deftly imply that Protestants might have to join the fray in defense of a Catholic candidate in the same way that Norris fought for Smith. He was anticipating the opposition he would face on a national ticket.

In the period between 1956 and his formal decision to run in 1960, Kennedy turned to a friend, Father John Wright, for political and religious counsel. Kennedy and Wright had met before World War II while Kennedy was at Harvard and Wright was a diocesan priest in Boston.[20] Both men would experience great success in their respective professions, and their relationship would prove to be a source of insight for Kennedy during his quest for the White House. Wright had been named auxiliary bishop in Boston in 1947 and was named bishop of the new diocese of Worcester, Massachusetts, in 1951. He would be appointed bishop of Pittsburgh in 1959 and in 1969 was made a cardinal. A month later, he was called to Rome and named prefect of the Sacred Congregation for the Clergy, becoming the highest-ranking American in the Vatican at that time. Among pre-Vatican II American bishops, Wright emerged as a type of public intellectual the church so badly needed. Meanwhile, the little-known relationship between the future cardinal and the future president blossomed in Wright's chancery office and apartment in Brighton, Massachusetts, in the heart of Kennedy's congressional district.

Wright aided Kennedy greatly in the early stages of his presidential aspirations. Perhaps Wright's most revealing insight was that Kennedy feared Protestant clergy and distrusted Catholic clergy. Wright argued that Kennedy's fear of Protestant clergy stemmed mainly from his ignorance of the complexities of the Protestant world. Kennedy feared Protestants in "a hundred ways." One of those he feared most was G. Bromley Oxnam, a Methodist bishop who served in Massachusetts and in Washington, D.C., during Kennedy's public life. Wright later recounted:

> During the period of World War II in Boston a great dragon-slayer was the Methodist Bishop G. Bromley Oxnam. Bromley was always pointing out where the long lean hand of Rome might be concealed at any given moment and always crusading for sympathy and understanding and making every effort to offset the fantastic manner in which the local Roman hierarchy were preventing such sympathy and understanding. Now Jack's father had an unholy horror of Oxnam. He looked upon him as a thoroughgoing bigot and as basically anti-Irish and anti-Catholic, and in all probability anti-Democratic Party, even though he might be elaborately backing Roosevelt or Truman or anything else.[21]

While John Kennedy shared his father's dislike of Oxnam, he saw him as someone who had to be placated. When Oxnam returned from a trip to Yugoslavia and announced that Josip Broz Tito had been treating the Catholic bishop Aloysius Stepinac fairly and sympathetically, Kennedy called Wright and told him that someone should meet with Oxnam and set him straight. Wright replied that he met with Oxnam frequently and so had the late William Cardinal O'Connell. Kennedy was incredulous:

> There was a long silence, he didn't believe me. And he said, "O'Connell and Oxnam talked?" I said, "For almost an hour, Jack." And he said, "What did they talk about?" I said, "All manner of things." I said, "I helped Oxnam on with his coat, and he informed me that he never liked to have people help him on with his coat because he had once been a great football player." And I said, "So far as I remember, the conversation with the Cardinal was that Oxnam was telling him that as he was driving through the streets in some of the neighborhoods where there were large numbers of Irish Catholics living, he had seen some anti-semitic [*sic*] chalk remarks on a wall, and he thought the

Cardinal should know about it." And the Cardinal had said, "Oh dear me, that was most unfortunate." It was bad enough for people of Oxnam's age to have those sentiments or the Cardinal's age to have them, but the children shouldn't have them. I said, "That's what they talked about." This sort of thing was unreal to him. He thought they never met. And I think he had a wholly admirable feeling that if he could bring it to pass that we would meet more often, he'd feel the world would be happier and better.[22]

Following Wright's advice, Kennedy would soon reach out to Oxnam and reap significant political benefits as a result. Oxnam was the closest thing to an American Protestant cardinal in the middle of the twentieth century. President of the Council of Methodist Bishops, he had been president of the Federal Council of Churches, the precursor to the National Council of Churches, and a founding member and vice president of Protestants and Other Americans United for Separation of Church and State (POAU). He had pastored a large Methodist church in California and served as a bishop in Omaha, Boston, and Washington. While liberal in theology and politics, he was a notorious critic of the Catholic church. In the late forties, he was a leading Protestant voice against federal aid to parochial schools and the appointment of a U.S. ambassador to the Vatican.[23] Both causes served as focal points for renewed Protestant anti-Catholic activism.

Oxnam also had the distinctly liberal honor of having directly challenged the House Un-American Activities Committee and lived to tell the story. His web of relationships with various liberal organizations from the 1920s forward had made him vulnerable to charges that he was a Communist. In July 1953, Oxnam met in public session before the committee and was vindicated.[24] While Nixon was vice president by this time, Nixon's earlier work on this committee during the Alger Hiss case may have fed Oxnam's hesitancy to flee Kennedy and move to Nixon during the 1960 campaign. Oxnam had been a staunch Stevenson supporter in the fifties and also held Hubert Humphrey in high esteem.

On June 16, 1958, Oxnam and Boston University president Harold Case met with Kennedy for lunch in the Capitol building. Oxnam recorded five typewritten pages in his diary on the meeting.[25] Case had approached the Kennedy Foundation for a gift to Boston University and Senator Kennedy had asked Case whether he knew Oxnam. Kennedy wanted to talk to Oxnam about some important problems facing his candidacy so that he might understand Protestant attitudes. Case told him that he and Oxnam were friends and that Oxnam would be eager to respond to an invitation from Kennedy. Kennedy invited them to his home for lunch, but at the last minute changed the meal to the Capitol since he was spending the morning on the Senate floor trying to fend off Republican attempts to amend his labor bill.

Oxnam was afraid that the meeting might become public, and his fear was almost realized when he and Case entered the Capitol and encountered his friend Glenn Everett, a reporter for the Religion News Service, who always wrote a story when a prominent religious leader met with a senator. Oxnam did not tell Everett where they were heading.[26]

Three months earlier, Kennedy had poked fun at Oxnam at the March 1958 Gridiron dinner, an annual Washington event where journalists and politicians make humorous speeches. Kennedy promised that, if elected president, his first act would be to make Oxnam his personal envoy to the Vatican and have him immediately begin negotiations for a transatlantic tunnel.[27] When Kennedy appeared on that day in June and invited Oxnam and Case into a private dining room, Oxnam asked where his credentials were. Kennedy replied that Oxnam did not need any credentials to eat in the Capitol. Oxnam said that he wasn't talking about those credentials, he was talking about his credentials as ambassador to the Vatican. Kennedy burst out laughing.

Oxnam apologized for not calling him before this meeting. He was afraid that Kennedy might think he was calling to follow up on a questionnaire that POAU had sent and might try to embarrass him. Kennedy put him at ease and said that he knew there were many fundamental questions in the minds of Protestants. He wanted to explore just what they might be.

Oxnam went through the usual Protestant litany of issues: federal funds to parochial schools, hierarchical control of politicians, mandatory attendance of Catholic children in parochial schools, birth control, appointing Catholics to offices over Protestants, his stand on Senator Joseph McCarthy, and his opinion about an ambassador to the Vatican. Kennedy answered his concerns directly.

Kennedy said that the Supreme Court had ruled out direct aid to parochial schools and that was settled. He did not believe that the church hierarchy had any say over elected officials on matters of policy despite what old canon law and papal pronouncements implied. He indicated to Oxnam that he had talked to Wright about these matters at some length. He also noted that American Catholics were free to attend public schools as he and his brothers had. Likewise, he added, it would not be good politics for a Catholic officeholder to hire only Catholics. He pointed to his own staff as proof. Regarding McCarthy, he told Oxnam that his public record was clear and fully known. He was opposed to all that McCarthy stood for. He felt that Eleanor Roosevelt's public statements that Kennedy had not opposed McCarthy were unfair and probably reflected her disagreements with his father. He planned on seeing her and straightening her out on the matter.

Oxnam reminded Kennedy that Harry S Truman had raised the ire of many Protestants when he tried to appoint General Mark Clark as ambassador to the Vatican. They discussed the constitutionality of such an appointment, which was disputed among scholars. Kennedy argued that the constitutionality of the post was not what was most important, but rather the question of whether or not it undermined the American tradition of religious liberty and separation of church and state. He thought that such an appointment would be politically unwise and that was why he would oppose it.

In terms of birth control, he did not believe that the church had anything to say that was binding in terms of "planned parenthood." He did not believe in planned parenthood personally, but it was a matter for the electorate to decide for itself in terms of limiting birth control clinics and the like. While he did not believe in birth control, it was not because his church said so or had any control over him.

Oxnam also recorded his personal impressions of Kennedy:

> There is extraordinary charm about this young man. He is honest about his self-interest. He took it for granted that we understood that he wanted to be president of the United States, and that we understood that the reason why we were there at luncheon was for him to explain his views upon some subjects and to ask questions. He gave no evidence of the heavy physical strain under which he labors. He had been in Wyoming the day before and had flown back through the night, getting in at four or five in the morning, and yet here he was on the Senate floor defending a most important bill and winning apparently. There is a boyish quality about him. But back of him lies war experience and excellent education.
>
> I found him a gentleman, honest, unashamed of wanting something as a politician, realistic in his political outlook, basically liberal, I think, somewhat puzzled by the fact that an American should be facing problems in the matter of political ambition because he belonged to a particular church, but I think down underneath well aware of what the church has done and is doing in certain controls.[28]

At the end of the meal, Oxnam asked him how much of the conversation he could share with the Council of Methodist Bishops. Kennedy said he was free to share anything he had said, but he also asked Oxnam to be discreet since he was running for reelection and that he would like to talk to Oxnam more on these questions in the future.

Kennedy's future relationship with Oxnam would be complicated with many twists and turns. Oxnam would invite Kennedy to speak to the Council of Methodist Bishops in Washington in 1959. Yet immediately after his public announcement of his decision to run in January 1960, Oxnam would express doubts about Kennedy to the national press.[29]

On the other hand, if the Democrats would nominate Stevenson with Kennedy in the second slot, they would sweep the nation. Yet he felt the Democrats would probably not be smart enough to do that. Kennedy had a certain charm which when combined with his courage and competency would make him a formidable candidate. Humphrey impressed Oxnam more, but he did not think he had a chance to win the nomination.

In July 1958, Kennedy wrote Oxnam a note to thank him for the lunch they had shared. Kennedy added that he hoped they would have more such opportunities in the future, and he encouraged Oxnam to get in touch at any time concerning any questions he might have.[30] Oxnam responded that he counted it a high privilege to meet Kennedy and appreciated "your frank and illuminating conversation." Oxnam assured Kennedy that he would not hesitate to contact the senator should important matters arise.[31] It appears the two made a positive political and personal connection that would blossom the following year.

The Oxnam connection paid some valuable public relations dividends on April 15, 1959, when he invited Kennedy to address 51 bishops of the Methodist church, who were meeting in Washington for their twice-annual Council of Methodist Bishops. Ever the political operator, Oxnam, who chaired the council, had arranged meetings with President Eisenhower, Vice President Nixon, Chief Justice Earl Warren, Secretary of Defense Neil McElroy, Secretary of State John Foster Dulles, Senator Hubert Humphrey, Senator Lyndon Johnson, and Kennedy. He apparently sent each person a list of questions that Oxnam wanted them to address. Despite meeting with such a long list of Washington elites, only Kennedy's session generated national public attention. The April 27 issue of *Life* magazine ran a half-page photo of a youthful Kennedy entering a Senate meeting room filled with somber Methodist bishops. The headline read, "Jack Kennedy Takes Two Tough Tests," and the subheadline stated, "Methodists Give Him Fair Grade, Wisconsin Voter an 'A.' "

The article called the meeting a critical test for the front-running candidate for the 1960 Democratic nomination. In submitting to the "going over" by the bishops, Kennedy directly confronted the leaders of the 10 million-member church, the country's largest Protestant denomination, and answered their questions. Kennedy said that he believed in a strict separation of church and state and opposed the use of federal funds for parochial schools and the appointment of an ambassador to the Vatican. He left a favorable impression on a tough audience.

Time magazine, which also ran a flattering photo, called the meeting a modern version of Daniel entering the lion's den. One bishop reported that Kennedy did not win over any of the hardliners, who strongly opposed a Catholic candidate, but some in the room did warm to him. The *New York Times* and the *Washington Post and Times Herald* also covered the 40-minute meeting. According to these reports, Kennedy emerged smiling and said, "There was a general discussion of public questions. It was very pleasant."[32]

Oxnam's diary accounts of these meetings are revealing.[33] After a glowing entry about the bishops' meeting with Hubert Humphrey, Oxnam described their discomfort when they arrived at the Old Senate Office Building to meet Kennedy and discovered the news photographers there. They refused to let the photographers into the meeting and thus the shots that made the press were taken peeking into the room, which heightened the inquisitional effect of the pictures, much to Oxnam's chagrin. Oxnam introduced Kennedy as cordially as he knew how but felt that Kennedy was on edge. Oxnam felt that Kennedy viewed the bishops with suspicion, which was unwarranted in Oxnam's view. He thought the bishops were eager to meet Kennedy and approached him with respect. Oxnam noted that, although Kennedy was young, he took up the questions clearly, succinctly, and courageously. Oxnam did observe with some irritation that Kennedy went out of his way to point out that he was a strong Catholic from a strong Catholic family. Afterward, Oxnam walked down the hall with Kennedy and explained the bishops' attitude to him. He hoped he had overcome any misgivings Kennedy might have harbored.

The next day, the Methodist entourage met with Vice President Nixon in the Capitol.[34] Oxnam noted that Nixon was well dressed and in complete control of himself. He outlined the critical issues that America faced in world affairs with considerable ability through a calm recitation of the facts without any appeal to emotion. Oxnam believed that his performance, beginning with a discussion of Berlin and moving to why America should not recognize China, illustrated Nixon's extraordinary strength. Yet Oxnam gained the impression that Nixon was a man who might "sell his abilities to the highest bidder and will do a first rate job." He was skilled, but Oxnam had doubts about his fundamental interests being too selfish, an impression shared by others.

In March 1960, Oxnam handicapped the presidential race in his diary. He described the field as it stood as an increasingly difficult political situation.[35] He did not question Nixon's ability, but he saw Nixon's political ascent as a series of strokes of good fortune. He was very uncomfortable with Nixon's tactics in his House and Senate races. He seemed too dedicated to political expediency and lacking in principles.

Wright related a conversation that Kennedy had with the presiding bishop of the Episcopal church, Henry Knox Sherrill. The two were on the same boat returning from Europe sometime before the 1960 convention. Kennedy mentioned that they had several conversations. He told Wright that Sherrill didn't think what "you people" think he thinks at all. Wright replied, "I don't think he thinks what you think I think he thinks at all, Jack." Wright went on to tell Kennedy that he knew Sherrill and had a pretty good idea what Sherrill's opinions were:

> Now all of his conversation indicated that he was very much afraid of what Sherrill thought. He didn't distrust him. In fact, he trusted him to act consistently with his attitudes toward Jack as a baptized Catholic, you see, he trusted him to do that. But he greatly feared what it might prompt him to do, do you see? He even said that. He said, "You can imagine that fellow," he said, "putting out a statement that I was for Franco. He might." I said, "I doubt that he would." I said, "He might have a hard time finding any reason to say so." But it was a fear, alright.[36]

Wright went on to tell Kennedy that Catholic and Protestant leaders were very good friends and that they were in conversation all the time. Wright argued that, while Kennedy understood very well the point of view of the average New England Catholic, he did not understand Protestants at all, and as a result he feared them.[37]

This stark portrait of Kennedy's view of Protestants is remarkable and makes Kennedy's subsequent efforts to reach out to Protestants all the more interesting. Kennedy did not allow his instinct to fear Protestants prevent him from eventually talking to them, and he did not allow the staggering volume of Protestant resistance he would encounter to feed his fear and impede his outreach efforts. Wright astutely observed that this fear led Kennedy to seek ways to placate the discontented Protestants. Here was Kennedy's political pragmatism at work. Rather than seeing the Protestant-Catholic divide as reason for despair, Kennedy saw it as a political problem calling for a strategy. Wright became some-thing of a tour guide and counselor whom Kennedy sought out as he began to contemplate running a national campaign.

Just before the 1960 convention, Kennedy dropped in on Wright in Pittsburgh. Kennedy was stunned to meet some local Protestant politicians who not only supported him in 1960 but had been for him in his brief run for the second slot in 1956. Kennedy was cautious with these local party chieftains because they were Protestants. Wright explained to him that they were Presbyterians of the Ulsterite tradition and while they were Calvinist, rich, and entrenched, many of them were Democrats. Kennedy was surprised.[38]

It is not altogether clear that Kennedy's experience in the 1960 election erased his fear. Wright detailed an episode during Kennedy's presidency when he invited a hundred religious leaders to the White House to talk about civil rights. Wright believed that Kennedy brought them there in order to pacify them in advance of doing any public work on civil rights out of fear that the religious leaders might oppose him. Wright observed that, ironically, all of the leaders were already active in fighting for civil rights.[39]

Under Wright's tutelage, Kennedy, along with his brother Robert, began something of a listening tour of Protestants. Wright relates that the two met with Oxnam, Sherrill, and Paul Blanshard, the general counsel of Protestants and Other Americans United for Separation of Church and State, among others. In each case, there were reasons in Kennedy's mind to doubt that they would ever support his candidacy. Wright's description of this effort is tantalizingly brief.[40] He observed that Robert Kennedy's responses to these Protestants were more per-ceptive than his brother's. The elder brother saw them as men who must be placated in order to prevent them from doing an awful lot of harm, while the younger brother sought to understand what made these men tick. This difference in attitude may account for why later, in the summer of 1960, Robert, who was the campaign manager, heeded Ted Sorensen's advice and hired James Wine of the National Council of Churches and John Cogley of *Commonweal* as full-time staffers to manage the religion issue. It may also explain the decision to make the famous speech in Houston (discussed at length below) before the Greater Houston Ministerial Association, despite significant internal dissent about its wisdom.

The younger Kennedy's political insight may have exceeded John's on the religion issue. The campaign would eventually have to move beyond the private courtship of Protestant elites to direct public engagement of Protestant discomfort with a Catholic candidate. But this realization came later as the Kennedy strategy evolved. This initial foray into private conversations with powerful Protestant leaders was the precursor to the later public efforts. In the long run, Robert's impulse to understand Protestants would yield more political fruit.

Perhaps the most intriguing visit in Kennedy's listening tour was a stop in Salt Lake City, Utah, for a visit with David McKay, president of the Church of Jesus Christ of Latter-Day Saints, in March 1959. Kennedy had met previously with McKay in 1957, when Kennedy spoke at a Democratic dinner on November 11.[41] On March 6 and 7, 1959, Kennedy gave two speeches in Salt Lake, and he and his wife, Jackie, met privately with McKay. Kennedy had sent McKay an autographed copy of *Profiles in Courage*, and McKay wrote to Kennedy, thanking him for the gift.[42] After the 1959 meeting, Kennedy wrote to McKay to say that they were deeply honored to have visited with him and that they had enjoyed the hospitality of the people of Salt Lake City. He went on to note that the work of "your church and its people in Utah, the United States, and throughout the entire world is, indeed, edifying. Its devotion to principle is a firm bulwark against any encroachment by the godless enemies of western and Christian civilizations."[43]

The immediate payoff of this initial effort to crack the Protestant mind is impossible to determine. But it did represent an affirmative step toward addressing the powerful accepted political wisdom that a Catholic could not win the presidency. The learning curve that the campaign faced would prove to be quite steep, but Wright's wise counsel nudged Kennedy in the right direction.

In the late fifties, once his name began to be mentioned as a likely candidate in 1960, Kennedy began receiving letters from around the country. Some mundane correspondence from this period reveals some themes that Kennedy would develop more fully in the glare of the campaign. One woman wrote to Kennedy after hearing him speak to the National Conference of Christians and Jews. She argued that a Catholic cannot honestly become president since the Catholic church had repudiated the separation of church and state.[44] Kennedy responded:

> I of course respect the position which you have taken in your letter, but I must frankly say that I cannot agree with your interpretation of the current situation. I have absolutely no hesitancy in stating to you that without reservation I subscribe to the principles of the First Amendment to the Constitution, guaranteeing as they do to every American the freedom to worship or not to worship as he pleases. I do not think that any majority having political control of this country

could morally or legally impose its own religious views on the minority. As I have repeatedly said publicly, and reiterate to you, I can conceive of no situation in which my religious convictions could interfere or conflict with the faithful exercise of any responsibility I might be called upon to assume in public life.[45]

This reply presaged half of Kennedy's famous statement at Houston in that he affirmed religious freedom in the First Amendment and strongly denied that he would have any conflict between his faith and his duties as president. Kennedy's mounting frustration with these sorts of arguments became clearer in another letter a few months later. In April 1958, E. Claude Gardner, dean of Freed-Hardeman College, a junior college in Henderson, Tennessee, affiliated with the conservative Protestant Churches of Christ, wrote to Kennedy to say that he was impressed with Kennedy on a recent broadcast of *Face the Nation*. The writer was impressed with Kennedy's wide experience, depth of discernment, and his record. Nevertheless, he expressed his hope that Kennedy would not get the nomination in 1960 because of his Catholicism: "There are many Americans that believe that the basic philosophy of Catholicism runs counter to many basic freedoms of our nation."[46] Kennedy replied in dismay:

> While my principal political objective at the present time is reelection to the United States Senate from the State of Massachusetts, I was very much disturbed to learn that you feel that any person would be denied public office because of his religious beliefs—whatever they might be. I had certainly thought that by this time, given our broad educational base, individuals who in other times might out of ignorance be misinformed about various religious faiths and their application to everyday life would now be better informed.
>
> In any event, I am sure that you join me in the fervent hope that a high degree of understanding and tolerance among men of every religious persuasion will be attained in the not too distant future.[47]

In addition to getting a hint of the grassroots opposition to a Catholic as president, Kennedy received a foretaste of the pungent public critique from one of the most powerful Protestant organizations in the country in the form of letters from Glenn Archer, executive director of Protestants and Other Americans United for Separation of Church and State, which had emerged as a unifying polemical force on behalf of a wide swath of Protestants. Archer's letters give us clues about the future fireworks.

Archer wrote Kennedy a flinty letter in April 1958 taking issue with Kennedy's characterization of POAU's questions about a Catholic candidate's handling of the conflict between the church's teaching and America's freedom of religion. Archer said that they were not infringing on Kennedy's beliefs by pressing this question on him. He concluded his note by saying that Kennedy's responses to POAU's questions are important to the "80,000 leaders" who comprise POAU.[48] Kennedy was not intimidated. He wrote back six weeks later that it was important for national leaders to be clear in their public policy ideas. He noted that Archer had unfairly characterized some of his positions and invited Archer to see him if he were ever in the Capitol.[49] Even though Archer worked in Washington, there is no evidence that he ever took Kennedy up on his offer.

In November 1959, on the cusp of Kennedy's public announcement of his formal presidential candidacy, Archer wrote again, this time trying to embarrass Kennedy by calling his attention to a recent statement by the U.S. Catholic bishops that they would not support any U.S. program, domestic or foreign, that would support artificial birth prevention. Did Kennedy approve or disapprove of this statement?[50] In addition, Archer included a copy of the latest POAU tract, *If the U.S. Becomes 51% Catholic!* written by POAU staffer C. Stanley Lowell. Kennedy's assistant David Hackett acknowledged receipt of the letter, but apparently Kennedy thought best not to reply. POAU was interested only in scoring polemical points, and Kennedy knew better than to continue the conversation.

In addition to skillfully using free religious media such as *Jubilee* magazine, the campaign also promoted Kennedy through the large-circulation glossy magazines of the era.[51] On February 16, 1959, Fletcher Knebel's aforementioned article on Kennedy appeared in *Look* magazine, and religion figured prominently. Kennedy took a clear line on the separation of church and state and added his usual positions against federal aid to parochial schools and opposing an ambassador to the Vatican. One statement in particular created a stir: "Whatever one's religion in his private life may be, for the officeholder, nothing takes precedence over his oath to uphold the Constitution in all its parts—including the First Amendment and the strict separation of Church and State."

Yet this time, Kennedy learned that his doubters on the religion issue were not all conservative Protestants, as several leading liberal Catholic publications protested his answers. Both *America*, the Jesuit magazine, and *Commonweal* chided Kennedy for giving too much ground to the Protestant worriers. Both publications argued that the Catholic church did in fact uphold the separation of church and state and that there was no conflict between a Catholic politician's faith and the upholding of the Constitution.

Suddenly a new front had opened up against Kennedy, and the assault was coming from progressive Catholics. The *New York Times* covered the story on March 1 under the headline "Catholic Censure of Kennedy Rises." The article quoted an editorial in *America* suggesting that, by answering the Protestants' questions, Kennedy had submitted to a religious test for office. The magazine was impatient with Kennedy's efforts to appease bigots and argued that Kennedy really did not believe that the oath of office takes precedence over one's faith. It argued that no religious person, Catholic, Protestant, or Jew, holds such an opinion. The article went on to cite several Catholic diocesan papers that offered similar critiques of Kennedy's statements.

Nine days later, the *New York Times* ran an article on a speech given by Richard Cardinal Cushing of Boston in which he defended Kennedy's answers. He knew without hesitation that Kennedy would fulfill his oath of office in obedience to the highest standards of conscience. He added that it was ridiculous to ask these questions of Kennedy given his length of public service and that it was a pity that Kennedy had to answer questions about his religion.[52] Cushing's intervention is a sign of his deep affection for Kennedy. It would not be the last time that Cushing felt the need to make a public statement. He would do so whenever he thought people were taking cheap shots at the senator.

This dust-up never developed into a full-blown anti-Kennedy movement among progressive Catholics, perhaps due to Cushing's strong intervention, but there would be wistful comparisons in the minds of some in this camp between Kennedy and Senator Eugene McCarthy. John Cogley's presence in the campaign would eventually help to solidify Catholic intellectuals for Kennedy. But in 1959, that support was not assured, and the efforts to reach out to Protestants threatened to undermine Catholic support as Kennedy appeared to pander to anti-Catholic conservative Protestants.

Indeed, many liberal Democrats were deeply suspicious of Kennedy for four reasons. First, there was the historic distrust of the Catholic church. Many progressives saw the church as an authoritarian institution intolerant of ideas at odds with its teaching. Second, many liberals viewed Kennedy as a superficial playboy who relied on his good looks and charm. Third, Kennedy was a threat to a third Stevenson campaign. Since Stevenson was the patron saint of many liberals, any candidate who rivaled Stevenson would face some liberal ire. And finally, some liberals, such as Eleanor Roosevelt, distrusted Kennedy because they felt he had dodged the McCarthy controversy earlier in the decade. This dovetailed with liberals' distrust of his father.[53]

In April 1959, Kennedy made a seven-speech, three-day tour through Wisconsin, the site of an early presidential primary in April 1960. At this stage, Kennedy had not yet decided if he were going to challenge Minnesota senator Hubert Humphrey in the primary there. The tour allowed Kennedy to test the waters and set the stage for a possible challenge to Humphrey a year later. The *New York Times* highlighted Kennedy's Catholicism with the headline "Kennedy Regards Religion as Issue."[54] Kennedy took the flap over his *Look* remarks in stride, saying that religion was a proper matter for discussion in political campaigns. Disagreeing with Cushing, Kennedy acknowledged that he had to confront these questions directly in order to reach persuadable Protestants. He did not want to repudiate these questions in public and risk alienating the Protestants for whom they were important.

In May, George Gallup released the results of a nationwide, 9,000-person survey on what effect Kennedy's Catholicism would have on the 1960 presidential race. The size of the project devoted exclusively to the question of Kennedy's religion showed that early on this was the defining issue of the 1960 election. In a week-long, five-part series syndicated in newspapers throughout the country, Gallup painted a mixed political picture. In the initial article, Gallup drew two major conclusions. First, Catholicism had retreated as a negative issue, but it could still give Kennedy trouble; and second, Kennedy could draw Republican Catholics into the Democratic column.

A great majority, 62% of Americans, said they would vote for a well-qualified Catholic while 28% said they would not. Opposition to a Catholic president stemmed from two major fears: that a Catholic president must serve two masters and that such a president would introduce a sort of Catholic spoils system.

Gallup identified a powerful loyalty among Catholic voters, who were willing to vote for a well-qualified Catholic on either ticket. Ninety-five percent of Catholics said they would vote for their party's nominee if he were Catholic, and 52% said they might vote for a Catholic nominee from the other party. For the Democrats, who had a larger proportion of Catholics within their rank and file, this meant that almost all Catholic Democrats were safe while they might pick up half of all Republican Catholics, or about 1 out of every 14 Republican voters. For Republicans, choosing a Catholic nominee might mean picking up half of the Catholic Democrats, or 1 in every 7 Democrats.

At the end of the series, Gallup concluded that, when all of the factors were weighed, Kennedy was hurt more than helped by his Catholicism. In a trial heat against Vice President Nixon, when the religion of the candidates was not called to voters' attention, Kennedy led Nixon 57% to 43%, but less than half of the voters knew that Kennedy was Catholic. As this became known, it had negative results in different regions. Only 42% of Protestant voters knew his religion. In the South, only 30% knew. Factoring in those voters who favored Kennedy and yet said they would not vote for a Catholic, the trial heat was dead even. The more people who knew that Kennedy was a Catholic, the closer the election would be.

The Gallup poll began to establish some of the emerging parameters of the upcoming election. On the one hand, Kennedy was announced as the Democratic frontrunner, and he polled well against the likely Republican nominee. Yet his religion produced mixed results. Democratic Catholics might return to the fold and significant numbers of Republican Catholics might defect to the Democrats. Yet, as Protestants learned of his religious affiliation, they might defect in such large numbers that the race would be a dead heat.

Two religion stories in 1959 would later figure prominently in the general election. On May 21, the Southern Baptist Convention elected Ramsey Pollard to succeed Brooks Hays as president of the denomination. Pollard, a pastor in Knoxville, Tennessee, defeated a more moderate candidate. The *New York Times* quoted Pollard as saying, "There is a great deal of feeling among many good people that Kennedy would meet with severe opposition in many circles consonant with Baptist life."[55] Hays had been a racially progressive Arkansas Democratic congressman. Pollard would actively work in Southern Baptist circles to oppose the Kennedy candidacy in 1960. The Democratic National Committee took note of this transition by clipping and saving the *Times* article.[56]

The second, less obvious story was the quiet work of the National Council of Churches, an ecumenical umbrella organization composed of 33 Christian denominations, including the mainline Protestant denominations. The NCC distributed a biweekly newsletter summarizing religious news from mainstream national news outlets. The April 2 issue was devoted exclusively to the question: How has religion influenced presidents? The May 23 issue was dedicated to "The Big Issue: Religion and the Presidency." Both treated the prospect of a Kennedy candidacy with respect bordering on hope. At this point, the NCC was clearing ground among its powerful mainline Protestant stakeholders for a possible Catholic candidacy. Religious battle lines were being drawn well in advance of the formal campaign.

On October 28, 1959, a year and 11 days before the 1960 election, Kennedy's inner circle met at Robert Kennedy's home in the Kennedy compound in Hyannisport, Massachusetts, to draw up the initial plans for John Kennedy's race. The 16 attendees included the senator, his father, both brothers, Robert and Edward, and trusted advisors such as Steve Smith, Ted Sorensen, Larry O'Brien, Bob Wallace, Ken O'Donnell, Governor John Bailey, Governor Denny Roberts, pollster Lou Harris, and Pierre Salinger.[57] Theodore White has argued that this assembly of 16 displayed craftsmanship and vitality in creating the Kennedy presidency with greater precision against greater odds across more contrary traditions than had been shown by any group of amateur president-makers since Abraham Lincoln's backers.[58]

A survey meeting had convened in Palm Beach, Florida, back in April, and Steve Smith had established a small Washington office, but this was the first time the whole team had gathered to formally set up the strategy for the nomination process. Here in Hyannisport, official duties were assigned. Sorensen shifted from the de facto campaign manager to national policy chief. Robert Kennedy became the operational and campaign manager. The relationship between Sorensen and RFK was a crucial one for the management of the religion issue. Their mutual agreement on a revised religion strategy at the outset of the general election was vital to Kennedy's ultimate electoral success. White's portrait of Sorensen is revealing:

> There was, next, sitting beside the candidate, Theodore C. Sorensen, then thirty-one. If O'Donnell and O'Brien were stewards of Kennedy's political personality, then Sorensen was steward of the candidate's intellectual personality. "My intellectual blood bank," Kennedy styled him late in the campaign. Tall, handsome, even more youthful in appearance than his age, quiet-spoken, shy, Sorensen perhaps as much as any man, had helped educate the candidate to his present views. A gut-liberal (his father, in Nebraska, had been George Norris' campaign manager), Sorensen had now been with Kennedy for seven years; his introspection, his reading, his elegant writing, had stimulated many of Kennedy's finest thoughts and expressions. Hired originally as little more than an intellectual valet by the young Senator from Massachusetts in January, 1953, just after Kennedy had been elected to the seat, Sorensen had, by his learning, his dedication, his total devotion to his chief, become almost a lobe of Kennedy's mind. Through Sorensen were to filter, in the coming year, all major policy decisions on matters of national or international importance.[59]

Sorensen outlined the three major hurdles facing his boss. First, the country had never elected a Catholic. Second, it had never elected a 43-year-old. Third, only one sitting senator had been elected president in the twentieth century. Sorensen told White:

> This being true you had to examine the nominating process, which is not a free open popular vote, but a process which is dominated and influenced by all the groups in the Democratic coalition—the farmers, labor, the South, the big city people, et cetera. These groups are more influential in a convention than they are in the country as a whole. Therefore he had to prove to them that he could win. And to prove that to them, he'd have to fight hard to make them give it to him, he couldn't negotiate it. If the Convention ever went into the back rooms, he'd never emerge from those back rooms. So it evolved from the top down that you had to go into the primaries.[60]

The bulk of the three-hour meeting in the morning consisted of John Kennedy marching state by state, surveying the political terrain and assigning duties to the assembled staff. Only by virtue of winning primaries beyond New England's Catholic Democratic enclaves could Kennedy demonstrate that his candidacy was not hopelessly flawed because of his Catholicism. There is no record of any talk of just how the Catholic issue would be addressed in these primaries. For the moment, while the talk was strategic and analytical, religion was not discussed at length. In the afternoon, Robert Kennedy conducted an operational discussion. He chose seven state primaries to enter. Interestingly, West Virginia was listed as a possible primary entry, but that decision was postponed until Lou Harris had done his polling there. The prospect of campaigning in an overwhelmingly Protestant state did not appear attractive at the outset. If Kennedy could defeat Minnesota senator Hubert Humphrey in neighboring Wisconsin and drive Humphrey out of the race, a battle in West Virginia might be avoided. The real scenario in Wisconsin and West Virginia would subvert this early hope.

On January 1, 1960, 70,000 letters were sent to Kennedy supporters, announcing that Kennedy was running and that their support would be appreciated. The next day, John Kennedy formally announced his candidacy for the presidency in a Senate caucus room. His short statement made no direct reference to his Catholicism. It did outline what Kennedy saw as the crucial decisions of the century that had to be made in the next four years. The last of these he called "how to give direction to our traditional moral purpose, awakening every American to the dangers and opportunities that confront us." He went on to call for all Democratic aspirants to submit their views and records to the voters in the primary process. He closed his remarks with an image of America as he saw it:

> For 18 years, I have been in the service of the United States, first as a naval officer in the Pacific during World War II and for the past 14 years as a member of Congress. In the last 20 years, I have traveled in nearly every continent and country—from Leningrad to Saigon, from Bucharest to Lima. From all of this, I have developed an image of America as fulfilling a noble and historic role as the defender of freedom in a time of maximum peril—and of the American people as confident, courageous and preserving.
>
> It is with this image that I begin this campaign.[61]

By indirection, Kennedy laid claim to being able to lead the country morally and to preserve its freedoms, including its freedom of religion. The hypothesis that a Catholic could defend religious freedom in America would be severely tested. Arthur Schlesinger, Jr., gave a revealing report on Kennedy's mood at a private dinner with him and John Kenneth Galbraith in Boston at the venerable Locke Ober restaurant that night:

> I noted of Kennedy later, "He was, as usual, spirited and charming but he also conveyed an intangible feeling of depression. I had the sense that he feels himself increasingly hemmed in as a result of a circumstance over which he has no control—his religion; and he inevitably tends toward gloom and irritation when he considers how this circumstance may deny him what he thinks his talent and efforts have earned." The religious issue, he said, left him no choice but to go into Wisconsin. It would be a gamble, but his only hope of forcing himself on the party leaders was to carry the primaries. A victory over Humphrey in Wisconsin would make his case irresistible.[62]

So, at the outset of his official public pursuit of the White House, Kennedy was depressed by the stumbling block that his Catholicism placed in his way. But neither he nor his circle of advisors remained passive in the face of this challenge. In fact, there was already a political strategy in place within his brain trust.

The strategy had developed in the three-year period between the 1956 Chicago convention and his announcement. But it would require evaluation and revision. As they were about to learn the hard way, the religion issue grew and mutated and was subject to outside forces that wrested any control of it out of their hands. Kennedy's flexibility and risk-taking capacity served him well during the whirlwind that surrounded religion through the remaining 11 months of the election cycle.

The early Kennedy strategy on religion was too political, too focused on placating Protestant elites, and too blind to the complexities of Protestant anti-Catholicism. The debate that emerged among Protestants and between Protestants and Catholics in the late fifties over the role of the Catholic church in American public life provided clues that might have been useful to Kennedy had he been following the debate. But he had not been. With his formal entry into the race, the debate would come to him in the form of resistance to his candidacy from all over the Protestant map.

The depth and complexity of the vociferous Protestant intramural squabble over what to make of the American Catholic church was far too large to be managed by a national political campaign. The reaction of Kennedy and his advisors to this debate would prove to be decisive for his election prospects. The best way to grasp what was at stake is to track the controversy as it played out in the competition between the two flagship periodicals of midcentury mainline Protestantism, the *Christian Century* and *Christianity and Crisis*.

2

THE LAY
OF THE LAND

· ·

Harold Fey was not a typical player in American presidential politics. Yet the exceptional circumstances of 1960 thrust him into the arena by virtue of his prominent position within liberal Protestantism. In 1959, the *Christian Century* was the most important publication in the American Protestant world.[1] Fey was coming into his prime, having taken over as editor in 1955. Paid circulation was at 35,000, and the magazine was planning a fundraising campaign to establish a $500,000 sustaining fund. In a 1958 speech to the magazine's stakeholders, Fey described his position as editor as free from outside influence.[2] As he saw it, the Chicago-based magazine's role included forging a Protestant consensus on the issues of the day, including the separation of church and state, promoting Christian unity and ecumenism, raising issues of religious and civil freedom, and offering a Christian commentary on national and international affairs.[3] Interestingly, Fey saw the *Century*'s primary journalistic competitor to be not the New York–based *Christianity and Crisis*, led by the intellectual giant Reinhold Niebuhr, but the newly launched evangelical magazine *Christianity Today*.

The membership lists of the Christian Century Foundation Board and the foundation itself read like a who's who of the American Protestant establishment.[4] Fey was thus well positioned to shape Protestant opinion on Kennedy's candidacy directly in terms of explicit editorial opinion and indirectly as the magazine reflected the state of liberal Protestant thought. As thousands of clergy, professors, and lay members read its pages, Fey's influence on liberal Protestant views of

Kennedy's Catholicism and presidential candidacy was immense and wide ranging.

During 1959, the *Christian Century* displayed a range of dispositions toward the still-theoretical Kennedy campaign. In February, an unsigned editorial briefly commented on the pope's announcement of an ecumenical council by noting that, in the last two such councils, the Catholic church had promulgated the doctrine of papal infallibility, approved the antidemocratic Syllabus of Errors, and took a dim view of democracy as a political movement.[5] All of these would become major issues surrounding Kennedy's candidacy. Until the infallibility of the pope was repudiated, the editorial argued, all efforts toward reunion with Protestants were simply idle gestures. This revealed a baseline of skepticism on Fey's part toward Catholics in general and Kennedy in particular.

The issue of Kennedy's candidacy and his religion became explicit in an editorial in March that commended Kennedy for telling *Look* magazine that, as an officeholder, nothing would take precedence over his oath of office to uphold the Constitution.[6] But its author regretted that the church itself was equivocal on questions of the separation of church and state and religious pluralism. The problem, according to the editorial, was that Catholicism saw itself as the one true church, which had the right and duty to require the state to employ its power on behalf of this truth. On the contrary, Fey argued, in a democracy no church should use its advantages and freedoms to undermine the rights and liberties of other churches.

The editorial concluded by commending Kennedy's opposition to using federal funds for churches or church schools and his opposition to the appointment of a U.S. ambassador to the Vatican. Its author hoped that other Catholic politicians would follow his lead and "go farther." The final paragraph established what would become a common refrain among many Protestants during the campaign:

> The fact that these questions have to be asked does not prove that the askers are bigots. The fact that such questions have to be answered does not prove that those who answer must demonstrate their patriotism is above suspicion. Imputations of bigotry or lack of patriotism are equally out of order. The difficulty and embarrassment are not of that sort. Rather they derive from the presence and growth in our secular political order of a church which does not accept the pluralism which is essential for the separation of church and state. Since that is the case, we have to settle these issues without the help that that church should provide.[7]

This position, which separated Kennedy's views from his church's views, would hurt him all through the election. It perpetuated the belief that his personal views as president would not matter because his church would require him to adhere to its views. It is hard to overstate the exasperation this caused the Kennedy brain trust.

Within a matter of days, associate editor William Coolidge Hart wrote to Senator Kennedy, asking him to participate in an anticipated series of interviews with various men whose names were being prominently mentioned as potential presidential candidates in order "to gain additional insights for formulating our editorial policies."[8] He added somewhat sheepishly that Kennedy should be assured that they have "no motives in seeking such an interview but to do our job more creditably." The fact that Kennedy apparently did not grant this interview may indicate that he saw other motives at work. In 1956, the journal had not endorsed a candidate even though Adlai Stevenson was the staff's preferred candidate. In mid-1958, Stanley Lowell of POAU lobbied Fey to endorse someone—Republican or Democrat—in the coming election, reminding Fey that responsible political action consists in taking sides.[9] This may have been POAU's indirect way of testing Fey's willingness to join in their anti-Kennedy crusade, but Fey resisted taking an overtly anti-Kennedy stand early on.

Fey's skepticism about the emerging American Catholic position on religious freedom came out in a letter thanking a reader for calling his attention to a recent column by John Cogley in *Commonweal*:

> It sounded as though Cogley was doing a little bit of condescending to his low-brow Protestant brothers in writing in so lofty a tone concerning the Catholic authors who have got all the issues concerning church and state properly worked out.
>
> What if John Courtney Murray does have it all worked out if the hierarchy goes on conducting the affairs of the church along the lines of its historic aggressiveness? Murray's position doesn't add up to much except as a smoke screen to confuse Protestants.[10]

In a long editorial, Fey reviewed *Christianity and Crisis* editor John Bennett's book *Christians and the State* and in the process illuminated some of the differences between the publications.[11] He congratulated the Union Seminary professor for raising all of the right questions, even if he did not give all of the right answers. Fey was most critical of the portion of the book dealing with church-state relations. Bennett denied that there was a single Protestant doctrine of church-state relations, but he did cite the influential Baptist version of strict separation. Bennett preferred independence to separation and maintained that there were good reasons for supporting the independence of church and state: It was the only way of assuring the complete freedom of the church, and it preserved the state from control by the church. Fey agreed with Bennett.

Fey then concentrated on Bennett's discussion of Protestant angst over perceived Catholic threats to separation. With Catholics growing in cultural and political power, their intolerance on dogmatic issues and the tension between an authoritarian church and an open, pluralistic, democratic society was becoming a cause for concern to many—including Bennett. Catholic threats to religious liberty came from its flexible interpretation of the First Amendment; its support of birth control legislation, rigid divorce laws, and censorship; its attempt to control the public school system, including support of discrimination against non-Catholic teachers and opposition to bond issues needed by public schools; boycotts of media such as movies and newspapers; and pressure for preference toward the Vatican and Catholic countries in foreign policy.

In spite of this laundry list, Bennett urged Protestants not to worry. There were, he argued, four characteristics of Catholicism that Protestants tend to forget. First, Catholicism differed from culture to culture and from country to country. Second, Catholics in the United States had to win their way against social and cultural odds, and they showed the effects of this struggle. Third, the Catholic church was divided in America and abroad on matters of religious liberty. Finally, Catholics did not agree on social or political matters. Bennett feared that exaggerated Protestant fears might kill any chance for mutual understanding.

Fey agreed with Bennett's diagnosis but not his prescribed treatment. Catholics were becoming more powerful politically, and something besides passive acceptance was needed. He concluded ominously: "Persons who do not agree with his prescriptions as how to deal with this situation had better change the situation or come up with a different answer soon. Time is running out, and Dr. Bennett is growing more nearly right every day."[12]

To his credit, Fey did not take a bigoted stand against Catholics running for public office, but he was clearly troubled at the prospect of the church's influence on elected Catholics. He would later give a platform to writers who shared his anxiety and who offered a variety of prescriptions. But at this point, he was not staking out a hard and fast position against Kennedy or anyone else.

The next noteworthy installment in the *Christian Century* was a long excerpt from Jaroslav Pelikan's book *The Riddle of Roman Catholicism.*[13] Early in the article, Pelikan argued that, in order to fully engage in any analysis of the divide between Protestants and Catholics, one had to offer an honest assessment of the Reformation. What followed was a detailed analysis of the Reformation and its consequences. The enduring tragedy of the Reformation, Pelikan argued, was that the Catholic church excommunicated Luther for "being too serious about his catholicism while it retained within its fellowship the skeptics and scoffers who did not bother to defy its authority."[14] Ever since then, he argued, Roman Catholics had displayed an astonishing incapacity to understand the Reformation and an unwillingness to admit that the religious convictions of the Reformers were animated by their fidelity to Catholic ideals.

This was an oversimplification and a terrible burden to place on contemporary Catholics. While there was undoubtedly widespread agreement on both sides that there had been mutual misunderstanding during the Reformation, this analysis overlooked the complex social, political, philosophical, and theological reasons for the gulf between the traditions. But what Pelikan did provide was ammunition from an eminent Lutheran church historian for Protestants, liberal or conservative, who sought to place blame for the current enmity between Catholics and Protestants at the feet of Catholics.

The low point in the *Christian Century*'s coverage of the divide between Catholics and Protestants came in two articles by Paul Blanshard, special counsel for POAU. These articles were melodramatic accounts of Spanish Protestants being mistreated in the courts of Franco's Spain, where the Catholic church had a concordat with the government.[15] The clear implication was that injustice toward Protestants was the norm whenever the Catholic church got its way.

The first article was an account of a man facing the possibility of three months in prison for misleading the census about his marital status. He had been married by a Protestant pastor and reported that he was married. But because his marriage was not performed—and therefore not recognized—by the Catholic church, he was charged with lying to the census. According to Blanshard, the defendant was acquitted on a technicality thanks only to the brilliance of his Protestant lawyer. Blanshard hailed the victory since it might help the thousands of other former Catholics in Spain who were being denied the right to leave their faith without civil penalties by an authoritarian church in league with an authoritarian government. The second article told the story of a Baptist who reopened a church five years after it had been shut down by the police. Similarly, the defendant prevailed and was not imprisoned for violating the illegal proselytizing laws. The Catholic church, it seemed, had the power to harass and imprison Protestants for trying to worship publicly—but not to prevail in court.

Whatever the merits of these cases, their function for Blanshard was to remind American Protestants that the authoritarian political nature of the Catholic church was not American. Europe was full of examples where the church had not supported religious freedom and pluralism. It could happen in the United States if Protestants were not vigilant.

The web of relationships between the *Christian Century* and POAU reveals a lot about the coverage of the election in the pages of the magazine. Both organizations owed their existence to Charles Clayton Morrison.[16] Morrison became editor of the struggling magazine in 1908 and rescued it from fiscal disaster while transforming it from a small denominational periodical representing the Disciples of Christ into a leading Protestant publication. In the late 1940s, Morrison penned a "manifesto" in response to accusations of anti-Catholicism leveled at various Protestants who opposed an American ambassador to the Vatican. This manifesto was the founding document of Protestants and Other Americans United for Separation of Church and State.[17]

The Catholic response to the manifesto was swift. The Catholic Welfare Conference issued a lengthy riposte in which it disputed POAU's interpretation of the Catholic position on the separation of church and state.[18] Thus, POAU was born in a battle with the Catholic church. Their mutual animosity would reverberate throughout the campaign.

As editor, Fey continued the close relationship between the magazine and POAU. In 1948, he had written an article entitled "Can Catholicism Win America?" It concluded with the words "Yes, it can." Ten years later, Stanley Lowell of POAU invited Fey to update his thoughts for POAU's 11th National Conference on Church and State.[19] POAU reprinted Fey's speech and distributed 100,000 copies.[20] Fey showed some independence from POAU during the course of the campaign, but he and the *Christian Century* were much more closely aligned with POAU and its constituency than was *Christianity and Crisis*. In early 1960, he reviewed a Catholic book, *United for Separation*, written specifically to counter POAU's anti-Catholic efforts.[21] Calling the book a debater's manual that put POAU in the worst possible light, Fey said the book ignored the real historical cases of Catholic abuses of the separation of church and state, which showed the need for POAU. He wrote:

> I am not and have never been a member of POAU and have no brief
> for everything it is or does. But I consider that the defense of the
> principle of separation of church and state requires an organization,
> just as the defense of civil liberties requires an organization. I consider
> the national POAU a useful organization, particularly in relation to
> its main function: legal defense of church-state separation. POAU is
> not entitled to speak for Protestantism, but it may speak to both Prot-
> estant and Catholic churches on behalf of the [C]onstitution and it
> constantly does so.[22]

His parting shot was to observe that the book carried the *nihil obstat*
and imprimatur, meaning it had been certified to be free of doctrinal
and moral error by church authorities and thus reflected Catholicism's
official teaching on the separation of church and state.

The last major coverage of Catholic and Protestant relations in this
period came in the form of two articles that examined the case of St.
Louis University's acquisition of land through public condemnation
and sale. The first piece was yet another essay in the genre of "look at
what those Catholics do at the local level when their politicians are in
power." Entitled "An Unhallowed Perversion: A Flagrant Violation of
the Constitutional Requirement as to Church-State Separation Is Soon
to Be Contested in St. Louis, Missouri," it alleged that the Jesuit-run
St. Louis University was about to acquire blighted land valued at $8
million for pennies on the dollar as a result of a no-bid sweetheart
deal with the St. Louis Redevelopment Authority.[23] The episode was a
launching pad for a rehearsal of the sad history of the Roman Catholic
church on church-state separation.

Citing Pope Pius XI's 1929 encyclical *Christian Education of
Youth*, the article argued that the church demanded public funding
for its schools and claimed that arguments to the contrary based on
the separation of church and state reflected a prejudice against Roman
Catholics. The author cited this from a 1948 article in the Jesuit magazine *La Civiltà Cattolica*:

> The Roman Catholic Church, convinced...of being the only true
> Church, must demand the right of freedom for herself alone, because
> such right can only be possessed by truth, never by error. As to other
> religions, the Church...will require by legitimate means that they shall
> not be allowed to propagate false doctrine. Consequently, in a state
> where the majority of people are Catholic, the Church will require
> that legal existence be denied to error.... In some countries Catholics
> will be obliged to ask full religious freedom for all, resigned at being
> forced to cohabitate where they alone should rightfully be allowed to

live. But in doing this the Church does not renounce her thesis which remains the most imperative of her laws, but merely adapts herself to de facto conditions which must be taken into account in practical affairs.... The Church cannot blush for her own want of tolerance, as she asserts it in principle and applies it in practice.[24]

This quote, and others like it, fed the American Protestant fear of what the Catholic church was really up to with the Kennedy candidacy. Progressive Catholic voices such as John Courtney Murray, Gustave Weigel, and John Cogley had to contend against the intellectual paper trail laid down by various European Catholic predecessors. Articles such as these undermined the argument, advanced by these progressives, that in America Catholics view religious freedom differently.

Five weeks later, another article, written by a Protestant, directly challenged the facts as presented in the first article.[25] The writer showed that St. Louis was not dominated by Catholic politicians and that the redevelopment plan adopted was supported by numerous Protestant and Jewish groups. Instead, the false arguments represented a summation of the stance of groups that were opposed to a bond referendum that paid for much of the redevelopment of downtown St. Louis. But this late reply may not have blunted the effect of the initial piece.

The second article concluded on a very interesting note when it said that Catholic-Protestant differences were deeper than property disputes. They were separated by a great gulf, including mounting Mariolatry, the materialism of the mass, the claims of infallibility by the pope, and the insistence that the Catholic church was the one true church. The writer was convinced that, on all of these issues, Protestants were in the right. Because of this, Protestants needed to speak the truth, with love, to Catholics and engage in a ministry of reconciliation. It was both a rebuke to the sentiment of the first article and a call to hold fast to Protestant resistance to perceived Catholic errors. But it did not offer a way out of the disputes.

The closing days of 1959 brought more mild treatments of Catholicism in general—and Kennedy specifically—to the *Christian Century*. Jaroslav Pelikan reviewed *The Twentieth Century Encyclopedia of Catholicism* and extolled the changes in the European Catholic church.[26] Protestants should study this set of writings because it demonstrated "new and deep stirrings within the Roman Catholic Church." Pelikan predicted that some Protestants would respond with disappointment because stereotypical anti-Catholic polemics no longer applied. Some would respond with fear in seeing Catholics react to modernity in a manner that Protestants thought only Protestants could. Some would respond with gratitude because the Holy Spirit was at work. Others would respond in hope and trust. His final sentence asked, "Will American Protestantism be ready when someone suggests that the time has come for conversation?"[27]

The changes unfolding within Catholicism leading up to Vatican II were becoming clear to some of the writers in the *Christian Century* fold. But the magazine itself did not seem to fully realize the scope of the changes and their implications for presidential politics. An unsigned editorial reflecting on the significance of Pelikan's book *The Riddle of Roman Catholicism* acknowledged that the cold war among Christians was thawing.[28] The signs of the thaw included the liturgical movement in the Catholic church as it rediscovered "the separated brethren" of Protestantism, the ecumenical work of biblical scholars, and the increasing number of ecumenical conferences and books in the United States. And yet the essay expressed a deep hesitancy:

> The Reformation has entered into a new phase. The "cold war among Christians" is not as cold as it was. We can gratefully take account of this development, and we should do what we can to advance it. But the surest way to end it is to infer from it that reunion is just around the corner, that the deep gulf which separates Protestant and Catholic is about to be bridged or filled up. Indeed, nothing serves so well as a rapprochement to demonstrate how great are the differences—theological, ecclesiastical, cultural, historical, and even political—which continue to divide us.[29]

In another unsigned editorial, the magazine congratulated the weekly Catholic publication *Commonweal* on its 35th anniversary.[30] Calling it "our younger colleague in the field of what for want of a better term is referred to as 'liberal religious journalism,'" the essay commended the Catholic journal for its commitment to political democracy and its criticism of Catholics who discuss politics as if nothing had happened since the French Revolution. Citing a recent editorial in which *Commonweal* stated that Catholics had not given enough thought to what it means to live in a pluralistic society, the writer wished *Commonweal* more success in serving this commitment.

The year ended with two editorials on the issue of the Catholic bishops on birth control and whether or not their stance was binding on Kennedy and other Catholic politicians. The bishops opposed the use of public funds to promote artificial birth control at home or abroad. The first editorial called this action an attempt to subject U.S. foreign policy to sectarian control.[31] The second editorial reported on Episcopal bishop James A. Pike's question as to whether this pronouncement by the bishops was binding on Catholic candidates for public office.[32] Kennedy was quoted in a *New York Times* article as evading the issue when he said that he agreed with the bishops but had held his view before they pronounced it. He elaborated that, if the U.S. government were to impose birth control measures on Asia, the country would be departing from precedent, since Americans did not advocate this for Europe or themselves. The editorial chided Kennedy for missing the point. The real point was whether or not the U.S. government would support research for cheap and easily dispensed birth control methods. If they became available, it would be up to individual countries to adopt them. The editorial concluded by congratulating Senators Hubert Humphrey and Stuart Symington, two likely Democratic presidential candidates, for their forthright embrace of making birth control information available if other countries asked for U.S. assistance. In early 1960, the magazine ran an excerpt from an essay by liberal Presbyterian Robert McAfee Brown from a book co-written with Gustave Weigel, which took a moderate stand, encouraging Protestant-Catholic dialogue.[33]

Under Fey's editorship, the *Christian Century* mainly published editorials and articles that were skeptical of Catholic progress on the separation of church and state and on religious freedom, anxious about what European examples of Catholic political behavior portended for American pluralism, and critical of liberal Protestant voices that argued the Catholic church in America was changing for the better. While it was hospitable to the views of the ever-vigilant POAU, it was not blind to Kennedy's attempts to distance himself from the medieval political views imputed to him by some Protestant critics. Fundamentally liberal politically, as seen in their support for liberal Democrats such as Stevenson and Humphrey, Fey and his associates were not drawn to Nixon, hence they maintained what might be called a skeptical openness to Kennedy should he become the Democratic nominee.

But the *Christian Century* was not the exclusive voice of liberal Protestantism. It shared the field with *Christianity and Crisis*, the New York publication that Reinhold Niebuhr helped to establish when he broke with the *Christian Century* and its pacifist stand two decades earlier. These two publications engaged in a heated debate over the desirability of a Kennedy presidency and set the tone for huge segments of Protestant America. Nothing short of the fate of the election was at stake. The readerships of these two magazines were key constituencies for both Kennedy and Nixon. For Nixon to win, he needed to claim these voters to offset the likely Catholic migration to Kennedy. Kennedy needed to keep these liberal Protestants from defecting to Nixon.

During 1959, *Christianity and Crisis* set a different tone from the *Christian Century* by sponsoring a Protestant-Catholic dialogue.[34] While the purported rationale for the exchange was to improve ecumenical relations, it became clear that the looming Kennedy candidacy was the real reason. Both sides in the dialogue understood that Kennedy's faith and possible candidacy could exacerbate the problems between Protestantism and Catholicism or it could be an opportunity for progress between them. The exchanges in this conversation ranged from hopeful to testy.

Robert McAfee Brown, an editorial board member of *Christianity and Crisis*, launched the exchange on an inauspicious note by chiding Kennedy for attempting to put the religion issue to rest with his interview in *Look* magazine.[35] Brown argued that Kennedy went too far and privatized his faith when he said that, for an officeholder, nothing took precedence over his oath to uphold the Constitution. No true Christian, Catholic or Protestant, Brown felt, would say this. By trying to defuse the religion issue, Brown argued, Kennedy had adopted a secularist position.

In a demonstration of just how closely the Kennedy side monitored these matters, a few weeks later Arthur Schlesinger issued a swift rebuke in a letter to the editor. Schlesinger called Brown's reaction "strange" and "mysteriously vehement."[36] He argued that Kennedy's call was for officeholders to affirm that nothing would take precedence over their oaths to uphold the Constitution. It was not a universal principle for all citizens. He turned the tables on Brown and argued that those officeholders who allowed other principles to take precedence over upholding the Constitution pose a greater threat to "our freedom."

After this initial foray into the controversy surrounding Kennedy's Catholicism, the magazine shifted into an activist mode by inviting three prominent Catholic intellectuals to initiate a conversation in its pages. While Kennedy was not the focus of this exchange, his anticipated candidacy lurked near the surface. The first contribution was from the Jesuit Gustave Weigel.[37] He wasted no time in knocking down one of the primary Protestant fears by assuring his readers that America was not becoming a Catholic nation. The percentage of Roman Catholics in the American population had not grown much in years.

Weigel made two larger points. The first was that the history of Catholics in the United States could be divided into two periods. In the nineteenth century, European Catholics came here in ignorance and hardship, but they were equipped with a readiness to work hard to improve their conditions. This pursuit of the American dream in turn produced a unique American Catholicism. Weigel directly addressed the fear that Catholicism represented a European invasion that would ultimately undermine American democratic values. Then, after World War I, American Catholicism "arrived." A cocky adolescent pride infected Catholics, and their earlier resentment of Protestants turned into "an edgy aloofness." The pain of Al Smith's defeat in the presidential election of 1928 launched some introspection, but it was not widespread.

Currently, American Catholics were neither a harassed minority nor a triumphalist majority. They were more prone to conservatism than to radical change, more jingoistic than anti-American. He summarized this first point by saying that the Catholic church—in its generosity, activism, and optimism—was probably more American than Catholic. Weigel then segued to his second point. He argued that Protestants had been slow to recognize that American Catholics were not a threat and had no wish to become one. In fact, Catholics were largely ignorant of Protestantism.

Catholics, Weigel argued, simply were not preoccupied with things Protestant, again refuting a common Protestant fear that Catholics were conspiring to take over America. At this point, he worked in a direct shot at POAU, calling it a nuisance that Catholics did not identify with the Protestant community as a whole. Weigel wryly put the organization down by saying that it must be embarrassing for many Protestants to see POAU use the proper name "Protestant" when that label is so much bigger and means better things than what POAU stands for.

But his main point was that Catholics were simply ignorant about Protestantism—and, by implication, Protestants were equally ignorant of Catholicism. The result was that Catholics were totally unprepared for ecumenical dialogue. They were not hostile to it, they were simply not ready. He ended his conciliatory piece with these paragraphs:

> The electoral campaign of 1960 is already aborning. The presence of Senator John Kennedy among the possible candidates will produce intranquility [sic]. In God's goodness it may be the occasion for Catholic ecumenical action. Perhaps it may even do the contrary.
>
> Certainly the ecumenical council to be summoned by Pope John XXIII should produce some good fruits, at least in the world-wide preparations for the council sessions. Just now, with these possibilities before us, we must wait, hope and see.[38]

The second article to appear in the series was by Thomas O'Dea, a sociologist at Fordham. O'Dea offered a darker portrait of two ideological camps, one Catholic and one Protestant, which threatened the nascent ecumenical dialogue.[39] His contention was that the bridges between the two branches of Christianity were weak, and each branch housed a group that drew satisfaction from keeping the enmity alive. Like Weigel, O'Dea argued that the impending Kennedy candidacy had to be seen against the wider backdrop of Catholic-Protestant relations.

On the one hand, Catholic "hyper-integralists" wanted two incompatible things: to preserve some kind of Catholic ghetto while simultaneously seeking to identify Catholicism with America and Americanism, understanding these especially in terms of right-wing politics. They saw no need for genuine dialogue with Protestants to solve pressing social problems. He traced the origins of this movement to the perils of being an immigrant group and the struggle against secularization and assimilation into American culture.

On the other side was a Protestant camp that he called the "hyper-reformationists." This group was reacting to the loss of Protestant cultural hegemony. Every gain for Catholics was seen as a loss for Protestants. They were not willing to move over a bit to make room for other ascendant groups. They saw their chief task as carrying forward the anti-Catholic aspect of the Reformation.

What these ideologies have in common is that they provide their adherents with a simplified and manageable diagnosis of the world in which they find themselves. While neither represents a majority view within their religion, they are hardly the lunatic fringe and wield considerable power. O'Dea argued that both groups were a problem for intelligent Catholics and Protestants and should not be allowed to define the debate. O'Dea dreaded that the impending Kennedy candidacy might allow just that.

In his conclusion, O'Dea cut to the chase and assessed the problem that Kennedy posed. He expressed surprise at how tense and disproportionate the conversation had already become surrounding Kennedy. No Catholic president could or would alter the Constitution or its interpretation. There were effective controls against this. He believed that Catholics as a religious group would have less influence on a Catholic administration because a Catholic president would have to bend over backward to avoid the suggestion of favoritism. But he was keenly alert to the fact that symbolism and ideology might trump reality. The only antidote to the fantasies and fears of the extremists was to extend the

Catholic-Protestant dialogue between theologians and biblical scholars to wider audiences.

William Clancy, a former editor at the Catholic magazine *Commonweal*, wrote the final installment. He began by citing Niebuhr, who wrote that the relations between Catholics and Protestants in America "are a scandal and an offense against Christian charity."[40] Clancy then offered three important insights for understanding the state of those relations. First, for most Catholics, a principled skepticism was easier to understand and accept than Protestantism. That is, for Catholics, the only alternative to the church of Rome was unbelief. Protestantism, with its innumerable denominations, represented at best a compromise and at worst chaos. Catholics thus tended not to take Protestantism seriously as a genuine Christian enterprise even in social and political arenas. The result was much religious misunderstanding. Clancy's insight helps to explain the intense frustration of many Catholics with the unfolding Protestant responses to Kennedy's candidacy. The gulf between the faiths was huge, and it cut in both directions.

Second, he argued that many of the controversies were conducted on the level of caricature. Protestants approached Catholicism with unreasoning suspicion, and Catholics avoided real issues, approaching Protestantism with fatuous condescension. This observation was a dark harbinger of the next year and a half of American presidential politics. Finally, Clancy observed ironically that "those Protestant groups" that were keenest on separation of church and state—obviously, he meant POAU and the like—and most worried about the Catholic threat to separation were the groups that sought to impose a Protestant ethos on the community through civil law wherever possible. That is, while they supported separation, they assumed that the state would remain implicitly Protestant. Clancy was quite right about the separationists, but he was wrong to conclude that this anti-Catholicism was vestigial and dying. Its potency was about to be tested, and the pages of *Christianity and Crisis* would provide ample testimony to its vitality.

These essays sparked quick reactions. POAU responded in a letter to the editors with a strong ad hominem attack on Weigel. Stanley Lowell, POAU's associate director, wrote:

> [Father Weigel] displays a mentality that we in POAU have grown accustomed to when he speaks snidely of our organization and attempts to pass it off with a sneer. It is, alas the attitude of a man—and a church—so smug and insulated that it cannot even conceive that there could be any validity to concerns and questions that millions deeply feel.[41]

Lowell asserted that, contrary to Weigel's belief that POAU did not represent Protestantism, it actually had broad support. He concluded his broadside by noting that one reason Roman Catholics were so ignorant of Protestantism was that the rulers of the Catholic church forbade attendance at Protestant worship and reading Protestant books. One pole of the debate was set here by POAU. It would have no truck with dialogue in any normal sense. Its members would remain polemicists on the sidelines, hurling rocks at those who sought substantive conversation.

Other Protestant responses to these Catholic essays came a few weeks later from Henry P. Van Dusen, the president of Union Seminary in New York, and Claud Nelson, a staffer at the National Council of Churches. Van Dusen's reply is particularly interesting. He was so thrilled that a conversation had begun, he wrote, that he had to resist the urge to temper his remarks.[42] He directly questioned whether there was parity between liberal Catholics and liberal Protestants: Protestant liberals had substantial influence while Catholic liberals did not. In fact, the tide within the Catholic church was running toward the reactionaries. Van Dusen would be proven wrong after Vatican II, when the church embraced John Courtney Murray's tolerant position on religious freedom, but it was significant that such a progressive Protestant figure harbored this pessimistic view.

Van Dusen bore in on two issues: the relationship between church and state and reactionary Catholic dogma. He rejoiced that there was a liberal Catholic view on church and state that modified what he called the "old thesis" advanced by the Catholic scholar John Ryan. That thesis, according to Van Dusen, stated that when Catholics were a minority in a country, they were under obligation to conform to the prevailing law regarding religious liberty and the status and privileges of religious institutions. When Catholics were an effective majority, they had a duty to seek to bring law and practice into accord with Catholic principles, allying the state and the church under the guidance of the church's leadership.

Van Dusen acknowledged that the American bishops had made "reassuring statements" regarding Catholic loyalty to the Constitution, but he observed that there had been no change in official Roman Catholic principles and policies. Here, in his estimation, was the crux of the issue for Kennedy. Kennedy might disavow the Ryan thesis. He might be the type of shrewd politician O'Dea talked about in his essay: "But, 'political shrewdness' can be expected to exercise constraint only so long and so far as expediency dictates."[43] In other words, Kennedy would not press the issue any further than necessary to get elected.

This was as direct a statement of liberal Protestant fear as can be found in the early days of the 1960 campaign. Van Dusen recognized that liberal Catholics had a much better approach to democracy and universal religious freedom than traditionalist Catholics. Yet to envision an actual Catholic president practicing something akin to a Protestant understanding of independence from papal political authority required liberal Protestants to suspend disbelief in a manner that might come back to haunt them later. Van Dusen was hesitant to take this step.

But he was not finished. If these liberal Catholics were increasingly reasonable on church and state questions, the Catholic church as a whole was increasingly reactionary when it came to doctrine. Van Dusen was particularly offended by the doctrine of the Assumption of Mary, promulgated by Pope Pius XII in 1950, which stated that Mary was taken up, body and soul, into heaven. These sorts of pronouncements only served to widen the gulf between Protestants and Catholics. While Clancy felt that many Catholics cannot imagine how a person of integrity and intelligence could be a Protestant, Van Dusen thought the opposite was true. Many Protestants could not imagine how their intelligent Catholic friends could affirm such incredible, unhistorical doctrines.

The main value of Claud Nelson's contribution was that it reminded readers that all sorts of conversations were popping up between Protestants and Catholics in a variety of settings: the Fund for the Republic, the Methodist church, the Villanova Institute, and the National Conference of Christians and Jews.[44] He interpreted all of this activity as a sign of the maturity of American pluralism. If he was a bit too sanguine about what the conversations signified, he was right that something was in the air and the candidacy of John Kennedy was woven into much of it.

This initial dialogue set off an interesting exchange of letters to the editor that indicated that the series was being carefully followed in different and important camps. Monsignor Francis J. Lally offered a prickly response to Van Dusen.[45] As editor of the Boston archdiocese's newspaper, the *Pilot*, he was no ordinary priest; he was the confidant of Cardinal Cushing, the powerful bishop of Boston and a supporter of John Kennedy. Lally began by disputing the distinction between "liberal" Catholics and the "official" Roman Catholic hierarchy. For those with ears to hear, Lally was saying that Cushing supported the emerging liberal Catholic view of Murray, Weigel, and others, and affirming that American Catholics respected the freedom of the democratic state from religious domination. Lally argued that, outside of the domain of faith and morals, there were a variety of viewpoints on numberless matters. But even liberal Protestants would have a hard time accepting this distinction between faith and morals, on the one hand, and issues like the separation of church and state, on the other.

He then took up the so-called Ryan thesis by noting that Ryan, 15 years dead, never saw himself as the official church-state theologian for the American church. Lally noted that there were many more Protestant-established churches around the world than Catholic ones. Even in Massachusetts, political leaders reacted to the pronouncements of the Catholic church in the same way that political leaders in other places reacted to Protestant church groups' public pronouncements. In other words, nowhere in the country did politicians get trumped by religious leaders, no matter how numerous their followers.

Next, Lally testily replied to the alleged flouting of historical truth in the adoption of theological doctrines such as the Assumption of Mary. Such indictments "are the same charges the nineteenth century scholars brought against the Virgin Birth, the Resurrection and Divinity of Christ. If 'reactionary' means old, we must allow that the dogma of the Assumption is very reactionary, going back even to apostolic times."[46]

He closed on a more conciliatory note, writing that all of this showed the need for true dialogue, not just a double soliloquy. Such a dialogue would require both sides to speak and listen, to learn and unlearn a great many things before Catholics and Protestants would know "how the lines are drawn among us." That Cushing's best communicator would join this forum illustrates yet again the high importance that various actors were placing on this magazine.

Stanley Lowell of POAU reacted swiftly to Lally in a letter to the editor.[47] He asked why there should be any confusion on the point of Catholic teachings on church-state relations. He argued that the Catholic church was an authoritarian body and while individual Catholic thinkers like John Courtney Murray were interesting, the pope had not endorsed his views. Until that time came, Lowell wrote, the issue was fair game and POAU intended to keep raising it: "If the Pope does indeed believe in liberty for all faiths, why doesn't he just say so?"[48] *Christianity and Crisis* would consign POAU's responses to the letters section throughout the campaign, and POAU would play its agitator role in that forum. But in the early days of the quest for the White House, everyone seemed to recognize that something important was being played out on those pages.

On a more substantive note, William Clancy responded with a lengthy letter in which he nailed Lowell and engaged Van Dusen.[49] He stressed that POAU had no capacity to understand the slow but real development of doctrine in the Catholic church. It was not the case that the pope simply had to speak and doctrine changed. Clancy argued that religious liberty was one of the most discussed theological problems in contemporary Catholicism, and he further noted that John Bennett, one of *Christianity and Crisis*'s two chairs, had stated that for every book by a Catholic defending the traditional view of religious liberty, there were 10 defending religious freedom. POAU's problem was that it saw the Catholic church as a frozen authoritarian institution incapable of self-criticism and adaptation, no matter how much evidence there was to the contrary.

He saw Van Dusen's view as much more nuanced. Clancy argued that liberal Catholics—a term he didn't like but accepted—saw themselves not as a beleaguered minority, but as participating in a major adaptation of Catholic thought to the realities and truths of the current age:

> I cannot think of a single major Catholic thinker of the twentieth century who does not support the "liberal" view of religious freedom, and the "official" pronouncements of the recent Popes have been clearly, however cautiously, moving in this direction. And one now hears that a re-examination of religious tolerance will be one of the major questions before the forthcoming ecumenical council. Rome moves slowly but it does move.[50]

These exchanges did a remarkable job of establishing the parameters not only of the debate that would emerge during the presidential campaign but also of the changes in Catholic doctrine over the next few years, through the Second Vatican Council. The timing could not have been better for John Kennedy. If this liberal Catholic movement had not started by this time, it would have been hard to convince even liberal Protestants, much less more conservative ones, that a Catholic could be trusted to be president of all the people. The leaders of *Christianity and Crisis*, due to their proximity to eastern Catholic public intellectuals and because of their intellectual prowess, knew that the Catholic church was changing and that liberal Protestants needed to know this, especially in light of the possibility of Kennedy's candidacy. As Bennett noted, the journal made much of the fact that in the Catholic church there was a serious attempt to develop a doctrine of religious liberty that was consistent with the principles of democracy.[51]

Samples of most of the major forms of twentieth-century anti-Catholic arguments could be found in the pages of these two magazines in this short time frame. The analyses of two scholars in particular,

Mark Massa and John McGreevy, shed light on Protestants' fear of Catholic power. Massa argues that there have been three basic sets of explanations for the deep seated anti-Catholic strands in American history: cultural, intellectual, and social scientific.[52] The cultural explanation for anti-Catholicism is perhaps the oldest and most revered.[53] These explanations presume that North American public culture in its concrete political democratic processes, the protocols of capitalism, and its work ethic are all rooted "in a profoundly Protestant ordering of human society."[54] Some historians point to the Puritans' distrust of Catholicism as the origin of these feelings while others point to the two Great Awakenings as the engines of this phenomenon. Massa observes that, in the twentieth century, the great Harvard sociologist Talcott Parsons argued that Anglo-Saxon Protestant traditions, such as the Protestant work ethic, separation of the federal political powers, and a devotion to experimental science, provided the most reliable barriers to the threat of American fascism embodied by figures like the Catholic priest Charles Coughlin.

This is the proper category for the arguments advanced in the two magazines that concentrated on the European political behavior of the Catholic church. The essence of these arguments was that Catholic political thought and behavior were too European and not sufficiently appreciative of the American values of democracy and individual freedom. A Catholic president, by implication, would not be able to fully protect these values against the coercion of a European-based, rigidly hierarchical ecclesiastical organization.

The intellectual explanations for the anti-Catholic impulse posit a set of epistemological or philosophical ideas that underlie the American ideal, to which Catholic theology and piety are hostile. The actual contents of these core ideas varied with different thinkers, but they tended to include ideas of religious liberty, the inviolability of individual conscience, the free expression of personal opinion in speech and print, the separation of the church from the secular state, and a belief in American manifest destiny or exceptionalism.[55] There have been both Protestant and secular versions of this critique of Catholicism. McGreevy has shown that these intellectual arguments were even more powerful than the cultural explanations in the 1930s through the 1950s as a raft of secular intellectuals constructed a view of democracy that would be undermined by the hierarchical, monolithic, and authoritarian Catholic church.[56] This is where the bulk of the Protestant attacks in the pages of these two liberal magazine should be placed.

Massa's third set of explanations for the American anti-Catholic impulse is rooted in the social sciences, often under the rubrics of nativism or secularization. *Nativism* is a fear of outsiders by cultural insiders. Drawing on the work of sociologist Emile Durkheim, this view posits that societies establish boundaries that define the group. Deviance is an invented property that is conferred upon certain political, religious, or racial groups to demonstrate those behaviors that are outside the boundaries of the group. Anti-Catholicism can be interpreted as a function of boundary maintenance on the part of Protestants.[57] The other sociological explanation for anti-Catholicism is rooted in secularization theory. In modern Western societies, religious claims get moved into a private sphere in order to gain political peace, social comity, and civilized public discourse. Catholicism presents, in Massa's analysis, a special problem for this orientation since it is a magisterial religious tradition that "resolutely refuse[s] to play by the rules of the privatized religious game."[58]

McGreevy's account pushes further. He argues that the anthropological conceptions of culture that emerged in American thought by the 1930s form the backdrop for understanding this period of anti-Catholicism. By this time, *culture* "meant the web of meaning supporting the seemingly disparate practices in a particular society."[59] Widespread philosophical and institutional separatism cast Catholics as a problem group that resisted "integration" into American culture. Liberal intellectuals such as John Dewey saw the church as a barrier to the democratization of its communities. Around this time, McGreevy argues, a series of issues and themes emerged that raised new questions about the relationship between Catholicism and democracy. Several of these deserve mention because they form the background and much of the content of the Protestant critique of Kennedy's Catholicism and potential presidency.

McGreevy notes that, for many American liberals in the late 1930s, the importance of issues such as economic planning and redistribution of wealth began to recede in the face of a growing emphasis on individual freedom. These liberals drew constant distinctions between American civil liberties and fascist repression elsewhere. With the church in Mexico battling the administration of President Plutarcho Calles—who enforced measures against the Catholic church with the support of many American liberals—and with Catholic willingness to accommodate European fascist regimes, liberals saw a Catholic church out of step with democracy.

The Spanish Civil War was a crucial issue, as most American intellectuals found it impossible to believe that people of good will could support General Francisco Franco's regime. American Catholic support for Franco fed liberal suspicion. McGreevy argues that the cumulative effect of these cases led to extensive press coverage of the connections between Catholicism and fascism and to the conclusion of many liberals that, as Reinhold Niebuhr put it, "the Catholic Church has cast its lot with fascistic politics."[60]

The defining of "Americanism," according to McGreevy, became a central project for intellectuals concerned about Catholic power from the mid-1930s through the early 1950s. These thinkers sought to demonstrate the nonhierarchical sources of American culture, with Catholicism a convenient target of criticism. Catholic authoritarianism might repress the scientific spirit, produce adults incapable of psychological autonomy, and undermine national unity due to the growing number of children being educated in Catholic schools.[61]

Democratic institutions were linked by a number of prominent historians to the work of the Protestant Reformation, thus distinguishing what was Catholic from what was American. Talcott Parsons, who translated Max Weber's famous work *The Protestant Ethic and the Spirit of Capitalism*, stressed that it was America's Anglo-Saxon Protestant traditions, including a concern of civil liberties, that provided the strongest barriers to fascism. He expressed concern that the authoritarian structure of the Catholic church might weaken these traditions.[62]

In a similar vein, liberals argued that a crucial trait of democratic culture was an enthusiasm for science. The scientific impulse was seen as an outgrowth of Protestantism, and the Catholic church was portrayed as being a hindrance to science. And just as Catholic authoritarianism undermined the intellectual autonomy necessary for scientific research, Catholic families might destroy psychological independence. Overly restrictive Catholic families might produce children who would channel their frustration into fascist politics.[63]

In the realm of American politics, concrete issues emerged at the nexus of Catholicism and democracy, most notably federal aid to parochial schools. McGreevy demonstrates how many Catholic leaders had resisted government intrusion in parochial schools. But by the 1940s, these leaders came to see that the property tax increases necessary to pay for the expanding public school systems would make it harder for Catholic parents to afford parochial schools, and Catholic arguments evolved.

Two landmark Supreme Court decisions—*Everson v. Board of Education* in 1947 and *McCollum v. Board of Education* in 1948—addressed related issues. In *Everson*, the Court found that the busing of Catholic children by a New Jersey township did not violate the wall

of separation between church and state. A firestorm of Protestant complaints emerged, leading to the founding of POAU. In the *McCollum*
case, the Court ruled that a local program to provide "release time" for
students to receive religious instruction from clergy in public school
classrooms was an unconstitutional establishment of religion.[64]

Against this background, the liberal Protestant voices of these two
publications were typical for the era. So this initial phase of the campaign
ended with the two major Protestant journals of record staking out their
initial coverage of the emerging religion issue and taking their first editorial stands. The major differences between *Christianity and Crisis* and
the *Christian Century* were twofold. First, *Christianity and Crisis* was
more optimistic that the changes afoot among Catholic theologians on
religious freedom signaled real change. While the *Century* acknowledged
that change was in the air, it remained skeptical that Kennedy would be
free of Vatican interference. Second, *Christianity and Crisis* was not content simply to report the development of Catholic thinking, it wanted to
help move it along through dialogue. The *Christian Century* took a less
activist role.

In the early months of 1960, the political trajectory of the campaign and the intellectual trajectory of liberal Protestantism (and conservative Protestantism) set these two forces on a collision course. As
Kennedy sought votes in the primary season and as wary Protestants
witnessed his progress, they would meet head on.

3

FIRST SKIRMISHES
··

In January 1960, a few days after the formal launch of Kennedy's campaign, the Journalism Department at Columbia University sponsored its second annual conference on religious journalism. The staffs and supporters of three religious magazines—the *Christian Century*, *Commonweal*, and *Commentary*—were featured (it was quickly dubbed the Four Cs conference).[1] Many *Christianity and Crisis* staff also attended. Kennedy's candidacy was on the docket for discussion. After the conference, *Christianity and Crisis* managing editor Wayne Cowan wrote to *Christian Century* editor Harold Fey:

> I found myself agreeing with your summary statement where you pointed out the inevitability of problems being laid at the feet of prejudice against Roman Catholics when, in fact, it may merely be the result of honest efforts that choose not to support Kennedy on other grounds entirely. I suspect the opposite will be true, too, in terms of those Catholics who choose to support Kennedy for the best of reasons.[2]

As the campaign got under way, Fey would retreat from this position and come to believe that Catholic bloc voting for Kennedy was a critical problem for Protestants. Cowan's argument that not all Catholics were voting for Kennedy for sectarian reasons failed to convince him.

The Four Cs conference demonstrated that the intellectual world of these liberal journalists and theologians was small. They knew one another and were in contact often. They all rubbed shoulders in the nascent ecumenical movement of the late fifties and early sixties, much of it centered in New York City.

From the beginning of 1960 through the summer nominating conventions, nostalgia for Adlai Stevenson filled the pages of *Christianity and Crisis*. In the first issue of 1960, the magazine took the unusual step of printing Stevenson's address on the national steel strike along with separate commentaries by John Bennett and Reinhold Niebuhr.[3] The editors justified this move by saying that the speech deserved the widest possible circulation because its major emphases transcended partisanship and because it touched on fundamental concerns of the magazine. The whole exchange seemed artificial and out of proportion to the actual importance of the speech, which was a pretty mundane policy address. More likely, the editors of the magazine were goading Stevenson to jump into the race, and Niebuhr and Bennett were signaling to Stevenson that they remained loyal supporters.

Later in January, the actual events of the campaign interrupted the will-he-or-won't-he drama surrounding Stevenson when New York governor Nelson Rockefeller withdrew from the race, leaving Nixon as the only Republican candidate. Bennett wrote that Rockefeller's exit left only a candidate "who until recently appealed only to the narrower and more conservative type of Republican."[4] For Bennett, Rockefeller's withdrawal was a failure of democracy:

> A strong bid by Nelson Rockefeller would have done much to stimulate thought about real issues and it would have forced Nixon to declare himself early enough to enable the people to take his measure. The chief impression that is left by all that has happened is that Nixon is as skillful a political operator as one can expect to find.

With Nixon free to concentrate on the general election, the eventual Democratic nominee's task became that much harder.

Bennett went on to say that Nixon's unscrupulous campaign tactics in past races showed serious defects of character. The balance of the article questioned his suitability for the presidency based on his McCarthy-like anti-Communism and his ties to questionable right-wing California businessmen.[5] Future U.S. senator John C. Danforth wrote a heated reply in which he accused Bennett of engaging in McCarthy-like tactics himself.[6] Bennett replied prophetically that Danforth's letter was an indication of the differences of opinion that "we can expect during the coming campaign."[7]

In February, Niebuhr penned an article marking the 20th anniversary of *Christianity and Crisis*. In it, he asked if the title of the

magazine—which was originally a reference to the crisis of Nazism—
was still apt. Niebuhr acknowledged that, for the most part, the magazine had focused on international problems and political problems.
Increasingly, though, the attention of its writers had turned to cultural
issues. Among those that Niebuhr identified, one was directly relevant
to the presidential race:

> Part of the mission of this journal to the Christian community has
> been to assuage the animosity between Protestantism and Roman
> Catholicism, without sacrificing the achievements of the "free"
> churches. These two forms of Christianity have "coexisted" for a long
> time, since the end of the religious wars in the seventeenth century.
> Still there is a problem of achieving genuine charity and of preventing
> Protestantism from becoming mere anti-Catholicism.[8]

Christianity and Crisis did not abandon the Protestant-Catholic
dialogue to its rival publication in Chicago. In March, Bennett wrote a
lengthy piece addressing the whirlwind surrounding the possibility of a
Catholic president.[9] Bennett issued the closest thing to an endorsement
of Kennedy to appear in any influential Protestant periodical. He began
with an important thesis:

> The issue raised by the possibility of a Roman Catholic candidate for
> the Presidency is the most significant immediate problem that grows
> out of the confrontation of Roman Catholicism with other religious
> communities in the United States. There are a great many Protestants
> of influence who are inclined to say that they would never vote for a
> Roman Catholic for President. Many of them refuse to say this with
> finality, but there is a strong trend in this direction. Our guess is that it
> may be stronger among clergy and among official Protestant spokes-
> men than among laity.[10]

The headline was marked by an asterisk with a notation at the bottom
declaring that the editorial was written in the hope that it would clear
the air regarding general principles, and it was not intended to support
any particular candidate.

This was the most direct statement of the problem to date. Bennett
had managed to cut through any clouds surrounding Kennedy's candidacy. Kennedy faced a huge political problem with Protestant leaders,
and he could not rely on the Protestant establishment for extensive help
in reaching out to the laity. Bennett proceeded to do the Kennedy campaign a huge favor by dissecting all types of Protestant anti-Catholicism.
He acknowledged that crude prejudice combined with a reluctance to
accept the fact that this was no longer a Protestant country accounted

for some forms of Protestant anti-Catholicism. But Bennett did not dwell there because his counsel would be of limited or no value with those constituencies. Rather, he turned to what he might have called persuadable Protestants.

Two substantive considerations were feeding their fears. First, the traditional teaching of the Catholic church was at variance with American conceptions of religious liberty and of church-state relations. Might a Catholic president be used by a politically powerful church? Second, there were policy issues on which there was a Catholic position, and a Catholic president might steer national policy in those directions.

Bennett's response had three main planks. First, if the American people made it clear that a Catholic could never be elected president, this would suggest that Catholics could not fully participate in U.S. political life, which would be an insult to the 39 million Catholics in the country. It would "wound our common life and damage our institutions" far worse than anything a Catholic president might do. He was shocked that so many Protestants were unwilling to consider this.

Second, people were not justified in asking what a particular Catholic candidate believed regarding church and state relations. There was no need to grill a candidate on this matter since his years of public service would tell the story. He then traced the two dominant, well-documented Catholic views on the matter. In the traditional view, the church is in a privileged position and there is at least some curtailment of the liberties of non-Catholics. This view was inherited from an earlier era and was rejected by "many Catholic theologians and ecclesiastical leaders." They believed in religious liberty for non-Catholics on principle and not merely as a pragmatic adjustment to American reality.

This liberal view, according to Bennett, was held not only in America, but also in Western Europe and by some in the Vatican. Some of the latter believed that Pope Pius XII had at least been open to it and were "even more sure that this is true of his generous-minded successor." In addition, the American laity emphatically accepted this liberal view, and Senator Kennedy embraced it as well. Bennett concluded the point by arguing that it was quite possible that a Catholic president who was liberal on this point might be better able to deal with Catholic pressures than a Protestant. This was the ultimate heresy to both the hard-line Protestant view of POAU and the skeptical moderation of Harold Fey.

Bennett's third and final argument was that, while there were some specific issues on which there was a known Catholic position, few of these would ever reach the president since they were dealt with at lower levels of government. But he quickly conceded that birth control was a vexing issue. As a domestic issue, it belonged primarily to the states, but there was also the question of foreign aid. Bennett suggested a hedge for a Catholic president in a thinly veiled piece of advice to Kennedy:

> There is general agreement that this country should not urge on another country a birth control program but that it should cooperate with a country that desires it. The birth control feature of a broader program of economic development could be paid for by the government of the aided country while the United States Government would support the program as a whole. This merely suggests a possibility that might enable a Catholic President to handle this issue constructively.
>
> However, it must be noted that the issue of birth control must be weighed along with all the other issues that are at stake in an election. Even if a Catholic candidate were to take a line here that we might regret, this would not necessarily outweigh all the other considerations of which we need to take account. Furthermore, we do not know what line a Catholic President would take in a complicated situation, for Catholic moral theology gives a high place to the virtue of prudence.[11]

Bennett concluded on a positive note, observing that a Catholic president who was well versed in the moral teachings of his church would have certain assets, including a better perspective on social justice than many Protestants and the restraining guidance of the just war tradition. He also noted that there were elements in Catholic moral doctrine that he rejected, "but Catholic teaching has its better and more humane side, and it is a repository of much wisdom that could stand a Catholic President in good stead."

This was an astonishing piece of writing. Not only did it take the fight to the dominant Protestant positions against Kennedy and any Catholic, it made a case for why a Catholic might even be desirable for the country. Bennett candidly admitted that there were troublesome issues, such as birth control, while reminding readers that it was simply one issue among a host of important ones. While Adlai Stevenson might be the hero of the magazine's leaders, at least some of them were beginning to see the merits of Kennedy's candidacy. There would be no further cheerleading for Stevenson to jump into the race. The primary season unfolded with little comment from the magazine. Only after the Democratic convention in Los Angeles did the old feelings for Stevenson come back for one last visit.

The depression expressed by Kennedy on the night of his announcement could only have been compounded by a story that broke in which the Reverend Daniel Poling charged Kennedy with being unduly influenced by the Catholic hierarchy in an episode almost a decade earlier.[12] While Poling held no official leadership role in the Christian Reformed church, as editor of the *Christian Herald*, with its circulation of over 400,000, he held great power and influence among moderate evangelicals. And he claimed to hold the smoking gun that proved that Kennedy was indeed unduly influenced by the Catholic hierarchy. If his charges stuck, Kennedy's nascent candidacy would be finished among Protestants.

During World War II, Poling's son, a military chaplain, was one of four chaplains who went down on the USS *Dorchester*. The four chaplains—one Jewish, one Catholic, and two Protestant—gave their life preservers to others and died as a result. After the war, the Reverend Poling began raising funds to build a memorial chapel in the Baptist temple at Temple University. Construction was completed in the early 1950s, and Poling invited Representative John Kennedy to be one of the speakers at a dinner in a Philadelphia hotel. In Poling's autobiography, *Mine Eyes Have Seen the Glory*, published in late 1959, he claimed that Kennedy withdrew as a speaker at the request of Dennis Cardinal Dougherty, the Roman Catholic bishop of Philadelphia. Poling also ran an article about the incident in the December issue of the *Christian Herald*. This was clear proof in Poling's mind that Kennedy had acted under direct orders of the Catholic hierarchy, and if he had done so in the past, he could be expected to do so in the future. Protestant fear of undue clerical influence on Kennedy was not based on a hypothetical; it was grounded in experience.

Kennedy's first response had been to downplay the story and hope it would disappear. In December 1959, he refused to comment to the *Christian Science Monitor*, and later that month, his father told the *New York Times* that the reporting was inaccurate. But the national press picked up the story, and Kennedy could not make it go away.

Bishop Oxnam heard of the story and wrote to Poling to say that, while he liked Kennedy and had met him, he had grave doubts that any Catholic politician could be free from the pressure of the hierarchy. He told Poling that his account was the first and an "almost conclusive" statement of the Catholic hierarchy's pressure upon an individual. In Oxnam's estimation, it was a significant and compelling episode. He asked Poling if he knew of other circumstances involving the senator and the Catholic hierarchy.[13] Poling responded that he did not.[14]

Oxnam, despite his budding relationship with Kennedy, went public with his doubts, and as a result the story exploded. A day after

Kennedy's formal announcement, Oxnam told the national press that, as a result of the Poling incident, he had doubts about Kennedy's freedom from the Catholic hierarchy. The *New York Times* quoted Oxnam: "I had thought he could exercise independent judgment as an American citizen until I saw a report that he had canceled an interfaith speaking engagement because a Cardinal had insisted he do it."[15]

Kennedy told his side of the story at a National Press Club event. Kennedy said that he had been asked to attend as a representative of the Catholic church and not as a congressman. Then Cardinal Dougherty informed him, indirectly, that he did not have any credentials to do this. In addition, the chapel was located in a church of a different faith. Kennedy said that he told Poling that he would like to come, but he could not attend as a representative of the Catholic church. He also expressed dismay that Poling had waited nine years to lodge his complaint.

Poling continued to press his case by trying to rebut Kennedy in opinion columns in the February and March issues of his magazine, but the steam seemed to be escaping the controversy. Kennedy and Poling exchanged letters throughout the spring. By September, Poling was still in a fighting mood and joined forces with other prominent Protestants, including Norman Vincent Peale, to try to stop Kennedy. But in his final column before Election Day in November, Poling wrote that he had asked Kennedy whether he would have come to the dinner for the chapel if he had been invited as a congressman and Cardinal Dougherty had objected. Poling wrote that Kennedy's answer was "forthright and significantly American."[16] Presumably, Poling was placated, and the charge that Kennedy was a pawn of the Catholic hierarchy was finally laid to rest in his mind.

After the Poling controversy blew over, Kennedy exchanged letters with another unlikely correspondent, E. S. James, another editor-bishop, this time a Southern Baptist who ran the highly influential Texas magazine the *Baptist Standard*. Someone in the Kennedy camp, perhaps Sorensen, was paying close attention to some of the farthest corners of "yellow-dog Democrat" country at an early point in the presidential derby. In the February 17, 1960, issue of his magazine, James wrote an editorial entitled "Mr. Kennedy's Candidacy." James noted that it looked like Kennedy was going to be the Democratic nominee and if Baptists were going to oppose any man for his religious attachments, it should be before the convention. He elaborated:

> The *Standard* regards Mr. Kennedy as a clean young man with intelligence, ability, and competence. He has a pretty good political record.

He should be commended for his affirmation that if he were President he would abide by the [C]onstitution regardless of the attitude of his church. The statement brought upon him the condemnation of the hierarchy, and this is understandable because the Catholic clergy always reserves to itself the right to control every action of all its subjects. If we must have a Catholic as President, perhaps Kennedy would be as good as could be found; but until two things are done this country must never elect to this high office a member of that faith.

There must be a renunciation of allegiance to the foreign religio-political state at the Vatican, and there must be a declaration of freedom from the domination of the clergy by American Catholic citizens. If that were done we know of no reason why a Roman Catholic should not have the support of voters of all faiths. Until it is done, many of us will oppose the election of any of them to the office of national leaders. If they want to hurl anathemas at us, let them proceed.[17]

Twelve days later, Kennedy replied in a letter. He thanked James for his generous statements about his record and views. He then noted that he thought his previous statements had made it clear that in public office he was guided by the best interests of the country and that he would not be dominated by any source. He concluded by saying that he should be held responsible only for his own views and conduct and that any predictions about his future behavior should be based upon his own record. The tone was friendly, and it seems as if Kennedy felt that James was someone to whom he could talk frankly.[18]

James responded quickly and with some measure of grace. He reiterated that he liked Kennedy and his record and was grateful that Kennedy wrote to him directly. His problem was not with Kennedy or with Catholicism per se. Rather, he disagreed with the control that Catholic clergy exercised over the morals of its membership. Since government acted primarily in the realm of morals, he did not see how it was possible for a man to faithfully exercise the tenets of Catholicism and still be absolutely free to exercise his own judgment rather than the judgment of his church's hierarchy. He informed Kennedy that he would be happy to publish Kennedy's letter for the millions of readers of the *Baptist Standard* if Kennedy were willing to give his permission.[19]

There is no evidence that Kennedy did so, and this correspondence produced nothing in the short run. But this initial exchange of views and mutual respect laid the foundation for an exchange of opinions on specific policy issues later in the campaign that would pay huge, perhaps even crucial, dividends for Kennedy. This episode illustrates yet again Kennedy's willingness to engage his religious critics directly when it seemed politically prudent to do so. He did not retreat in fear in the face of strong conservative Protestant criticism.

At about the same time, Sorensen gave a long speech on "The Catholic Issue in American Politics," which was a snapshot of the campaign's thinking just as the primary season was starting.[20] Certain themes emerged in the speech that, not surprisingly, Kennedy would later use himself. Sorensen admitted that there were some legitimate issues touching on religion, such as public education, an ambassador to the Vatican, religious liberty, the doctrine of the separation of church and state, and foreign aid for birth control: "No one should feel bigoted about raising them—and no candidate for public office should feel persecuted if he is asked them."

The real issue, he asserted, was Kennedy's record. He invoked Bishop Oxnam and Paul Blanshard, who had praised Kennedy's answers to their legitimate questions. Sorensen denied in strong terms that, as president, Kennedy would be subject to any ecclesiastical pressure, divided loyalty, or religious obligation. In fact, he would be less vulnerable to any possible political pressure from the so-called Catholic vote than some non-Catholic politicians who might feel the need to cater to Catholics.

Sorensen then directly addressed the sort of preemptive argument advanced by some Protestants that Kennedy's personal views did not matter; if he wanted to stay in the good graces of the church, he had to do its bidding. This so-called Catholic view had nothing to do with Kennedy's own positions. He elaborated:

> Contrary to what is popularly believed, as a Catholic, he takes no vow to any foreign power. He binds himself to no manifestos on public policy—and he is in no danger of excommunication for any conceivable act he may perform, or any view he may express, or any law he may enforce, as President of the United States—regardless of what some Pope may have done to some other ruler in some other land at some other time. Any American Bishop, Archbishop, or Cardinal who might dislike his conduct of office has only one remedy—to vote Republican at the next election.

Then Sorensen went on the offensive against the Reverend Poling. He noted that, in Poling's original account of the incident in his autobiography, he had written that he invited Kennedy to the ceremony in 1950 as a spokesman for his Catholic faith. When Kennedy learned that the Catholic church was not participating in the ceremony because it involved a revolving three-part altar in a Baptist church, which was not in keeping with Catholic practice, Kennedy withdrew without any orders from the cardinal because he did not have the authority to represent the Catholic church. He could represent Massachusetts or even Congress, but not the church.

Sorensen closed the speech by addressing the pragmatic question of whether or not a Catholic could win the presidency in 1960 by emphasizing three points. First, 1960 was not 1928. Contemporary polling showed that Catholicism had declined as a factor in American elections. Second, Kennedy's Catholicism would doubtless hurt him some in the deep South, but not enough to affect the electoral vote. Better to discuss Kennedy's Catholicism openly now and get it out of the way. And third, when all of the candidates were better known, there would be less emphasis on "the Catholic candidate."

The speech was a combination of stark political realism and wishful thinking. Kennedy and his campaign had done a lot of work to defuse the religion issue. Their efforts were about to be put to the test in the primaries. While the speech acknowledged the reality Kennedy faced, it also signaled to the world that Kennedy had a strategy for facing the negative role his faith might play.

Meanwhile, the *Christian Century*, too, was deeply involved in the nomination process. Between January 1960 and the Republican convention in August, the magazine published over 20 articles related to presidential politics. One constant theme was a negative portrayal of Kennedy. There were many different shades and nuances in these portraits, but the overall impression was unmistakable. The coverage began with a brief notice of Rockefeller's withdrawal and Kennedy's formal announcement.[21] The article noted that Kennedy would put the Democrats in a difficult situation if he were nominated, not because of his youth and inexperience, but because he was Catholic. Democrats would risk alienating the Catholic vote if the party rejected him.

In the next issue, the magazine reprinted a negative account of Kennedy from the British magazine the *Economist*.[22] The candidate was described as wily and coldly calculating, a spiritually rootless man who only performed the prescribed devotions of his Catholic faith. He was distrusted for his Catholicism, for the influence of his father, and for his dismaying record of retreating under political pressure. His approach to public issues was almost wholly cerebral, and he had no reservoir of deep feelings about any issue. He had no executive experience and had no prospect of gaining any unless the Democrats, for "vote catching purposes," consign him to "the dusty futility of the vice-presidency." Under the guise of running an article showing a foreign view, the magazine was able to print things that none of its own writers could possibly have gotten away with.

Later in January, the *Christian Century* ran a news story highlighting the Poling charges and Kennedy's explanation at the press conference at the National Press Club.[23] The upshot, for the magazine, was that if Kennedy were president, "he would be subject to the same kind of discipline that he acknowledges as Senator."[24]

As the formal campaign for the Democratic nomination got under way, the real world of politics and the clubby world of mainline Protestant journalism moved closer together. As Kennedy was put to the test by actual voters, the debate in the Protestant press took on a new urgency. The first of 16 Democratic presidential primaries was in New Hampshire on March 8, and Kennedy won overwhelmingly against only token opposition.

The first real contest was in the Wisconsin primary on April 5, where Kennedy went head-to-head with Minnesota senator Hubert Humphrey. Wisconsin was a large state, adjacent to Minnesota, with a diverse religious and ethnic population that presented challenges to Kennedy. The state's 31 delegates would be apportioned by a formula granting 10 on a statewide, winner-take-all basis, 20 (2 each) from the 10 congressional districts, and the remaining delegate split between the national committeeman and committeewoman. In theory, a candidate could lose the popular vote and still win the most delegates. Wisconsin, where the presidential primary had been invented in 1903, held an open primary, allowing people from either party to vote in the other's primary. Thus, the exact force of the religion issue was open to question. Protestant Republicans could vote for Humphrey to frustrate Kennedy while Republican Catholics could vote for Kennedy out of religious loyalty.

All of these variables made some in the Kennedy circle wary of challenging Humphrey so close to his home. By contrast, Kennedy himself believed that he needed to show his ability to win against Humphrey in hostile territory. As one staffer put it, Kennedy was looking for reasons to run there while the men around him were looking for reasons not to.[25] The anxiety over religion played a role in the staff's doubts. Despite their anxieties, he insisted on entering the Wisconsin primary. If he could win decisively there, he could knock Humphrey out and run the table of remaining primaries. Since the spring of 1959, Kennedy had been campaigning unofficially in Wisconsin and, based on the reception he had received, he felt confident.

On December 22, 1959, Pat Lucey, chair of the Wisconsin Democratic Party, wrote a passionate four-page memo to Ted Sorensen, arguing that Kennedy should enter the primary.[26] His argument had three main points. First, Kennedy was leading Humphrey in the November Harris poll. Second, Humphrey was drawing tiny crowds and minimal press coverage, and his volunteers were already demoralized. Finally, Lucey had surveyed the Democratic establishment and the state press, and both were favorably disposed toward Kennedy. Religion did not come up.

But Kennedy left nothing to chance. He announced his entrance in the primary on January 21 and moved his entire campaign apparatus to the state on February 1. The massive operation would be on the ground for more than two months before the primary itself. Simultaneously, Kennedy engaged the Harris polling firm to ply its trade in what may at the time have been the largest concentration of presidential polling in one state. Harris produced two reports that revealed many things about the campaign, including its nervousness over Kennedy's Catholicism.

In the first of two confidential memos to Kennedy, Harris wrote on February 13 that, in 15 years of polling, he had never seen a state like Wisconsin, where half of the congressional districts were stable while the other half were extremely volatile.[27] Harris had conducted a statewide survey with a large sample of 1,564 likely Democratic primary voters in addition to a survey of 1,230 potential crossover Republican voters. He sought a direct reading of the extent to which voters felt strongly about a Catholic running for president. His bottom line was that Kennedy could be confident of winning the overall vote, but given the quirks of the system for assigning delegates, the volatility of the voters in half of the state, and the unknown religion factor, arduous and careful planning and campaigning were needed. Kennedy's congressional district tally could range from a high of nine to as low as five.[28] But Harris thought a 9–1 congressional district win was possible. That would put an end to Humphrey's challenge and greatly boost Kennedy's chances of securing the nomination.

In the course of his analysis, Harris put his finger on the very problem that would emerge on primary night:

> There is one consideration, however. Most observers have written off the three western-most districts, the 3rd, 9th, and 10th as being virtually "sure" Humphrey country. Along with the 7th, they are thought to be the heart-land of the state's dominantly rural vote. Were Kennedy to win six districts but lose these four to Humphrey,

undoubtedly the cry will go up that Kennedy is strong in industrial and Catholic areas, but shows weaknesses in the rural and Protestant areas. Therefore, it becomes of the utmost urgency to break through in at least one, perhaps two, and obviously preferably in all four of these rural areas.[29]

Harris then turned to an extensive analysis of the religion issue. He saw that Kennedy was winning a massive proportion of the Catholic Democratic vote (81% to 19% for Humphrey) while holding the Protestant vote against him down to manageable levels. His fear was that the large Lutheran vote might begin to break against Kennedy in large numbers. But so far, Lutherans were running just 56% to 44% for Humphrey.[30]

Harris concluded with some analysis of the likely turnout by religious affiliation and offered some final advice. For the time being, Catholics in both parties were likely to vote for Kennedy in the Democratic primary while Protestant Republicans were not likely to cross over and vote against Kennedy to protect Nixon. Religion had not yet become an overt factor in the race. Harris thought that Humphrey was unlikely to raise the religion issue out of fear that Catholic Republicans might retaliate against him and cross over to vote for Kennedy. Harris observed:

> The fact is that the Catholic vote is solid for Kennedy and the big potentially anti-Catholic Lutheran vote plans to vote for the most part in the Republican primary. The danger, of course, is that at the last minute the religious issue will be stirred and when it does, it will drive Republican Lutherans over to the Democratic primary to vote against Senator Kennedy. There are no signs of this now, and certainly it would be most unwise of the Senator to raise the issue himself in any shape, manner, or form. With the continuing, ongoing work we shall be doing, we will be able to measure any raise [sic] in religious feeling and then the situation can be reassessed.[31]

Two weeks later, Harris offered a report on three of the four congressional districts he had recommended for extra attention.[32] The sample size was huge, as was the army of Harris employees who had gone into the field to interview 2,571 individuals in every county in these three districts. The large sample was necessary, Harris argued, in part because of the complexities of the religious landscape and in part because of the fluidity of support among the candidates. Five weeks before the primary, Harris was confident that Kennedy had substantial leads in the Third and Seventh Districts and a smaller lead in the

Second District. These districts held the smallest percentage of Catholic voters in the state.

Harris highlighted a phenomenon he had never seen before: the selective turnout of Catholic voters of both parties for Kennedy. In these three rural districts, 80% of Catholics intended to vote in the Democratic primary whereas only 45–55% of them would usually vote Democratic. Harris had a few theories about this. First was the simple straightforward attraction of Kennedy, first as a person and only secondarily as a Catholic:

> Today in Wisconsin, there is scarcely a Catholic voter who is unaware of the fact that 1960 might see the first man of the Catholic faith elected to the nation's highest post. We are quite certain that this turnout would not take place for any Catholic regardless of his personality and what he stands for. Senator Kennedy has a remarkable capacity to make Catholic voters feel that he represents the "best" of their group. His fine family background, his upper class demeanor, and his wealth all label him with the Catholic group as what they all would like to see a representative of their own group to be.[33]

What helped to crystallize the Wisconsin Catholic vote was the view, expressed in the survey, that if Kennedy were to win the nomination, he would need every possible vote he could garner. Catholics identified with Kennedy and felt they must rally to one of their own, since if they didn't, no one would.

Harris had one fear, which was the possibility that Catholic voters would come to believe that if Kennedy did not win, it would be because of Protestant bigotry. Harris did not see much evidence of this yet, but it might arrive in the next month "without any great difficulty."[34] If the Catholic community were to dig in for a last-ditch battle against the rest of the polity, it might cause a massive Protestant counterreaction in which a "sleeping Lutheran and other Protestant majority" would be aroused and would move into the Democratic primary in larger numbers to vote against Kennedy.

In light of this possibility, he argued that Kennedy had to bend over backward not to demonstrate any pro-Catholic bias in his campaigning. No local appearances with Catholic clergy or at Catholic venues must be allowed. No final church-state speech should be made. If questioned at local appearances about his Catholicism, he should answer unequivocally, as he had been doing. Harris felt that Kennedy had enjoyed the optimum conditions on the religion question so far in Wisconsin: Catholics were drawn to him in record numbers, and Protestants did not seem to be inclined to cross over from the Republican side to vote against him. He counseled extreme caution from the campaign so as not to provoke a shift in the status quo.

This was an early sign of the Kennedy campaign's pragmatic, case-by-case approach to the whole nexus of religion issues it faced. As the campaign progressed, Kennedy and his advisors demonstrated great dexterity. By framing the stakes early on, Harris did Kennedy a great service. Kennedy's delicate task was to attract Catholics without alienating Protestants in the process. Yet he also had to be careful not to allow Catholics to raise charges of anti-Catholic bigotry, lest they provoke a Protestant backlash. This sort of issue management might have been possible in rural congressional districts in Wisconsin, but it would be impossible to control the discourse at the national level.

Harris's prediction of the volatility of the voters proved to be true, while his prediction of a possible congressional district sweep for Kennedy did not. While Kennedy beat Humphrey convincingly in the popular vote, 56.3% to 43.5%, the congressional districts split 6–4, with Kennedy losing the three most populous Protestant districts, which comprised Wisconsin's border with Minnesota. Pollster Elmo Roper told Walter Cronkite during the CBS network's special coverage of the primary that the religion issue was the single most important issue in the race.[35] He reported that the Catholic vote was going 3–1 and 4–1 for Kennedy in some places, while Protestants were going for Humphrey at 3–2. But what seemed to be a problem for Kennedy was that the religion issue grew in prominence in the last few weeks of the campaign, apparently eroding some of the support that Harris had found for Kennedy among Protestants. Roper theorized that, as Protestants heard that Catholics were breaking 4–1 for Kennedy in the days leading up to the primary, Protestant groups began to turn to Humphrey. While it was not the large-scale Lutheran rebellion that Harris had feared, it was significant enough to deny Kennedy a knockout blow against Humphrey, which might also have put the religion question to rest for the balance of the primary campaign.

Publicly, Kennedy took the high road. He told Cronkite that he did not think the religion issue should be part of the analysis of how voters chose in Wisconsin. He pointed out that Humphrey's strong farm record had helped him in western Wisconsin. And he went on to say that he did not think that religion would play a large role in the next contested primary, West Virginia.[36] Privately, Kennedy was frustrated. A thousand-vote shift in Madison would have given him the Second District. The campaign had invested heavily there. Kennedy had stolen

Wisconsin senator William Proxmire's campaign aide Jerry Bruno and put him in the field in July 1959. He had dispatched his confidant Ken O'Donnell to Wisconsin in January 1960, and his full campaign operation had been there since the beginning of February. And yet Humphrey had lived to fight another day and Kennedy's Catholicism was still an issue. Kennedy aide Dave Powers reported that, when Kennedy's sister Eunice asked JFK what the returns meant, he said angrily that it meant they had to do it all over again, go to West Virginia the next day, and win all of the primaries from there to Los Angeles (where the Democratic convention would be held).[37] Kennedy and his staff would come to view the outcome in Wisconsin quite differently in time, but for the moment they were extremely frustrated.[38]

Meanwhile, the drumbeat continued in the *Christian Century*. In February, it had run a two-part series entitled "Religion and the Presidency," which examined the 1928 Al Smith case, among many others.[39] While not overtly hostile to Kennedy, the series argued that historically Americans have seemed to want an embodiment of themselves in a president, which meant that no candidate could disagree too sharply in his religious views. Atheists, Roman Catholics, Jews, Mormons, Christian Scientists, and any number of small groups had been disqualified. It did not seem likely that the American people would elect a Catholic president in the near future.

Fey warned in a private letter, "If the Roman Catholics of Wisconsin turn out to support Kennedy in wholesale fashion, it will be a warning to Protestants which we will be foolish to ignore."[40] While Kennedy had won in Wisconsin, you wouldn't have known it from reading the magazine:

> The magic went out of the presidential campaign of Senator Kennedy in Wisconsin's primary election. After the votes were counted it was clear that no miracle had taken place. Personable Jack Kennedy, with plenty of money and relatives to assist him, was not quite able to pull off the expected Hollywood finish. The combined efforts of his public relations staff, his political machine and his support from fellow Roman Catholics failed to start his bandwagon in an irresistible sweep toward Los Angeles....
>
> If "bigotry" was significantly present in the Wisconsin primary—which is doubtful—the outcome suggests that it was more in evidence in Catholics' crossing party lines to vote for Kennedy because he was a Catholic than in Protestants' voting against Kennedy on that ground. However, the unquestioned fact that Catholics did in large numbers apply a religious test to a candidate for the office of President is bound

to have its effect on the remainder of the campaign. Non-Catholics will expect Catholics in other places to follow the example of their fellow churchmen in Wisconsin. It would be wrong for them to ignore this probability in making their own choice of candidate. It would also be wrong for non-Catholics to ignore the obligation which would be imposed on a President if he won a national election with the kind of support Senator Kennedy received in Wisconsin.[41]

This analysis strains credulity. Catholics were seen as incapable of independent political judgment while Protestants, by definition, practiced it. The magazine continued to advance the argument that, when Catholics vote for Kennedy, it is reverse bigotry. The Wisconsin primary represented a missed opportunity for the magazine's favorite Democrat, Hubert Humphrey, to damage Kennedy.[42] In this desperate hour, it now embraced what had only been debated so far: Kennedy as president would be under an "obligation" to the Catholic church.

On April 11, W. H. Lawrence of the *New York Times* trenchantly described the dangerous political terrain for Kennedy in the upcoming West Virginia primary.[43] West Virginia senator Robert Byrd was urging a coalition of "stop Kennedy" forces in support of Humphrey for the May 10 primary. Byrd warned that the primary might be the last chance for supporters of Lyndon Johnson, Adlai Stevenson, or Stuart Symington to stop the Kennedy nomination. Since only Humphrey and Kennedy were on the ballot, Humphrey would have to be the surrogate for all of the others.

Lawrence went on to note that Kennedy had said he had to win all of the primaries he entered in order to secure the nomination, so West Virginia represented a make-or-break moment. Yet Kennedy faced many difficulties in West Virginia, the largest of which was his Catholicism. Catholics made up less than 5% of the state's population, and the old Ku Klux Klan was strong there. A whispering campaign among Protestants urged them to oppose Kennedy and the Catholic bloc voting that had propelled him to victory in Wisconsin. Lawrence also noted that, if Kennedy could win there, it would demonstrate to the country that he was not dependent upon a Catholic crutch. So Kennedy's religion was at the heart of the primary there, and whatever strategy he chose to employ would have to directly address his Catholicism.

The *Christian Century*'s coverage of the West Virginia primary began in late April.[44] The magazine rightly noted that the May 10 primary there might halt either the Humphrey or the Kennedy campaign. They argued that the primary would be difficult for Kennedy for two reasons. First, West Virginia had the highest unemployment in the country. Humphrey had the stronger record on the problems of labor and unemployment, was close to the common people, had an ability to speak to their needs in their own language, and had a record of championing federal aid for regional problems. Second, in West Virginia, less than 5% of the voting population was Catholic, and they were concentrated in the northern panhandle of the state: "So it would seem that prospects for victory in West Virginia are brighter for Humphrey than for Kennedy." The first observation was debatable while the second one was dead on. Everyone knew the difficulties that West Virginia posed for Kennedy—and that makes his victory there all the more remarkable.

These two themes were combined in an editorial in the next issue entitled "Moratorium on Bigotry."[45] The drumbeat against Kennedy continued, as the writer began by noting the possibility of the religion issue dividing the country. Roman Catholic bloc voting for Senator Kennedy in Wisconsin might provoke bloc voting against Catholics. Even worse, there were predictions that the margin of votes provided by Catholics in major cities and key states might be sufficient to win the Democratic nomination as well as the election. It was hard for the author to see how this could actually be true. Granted, a concentration of Catholic support might give Kennedy wins during the primary season, but in the general election, if Catholic support for Kennedy were to drive Protestants to Nixon, Kennedy would be soundly defeated.

West Virginia's primary now took on even greater significance, and the journal made it clear, indirectly at least, what it thought of Kennedy:

> Of course the relation of religion to the presidency must be taken into account. In our view the President will be a better head of state if religious faith gives him inward strength, poise, insight, sensitivity, sympathy. However, we are compelled to recognize that religion may be nothing more than a device by which a candidate, often with the help of clergy and laity, marshals church and religious pawns for the chess game of politics. West Virginia Protestants should try to decide whether Senator Kennedy is a believer in or an exploiter of his faith, and act accordingly. The same applies to other candidates.[46]

The piece concluded with the defensive complaint that the label "bigotry" was only applied to Protestants despite the fact that Wisconsin Catholics were the ones who had actually displayed the dictionary definition of bigotry in their voting behavior.

Kennedy had been eyeing West Virginia warily since April 1959. The combination of his early polling efforts there and its overwhelmingly conservative Protestant population made Kennedy anxious. In April 1959, Sorensen had crossed the state, holding a series of meetings to court Democratic Party leaders and assessing the political landscape. In a lengthy memo to Kennedy, Sorensen reported his results, breaking down the state by congressional district.[47] Part of his pitch to the local politicos was to argue that Kennedy's youth and his religion were going to be assets in the general election and to counsel that coming out early for Kennedy would be to their advantage. Individual support was sought and potential campaign leaders were recruited. Sorensen concluded that, while the governor would support Kennedy, the two U.S. senators were for Johnson. The number one issue in the state, in Sorensen's view, was the Depressed Areas Bill, since West Virginia had the highest unemployment rate and the highest percentage of persons on relief of any state in the country. There was no mention of religion.

Kennedy aide and West Virginia native Matt Reese explained that the statewide leadership of the Democratic Party was skittish toward Kennedy, and as a result the campaign had to rely on more county-level officials to ramp up the campaign. The major source of anxiety was Kennedy's Catholicism.[48]

Beginning in October 1959, Kennedy began to make trips to the state, raising money and making speeches. Everywhere he spoke to the press, the first question was inevitably about how much he thought his Catholicism was going to hurt him in the state.[49] The Kennedy camp learned the hard way about the volatility of polls. A November 1959 poll showed that he would run strong in the state while a poll in April 1960 had him at 40%. Two weeks before the primary election, another poll showed him gaining some ground but not enough to win. His religion was the primary reason for his trouble.[50]

Early staff analyses had barely registered religion as an issue in West Virginia. One internal memo, written the day after the Wisconsin primary, listed seven pages of relevant issues while devoting only eight lines to religion. It did contain a prediction from a Humphrey operative that Kennedy would be "whipped" in West Virginia because he was Catholic. But it did not offer any specific tactics for confronting the issue.[51] That changed less than two weeks later when Sorensen penned a strategy memo to the senator and his brother Robert, outlining a series of possible approaches to the religion question.[52] Seven specific actions were proposed:

1. A national statement by prominent clergy deploring the issue mailed to every Protestant minister from the signers, not the campaign

2. Television shows in question-and-answer format with 50% of the questions on religion
3. A letter from Kennedy to every Protestant minister and editor with a sheet documenting his record on religion
4. A brochure on the religious issue with photos of Kennedy in uniform
5. A series of Sorensen meetings with clergy in each West Virginia community of notable size
6. Television and newspaper ads on the religious issue
7. A Kennedy letter to every registered Democrat in the state

After internal deliberations, the letter to all Democrats and the religion brochure were rejected outright, and the Sorensen meetings and television ad buys were put on hold. This left a national statement by clergy, a single television show highlighting religion, and a letter to Protestant clergy from Kennedy as the only strategic efforts on religion.[53] Yet the issue would not go away, and the ferment within the campaign continued. After studying this initial analysis and advice from his staff, Kennedy decided in mid- to late April to confront the religion issue head on.[54] Three days after this memo, on April 21, Kennedy stopped campaigning in the state and gave a major address on religion to the American Society of Newspaper Editors in Washington, D.C.

Kennedy began his long speech by acknowledging the prominence of the religion issue in the press and the need to address it directly.[55] The first part of the speech sought to establish just what the real issue was. Kennedy argued that none of the candidates for president differed on the role of religion in American politics. They all supported the separation of church and state, they all sought to preserve religious liberty and end religious bigotry, and they all supported the total freedom of the officeholder from any form of ecclesiastical control. Kennedy asserted his independence from any Vatican pressure while he affirmed traditional American political doctrines. Similarly, he denied that "any candidate" was exploiting his religious affiliation. Kennedy elaborated on this point by denying that he was fanning sectarian flames in order to drum up Catholic support. The real religion issue, then, was not his views but others' misunderstanding of his views. He then segued to the role of the press in covering the race.

This proved to be a strong rhetorical move. Kennedy called for the press to be the honest brokers in the election. By focusing on the media, he was able to address the issue without having to launch specific charges at any fellow Democrats, any specific religious leaders, or any Republicans. And he was able to outline the boundaries of how the religion issue should be framed and assessed. He argued that the press had a responsibility not to magnify the issue beyond its importance while ignoring more pressing public issues, as he felt they had done in Wisconsin and West Virginia. He then turned the tables and asked a series of questions of the press.

He asked, first, whether religion was a legitimate issue in the campaign. As far as he was concerned, there was only one legitimate question underlying all the rest: Would he be responsive in any way to ecclesiastical pressures or obligations that might influence or interfere with his conduct as president? His emphatic answer was no. He was frustrated that although he had given a clear answer to this, that did not prevent the charge being made against him. This shows that Kennedy did not retreat into a cocoon, claiming that his religious views were private and therefore not fit for questioning in an election. Rather, he addressed his faith forthrightly and denied that his religious convictions conflicted with the duties of the presidency. In fact, he claimed that his religious views supported traditional American political values.

He did offer that there were legitimate issues of public policy that were of concern to different religious groups. It was fair to raise questions about them, and in no way did doing so make one a bigot. Here, he listed federal aid to parochial schools, which he rejected; an ambassador to the Vatican, which he opposed; and the issue of foreign aid funds for birth control. Kennedy argued that it was unlikely that any president would face signing such a bill, but if he did, he would decide it on the merits without regard to his religious views. Kennedy agreed that, although these were legitimate inquiries about real questions which the next president might have to face, "I have made it clear that I strongly support—out of conviction as well as Constitutional obligation—the guarantees of religious equality provided by the First Amendment—and I ask only that these same guarantees be extended to me."[56]

His second question was: Can we justify analyzing voters as well as candidates strictly in terms of their religion? Here, Kennedy argued that Wisconsin voters objected to being labeled solely by their religion. Voters were more than their religious affiliation. To apply a religious test to candidates was unfair; to apply one to voters was divisive, degrading, and wholly unwarranted.

Kennedy then came to his third and final question: Is there any justification for applying a special religious test to only the office of the presidency? He noted that no one paid attention to his religion when he took his oath as a military officer, a congressman, or a senator: "What is there about the Presidency that justifies this constant emphasis upon a candidate's religion and that of his supporters?"[57] Some people answered that we treat the presidency differently since there has only been one Catholic candidate in the past. Kennedy expressed his irritation with this answer, saying that he was weary of that because he was not the Catholics' candidate for president. His stances on aid to education and a whole host of other issues had upset prominent Catholic clergy and organizations and been cheered by others. He elaborated:

> The fact is that the Catholic Church is not a monolith—it is committed in this country to the principles of individual liberty—and it has no claim over my conduct as a public officer sworn to do the public interest. So I hope we can see the beginning of the end of references to me as "the Catholic candidate" for President. Do not expect me to explain or defend every act [or] statement of every Pope or priest, in this country or some other, in this century or the last.[58]

Kennedy saw two options for his candidacy. Some had suggested that he withdraw from the race to avoid a dangerous religious controversy. Clearly, he rejected this outright. On the other hand, he could stay the course through the primaries and on to the convention: "If there was bigotry in the country so be it. If that bigotry is too great to permit the fair consideration of a Catholic who has made clear his complete independence and his complete dedication to separation of church and state, then we ought to know it."[59] But he did not think this was the case. He believed that the country was more concerned about his views than about the church to which he belonged. His job was to face these issues fully and frankly, and the press's job was to treat it fairly, in perspective and in proportion. The press was to refute falsehood, to inform the ignorant, and to concentrate on the issues, the real issues, in this hour of the nation's peril.

It is impossible to say what the impact of this speech was in West Virginia, in the country, or in the press. But it did mark a dramatic shift in strategy for Kennedy. He now addressed the religion issue more directly and aggressively. The next few weeks saw a shift toward Kennedy in West Virginia.

Kennedy made some effort to reach out directly to the state's religious leaders. He met with retired Episcopal bishop Robert E. Lee Strider. The cleric was favorably impressed and after the meeting told the press he saw no reason that a Catholic should not be elected to the White House. However, Kennedy did not consult with Roman Catholic bishop John Swint in Wheeling, who was rumored to be a staunch Republican and not a Kennedy supporter.[60]

Two days after the speech to the press, staffer Robert Wallace urged that the letter from Kennedy to West Virginia clergy be pulled back. He agreed that they had to confront the religion issue head on, but "having gotten into the ring with the bull, however, I don't think he should wave a red flag at it."[61] Wallace noted that a direct letter invited a direct response in the Protestant pulpits, since most Protestant clergy saw Catholicism as their competitor. The campaign had made its point. If the sentiment were to send the letter anyway, Wallace wanted to run the draft by 10–20 clergy first and gauge their reactions. Wisely, the letter was scuttled.

Yet the indirect letter by surrogates to the clergy did go forward on May 3. The letter was signed by a who's who of American Protestantism, including G. Bromley Oxnam, who had apparently recovered from whatever doubts had arisen over the Poling affair. The other signatories included the president of the National Council of Churches and the heads of the Evangelical and Reformed church, the Congregational church, the Disciples of Christ, the Episcopal church, and the United Presbyterian church, and prominent clergy such as Harry Emerson Fosdick of Riverside Church in New York, Edward Pruden of First Baptist Church in Washington, D.C., and Francis Sayre, dean of the National Cathedral.

The letter itself was a masterpiece—propaganda for Kennedy masquerading as a neutral letter.[62] Addressed to "Fellow Pastors in Christ," it began by saying that it had been reported in Wisconsin and West Virginia that unnamed Protestants had been drawing religious lines in the primaries in a manner that could only lead to injurious dissent among the people. Both secretly and in public, "one of the candidates" had been attacked and also supported by some simply because he was a Catholic. The letter went on to decry this type of attack and asked that each candidate be judged on the issues: "We are convinced that each of the candidates has presented himself before the American people with honesty and independence, and we would think it unjust to discount any one of them because of his chosen faith." The letter concluded by asking the ministers to use every chance they had to commend to their flocks that "charitable moderation and reasoned balance of judgment which alone can safeguard the peaceful community of this Nation."

Without once invoking Kennedy's name, these prominent national Protestant leaders called on the anti-Catholic forces at work in West Virginia to cease and desist. By engaging these influential and learned surrogates to fight the antibigotry campaign on their behalf, Kennedy's forces had found a powerful resource to turn the religion issue into one of resisting bigotry. Mainstream Protestant leaders were now on record as opposing the type of whispering campaign that had reached a boil in the state. Avoiding a letter from the candidate himself and instead using surrogates was a powerful strategic move.

On May 8, the campaign bought statewide television time to air an interview of Kennedy by Franklin Roosevelt, Jr. A significant amount of the broadcast was dedicated to questions pertaining to religion. The religion questions ranged from "Will your church ever influence you in any way in the White House?" to "What do you say to those who say the pope will be telling you what to do?" These questions reflected the real concerns of voters, and the answers were designed to debunk Protestant fears.[63] Thus, the campaign drew on multiple forms of mass communication to implement its religion strategy. Direct mail to clergy, a national speech to the press itself on the topic of the media's coverage of religion, and a statewide television show devoted primarily to addressing the religion issue all combined to turn things around for Kennedy in West Virginia.

The final two weeks of campaigning saw Kennedy in the state almost full time. During the final days, the staff began to sense that all of the campaigning, especially on the religion issue, was beginning to pay off. Momentum seemed to be tilting toward Kennedy.[64] On primary day, Kennedy prevailed decisively, 60.8% to 39.2%. In retrospect, Humphrey's survival in the Wisconsin primary turned out to be a stroke of good fortune. Kennedy's camp felt that, by being forced to compete in West Virginia, Kennedy had shown the party and the country that he could win in an overwhelmingly Protestant state. If Humphrey had withdrawn after Wisconsin, the West Virginia primary would have been uncontested and thus meaningless.[65]

After Kennedy's important victory in West Virginia, the *Christian Century* continued to press him. The major lesson it had drawn from his win was that the accusation that Protestants were bigoted had been decisively refuted.[66] Any further charges of religious bigotry would be despicable. Here, the editors anticipated a key Kennedy strategy late in the general election. The charge of being a victim of religious bigotry might drive undecided voters into the Kennedy camp. Eventually, the Kennedy campaign would embrace this logic and begin to promote his religion, but this strategic shift came later.

In the *Century*'s next editorial, however, Kennedy was directly challenged.[67] Dredging up the argument that the Kennedy camp had advanced, unsuccessfully, to Adlai Stevenson (and the whole Democratic Party) in the 1956 Bailey Memorandum—that Kennedy would

attract Catholic voters back to the party and away from Eisenhower—
the editorial asked whether Kennedy would repudiate such religious
bloc voting. In 1956, he had argued that his religion would be such an
asset that he should be added to the ticket. He now said that religion
should not be a factor. It is far from clear just what action Kennedy
could take to answer this bizarre analysis, short of asking Catholics to
vote for anyone but him.

Christianity and Crisis did not reengage with the presidential race until
after the Democratic convention. William Lee Miller wrote a reflection
piece on the convention, and his opening words are worth quoting at
length:

> The extraordinary speech by Senator Eugene McCarthy in nomina-
> tion of Adlai Stevenson was the high point and most moving moment
> of the Democratic Convention in Los Angeles. It outshone the
> more-than-adequate speeches of the nominee and the keynoter, and
> increased our already great respect for the Minnesota Senator. By call-
> ing attention again to the significance of Adlai Stevenson's unusual
> and important career, it also furnished a backdrop of contrast against
> which to interpret the events of the convention (world affairs pro-
> vided another, more somber backdrop).
>   The contrasts were plain. Where Stevenson had humility or self-
> deprecation to a fault, Kennedy said forthrightly, after he had been
> nominated, "I *will* be worthy of that trust." Where Stevenson and
> company have regularly been accused of amateurism and ineptitude
> in political organization, no such charge could be made against the
> Kennedy forces. Most important, where Adlai Stevenson shunned
> power, John Kennedy sought it.
>   It was this last contrast that Senator McCarthy touched on in his
> forceful speech. Arguing with delegates already committed in great
> numbers to Senator Kennedy, that they should think again and turn
> to Mr. Stevenson, he presented his man (rightly, it seems to us) as a
> kind of "prophet," "one man" speaking out against the complacent
> materialism of the Eisenhower era, counseling the unheroic virtues
> such as patience, "talking sense to the American people." Arguing
> for Stevenson and by implication against Kennedy, Senator McCarthy
> said that those who seek power are not always those who use it wisely;
> that those who do not seek but are sought out by it might use power
> more responsibly. It was a strong speech, unusual in party conven-
> tions because it was shaped by a conscious intelligence.[68]

But Miller then pivoted back to political reality and took a shot at
Stevenson by admitting that self-doubters who avoid power may not be

the ones to whom to give great responsibility. Lonely prophets may not make the best politicians or statesmen. There may be nothing wrong with Kennedy's four-year quest for the presidency. While he argued that Kennedy lacked traits that Stevenson had, such as (of all things) charisma and an ability to articulate the deepest national ideals, he already had some qualities that Stevenson did not possess, such as a direct, uncomplicated, objective executive force.

In the last third of the article, Miller examined Kennedy as the nominee and explored the purposes that would guide and restrain his seeking of power. Kennedy's ideas were good ones, and he had connections to the best policy thinking of the Democratic Party. His platform on security, taxes, civil rights, foreign policy, and economics was very strong. One result of the convention might be that the next decade would bring a linking of the intellectual thinking associated with Stevenson with broader support within the party, a trend that Miller thought Kennedy had already started. He concluded by quoting Stevenson from 1952, "*who* leads us is less important than *what* leads us—what convictions, what courage, what faith."[69]

Niebuhr also offered a brief but revelatory postmortem of the epochal shift represented by the Democratic convention.[70] By virtue of being in California during the convention, apparently working for the Fund for the Republic, and having access to journalist and political friends who were at the convention, he recorded six brief paragraphs of impressions. He decried the methods employed by the "new generation": efficient organization, intelligence and shrewdness, unscrupulousness, and more money than should be used in politics. The Kennedys had brilliantly picked off the political bosses one by one and had promised the vice presidency indirectly to at least a half dozen. But Niebuhr could not fully rest in this zone of sentimental and nostalgic fog:

> Those of us who favored Stevenson found that we were in the camp of the "old fogies," who preferred genuine eloquence touched with real compassion, a certain moral scrupulousness. We also found ourselves in a category of idealists who were not prepared to accept politics as it has always been practiced, as F.D.R., the hero of many of us, had practiced it, with astounding efficiency.[71]

These were remarkable insights for several reasons. First, Niebuhr rightly perceived that Kennedy represented a generational change for the party and the country. Second, even when he was tempted to lapse into idealistic bitterness at the failure of his hero, Stevenson, he astringently noted that the Kennedys practiced a form of political realism that he, Niebuhr, had long embraced and advocated.

Niebuhr observed that the civil rights plank in the platform was the stiffest the Democrats had ever adopted, and Kennedy showed courage in supporting it against both North and South—which opposed it for different reasons. The race issue was not solved, but the battle was essentially won, and southern Democrats could not stop the gradual chipping away of their position. This was a remarkable prophecy. Niebuhr concluded, "[I]t will be interesting to watch a campaign between two such 'cool' operators as Kennedy and Nixon."[72]

The *Christian Century*'s coverage of the Democratic National Convention vented a lot of spleen.[73] Kennedy's win was seen as the "capture" of the Democratic Party. The *Century* called his victory the smoothest political operation of recent American history in which nothing was left to chance. Party stalwarts like Sam Rayburn, Eleanor Roosevelt, Stevenson, and the southern governors were all buried in the process. All of this was made possible by limitless ambition and funding. The elements of the party that made his victory possible were northern big-city and state machines, "dominated in almost every instance by Roman Catholic politicians." The big element of the party that was missing was the South, and Kennedy made up for this by selecting Senator Lyndon Johnson from Texas as his running mate. The editorial did speak well of the party platform and especially its plank on civil rights:

> Its most courageous pledge is that the resources of the central government will be used through civil suits to prosecute those who deny Negroes the right to register and vote. Congressional liberals have not yet been able to move Congress this far in civil rights legislation; the platform commits the party to battle this issue to a successful conclusion in congressional debate. If the party is in earnest, if it is promising the Negro deeds rather than dreams, the civil rights plank is to its credit whether it win or lose in November.[74]

Whatever misgivings they might have had about a Catholic president, these were still liberal Protestants. Their liberalism was nowhere clearer than on race. Indeed, Martin Luther King, Jr., was a contributing editor to the magazine, and his activities were monitored closely in its pages. Kennedy's unattractiveness had not yet pushed them into Nixon's camp. Commenting on the upcoming Republican gathering, the article stated:

> Most Americans will remember the Los Angeles convention for its phoniness, its pretense; the coming assembly in Chicago could, but

probably will not, offer a startling contrast. The Republican convention will be in progress when this editorial is read; it may provide a spectacle even more appalling of planned politics, of powerful political bulldozers pushing people around. On the other hand, it may afford a welcome contrast, yet present the voters with a less attractive choice.[75]

The conundrum for the editors was displayed clearly in the title of the article reporting on the Republican results: "No Political Messiahs."[76] Each party had shunted aside its best man—Stevenson and Rockefeller, respectively—and instead chose a political manipulator. While the Republicans put on a better show, both conventions had produced a fog of self-righteousness. The voter had "to slap himself back into contact with reality" and face a decision between two shades of gray. Nixon and Kennedy had much in common: They were tough, articulate, ambitious infighters of the brass knuckle school of politics; each was essentially a secularist; and both picked good running mates. In the end, voters should base their votes on concrete evidence of what was best for the country and the world. The editorial did not betray who was the best choice.

Kennedy had displayed a nimble and sophisticated grasp of the anti-Catholic forces he faced. The emerging strategy contained many elements that had served him well and would be sorely tested in the general election. Kennedy showed a willingness to admit his vulnerability regarding his Catholicism, to reach out to anti-Catholic Protestants under Bishop Wright's tutelage, and to learn more about them. These listening sessions produced some direct public dividends, but they also gave the campaign insights into just how serious they had to take the threat. Facing such a massive threat, the campaign dedicated resources from Lou Harris's massive polling effort in Wisconsin to making national speeches aimed at knocking down the arguments that were coming out against Kennedy. Sometimes the responses were direct, and sometimes they were issued through surrogates, such as Sorensen, or through clergy, as in West Virginia.

The campaign was also sophisticated in its use of the media. From the 1959 interview with Fletcher Knebel in *Look* to the hour-long statewide television interview with Franklin Roosevelt, Jr., the campaign spread its message on Kennedy's religion in cutting-edge form. This foreshadowed the general election campaign, in which electronic media would play a huge role. But perhaps the greatest skill the Kennedy camp displayed in this time frame was its ability to debate internally and to adapt its tactics to different times and places. By showing the flexibility to run in Wisconsin on a strategy of downplaying Catholicism while directly addressing the overt anti-Catholicism in West Virginia, the campaign signaled that it was adept at changing tactics as the terrain demanded.

As the nomination process came to a close, the Kennedy camp breathed a sigh of relief. The team had confronted the religion issue directly in the media and at the grassroots level. It could be forgiven for believing that it had put the issue behind it. But to do this was to overlook two factors. First, it ignored the fact that Protestant anti-Catholicism ran far deeper in the whole country than just the limited pool of Democratic primary voters in West Virginia. The legions of Protestantism were only beginning to organize their troops by the time Kennedy won the nomination, and the type of retail politicking they did in the five weeks leading up to the West Virginia primary could not be duplicated across the country. Likewise, any feeling of satisfaction on the part of the Kennedy camp ignored the formidable political cunning of Richard Nixon. Whatever satisfaction Kennedy and company may have rightly felt about how they managed the religion issue after securing the nomination was to be dashed before summer's end.

Now, the political stage had been set, the combatants were known, and the real battle was about to begin.

4

PREPARING FOR
BATTLE

. . . .

Nixon's religion problem in the 1960 election was the converse of
Kennedy's. That is, how could he stave off a massive movement of
Catholic Republicans to his opponent while simultaneously appealing
to Protestants, all without appearing to be a religious bigot? Nixon
came to the campaign with significant preparation in discussions of
religion.

Nixon offered his own account in a 1962 book entitled *Six Cri-*
ses. Nixon began writing the book almost immediately upon leaving
office in 1961. In retrospect, it reads like the opening salvo of Nixon's
(hypothetical) 1964 campaign for the presidency. According to Nixon,
in April 1961 a representative of Doubleday and Company came to
see him in California and asked him to consider writing a book. Nixon
proposed that he write a book analyzing six crises that he had faced
in order to distill a few lessons for handling them.[1] For Nixon, these
lessons were personal. He believed that it is in moments of crisis that
one sees the true character of a leader, his morals, faith, strengths, and
weaknesses. The greatest of these strengths is selflessness. Confidence
is necessary and comes from preparation. Serenity comes from religious heritage. Courage is the product of discipline. And experience
is vitally important because it empowers a leader not to be distracted
by tension.[2] These traits are usually acquired and not inherited. All of
these statements were extensions of arguments he had lodged against
Kennedy during the campaign—and would presumably have used again
in 1964 if he had the opportunity. The book also allowed him to retell

his political biography in a fashion that highlighted his successes under the guise of a personal study of leaders in times of crisis.[3] The last of the six crises was the campaign of 1960. In this chapter, Nixon gave his account of how religion played a pivotal role in his loss to Kennedy.[4]

In September 1961, Nixon wrote a memo to his staffers Agnes Waldron and Chuck Lichenstein summarizing the research help he wanted for this chapter. He wanted three religion-related things from his aides in a short memo. First, he wanted to show how Kennedy and his campaign had used religion to Kennedy's advantage. Second, Nixon wanted a summary of how he handled the issue, pointing out that from the Republican convention forward, he maintained the public position that religion was not to be discussed. And third, he wanted a summary of how the religion issue helped Kennedy more than it hurt him. Nixon did not want these words to come from him but from pollsters such as Gallup and Roper. Nixon noted that he got approximately 22% of the Catholic vote, the lowest in modern history for a Republican candidate.

Nixon's purpose, he wrote, was not to condemn Catholics for voting the way they did but "objectively to point out that I probably made a mistake in resisting the strong recommendations of virtually every one of my advisers two and a half weeks before the election that I should take the issue on frontally rather than to continue to ignore it."[5] By the time the book was done, Nixon had decided not to second-guess his strategy. But he was definitely thinking about it shortly after the election.

In January 1960, with the nomination a foregone conclusion, the Nixon brain trust met to plot a general election strategy.[6] Even at this early date, Nixon was sure that Kennedy would be the Democratic nominee. He thought Kennedy had intelligence, energy, and an effective television personality. Along with his unlimited money and resultant large skilled staff, Kennedy would dominate the weak field of Democrats. While Nixon's pollster, Claude Robinson, saw potential liabilities in Kennedy's youth, inexperience, wealth, and religion, Nixon felt that a skilled politician could turn each of these into an asset.

His take on Kennedy's religion was interesting and even prescient. It tracked remarkably closely the arguments of the Bailey Memo. Nixon did not buy the argument that the lesson to be drawn from 1928 was that residual anti-Catholicism was so strong that a Catholic could not get elected. While some of his aides disagreed, he believed that Kennedy's religion would hurt him in states he could afford to lose anyway and help him in states he needed to win. Nixon vowed never to raise the religion question, directly or indirectly, nor to allow anyone in his campaign to do so. Nixon believed that the Bailey Memo had predicted the 1960 presidential results in that Kennedy racked up impressive totals in northern cities—in states with large numbers of electoral votes—as a result of Catholic bloc voting. Nixon's conclusion about the role of religion in the campaign is revealing:

> As far as the religious issue is concerned, I must admit that I am at a loss to know how I could have treated it differently. Gallup, Roper, and the other pollsters reported after the election that I got the lowest percentage of the Catholic vote of any Republican presidential candidate in history (22 per cent) and that there was no a corresponding and balancing shift of Protestants away from Kennedy. But I still believe my decision was right, and I can take some satisfaction from the fact that this was probably the last national election in which the religious issue will be raised at all.[7]

There is the scent of reelection strategy in this passage. Nixon's hope that the religion issue would not reappear included, presumably, a rematch with Kennedy. But what the passage hinted at, but did not elaborate, was the extent to which he engaged in a campaign to aid and abet a shift of Protestants away from Kennedy. If Nixon could have marginally blunted the feared Catholic bloc voting and fed a Protestant flight from the Democratic Party, he would have been elected. The extent to which Nixon pursued such strategies sheds a different light on his post-election claims to purity.

Perhaps the most surprising aspect of Nixon's religion strategy was his outreach to Catholics, thanks to his long-standing relationship with a Catholic priest, Father John Cronin. Nixon first became acquainted with Cronin during the Alger Hiss episode in the forties. What united this unlikely pair, the Quaker and the Catholic, was their mutual anti-Communism. Soon thereafter, Cronin became a regular speechwriter for Nixon. When Nixon went to battle with Kennedy, he turned to this trusted aide, then working in Washington at the National Catholic Welfare Conference under the direction of the legendary priest George Higgins.

Their earliest available correspondence is a congratulatory letter from Cronin to Nixon celebrating Nixon's election to the Senate. The letter ends on a note of familiarity with Cronin offering to buy Nixon a victory dinner.[8] Two years later, Cronin wrote to vice president–elect Nixon, offering to put him in touch with possible leads who could help to clean out Communists from the government. According to Cronin, a number of government officials were now anxious and willing to talk after having been browbeaten in the Truman era. He especially wanted to introduce Nixon to "the official who was the anonymous source of much of the material which I used to supply to you." He, too, felt a little freer to come out in the open now that things had changed. Presumably, this was a person related to the Alger Hiss case, which Nixon had championed as a freshman congressman only a few years before.[9] Later, Cronin followed up on a conversation with Nixon by supplying the names of two Catholic judges, apparently helping the Eisenhower administration to compile a list of potential Catholic Supreme Court nominees.[10] All of these letters show a fairly substantial relationship between Cronin and Nixon that dated back into the forties and seemed to be based initially on their anti-Communism and in particular on the task of cleaning out Communists from the federal government.

By 1955, the relationship had begun to deepen, with Nixon asking Cronin for more direct political advice and research. In an otherwise inconsequential letter, Cronin told Nixon that the Democratic clamoring for Eisenhower to remove Nixon from the ticket in 1956 was a clever campaign move on their part. He promised to pass along his own informal poll to gauge reaction to speeches that Nixon had given across the country.[11] Soon thereafter, Cronin sent a list of seven Catholics as possible candidates to be the undersecretary of health, education, and welfare, apparently in response to a Nixon request.[12] Cronin also developed a reputation within Catholic circles as a conduit to Nixon. Ironically, Bishop John J. Wright, Kennedy's political and theological mentor, turned to Cronin to invite Nixon to speak at a national Catholic Youth Congress.[13]

In October, Nixon wrote to Cronin to thank him for his observations on how his performance as vice president was being interpreted by the press and radio. He concluded the letter with an open-ended invitation for Cronin to make any suggestions at any time and to stay in touch.[14] This was apparently a genuine request on Nixon's part, and Cronin certainly read it that way, as the paper flow between them increased exponentially in 1956.

Cronin's work for Nixon during the 1956 election season consisted of writing speeches, offering pragmatic political advice, and nurturing relationships between Nixon and various entities within the Catholic church. During this period, soon after it was written, Cronin obtained a copy of the Bailey Memo and passed it on to Nixon. It is not unusual that, given Cronin's prominent position, he had access to the Bailey Memo. What is fascinating is the analysis he sent to Nixon. In addition to passing on the Bailey Memo, Cronin sent Nixon a clipping of an Arthur Krock column from the *New York Times* that summarized the memo's findings and an article from the *Catholic World* written by a Paulist priest who disagreed with Krock (and the Bailey Memo) and challenged the very notion of a Catholic voting bloc.

Cronin noted that the truth about Catholic voters probably lay between the two extremes: "We should talk over this matter at your convenience. It may be a real tough problem."[15] It is impossible to know just how much stock Nixon ultimately put in the thesis of the Bailey Memo at the time. But his chief Catholic political guide clearly saw value in it, and ultimately Nixon followed its logic in his analysis of the 1960 race. So at a minimum, Nixon had his eye on Kennedy in 1956 and had a sense of the political threat that Kennedy's Catholicism might pose to him.

Cronin produced a series of political memos for Nixon that offered counsel on how to retain his spot on the ticket in the face of both Democratic and Republican pressure on Eisenhower to drop him. He elaborated this strategy in a memo in which he suggested that Nixon adopt two private attitudes and one public one.[16]

In private, toward the president, Nixon should state his personal loyalty and willingness to abide by Eisenhower's decision. At the same time, he should point out that if he were to withdraw, or be asked to do so, it would be indirect acknowledgment of the failure of the president and his policies. Toward party leaders, his stance should be that Nixon was being attacked by Democrats because his arguments were effective, and if he were forced off the ticket, the Republican Party would be badly divided.

In public, Cronin advised, Nixon should fight back hard in public addresses. One major speech devoted solely to the subject should launch the counterattack. Cronin drafted a speech in which he suggested that Nixon defend his record while refusing to campaign for the vice presidency. Instead, he argued, Nixon should simply acknowledge that his future was for others to decide.[17] The heart of Cronin's advice was for Nixon to review his anti-Communist record and his pursuit of world peace, domestic prosperity, and integrity and efficiency in government.

Throughout the summer and fall, Cronin wrote a series of speeches for Nixon while maintaining a steady flow of political analysis. In May, Cronin and Nixon had lunch to discuss politics and policy. They spoke about U.S. and Soviet policies and ways to widen the liberalizing trends they saw within the Soviet Union. They dissected the increasingly negative attacks on Nixon which, Cronin suggested, had the unintended consequence of magnifying Nixon's audiences when he did speak. Cronin counseled Nixon to maintain a calm, statesmanlike manner—in contrast to his shrill critics. He also recommended specific speech topics to the vice president and highlighted Nixon's need to reach out to religious communities in general and Protestants specifically.[18]

By this point, Cronin had become a major speechwriter for Nixon. He wrote speeches for appearances in Manila, in Miami, at Defiance College, at Lafayette College, before the Veterans of Foreign Wars, and at the American Legion.[19] He attempted to broker a lecture series at Harvard that would be turned into a book.[20] He even offered detailed advice to Nixon on public speaking and getting the proper rest before major speeches. One postconvention memorandum outlines over a dozen speeches on a wide variety of topics.[21]

Cronin also attended to Nixon's ongoing Catholic outreach. He made sure that Nixon was invited to the Pan-American Mass in Washington on Thanksgiving Day by auxiliary bishop Philip Hannan.[22] Cronin sent Nixon a copy of a speech that Washington bishop Patrick O'Boyle had delivered before the John Carroll Society. Nixon wrote O'Boyle a note commending his analysis of the issues of race and labor relations.[23]

All of this partisan work on Cronin's part did not escape the notice of Cronin's superiors. This would become an increasingly touchy issue as the general election of 1960 began to take shape. But even in the late summer of 1956, Cronin sent a signal to Nixon. Nixon's secretary, Rose Mary Woods, directed all staff that when sending any material to Father Cronin during the campaign, "please be sure to mail it in a plain envelope." And when calling his office, if one of Nixon's staff members had to leave a message, "just leave your name but do not say that the Vice President's office is calling."[24]

In 1957, Cronin began to push race relations, one of his favorite issues, with Nixon. Soon after the second term began, Cronin thanked Nixon for attending the annual Red Mass, which is held in Washington for government officials just before the beginning of a new Supreme Court session, and outlined ideas for a possible talk on race relations. Cronin had spoken to Agnes Waldron, a Catholic who would soon join Nixon's research staff and who had a keen interest in the pursuit of racial justice. For Cronin, solving the race problem was a profound moral issue. He noted that Nixon had already touched on this theme at the Al Smith Dinner, an annual event sponsored by the archbishop of New York. The speech that Cronin outlined would call for moderates to find solutions that extremists on both sides could not pursue. Cronin thought that such a speech should be given in the South, while Waldron disagreed. Cronin wanted to pursue the idea with other people and report their recommendations to Nixon.[25]

A few weeks later, Cronin told Nixon that he had some ideas for how Nixon might engage Martin Luther King, Jr., on a series of concerns raised by King.[26] Waldron took the initial talk with Cronin to heart and produced a draft report on race relations in the South for Cronin and Nixon.[27]

Cronin convened a series of meetings on race between Nixon and Harvard government professor William Y. Elliott and two members of the racially progressive Southern Regional Council, Paul Williams and Fred Routh, to see what actions Nixon might take. Elliott emphasized that Nixon was heir to the southern liberal vote that had supported Eisenhower and that he must not alienate these voters, especially since he doubted that Nixon could gain "the Negro vote." Nixon should stick to a centrist position and not try to outflank northern liberals on their left. Elliott suggested that, instead of a southern speech on race, the Commission on Government Contracts might schedule a meeting in the South that Nixon could address as a way to avoid the backlash that might be sparked by an overt speech on race.

Paul Williams of the Southern Regional Council argued strongly against a southern speech, fearing it might stir up deep resentment at an outsider telling southerners what to do. He endorsed the idea of a commission meeting and suggested Atlanta as the ideal site. Waldron echoed these sentiments and endorsed the commission idea as a way to advance the economic well-being of blacks.[28]

A few days later, Cronin met with Fred Routh, assistant director of the Southern Regional Council, to explore this idea. Routh was in wholehearted agreement. A lecture tour would be fatal for Nixon. Routh suggested that the council could help to convene private and public meetings with leading businessmen in the South, including Robert Woodruff of the Coca-Cola Company in Atlanta, Stanley Marcus of Houston, and Winthrop Rockefeller of Arkansas. The issue was settled, and the tour idea was scuttled.[29]

Cronin saw this type of outreach as one part of a broader political strategy aimed at positioning Nixon to run for the White House in 1960. In early 1957, at Nixon's request, Cronin outlined a series of suggestions for the next two years.[30] He offered pragmatic political advice on what Nixon needed to do to solidify his base in the Republican Party, to separate himself from Eisenhower in the public's mind, to build staff and resources, and to woo groups that had not been favorable toward him in the past. Cronin was no longer just a speechwriter. He had taken on a much more prominent political role.

All along, Cronin kept Kennedy firmly in view. In addition to Nixon's traveling to Harvard to talk to Elliott about race, Cronin also mentioned the idea of Nixon doing a series of lectures at Harvard as part of the summer school program that Elliott directed. Such lectures were ordinarily published in book form. Cronin noted that, as vice president, Nixon did not have a formal voting record, which might prove to be a liability in 1960. These lectures would be a way of establishing centrist positions on a range of domestic and international issues.[31] In a handwritten note, Cronin wrote of a potential book, "This can be important competing with Kennedy."

At the same time, Cronin continued to build Nixon's exposure in the Catholic world. In April 1957, Nixon traveled to the Vatican to meet with Pope Pius XII. Cronin wrote to Father Martin J. O'Connor, rector of the North American College in the Vatican, expressing his thanks for all O'Connor had done to make Nixon's trip a success. Cronin noted that Nixon said that the visit with the Holy Father was the highlight of the trip and that Nixon was impressed with his conversation with the pope.[32]

In April, Nixon was invited to the celebration of the 25th anniversary of Cronin's ordination.[33] In November, Nixon delivered remarks at the annual National Council of Youth convention in Philadelphia. Lauding Pius XI's encyclical *On Atheistic Communism* as one of the most remarkable examples of historic prophecy, Nixon went on at length to commend the Catholic church on its strong anti-Communist stance. John Cardinal Spellman, the archbishop of New York, and Archbishop Leo Binz were in attendance. Cronin almost certainly arranged the invitation to speak, and he wrote the speech.

While Cronin maintained a heavy workload for Nixon, he did harbor some anxiety about allowing his role to be made public. In the middle of the year, he expressed this anxiety to Nixon after Earl Mazo, who was writing a biography of the vice president, called him and asked about their relationship:

> When Mr. Earl Mazo called me in reference to your biography, Rose said to tell him nothing that I would not like to see in print.
> However, I soon found out that he knew enough to write up my relationship with you, even if I did not co-operate. Hence I considered it a better policy to work with him and thus be in a position to read in advance what he writes, and suggest changes.

In our discussion, and in a letter I wrote to him, I emphasized these points:

1) We have been discussing social and economic problems practically since you first arrived in Washington.
2) Our relationship is personal, not political.
3) You prefer to have memoranda of conversations, so you can study them later.
4) When topics related to a public speech have been discussed, these memoranda in more recent years have been tailored to help in the earlier drafts.
5) With only the rarest exceptions, you work for two or three days on all your major speeches.

I would have preferred to have remained in relative obscurity. But I am known on the Hill and by the press, and some public comments on our contacts seem to be unavoidable. It is probably better to have them in a friendly context, rather than the reverse.[34]

In 1958 and 1959, the relationship continued along similar lines. In late 1958, Cronin sent Nixon an advance copy of the Catholic bishops' statement on race, which Cronin undoubtedly wrote.[35] The statement is a powerful theological and philosophical document that lauds the racial progress in America in the aftermath of World War II while simultaneously decrying enduring racism and discrimination. It sets out both a biblical and a natural law case against racial discrimination. But at the end of the document, when it turns to ways to address the problem, it goes soft:

We urge that concrete plans in the field be based on prudence. Prudence may be called a virtue that inclines us to view problems in their proper perspective. It aids us to use the proper means to secure our aim.

The problems we inherit today are rooted in decades, even centuries, of custom and cultural patterns. Changes in deep-rooted attitudes are not made overnight. When we are confronted with complex and far-reaching evils, it is not a sign of weakness or timidity to distinguish among remedies and reforms. Some changes are more necessary than others. Some are relatively easy to achieve. Others seem impossible at this time. What may succeed in one area may fail in another.

It is a sign of wisdom, rather than weakness, to study carefully the problems we face, to prepare for advances, and to by-pass the nonessential if it interferes with essential progress. We may well deplore a gradualism that is merely a cloak for inaction. But we equally deplore rash impetuosity that would sacrifice the achievements of decades in ill-timed and ill-considered ventures. In concrete matters we

distinguish between prudence and inaction by asking the question:
Are we sincerely and earnestly acting to solve these problems? We distinguish between prudence and rashness by seeking the prayerful and
considered judgment of experienced counselors who achieved success
in meeting similar problems.

For this reason we hope and earnestly pray that responsible and
sober-minded Americans of all religious faiths, in all areas of our land,
will seize the mantle of leadership from the agitator and the racist. It
is vital that we act now and act decisively. All must act quietly, courageously, and prayerfully before it is too late.[36]

It is interesting to ponder what Nixon made of this. On the one
hand, Democrats since Franklin Roosevelt had captured the black vote
away from the party of Lincoln. Cronin felt that Nixon could successfully
woo these voters, but Nixon's circle of advisors doubted that. What Cronin missed, and Nixon probably saw, is that in order to win an offsetting
percentage of Protestants to balance Catholic bloc voting for Kennedy,
Nixon had to win a large percentage of conservative white southern voters, who would not be moved by the Catholic bishops' rhetoric or theology. Nixon simply could not be perceived as progressive on race and
have any chance at these voters, who historically voted Democratic. In
a contest between racism and anti-Catholicism in the hearts and minds
of these voters, there was no guarantee that enough of them would vote
their church and not their race. Kennedy would have to perform his own
tortured dance on race, but this was Nixon's. Perhaps unwittingly, Cronin provided Nixon cover on race by offering a gradualism based on
economic evolution and not legal or legislative activism.

Nixon embraced this strategy at the gathering of religious leaders
convened by the president's Commission on Government Contracts.
The meeting took place on May 11, 1959, in Atlanta, with Nixon
and Martin Luther King, Jr., as the primary speakers.[37] The conference had two parts, a morning session that ended with lunch and an
afternoon session with five workshops followed by reports from the
chairs of each workshop. Nixon spoke in the morning and at the close
of the day, and King gave an address in between. Nixon explained that
the purpose of the committee was primarily educational. It sought to
establish a pattern of compliance with the standard government contract clause that called for nondiscrimination in hiring. Nixon claimed
that it was rare for contracts to be refused or terminated because
of racial discrimination. In the afternoon session, Nixon argued that
racial discrimination, while both a legal and an economic problem,
was primarily a moral problem of the highest order. It conflicted with

an American sense of justice and brotherhood, and it made America vulnerable on the world stage to charges of not living up to its moral and religious convictions. Nixon called upon the religious leaders present to use all of their influence to bring about justice primarily at the community level. He did not call for state or federal legislation to address racial discrimination.

King's speech focused on illustrating the ill effects of racial discrimination upon blacks. But he also argued that racial hatred debilitated white people by creating a false sense of superiority, thus depriving them of genuine humility, honesty, and love.

The only negative feedback that Cronin received about the meeting came from some delegates who thought they should have adopted a ringing statement reaffirming basic religious principles on discrimination. He noted tersely that this was a minority view since most delegates had no authority to speak for their churches and the purpose of the meeting was informational and exploratory. All in all, it was a political victory for Nixon. Under the cover of a routine government committee meeting, Nixon had shared the podium with King and had reassured a gathering of progressive religious leaders that he saw racial discrimination as a moral evil. Yet there were no headlines in southern newspapers announcing this view. He had courted Catholic and Protestant liberals, reached out to the leader of the civil rights movement, and not offended the large white southern Protestant legions whose votes he needed to defeat Kennedy.

Cronin continued to help Nixon to cultivate Catholic connections. He secured yet another Catholic speech invitation for Nixon, this time at the 50th anniversary dinner of the Jesuit magazine *America* at the Waldorf Astoria in New York. Cardinal Spellman of New York and a host of prominent Catholics and friends of the magazine were there.[38] Cronin also recommended to Nixon that if he were to be Eisenhower's emissary to the coronation of Pope John XXIII, he should fly by jet and visit the French president, Charles de Gaulle, on the way home.[39]

At other times, Cronin's advice exceeded the limits of political reality. After the U.S. Catholic bishops issued a statement on birth control in 1959, Cronin penned a statement for Nixon to consider releasing. The page-and-a-half brief began with the overly dramatic observation that "for the unity and internal peace of our nation, it is essential to put this issue in its proper perspective."[40] The second paragraph descended into defensiveness: "Stating this more bluntly, it is time that some among us should stop baiting their Catholic fellow citizens and trying to reduce them to a second-rate status." From there, the tone was elevated, and an articulate case was made for the right of religious groups to enter the public sphere and to try and persuade others of the wisdom of their arguments. Religious majorities should not use political power to deny minority groups their rights. The killer statement came late in the document: "Specifically, I am convinced that Senator Kennedy, or any other Catholic in high office, would act like thousands of other Catholics have acted in public office, and millions of Catholics have acted in the armed services: for the best interests of our nation." The statement concluded with the observation that personal religious convictions should and will influence the judgment of politicians and that no loyalty oath should be required of any member of a church.

There is no record to indicate that Nixon ever released this statement under his name. While Nixon went to some lengths to solicit Catholic favor, he did not offer a specific defense of Catholic politicians like Kennedy. Indeed, he was dependent upon the likes of the *Christian Century* and POAU to advance precisely the kind of argument that Cronin decried in this statement. In this sense, Nixon chose a politically expedient route: trying to blunt Catholic bloc voting for Kennedy while simultaneously refraining from criticizing the conservative Protestant opponents of Kennedy.

In January 1960, Cronin met with Nixon staffer Robert Finch to talk about how to organize the campaign's research and speechwriting operations. In Cronin's summary memo to the vice president, he outlined three distinct tasks: building and maintaining an outside collection of experts, hiring a person to manage this group and to direct all internal research needs, and building a speechwriting team.[41] Cronin offered sage, pragmatic advice on how to organize these functions and offered his services to help to sift candidates for speechwriting.

Cronin continued to pen speeches for Nixon, including one on "a true conservatism" and apparently the one that Nixon gave at the 50th anniversary convention of the Catholic Association.[42] Among other topics, Nixon took the time to praise the Catholic press for strengthening the country's moral and spiritual awareness. But as the general election approached and Kennedy's candidacy seemed more assured, the paper trail drops off. The internal political and ecclesiastical pressure on Cronin from the National Catholic Welfare Conference and other groups within the Catholic church simply made it impossible for Cronin to continue an active role in Nixon's campaign.

Cronin sent Nixon a personal note after the Republican convention:[43]

Dear Dick,

I wish to congratulate you on a magnificent performance in Chicago. Your acceptance speech was deeply moving and by far the greatest of its kind in my memory, although possibly the situation in 1933 was made to order for dramatic appeal. Everything—content, tone, delivery, manner—added to its impressiveness.

Likewise I was struck by the skill used in uniting the factions of the Party. That Goldwater and Rockefeller could give warm endorsements on successive nights was fantastic. Republican chances look much better now than they did two weeks ago when Johnson cut off a number of Southern states you were counting on. Two Virginia Catholics told me, that, as of today, you have their vote. A surprising number of the clergy say the same thing, although I do not discount the pulling power of the idea of a first Catholic President.

As I watched the proceedings in Chicago, naturally I felt a desire to be with you. However, in God's Providence, I feel sure I can do more help by prayer and faithful adherence to the instructions of my superiors here about refraining from purely partisan activity.

I shall be following you closely and I have already applied for my absentee ballot.

Faithfully,

John F. Cronin

What does this extraordinary relationship signify? First, it shows that Nixon appreciated the power of the Catholic vote in general and the threat that Kennedy posed in particular. Eisenhower had made significant progress in wooing Catholics to the Republican Party, and Nixon wanted to hold on to as many of them as possible. Second, Cronin's work for Nixon graphically illustrates Kennedy's vulnerability among Catholic intellectuals. Cronin was a leading authority on Catholic social teachings, and he mined that tradition as he wrote for Nixon and pushed him on race and on the right and competency of the church to enter into public life. Third, it is not at all clear that Nixon took anything other than an instrumental view of Cronin's work on these two points. In other words, he appreciated the open doors and speaking engagements that Cronin provided. It is a mystery whether Nixon ever really bought the arguments on race or felt any attraction to the teachings of the church per se. The archival record just does not offer any insight here. But the fact remains that one of his inner circle of advisors and writers was a leading Catholic intellectual of the era.

At the same time, Nixon was doing extensive outreach to the conservative Protestant world. While the problem with Catholics was trying to prevent a stampede to Kennedy, the problem with Protestants was trying to start a stampede away from Kennedy without being seen as an anti-Catholic bigot and instigator. It would prove to be a delicate procedure.

Nixon had relationships with an interesting array of conservative Protestant luminaries, such as Harold Ockenga, Norman Vincent Peale, Frank Gigliotti, and Billy Graham, as well as the relatively unknown Orland "O. K." Armstrong. The Nixon camp's grasp of the unfolding religious currents can be seen as early as February 1960. Nixon pollster Claude Robinson surveyed in Wisconsin just before the primary there and reported some interesting results. Since Wisconsin was an open primary, both parties were keenly attuned to how many Republicans might cross over into the contest between Kennedy and Humphrey since Nixon was running unopposed.

Robinson's polling indicated that 20% of Republicans were going to vote in the Democratic primary and 80% of these were going to vote for Kennedy.[44] Virtually all Catholic Republicans planned to vote for Kennedy. The Protestant Republicans who crossed over would split their votes evenly between Kennedy and Humphrey: "Generally, speaking, it is the Catholic vote switching for Kennedy in Wisconsin." Months before either convention, in a remarkable bit of political prognostication, Robinson ran a nationwide poll pitting Johnson and Kennedy against Nixon and Lodge. He did not poll for any other pairings of hypothetical tickets. Johnson and Kennedy led Nixon and Lodge 51% to 49%.

A memo summarized the analysis that Robinson passed on to Finch via Nixon aide Len Hall:

> He [Robinson] thinks that already the Catholic people are moving. He is satisfied that there is a general swing of Catholics all over for Kennedy.
>
> The reaction to this is bound to be a swing by Protestants for Nixon.
>
> Claude is in Florida now and he says the Protestant ministers are already beginning to worry. He feels that a smashing victory by Kennedy in Wisconsin will further alert these Protestants and it looks like a religious fight coming up.
>
> In the final analysis RN will not be hurt because there are more Protestants than Catholics but it is not good.[45]

Thus, early in the election cycle, Nixon and his camp understood the Catholic migration to Kennedy and posited a Protestant defection to Nixon. But Robinson's contradictory analysis—that this was not good but would be all right in the end—reflects the unease with which

Nixon faced the campaign. When the vote was tallied in Wisconsin, both camps were agitated about religion and both camps rightly saw that Protestant reaction to Kennedy's Catholicism might prove to be the key to the election. This is the background against which Nixon went to work with Protestants. It is also worth noting that Nixon had known this was likely to be the dynamic in a race against Kennedy since the Bailey Memo. His pollster's data simply confirmed what he thought all along.

The same memo to Finch reported some information from Nixon supporter Charles Lucey in response to questions about how Kennedy was doing physically. Lucey reported that Kennedy was acting as though everything was wonderful, and he was having fun as far as an observer could see. So it appears that the Nixon camp had heard rumors about Kennedy's ill health. Lucey also reported that Bobby Kennedy was hurting his brother by throwing his weight around. He added, "The little girl—the wife—is not going over in Wisconsin. There was an editorial to this effect and she cried and stayed behind for several days."[46]

Nixon's courting of Ockenga, pastor of the historic Park Street Church on the edge of Boston Common, began in earnest in February 1959 when Nixon sent Ockenga a telegram to congratulate the congregation on its sesquicentennial.[47] Ockenga wrote a warm reply, thanking Nixon for his gesture and reaffirming his political loyalty to Nixon. "If there is anything I can do in the advancement of your candidacy for the President of the United States," he wrote, "I should be glad to do it and I assure you that you will have the loyal support of thousands of people in our own constituency."[48] Ockenga would have the opportunity to show that support within 18 months, but for the moment Nixon had to take comfort in the fact that the leading evangelical voice in Kennedy's home state of Massachusetts was pledging his political support.

In July, Nixon was awarded a Christian Endeavor citation—apparently at Ockenga's behest—by Gordon College, a fledgling evangelical school championed by Ockenga and Billy Graham. Ockenga praised Nixon for his remarks, which highlighted the contrast between the American and Soviet systems. Nixon was about to embark on his famous trip to the Soviet Union, and Ockenga wished him divine protection and guidance. He also thanked Nixon for agreeing to serve on the board of the college. He then went to work trying to set up a meeting time in Washington for himself, Nixon, and Graham. Ockenga wanted to convey to Nixon their vision for the college as it moved to its new campus on 800 acres northeast of Boston. They sought to build a school "that would be grounded upon sound Christian and political principles which would turn out men and women in every walk to life who are aware of the essence of our heritage who are prepared to promote this."[49] Nixon's staff set up the meeting for November 23, 1959.[50]

Nixon also maintained a relationship with Frank Gigliotti, who was a leader in both the Masons and the National Association of Evangelicals. Gigliotti wrote to Nixon that he "talked with some of the men in his office" and told them that the Masons would do all they could for Nixon in the "great fight ahead." He went on to say that the NAE would like to help quietly and explained that the NAE represented about 10 million people.[51] About three weeks later, he wrote to Nixon on NAE letterhead and elaborated that both organizations would leave no stone unturned on Nixon's behalf. Judge Luther A. Smith, the sovereign grand commander of the Southern Masonic Jurisdiction, and the Honorable George Bushnell, the sovereign grand commander of the Northern Masonic Jurisdiction, both Democrats, wanted to meet Nixon privately and discuss how they were going to help the campaign. Apparently, because of Nixon's flare-up of phlebitis, the meeting never took place, but the Masons were in the field on his behalf.

Gigliotti was more elusive when it came to just how the NAE was going to help. The NAE's work on Nixon's behalf would become clearer soon, but he stated his belief that, under God, Nixon would render a great service to "our people" and added that "we" did not oppose Kennedy on religious grounds.[52] It is impossible to ascertain at this historical distance the full range of work done by the Masons or by the National Association of Evangelicals. What is clear is that they were eager to help and eager to make sure that Nixon knew something of their work. Both organizations would figure in the single most public enclave of conservative Protestants to oppose Kennedy, which would erupt in September.

Nixon also maintained a cordial relationship with Norman Vincent Peale, the apostle of positive thinking and the senior minister at the Marble Collegiate Church in New York City. Their relationship dated back at least to 1955, when Peale had traveled to Europe for a summer trip, and his assistant had asked Nixon for introductions to the American ambassadors in London and Paris, writing that "any attention which you could arrange for Dr. Peale in London and Paris would provide him with rich illustrative material for his sermons."[53] Scrawled atop the letter in Rose Mary Woods's handwriting are the words, "Bob, Let's make an exception on this." A few days later, Woods wrote a

directive to a staffer noting that Peale was a good Republican and outside of Billy Graham probably the most influential Protestant preacher
in America, so while they did not normally do this sort of thing, they
were going to notify the ambassadors of Peale's trip.[54] Nixon wrote
letters to introduce Peale to C. Douglas Dillon, the ambassador to
France, and Winthrop Aldrich, the ambassador to England, and asked
Dillon to invite the Peales to a July 4 reception at the embassy.[55] Nixon
clearly understood Peale's prominence and went out of his way to be
of service.

Nixon's courtship paid off. In April 1960, Peale wrote a fan letter to
Nixon, telling him what a great pleasure he had just had in sitting next
to Hannah Nixon, Nixon's mother, at a luncheon in Los Angeles:

> If only Americans everywhere could know your family, they would
> take you to their hearts with real affection. I think your mother is one
> of the sweetest, most genuine, lovable, Christian mothers I have met
> in many a day. In fact, I told her that if the entire American people
> could know her your election would be assured. Your family, in my
> judgment, ought to be made better known to the American people,
> for they typify the best in American life. They represent that vast
> body of fine, honorable, hardworking, God-fearing American families
> which is of the heart of the nation itself.[56]

Nixon's cynical political instincts kicked in once he read Peale's
treacle. He sent a memo to several aides with Peale's letter attached:

> I think he hits here upon a very fundamental point which we should
> bear in mind in the articles which we attempt to encourage in the next
> few weeks and months.
>
> Billy Graham hit this same line with me when he was talking
> with me a few days ago. It is that we should emphasize more the fam-
> ily background with its humble origins which would have emotional
> impact on people in general rather than putting as much attention
> as we have on the strictly political story and the issues. Of course, as
> we get into the campaign, issues will be predominant. At this point
> I feel the other aspects should be heavily emphasized. For example, as
> I have said previously, I think a good article on my mother for Ladies
> Home Journal or Good Housekeeping would be helpful. She told me
> on the phone that somebody by the name of Schreiber was writing
> one. This sounded to me like one of those freelance jobs and I would
> like to have it checked to see what the situation is.
>
> What I am talking about here is not the usual dissecting job a la
> the Maso [*sic*] book in setting forth all the controversial issues and
> aspects and trying to be objective in doing so. What we frankly need

here is some overtly favorable "corn" such as the liberal press wrote about Roosevelt and Truman, and now about Kennedy, Humphrey and Symington at the drop of a hat.

In any event, give me a report on what will be done with regard to an article or articles on my mother along the lines I have suggested.[57]

Later in the summer, Peale distributed copies of *The Real Nixon* by Bela Kornitzer to a circle of his friends in an effort to drum up support.[58] The book was a classic puff-piece campaign biography that contained Nixon's mother's cherry pie recipe. Nixon asked Peale to lead a prayer at the Republican convention, but he was unable to do so since he was traveling in Europe at that time.[59] Peale would continue to work on Nixon's behalf during the summer with explosive results after Labor Day.

But all of the relationships that Nixon maintained with Protestant leaders paled in comparison to the one he had with Billy Graham. While the correspondence between Nixon and Graham blossomed as the general election season began, the two had exchanged some interesting letters prior to the summer of 1960. In December 1957, Graham wrote a fawning letter to Nixon, telling him that he was one of the most thoughtful persons Graham knew and that he read Nixon's speeches word by word. He saw in Nixon's speeches precisely the kind of warnings the American people needed to respond to the dangers of the hour. Graham was particularly agitated that the peace of the world rested on Premier Nikita Khrushchev's shoulders.

With the ever-present prospect of nuclear war with Russia in mind, Graham reminded Nixon of how in 1956 they had spent an evening together (along with Senator George Smathers of Florida) during which Graham "opened some of the prophetic Scriptures" to them. It was amazing, according to Graham, how those scriptures were being fulfilled before their very eyes: "Sometime perhaps we will have opportunity to go over them again privately, because it may help you in determining future courses of action in case added responsibilities are yours."[60] There is no evidence in any of the Nixon-Graham correspondence to suggest that Nixon shared any of Graham's apocalyptic, premillennial theology. Yet he apparently did indulge Graham and let him make his case on such matters without indicating any skepticism.

In the same letter, Graham also did some political prognosticating. He thought that Nixon's political stock was extremely high, though there were factors working against any Republican in 1960. Not the least of these was the fantastic buildup that Kennedy was receiving in the press, which would help to make him a formidable foe. He ended with a note that prophesied his own work in the next three years, "Contrary to popular opinion, when the chips are down I think the religious issue would be very strong and might conceivably work in your behalf."[61]

Two weeks later, Dr. Nelson Bell, Billy Graham's father-in-law, called Nixon's office to ask Nixon to continue to intervene on behalf of *Christianity Today*, the flagship evangelical magazine, in its efforts to receive tax exempt status from the Treasury Department. Bell reminded the staffer that Graham had spoken to Nixon about their petition and that Nixon had prompted Treasury to expedite the matter. Bell had recently spoken to a young staffer, who told him that the ruling would be forthcoming. He was alarmed at the immaturity of the Treasury staffer and asked for Nixon to put in a good word. Nixon's staffer noted that he had told Bell that they didn't normally intervene in such cases but that he would bring it to Nixon's attention. The staffer didn't think there was anything to worry about at Treasury, but nevertheless he asked Nixon if they should do anything with Treasury about this and Nixon checked the "yes" box.[62]

Despite Nixon's multiple interventions, apparently the Treasury Department had sufficient qualms about the nonprofit status of the fledgling religious publication that the ruling was not forthcoming for some time. A follow-up memo in the file detailed a conversation with a Treasury staffer who said that the application was complicated because there seemed to be some indication of profit making.[63] This may account for why the magazine's coverage of the entire 1960 campaign was muted in comparison to the *Christian Century* and *Christianity and Crisis*. One would have expected *Christianity Today* to have taken a strong anti-Kennedy stand, yet engaging in what might appear to be partisan work might have impaired its ability to get nonprofit status. But Nixon clearly went the extra mile to help Graham's magazine to get its coveted tax exempt status.

While Graham was the most prominent evangelical leader to court and be courted by Nixon in this era, one of the least known conservative Protestants in the country cultivated a relationship with Nixon that would eventually pay some unlikely dividends. Orland K. "O. K." Armstrong, a former Republican congressman from Springfield, Missouri, and an editor at large for *Reader's Digest*, kept up a stream of correspondence with Nixon throughout the fifties. Armstrong and Nixon had been freshman congressmen together in 1947, but while Nixon's career steadily took off, Armstrong's ended after a couple of terms. Yet his loyalty to the GOP never wavered.

In early 1959, Armstrong began peppering Nixon and his staff with chatty, sycophantic letters telling of his work on behalf of Nixon's campaign. Armstrong wanted to meet Nixon when he was to visit Washington on business, but ended up meeting with Robert Finch instead.[64] Finch noted that "O.K. Armstrong, the perpetual freshman," came by and shared some gossip about Nelson Rockefeller's impending hire of a journalist for his campaign: "Naturally, O.K. Armstrong is anxious to get underway for Nixon as soon as possible."[65]

In April, Armstrong continued to detail his organizing efforts in Missouri's Seventh Congressional District and offered to plug a Nixon speech to the International Christian Leadership Prayer Breakfast as a potential article in *Reader's Digest*.[66] He told Nixon that, from time to time, he would report to Finch.[67] Nixon responded with what initially looked like a modified form letter, thanking Armstrong for his work on Nixon's behalf but noting that, for the time being, he should work for the good of the whole Republican Party. It was not a complete brush-off, though, since Nixon noted that, if "anything should develop along the lines you discussed, you may be sure I shall be in touch with you."[68]

In July, between the Democratic and Republican conventions, the tone of the correspondence changed. Armstrong wrote to Nixon's press secretary, Herb Klein, enclosing a summary of his work for Nixon (he also sent a copy directly to the candidate). He closed the letter, "See you in Chicago."[69] The actual report to Nixon was filled with fluff and a tally of random comments from various unnamed Republicans about whom Nixon should pick as his vice presidential candidate. Near the end of the letter, Armstrong told Nixon that he had conferred recently with Senator Thruston Morton, chair of the Republican National Committee, and A. B. Hermann, chair of the Republican Party Campaign, and would be taking leave from his work for *Reader's Digest* and be working full time for the campaign.[70]

So how did Armstrong go from "the perpetual freshman" to campaign employee in less than five months? The clue is to be found in his July 16 letter, in which he told Nixon that he had conferred at length with their mutual friend Billy Graham. Armstrong, because of his vast network of connections with Protestants like Graham, the leadership of the Southern Baptist Convention, and the leadership of POAU, was uniquely poised to serve as the campaign's secret intermediary. That is, he could work for the campaign in his natural element, the vast Protestant world, without any apparent link to the campaign that would be paying his expenses. The Nixon campaign had found its Protestant anti-Catholic strategy in the person of O. K. Armstrong. The saga of his work for Nixon reveals a hitherto unknown aspect of Nixon's anti-Kennedy efforts.

5

MOBILIZING THE
TROOPS

∙∙

The day before the West Virginia Democratic presidential primary in May, Nixon advisor (and eventual titular campaign manager) Robert Finch gave a brief speech to a group of supporters to outline the strategy for the coming campaign. Nixon's internal polls at that point showed him leading all of the possible Democratic nominees except Kennedy, who led Nixon 52% to 48%. The Nixon brain trust did not think that Kennedy would win big in West Virginia. In the unlikely event that he did, there would be no way to prevent Kennedy from winning the nomination. But without a large victory, they felt, the contest would be decided by the convention, and Stevenson would prevail. There would, however, be tremendous pressure for Kennedy to take the second slot. While they thought that Kennedy was the strongest vote-getter among the Democratic candidates, there was no way to know how many Catholic votes he would bring to the Democrats if he ran for vice president with Stevenson or Johnson atop the ticket.[1]

Finch promised that the Nixon campaign would be the most unorthodox in the nation's history. While he did not fully explain what this meant, he did note that Nixon would act as his own de facto campaign manager, consulting periodically with Senator Thruston Morton, chair of the Republican National Committee; Senator Barry Goldwater, chair of the Republican Senatorial Campaign Committee; and Representative William Miller, chair of the Republican Congressional Campaign Committee. Nixon would be his own chief advisor.

So as late as May, the Nixon campaign felt that Kennedy would likely not be at the top of the ticket. While this differs somewhat from Nixon's own analysis well after the election was over, it helps to account for why they did not have a fully developed strategy for addressing Kennedy's Catholicism. The problem of holding on to Republican Catholics while facilitating a mass defection of Democratic Protestants was a tricky one that they hoped to avoid. When Kennedy did win the West Virginia primary and emerge as the Democratic candidate, the religion issue moved to the forefront for both campaigns. Enter former Missouri congressman Orland K. Armstrong.

Days before the Republican convention opened in Chicago, Armstrong wrote to Albert "A. B." Hermann, a senior official at the Republican National Committee. Hermann would be named national campaign director for the RNC, and he would coordinate the day-to-day activities for the RNC and Nixon headquarters.[2] Armstrong outlined a series of steps that the campaign could take in order to exploit Kennedy's Catholicism among a wide range of Protestants. Hermann immediately wrote back and told Armstrong to contact him immediately after the convention.[3] But Armstrong could not wait. He phoned Hermann instead and got an employee pass to the convention.[4] On July 16, a week before the convention, Armstrong wrote to Hermann and reported that he was beginning to gather a mass of information on church leaders, meetings, conventions, conferences, and publications, "which will give us a powerful medium of expression." He added, "[P]erhaps Chairman M. [Morton] would like to glance at it."[5] He also promised to report to Hermann at the convention.

On the one hand, his age and his location in Missouri made Armstrong a highly unlikely candidate to become the off-the-record organizer of anti-Catholic forces for Nixon. On the other hand, he was the perfect person for the job. His biography was full of twists and turns, the sum of which proved useful to the campaign. Born in rural southwestern Missouri to a Baptist minister and his wife in 1893, Armstrong had earned an undergraduate degree from Drury College, a bachelor of law degree from Cumberland University, and a bachelor's and master's of journalism from the University of Missouri—all by 1925. A World War I veteran, he helped to found the Journalism Department at the University of Florida. In the thirties, he was elected to the Missouri House of Representatives and served several terms. In 1944, he was hired by *Reader's Digest* as a member of the editorial staff, a post he held throughout the remainder of his career. In 1950, he was elected to the House of Representatives from the Missouri Sixth District and served one term before redistricting merged his seat with one held by a Republican with more seniority.[6]

An active Baptist layman, he maintained a wide circle of contacts in the Protestant world, including Billy Graham; Harold Fey, editor of the *Christian Century*; and Glenn Everett of the Religion News Service. His frequent travels across the country and the globe as well as his brief sojourn in Washington had given him a wide range of acquaintances, while his work as a journalist gave him cover to travel the country without raising any particular suspicions. His sycophantic style also meant that he was relentless in the pursuit of what he wanted or what he thought other people needed. Hired by the Nixon campaign to aid the forces of anti-Catholicism across the country, he could contact the leaders of sympathetic organizations and offer his aid to them without ever having to directly reveal that he was on the payroll of the Republican National Committee. At the age of 66, Armstrong had found his highest political calling.

In one sense, Armstrong had already begun his work for Nixon at the annual meeting of the Southern Baptist Convention in May 1960. On the fourth day of the national meeting, Armstrong helped to pass a resolution that expressed deep reservations about Kennedy's candidacy without ever naming him. This would be a common strategy throughout the campaign. The resolution, titled "Christian Citizenship," proceeded in classic syllogistic fashion. It reaffirmed the Baptist faith in the separation of church and state as expressed in the Bill of Rights: that a man must be free to choose his own church and that his personal religious faith shall not be a test for his qualification for public office.[7] Then, it introduced the caveat that captured Senator Kennedy:

> Yet the fact remains that a public official is inescapably bound by the dogma and demands of his church and he cannot consistently separate himself from these. This is especially true when that church maintains a position in open conflict with our established and constituted American pattern of life as specifically related to religious liberty, separation of Church and State, the freedom of conscience in matters related to marriage and the family, the perpetuation of free public schools and the prohibition against use of public monies for sectarian purposes.[8]

The obvious conclusion was that a candidate's church was of concern to the voters. In all cases, a candidate should be free of sectarian pressure so he could make independent decisions consistent with the rights and privileges of all citizens. The resolution concluded by calling on every member of every church to pray for public officials and to participate fully in the democratic process, including voting and seeking divine leadership in the selection of public leaders.[9] Clearly, voting for Kennedy was not an option for the faithful in the massive Southern Baptist Convention.

Armstrong wrote Hermann a three-page memo that laid the foundation for his work in the field.[10] He had surveyed many Protestant leaders across the country, and they were tremendously concerned and ready for action. He drew a map for his handler that divided American Protestants into three blocs. Two were organized, and one was not.

The first was made up of the denominations that comprised the National Council of Churches, with almost 39 million members among 32 major denominations. The second consisted of the 12 million members of the denominations that made up the National Association of Evangelicals. These churches were intensely concerned about a Catholic running for president. The third was made up of churches that were not aligned with either of the first two formal associations. These included the Southern Baptist Convention, with almost 10 million members, Christian Scientists, Seventh-day Adventists, and Jehovah's Witnesses.

Almost all of these denominations had already taken a stand in resolutions and statements, some of them quite specific, on the question of a Catholic for president. Moving chronologically through the spring and early summer, Armstrong noted resolutions passed at the Southern Baptist Convention, the American Baptist Convention, the American Council of Christian Churches, the annual conferences of the Methodist church in Idaho and Washington, the Augustana Lutheran Church Convention, the Bible Presbyterian church, and the General Assembly of Regular Baptists. Scores of other denominations, he claimed, had passed similar statements.

How could they mobilize this grassroots anti-Catholic sentiment for Nixon? The way to proceed, Armstrong argued, was to contact religious leaders and encourage them to issue statements, print materials, and talk to political leaders in their states who would help to take the lead in spreading the word and influencing the public. The strategy would be to work only with official and trusted leaders and through them move to community action. With no sense of irony, the man who had helped the Southern Baptist Convention to pass a resolution calling for elected officials to be free of pressure and coercion from religious leaders set out a grand strategy to use religious leaders to build a grassroots campaign to pressure Protestants to vote against a Catholic.

Soon thereafter, Armstrong began to recruit leaders willing to work against Kennedy. A five-page confidential memo outlined the movement's organization and leaders, its plan of action, and its budget.[11] Armstrong would coordinate all of the efforts of the disparate Protestant groups working against Kennedy. Since so many churches had expressed misgivings about Kennedy, this coordination could solidify support for religious freedom and for the principle of the separation of church and state, and it could convince church members of the probable weakening of the First Amendment to the Constitution if Kennedy were elected. The campaign would not encourage religious bigotry or make false accusations against the Catholic church, but it would encourage factual and dignified discussions by Protestant ministers and church leaders throughout the country.

Armstrong had already contacted several outstanding Protestant leaders in order to give proper direction to "our movement." All of them were eager to lend their leadership and their organizations to the work at hand. He claimed that these leaders and their associates were in contact with at least 80% of all the Protestants in the country. While the range of leaders Armstrong would contact is impressive, he was undoubtedly exaggerating his own influence. He was quite careful never to explicitly reveal his formal relationship with the Nixon campaign. But at the same time, the leaders to whom he talked had to know that he had some official sanction, or they would have never given him the level of attention he was able to elicit.

"It is hardly possible to estimate the number of publications under control of these groups, but they run into the thousands. All have publications already in the work at hand, and all are ready to help throw the campaign into high gear."[12] These leaders and their memberships were, in his estimation, about equally divided politically. The election might hang in the balance.

Armstrong had already recruited eight organizations or leaders to join the effort. First on the list was Citizens for Religious Freedom, coordinated by Don Gill. This group was created by the National Association of Evangelicals specifically for the purpose of opposing Kennedy. It would concentrate on conferences, speeches, and the distribution of printed matter. Next were the Baptists, led by the Reverend W. O. Vaught, pastor of First Baptist Church in Little Rock, Arkansas, and vice president of the Southern Baptist Convention.

Third on his list were the Assemblies of God and the Reverend Thomas Zimmerman, who was the group's general secretary as well as the president of the National Association of Evangelicals. Fourth were the Reverend Gerald Kennedy, bishop of the Los Angeles area for the Methodist church, and Leland Case, editor of the Methodist publication *Together* and brother of U.S. senator Francis Case. Fifth was the National Association of Evangelicals, led by the Reverend George Ford as executive director and Dr. Clyde Taylor as secretary. Next was Protestants and Other Americans United for Separation of Church and State, represented by the Reverend Glenn Archer as executive secretary. POAU was involved in efforts to promote the separation of church and state among all denominations, including those in the National Council of Churches. They were "very vigorous in their speeches, printed material, etc."

Wrapping up the list were two groups Armstrong had contacted through Dr. Nelson Bell. As editor of the flagship evangelical magazine *Christianity Today* and Billy Graham's father-in-law, Bell would open doors to the magazine and provide access to Graham's mailing list. All in all, Armstrong had built an impressive informal network that reached into many corners of the Protestant world. But he was not content simply to drop the names of this list of recruits. He had to develop a plan of action.

With the help of several on his list, along with their associates, Armstrong had already moved to arrange important conferences or to coordinate meetings with "our overall program." He continued:

> During the last several days in Washington, I helped the newly formed Citizens for Religious Freedom arrange for a great meeting of religious leaders, Protestants of all denominations (some 30 denominations will be represented), in Washington, September 7. This meeting will set the key note for the entire campaign. It will select leaders who will go back to their communities and establish local units of the Citizens groups. Note that Dr. L. Nelson Bell, father-in-law of Billy Graham will be serving as Chairman.
>
> On the day previous, September 6, there will be a great rally of the Protestants and Other Americans United, with perhaps as many as 800 leaders present. I have been closely in touch with their principle [*sic*] associates and we expect that this meeting will be most outstanding. Leaders of this well known organization assure me that they can arrange at least 60 important meetings, in strategic areas, between now and November.[13]

At the end of the memo, Armstrong went into full fundraising mode. He argued that support was needed for this

> tremendously important part of the current campaign, for necessary items such as expenses for leaders who will organize nationally and work among the local units; for office expenses in Washington, for newspaper, radio, and television advertising; for meetings and

conferences in every area of the country; for printing and distribution of millions of pieces of literature written by church leaders and their associates; for distribution of P.O.A.U. films such as "Captured Schools"; and articles for all the religious [Protestant] press. . . . Your support is urgently needed!

Thus Armstrong entered the fray armed with an array of impressive contacts among Protestant elites from the mainline and evangelical worlds. He had a comprehensive vision for coordinating the grassroots anti-Catholic efforts of dozens of church groups. And he had a mandate to raise funds, to distribute them as he saw fit, to disseminate the message that Protestants were against Kennedy. With a commitment from Albert Hermann to pay his expenses, Armstrong hit the road.

He went first to Dallas, where over three days, August 16–18, he met with various people, most notably Carr P. Collins, founder of Fidelity Union Life Insurance—and a Democrat—who was president of Texans for Nixon.[14] Collins had a long-running feud with Lyndon Johnson dating back to a U.S. Senate race in the early forties in which Governor W. Lee O'Daniel had narrowly defeated Johnson. Collins, an advisor to O'Daniel, owned a Mexican radio station that broadcast into Texas. He had given the O'Daniel campaign a large, undisclosed gift of free air time. A Baptist who was instrumental in bringing the fundamentalist William Criswell to the First Baptist Church of Dallas, Collins also gave large gifts to Baylor University.[15] He was a logical starting point in Armstrong's search for support.

Armstrong asked Collins for $50,000.[16] It is impossible to determine whether Collins made a contribution. Indeed, the money question remains one of the most tantalizing unknown aspects of Armstrong's work. We can't know conclusively just how much money Armstrong was able to raise or whether the campaign itself contributed money to his efforts beyond paying his travel expenses.

After returning to Springfield, Missouri, Armstrong drove to Little Rock to meet with several people, including Vaught and W. R. Smith. Vaught was a prominent Southern Baptist minister and vice president of the Southern Baptist Convention. Smith was an aide to Democratic Arkansas governor Orval Faubus and a member of the Churches of Christ, a conservative Protestant sect with heavy concentrations of members in the politically crucial states of Tennessee and Texas. Smith had attended the Democratic convention in Los Angeles as a delegate from Arkansas pledged to support Johnson. As a southern Democrat and a member of the conservative Churches of Christ, Smith's disgust at Kennedy's nomination over Johnson was compounded by Johnson's acceptance of the vice presidential slot. With Faubus's permission, Smith decided to help the Nixon cause. He drew a political map of opinion leaders in the highly decentralized denomination and introduced Armstrong to one of its entrepreneurial young ministers, James Walter Nichols.[17]

Nichols was the founder of *The Herald of Truth*, the evangelical denomination's signature national television program, and editor of the *Christian Chronicle*, its highest circulating newspaper. He was also one of the most successful fundraisers and organizers in the Churches of Christ. Nichols would provide much help to the Nixon cause, recruiting major Church of Christ publications to publish articles against Kennedy.

Working with Vaught, Armstrong set up a public meeting in Little Rock in October at which Glenn Archer of POAU was the keynote speaker.[18] Vaught praised Armstrong for his work and spoke glowingly of the coverage the event had received in the *Arkansas Democrat*. He went on to mention his travels to Texas and California to organize and affirmed his own congregation's distribution of material for the upcoming Reformation Sunday efforts, which had been dubbed Religious Liberty Sunday. As vice president of the Southern Baptist Convention, Vaught's sway was considerable.

At the same time, Armstrong reached out to the Reverend Ramsey Pollard, pastor of the large Bellevue Baptist Church in Memphis and president of the Southern Baptist Convention. Armstrong went to see Pollard in Memphis and, at Pollard's request, drafted language, drawn in part from the resolution passed at the convention's May meeting, that Pollard might use in sermons and press releases. He told Pollard that he hoped for national publicity and prompted him to make a speech or hold a press conference so that other denominational leaders might make similar statements.[19]

The statement showed the sophistication of the anti-Catholic message that Armstrong marketed. It started with an urgent plea to all fellow Southern Baptist ministers to remind their members of the extreme importance of reaffirming Baptist faith in the separation of church and state. The source of the urgency stemmed from "our concern over the candidacy for the president of the United States of one who indisputably would be under pressure of his church hierarchy to weaken the wall of separation."[20] It called on every Baptist congregation to bring attention to the resolution from the May convention and to give all 9 million Southern Baptists a copy of it. It called for sermons to be preached on the topic and encouraged laypeople to discuss the subject in their homes and churches and "by every media of public information."

Pollard put this material to use. He told Armstrong that he had gotten good publicity during recent days and that the battle "is being handled about as well as possible."[21] Armstrong had succeeded in drafting the head of America's largest Protestant denomination into his orbit. By the end of his networking, Armstrong had established close ties to the clergy networks of two of the South's most prominent and conservative Protestant denominations, the Southern Baptist Convention and the Churches of Christ.

Armstrong's method of operation was multifaceted. At the macro level, Armstrong promoted two national efforts, one of which was the large meeting in Washington, D.C., on September 7, which would be chaired by the Reverend Norman Vincent Peale, the senior minister of the Marble Collegiate Church in New York City. The other was the promotion of Reformation Sunday, traditionally the last Sunday in October, as a day for Protestant clergy to promote anti-Catholic sentiments through sermons and printed materials.

At the grassroots level, Armstrong barnstormed the country, meeting with church leaders to promote the Nixon cause. He traveled to Dallas, Texas; Little Rock, Arkansas; St. Louis, Missouri; Washington, D.C.; Memphis, Tennessee; New York; Philadelphia; Chicago; Mobile, Alabama; Oxford and Jackson, Mississippi; Urbana, Illinois; and Fayetteville, Arkansas. In between, Armstrong raised funds for local and national efforts and cultivated national leaders in a variety of denominations. From August 15 through October 9,[22] he contacted leaders of 37 denominations and assisted them in their election strategy plans. He attended 48 conferences and meetings in 12 states, including the Peale meeting, at which plans were made for numerous rallies and the distribution of printed matter. He coordinated the distribution of statements for about 20 denominational leaders.

Rallies were to be held by denominational leaders, lay conferences were to be organized, and information would be provided in churches. Armstrong estimated that thousands of people would attend; 1,500 people came to hear Archer speak in Little Rock on October 3. The Reformation Sunday effort was being promoted by the Southern Baptists, the Assemblies of God, and the National Association of Evangelicals. Armstrong had about a dozen volunteers, many connected to church organizations, who were working their cities, states, and regions.

He had done the most work in Missouri, Arkansas, Virginia, Florida, Tennessee, Kentucky, Oklahoma, Texas, and Illinois. He would concentrate his work for the remainder of the campaign in all of these plus California, Ohio, Indiana, and North Carolina. He also requested funds to carry out the work of printing and distributing publicity materials on Reformation Sunday rallies, to put at least six people in the field for the remaining time, and to cover the strategic states of Illinois, Kentucky, Oklahoma, and Virginia. Kennedy had hired James Wine, formerly of the National Council of Churches, to organize Democratic Protestants. Nixon needed to counter this work.

The linchpin of this strategy was the national meeting at the Mayflower Hotel in Washington, D.C. As Armstrong had indicated, this was to be a centralized launching of a nationwide campaign where leaders would be given literature to distribute and local work would be organized. Unraveling the various threads of how this meeting was conceived, organized, and paid for is a complex and fragmentary exercise. There were at least five additional trails that led to the so-called Peale meeting. In addition to Armstrong and the Nixon campaign, there were Billy Graham, Norman Vincent Peale, the National Association of Evangelicals, the Masons, and Protestants and Other Americans United for Separation of Church and State.

POAU, a national organization with a large grassroots membership drawn from all sectors of American Protestantism, would put all of its assets into the game to beat Kennedy. POAU would be one of the last para-church organizations in the Protestant world that drew members from the full theological spectrum of Protestantism. The common anti-Catholicism of conservative, moderate, and liberal Protestants was the glue that held POAU together.

It was a young organization, established in the late forties, the brainchild of Dr. Rufus Weaver, a Southern Baptist and the former president of Mercer University in Macon, Georgia.[23] He was instrumental in the formation of the Baptist Joint Committee on Public Affairs, a cooperative effort of four Baptist denominations to establish a Washington presence. In 1946, Weaver initiated preliminary conversations that drew interested parties from the Baptists, Disciples of Christ, Seventh-day Adventists, Methodists, and the National Association of Evangelicals to a November meeting in Chicago, presided over by G. Bromley Oxnam. At that meeting, Charles Clayton Morrison, founding editor of the *Christian Century*, presented "A Manifesto," which was unanimously adopted by the 60 people present. The *New York Times* printed the statement in its entirety. It called for support for the distinctively American separation of church and state and endorsed religious liberty for all. It sought to redress grievances and to correct violations of the constitutional provisions for separation and for religious liberty. It denied any intent to attack (or promote) any specific church. From Morrison's manifesto, POAU was born.

The diversity of the group can be seen from its leadership. Its original president was Edwin McNeill Poteat, president of Colgate Rochester Divinity School, and its vice presidents were Morrison; John Mackay, president of Princeton Theological Seminary; and Louie D. Newton, president of the Southern Baptist Convention. Dr. Frank Yost of the Washington office of the Seventh-day Adventists wrote the constitution, and Sovereign Grand Commander John H. Cowles of the Scottish Rite Masons, Southern Jurisdiction, presented a check that assisted in paying POAU's first-year expenses. In July 1948, POAU hired Glenn Archer, dean of the Law School of Washburn University, as executive director.

By the end of 1960, POAU was perhaps the most comprehensive Protestant organization in the country. As ideological pressures mounted within Protestantism through the sixties and into the seventies, it would become increasingly rare to find conservative and liberal Protestants united for anything. But in 1960, they were united in their anti-Catholicism.[24] The theological range of its 130-plus-member national advisory council was breathtaking.[25]

From an institutional perspective, the candidacy of John Kennedy allowed POAU to have an astonishingly successful year in 1960. By Election Day, its finances, membership, and literature distribution reached record levels. At its board meeting in February 1961, Archer reported the numbers for 1960.[26] During that year, its flagship monthly publication, *Church and State Review*, had grown by 37,000 subscribers to a circulation of 100,000. Two other publications, *Church-State News* and *Church-State Digest*, had circulations of 750,000 and 500,000, respectively. Twenty-six press releases were written, primarily on election topics, and testimony was given before two congressional committees.

The group produced a wide range of pamphlets with titles such as *51%* and *Summons to Americans*, both of which passed the 2 million mark in circulation. They distributed reprints of past articles and new educational items such as *President Kennedy's Pledge*, *Protestants Unashamed*, and *How the Roman Catholic Church Would Change the Constitution*. Most important were publications bearing directly on the 1960 political campaign. This section of the 1960 annual report began:

POAU was eager to exploit the educational possibilities for separation of church and state which inhered in the unique 1960 campaign. We could not, under our charter provisions, take any partisan part. We tried to steer a careful course, steadily holding the church-state issues before the public and making every use of the frequent discussion these issues received during the campaign. Generally, we succeeded in being active without being classified among religious groups seeking to defeat Kennedy or among the so-called "hate groups."

For example, two articles were ghostwritten by POAU staff and published under the individual names of board members. "The Religious Issue" by John Mackay appeared in *U.S. News and World Report* (and was reprinted in the *Congressional Record*), and "A Protestant View of a Catholic for President" by Eugene Carson Blake and G. Bromley Oxnam was published in *Look* magazine. On September 6, POAU issued a press release which was printed in the *New York Times*. Several pamphlets directly addressed the election. *The Religious Issue in the 1960 Campaign* by POAU staffer C. Stanley Lowell hit 250,000 in circulation. Lowell's *51%*, which described the consequences for America if Catholics became 51% of the population, was reprinted in *Christianity Today*. Though POAU had promised to avoid direct partisanship, the report admitted that it had circulated (but not printed) an essay by a Methodist minister in Evanston, Illinois, entitled "Why I Cannot Now Vote for a Roman Catholic for President."

In October 1960 an internal memorandum projected, POAU would circulate a total of 8 million pieces of literature.[27] In the first eight months of 1960, POAU fundraising was up over 50% compared to the same period in 1959.[28] POAU had a payroll of almost 30 staffers and a half million dollars in the bank as it headed into the 1960 campaign.[29]

While opposition to the Catholic church in American politics was one of the central planks in POAU's platform, it could not pull the trigger on an overt and large-scale anti-Kennedy campaign until Kennedy actually secured the nomination. Since it was not clear that Kennedy would prevail at the convention until the floor vote, POAU could not leap into full action until the summer of 1960. But associate director C. Stanley Lowell attended the Los Angeles convention and produced an exhaustive analysis of Kennedy's victory that was circulated among major POAU stakeholders. The 21-page paper, "An Analysis of Catholic 'Power Politics' and Other Factors of Political Pressure in the First Ballot Nomination of Sen. John F. Kennedy for President," was the opening salvo in POAU's assault on Kennedy's candidacy.[30]

Lowell's gossipy accounts of each state delegation's voting and religious makeup was designed to impress the reader with Kennedy's sinister sectarian appeal and the ability of his henchmen to persuade fellow Catholics to support him. While the Kennedy forces at the convention were certainly not averse to using all sorts of pressure tactics to secure votes, Lowell could not provide one example in which a sectarian religious appeal was used. He merely listed the number of Catholics in a delegation and drew the conclusion that a lot of Catholics in a delegation meant a lot of votes for Kennedy. This was undoubtedly true. But it is not proof of Catholic pressure.

Lowell noted that religion was an important factor in giving Kennedy many votes from states with Catholic leaders, such as New York, the six New England states, Pennsylvania, Ohio, Illinois, and California. Looking toward the general election, he wrote:

> Kennedy's religion did not handicap him. In a very real sense, it was his biggest asset because so many of the kingmakers were Catholic, and of those men, every single one who had any real votes was with Kennedy. The Catholics who held out for others, Senators [Eugene] McCarthy, [Christopher] Dodd, and [Mike] Mansfield, and Governor [Joe] Hickey, couldn't deliver any votes. It was a combination of Catholic power plus shrewd political deals, but it would not have succeeded had his opposition united behind one man.
>
> A political lesson is apparent. If a Catholic candidate emerges who has strong support from the Catholic city bosses and Catholic governors in the North, he cannot be defeated unless the predominately Protestant Southern states unite with the other sections of the North and West to back a candidate mutually acceptable. When the South holds out for a sectional candidate like Mississippi's [Ross] Barnett, it plays into the hands of the opposition and any Catholic candidate who can line up big-state support will win. Southern sectionalism, plus Catholic concentrations in major cities, will equal a Catholic candidate, not just in 1960, but a succession of Catholic candidates from now on.

To Protestants, this was the most chilling conclusion possible: Catholic Democrats had discovered a formula to capture the presidential nomination for the foreseeable future. Thus, POAU painted a dire picture of the threat that Kennedy posed in the fall, but it also foretold Catholic domination of the Democratic Party. The leadership of POAU sprang into action and decided to use its board meeting in Washington in early September as a focal point for its formal organizing in the upcoming election. This date also coincided with the Peale meeting and that of the Baptist Joint Committee on Public Affairs. Coordination among the various Protestant forces against Kennedy would be concentrated in early September in the nation's capital.

On July 6, the executive committee of the board met in Washington to discuss a paper, "An Open Letter to Senator John F. Kennedy," by Charles Morrison. The committee decided to help Morrison make copies of the letter and find a place to publish it.[31] In a memo circulated before the meeting, POAU executive director Archer sounded a note of caution. The Fair Campaign Practices Committee, an independent citizens' watchdog group headed by Charles Taft, had been watching POAU, and some people associated with the committee were determined to "destroy our movement." Archer had worked for years to keep the National Conference of Christians and Jews from tagging POAU as a hate group. He reminded the board that the organization's tax-exempt status was very valuable. In spite of efforts of some Protestants to discredit them, the Methodists in their General Conference and the American and Southern Baptists had given them official recognition.[32]

Archer noted that the Morrison paper could probably pass muster as an educational and not a partisan piece. As long as POAU's approach was educational, it was on solid ground, even if its educational program ran counter to a certain candidate or political party. This was POAU's rationalization for distributing overtly anti-Catholic and anti-Kennedy material. But Archer seemed to know that the organization was skating on thin ice. He thought that POAU could use it as an official piece or Morrison could pursue its dissemination as an individual. The executive committee urged Morrison to publish it but decided not to run it as a POAU document. A version of it eventually appeared in *Christianity Today*.[33]

On July 18, Louie Newton, the president of POAU and former president of the Southern Baptist Convention, wrote to Archer because he was getting inquiries as to what POAU was going to do about Kennedy's nomination. He was organizing strategy among Baptists around Atlanta, including Senator Eugene Talmadge and Walter Pope Binns, chair of the Southern Baptist Convention on Public Affairs. Newton was torn between not acting fast enough and acting rashly. On the one hand, he hoped that Kennedy might say something inflammatory, and he wondered what the Catholic hierarchy would say in response to some of Kennedy's convention remarks. On the other hand, he had spoken with George Buttrick, the minister at Harvard Memorial Church, who was visiting in Atlanta, about what he thought of an open fight with Kennedy. Buttrick told him, "We cannot afford to lose."[34]

Archer was troubled by Newton's letter. He had fielded questions on the topic from *Christianity Today* and other media outlets.

He asked Newton if the board should meet in August to strategize or wait until its scheduled September meeting. He confessed that "it is a hard situation with Johnson on the ticket," showing that at least some of the southerners among the POAU crowd really wanted Johnson to be at the top of the ticket. Nixon did not have a natural appeal, at least among this slice of POAU.

Archer described the precarious path the group had to pursue against Kennedy. Its work to that point had "been purely educational." His best judgment was to wait and say nothing until Kennedy made a few more moves. By the time of the September board meeting, there would be a better basis for a POAU program. But then he turned somber:

> Somehow we must lay the groundwork for the defeat of Kennedy, but do it strictly in the ideological field without touching partisan politics or candidates. I don't know how this can be done. It takes a very deft touch and consummate skill.
>
> The real facts are that the Roman Catholic hierarchy is not entitled to a President, even though Kennedy is a pretty decent guy, until it cleans its house.[35]

Archer was sure that the Catholic hierarchy had told Kennedy to do whatever was necessary to get elected. Republican Catholics were moving to him because Catholics were hungry for the presidency. They expected to obtain it at all costs. He feared what a Catholic president would mean for American foreign policy, for the judicial system, and for state legislatures, among other things: "The Roman Catholic hierarchy has a box full of demands which violate our Constitution, and give a special privilege to them alone. The Presidency in the hands of the Catholics will further this legislative program."[36]

By early August, Archer was in full recruiting mode for the September meeting. He was especially keen on recruiting Southern Baptists to the gathering. In an internal memo to POAU staff, Archer told them that he had consented to inviting "a Mr. J. O. Wright" to sit in at the board meeting as a guest of Clyde Taylor, head of the National Association of Evangelicals' Washington office and a POAU advisor. This was actually J. Elwin Wright, the founder of the NAE. Wright and Taylor were calling on top NAE leaders to meet in Washington on the same day as the POAU board meeting. Wright wanted their strategy to "parallel" POAU's strategy, and Archer had consented to working together.[37] Coordination among Protestants began to emerge as large organizations such as POAU, the NAE, and leading Protestant clergy made plans to converge on Washington in early September.

In a similar manner, Archer wrote to Dr. William Givens of a local Washington Masonic temple, to say he was happy to learn that Givens would be speaking at the off-the-record luncheon during POAU's board meeting on September 9. He noted that Givens and Grand Commander Luther Smith of the Masons were doing "a mighty good work" and that he watched them with great interest and admiration.[38] Russell Hitt, editor of the influential evangelical magazine *Eternity*, told Archer that he planned on attending the POAU meeting because of "our deep interest in the pressing issued you'll be discussing."[39] *Eternity* had been founded by the popular Philadelphia Presbyterian minister and television preacher Donald Grey Barnhouse, whose television show, *Bible Study Hour*, was nationally syndicated.

The Baptist outreach effort was especially noteworthy. Jimmy Allen, director of the Christian Life Commission of the Baptist General Convention of Texas, eagerly accepted Archer's invitation to come to the September meeting, citing the need for national coordination "on this matter."[40] Two weeks later, Allen asked Archer to invite E. S. James, editor of the *Baptist Standard*, the highly influential magazine that went to tens of thousands of Texas households, to the meeting. "Since you are planning to spend some time in discussion of strategy for the coming campaign," Allen argued, James was an important person to have on board. James was going to be in Washington for the meeting of the Baptist Joint Committee, so Allen thought it logical to invite him to the POAU gathering.[41] James would later prove to be a crucial player in the outcome of the entire election.

Archer also invited W. O. Vaught. Vaught wrote to Archer to tell him that he was enthusiastic about the election because he believed there had been a large movement to Nixon recently. The *Dallas Morning News* had endorsed the Nixon-Lodge ticket on the front page. He was working hard on getting the Arkansas Democratic Party to endorse Nixon as well. He was convinced that POAU had a great opportunity and had to get into every state in the next few weeks to hold religious freedom rallies. To that end, he was looking forward to Archer's trip to Little Rock in October to headline a rally there.[42]

Louie Newton, the former president of the Southern Baptist Convention and current board president of POAU, also organized outreach for the meeting among Southern Baptists. Newton held a private caucus in Atlanta with a small circle of Baptist luminaries to strategize over how Baptist clergy should respond to Kennedy's candidacy.[43] One of the participants, Dick Hall, a vice president on the board of POAU, wrote to Archer describing their dilemma.[44] He said that many Baptist pastors remembered the negative reactions they got in their congregations in 1928 when they took a stand against Al Smith because he was a Catholic:

> I feel that there is certainly a question as to how far we as Baptists [*sic*] preachers can go in opposing such an election. To make speeches right now, which by implication at least would oppose his election, would to many be objectionable for a Baptist preacher whether in the pulpit or out of it. We can not oppose his election on Constitutional grounds and we have not opposed the election of lesser officials because of their religion. Kennedy has claimed that he would not do any of the things we claim as objectionable, such as the appointment of an ambassador—or asking [for] such an appointment—and allowing the Vatican to influence his actions as president.
>
> The organized rallies at this time would be construed as being in opposition to Mr. Kennedy, whether we mentioned his name or not. So, we are in a spot and I am not sure which way we should go.
>
> When the election is over, if Kennedy is in the White House, I want us to be able to continue to press the principle of the Separation of Church and State. We may be in a better position to do this if we have abstained from getting into what might be construed as a fight against a man.[45]

This prudent advice did not carry the day with Archer. But it did illustrate the disingenuousness in the POAU argument against Kennedy. The separation of church and state became the intellectual fig leaf to cover its anti-Catholicism, and at least some of the leaders of POAU understood this. Some Baptists remembered the fallout from 1928 and had to face congregations that contained more than a few members who were likely to vote for Kennedy.

The Baptist Joint Committee on Public Affairs was meeting in Washington on the day after POAU's meeting. Louie Newton went to work inviting other Baptists to the POAU meeting. Lowell wrote to Newton that there was little consensus on what should be done regarding the political situation. He mentioned that there were two strategies under consideration, both requiring an ad hoc committee to pursue either a campaign on religious liberty themes or "an all-out campaign against an R.C. sectarian in this post."[46] On that same day, Archer wrote to Newton and told him that a political action group was forming in Washington, and he had told its organizers that he would have to wait until after the September 6 board meeting before he could say what POAU might do for the effort.[47] This is the first indication that Archer and POAU knew about the Peale meeting. POAU, the Baptist Joint

Committee on Public Affairs, and the Peale group were meeting over back-to-back days in Washington, D.C. The common theme was what to do about Kennedy.

The official invitation letter to the national advisory council went out on August 9, 1960. Archer wrote that, with President Newton's approval, a few key leaders not affiliated with POAU's board of trustees would attend the board meeting: "These men have a real concern for religious liberty as it relates to religion and the presidency, and the desire to learn more about POAU's strategy to cope with this problem."[48]

The roster of attendees reveals 50 people from a wide swath of Protestant leadership.[49] There were representatives of eight religious publications: W. Melvin Adams, associate editor of *Liberty*, published by the Seventh-day Adventists; Gainer Bryan, Jr., editor of the *Maryland Baptist*; James Cole, editor of the *Baptist Messenger* of Alexandria, Louisiana; Russell Hitt, editor of *Eternity* magazine; John Hurt, editor of *Christian Index*; E. S. James, editor of the *Baptist Standard* from Dallas, Texas; Erwin McDonald, editor of the *Arkansas Baptist*; and Charles Clayton Morrison, founder and former editor of the *Christian Century*. There were mainline Protestants, such as Frank Blackwelder, pastor of All Souls Memorial Episcopal Church in Washington, D.C.; John Mackay, former president of Princeton Theological Seminary; Theodore Palmquist, pastor of the Foundry United Methodist Church in Washington, D.C.; and W. Stanley Rycroft of the United Presbyterian Commission on Ecumenical Mission in New York.

The Masons were represented by Willard Givens, former executive director of the National Education Association and then director of the Department of Education for the Scottish Rite Masons, along with Luther A. Smith, sovereign grand commander of the Scottish Rite Masons, Southern Jurisdiction. The National Association of Evangelicals sent its founder, J. Elwin Wright, as well as Clyde Taylor, secretary of public affairs and executive secretary of the Evangelical Foreign Mission Association.

Other notables among the group were Paul Blanshard, POAU special counsel; Foy Valentine, director of the Christian Life Commission of the Southern Baptist Convention; Charl O. Williams, former president of the National Education Association; Jimmy Allen, director of the Christian Life Commission of the Baptist General Convention of Texas; and C. Emmanuel Carlson, executive director of the Baptist Joint Committee on Public Affairs. At least 21 of the 50 attendees had an affiliation with the Southern Baptist church, but this was not just a meeting of Baptists. The forces gathered at the meeting came from across the Protestant spectrum.

The minutes of the meeting reveal a partial view of the electioneering that went on. The meeting began with the usual reporting of administrative minutia. The office manager reported that 688,721 pieces of literature were mailed by POAU in June, 788,828 in July, and 1,657,448 in August.[50] Judge Luther Smith of the Masons was one of the lunch speakers, and he spoke of his interest in the ideals of POAU, which he was "endeavoring to spread throughout the country."

Dr. Kenneth Haddock gave the report on the 1960 strategy proposals. He reminded the board that theirs was an educational, not a political, organization and thus POAU should hold to its present course. It could not endorse any candidate, but it could ask questions of candidates, publish their answers, and give reliable and accurate information about clericalism. It could urge people to vote and provide guidance to other groups that were springing up all over the country. He proposed a resolution:

> Resolved, that the POAU Board of Trustees hereby authorizes and directs the Executive Director of POAU to continue the policy, as set forth in the Manifesto, of educating the people of the United States of America on the whole problem of church-state relations, taking full advantage of the current paroxysms to secure nation-wide publicity for continuing church-state problems, by (1) Enlisting and assigning speakers who will, without campaigning for or against any candidate for public office, present to audiences, large and small, the facts of the Roman Catholic problem in America; (2) Forming new POAU chapters in every possible place and using them fully as educational units and sources of moral and financial support of National POAU; and (3) Strengthening and enlarging all existing POAU chapters and committees.[51]

A lengthy discussion of the motion followed. Clyde Taylor of the NAE then addressed the meeting on the topic of a proposed organization called Citizens for Religious Freedom, an ad hoc group that would be formed to correlate the literature of POAU and other organizations and to hold rallies. It would not represent any church but would simply be an independent organization that could step into the political arena. This was what would come to be known as the Peale group, the first meeting of which was scheduled to meet the next day at the Mayflower Hotel.

Foy Valentine expressed his reservations about any official representation from the POAU board at what was really an "anti-Kennedy meeting." Taylor claimed that the meeting was no such thing. Gainer Bryan, a Baptist from Maryland, said that since Kennedy had stated that he believed in the separation of church and state, he wondered if the stand that POAU had taken would become a religious test for public office. POAU staffer Stanley Lowell countered that the religion issue was bigger than Kennedy or any individual and that POAU should not silence itself because Kennedy had made some good statements. After further discussion, the resolution was read again and adopted unanimously.[52]

Perhaps sensing the ambivalence of at least some of the figures in the room, Archer stated that there might be some risks in his speaking at the Peale meeting the next day and asked the board for guidance. After some discussion, a motion to let Archer make up his own mind was passed. The board members assured him that they would stand behind him whether he spoke or not.[53]

The minutes thus portray a meeting at which some powerful forces across a significant spectrum of Protestantism decided to maintain a course of disseminating anti-Catholic literature at an astonishing volume and to allow its executive director to speak at the organizing meeting of the Citizens for Religious Freedom the next day, and it overcame modest internal dissent that these efforts were not appropriate. Nixon's man Orland K. Armstrong was in the room as was the chief organizer of the National Association of Evangelicals, Clyde Taylor.

The next day, POAU released a scathing press statement.[54] It began benignly enough, calling for calm analysis and sober speech about the religion issue. POAU had consistently criticized the literature of religious bigotry and scandal. POAU did not support or oppose any specific party or candidate: "Nevertheless, we cannot avoid recognition of the fact that one church in the United States, the largest church operating on American soil, officially supports a world-wide policy of partial union of church and state wherever it has the power to enforce such a policy."

A list of specific grievances followed: the 1948 statement of U.S. bishops that criticized a Supreme Court decision calling the separation of church and state a "shibboleth of doctrinaire secularism"; the bishops' call for full tax support of parochial schools; their rejection of public funding for birth control; and the prohibition of Catholic parents' sending their children to public schools. The tone then turned more pointed:

> These policies are clearly inconsistent with the American concept of
> separation of church and state, and, to the extent that any candidate

supports or endorses them, he is unfitted for the Presidency of the United States. To the extent that he repudiates these policies and demonstrates his independence of clerical control, he is entitled to our praise and encouragement.

We have repeatedly praised the candidate of Roman Catholic faith in this campaign for declaring frankly that basic government financial support for parochial schools is unconstitutional. We have likewise praised him for his opposition to the appointment of an American ambassador to the Vatican. We are skeptical about his equivocal words on birth control. We find that he has at no time stated simply that if Congress passed a law providing for aid in this matter that he would not hesitate to sign and administer it. We are skeptical, too, about his silence in regard to the official boycott of public schools contained in the Canon law of his church. We remain uneasy about the persistent denial of religious liberty to non-Catholics in some Roman Catholic countries such as Columbia [*sic*] and Spain, for we know that the Roman Catholic Church is everywhere committed to the doctrine that "error has no rights" theoretically....What effect, we wonder, would the election of a Roman Catholic as President have upon governments which practice such suppression with the knowledge and cooperation of the Vatican? To ask Protestant and Jewish people to take a light view of this matter or to disregard it entirely is to be unrealistic. For us this is a matter of self-preservation.

We deplore the evasive journalism of many American newspapers in handling the religious issue in this campaign. Many editors do not even recognize the elementary fact that one church in the United States has for centuries pursued a policy of partial union of church and state, and that the adoption of such a policy in this country would be a calamity of the first magnitude. When a candidate belongs to an organization which champions such a policy, it is not bigotry or prejudice to examine his credentials with the utmost care and frankness, and to ask how far this commitment goes.

We leave it to our members to decide for themselves, on the basis of all the evidence, whether the election of a Roman Catholic would promote or hinder the historic American principle of church-state separation. We recognize that millions of American Catholics are wholly loyal to this American principle and wholly loyal to the American way of life. We also recognize that there are other issues in this campaign beside the church-state issue, and that it is the duty of the voters to choose the man they consider best fitted to meet all the exacting demands of the office.[55]

One member of POAU's board, however, was not happy. W. Stanley Rycroft, an official of the Presbyterian church, later wrote to

Stanley Lowell to express his discomfort with some of what had transpired at the meeting and since. He was concerned about blatant electioneering and frustrated at POAU links to the Peale group.[56]

There is circumstantial evidence to suggest that Rycroft acted directly on his discontent over the events at POAU's board meeting. Between the end of the meeting on September 6 and the beginning of the Peale meeting on September 7, someone told the Kennedy campaign about the organizing against Kennedy by Protestant groups. But the full extent of this massive work would not be clear until the next day, when the Peale group convened.

6

GUERRILLA WARFARE

Every modern presidential election has a handful of defining moments. They are usually unplanned. Or they are the result of unintended consequences of planned actions. The Peale meeting, a gathering of Protestant ministers at the Mayflower Hotel in Washington, D.C., which was designed to put a public face on Protestant opposition to Kennedy's candidacy, was just such a moment.[1] It sent shudders through both the Kennedy and Nixon camps.

In the summer of 1960, Billy Graham had been in Europe, conducting a series of crusades. On August 17, he had convened a group of 25 American clergy in Montreux, Switzerland, to discuss the presidential race and to plan a response to Kennedy's candidacy. The gathering included Norman Vincent Peale, Daniel Poling (of the Four Chaplains affair), Clyde Taylor and J. Elwin Wright of the National Association of Evangelicals, Samuel Shoemaker, Harold Ockenga, and Graham's father-in-law, Dr. Nelson Bell. Peale sent Nixon a handwritten account of the meeting, describing the long discussion that took place among the selected group of "distinguished religious leaders."[2] According to Peale, the group was unanimously behind Nixon. Peale was part of a select committee chosen to meet with the vice president to convey the group's thoughts. Peale suggested September 8 as a possible meeting date. He concluded by telling Nixon that he would have been touched by the spiritual concern expressed for him by those in attendance. He also noted that Billy Graham was one of Nixon's biggest supporters.

Peale hoped that something constructive and wise could come of this meeting. He later claimed that he had nothing to do with organizing the Washington meeting. But since that meeting was planned at the gathering in Montreux, this could hardly be true.

Graham also wrote a letter to Nixon after the meeting, one installment in a regular correspondence between the two over the course of the summer and fall. Earlier in the summer, Graham had reported to Nixon that both Lyndon Johnson and Sam Rayburn had told Graham that if Kennedy were the nominee, the religion issue would be the paramount issue in the campaign.[3] At that point, Graham believed that Kennedy would garner 100% of the Catholic vote. At all costs, Nixon had to refrain from nominating a Catholic as his vice president and instead name someone Protestants could rally behind. Earlier in the spring, Graham had sent Nixon a clipping from the *Chicago Tribune* telling the story of how Graham had led the Southern Baptist denomination to pass a resolution that was a de facto repudiation of Kennedy as a presidential candidate and an endorsement of Nixon.[4]

In another long letter addressed to "Dear Dick," Graham outlined some observations that had emerged from the Montreux meeting.[5] Graham had been following the developments in the campaign with keen interest. He believed that God was giving Nixon "supernatural wisdom" to handle difficult situations. According to Graham, "a highly financed and organized office is being opened September 8 in Washington to supply information to religious leaders throughout the Nation." This refers to the National Association of Evangelicals' spin-off known as Citizens for Religious Freedom, which would be headed by Donald Gill, a Washington staffer for the NAE.

Next, he relayed the results of a recent poll of Protestant clergy that estimated 76% of them were supporting Nixon. Graham felt that this percentage would increase by Election Day, no doubt as a result of the massive efforts he was planning. Graham conceded that, while there would be a large Catholic bloc vote for Kennedy, it was not as large as some had originally thought, and he thought that by Election Day, Kennedy's share of the Catholic vote might be under 70%. Those gathered in Montreux believed that the Catholic vote for Kennedy had peaked whereas the Protestant vote for Nixon would gain momentum right up until the election.

Graham and the other clergymen thought that Nixon should emphasize the South and border states. The more conservative Republican platform combined with the religion issue could put some of those states in Nixon's column. They did not think that Johnson's presence on the Democratic ticket would trump the religion issue in these states. Graham's political advice then became more pointed. He and Peale urged Nixon to say more on religion in his speeches. There were real questions in the Protestant world as to Nixon's religious convictions. Graham had told the Montreux gathering of Nixon's reticence to use his religion for political gain. But the attendees did not think the country's Protestants would interpret Nixon's actions that way. They would insist that the people have a right to know a candidate's religious beliefs, "particularly at this uncertain hour of history." Graham urged Nixon "once again" to weave this into his addresses. Perhaps most important, Graham wrote:

> I have just written a letter to my mailing list of two million American families, urging them to organize their Sunday school classes and churches to get out the vote. Contrary to most people's thinking, my primary following lies in the Middle West, California, Pennsylvania and New York State. I think in these areas plus the South we can be of greatest help, though we have supporters on our list from every single post office in the United States. We are getting other religious groups throughout the Nation to do the same; thus many millions will be personally circulated. It is felt that the majority of these lists are Democratic or independent voters. It was also felt that this would bring about a favorable swing among these voters to you.

Graham concluded his epistle by announcing that Peale was planning to endorse Nixon in a sermon in early October. He also extended an invitation for Nixon to visit the Graham home in North Carolina in October. This would be a dramatic event that might tip North Carolina to Nixon and would highlight the religion issue nationally without any overt mention of the topic.

The next day, Graham sent a shorter letter with two other urgent matters he had omitted from the first letter. First, Graham had met Dr. Martin Luther King in Rio de Janeiro at the Baptist World Alliance meeting, shortly after King and Kennedy had met for three hours at Kennedy's home. According to Graham, King was impressed and "just about sold."[6] Graham fully realized what was at stake with King's blessing: "I think I at least neutralized him. I think if you could invite him for a brief conference it might swing him. He would be a powerful influence."

Second, Graham warned Nixon that the sense of his clergy war council was that the Kennedy campaign was better organized than Nixon's. One piece of evidence of this was that he was reading more about Kennedy in the American newspapers he got in Europe. And despite Nixon's lead in the Gallup poll, Graham thought Kennedy was still ahead. Yet he remained cautiously optimistic. He emphasized that the upcoming debates would be crucial.

A week later, an agitated Graham wrote to Nixon that open attacks by Protestants were solidifying Catholic bloc voting. The contest would come down to which Christian voting bloc was strongest. "At all cost," Graham counseled, "[y]ou must stay a million miles away from the religious issue at this time."[7] The day before, Graham had read a copy of what he called "a very dangerous letter." A Protestant leader had said that he had established underground communication with the Republican National Committee: "Even if it were true, I was shocked to see it in a letter for fear that if it ever got into the wrong hands it would do the Republicans great damage."[8] Graham realized that, if the level of communication and coordination going on between his associates and like-minded Protestants and the Nixon campaign ever became public knowledge, it could mean the end of Nixon.

In his reply to Graham, Nixon did not respond directly to the claim that relations existed between the campaign and Protestant organizers. After all, weren't Graham and Nixon carrying on an extended religious strategy discussion themselves?[9]

Thus, the most prominent leader of American evangelicalism recruited an all-star roster of clergy to plan, fund, and execute a strategy to raise the religion issue across the country on Nixon's behalf without directly endorsing Nixon. They tried to avoid the charges of religious bigotry by keeping Graham in Europe during the early stages of the post–Labor Day campaign. While Graham's fingerprints were all over the work of Citizens for Religious Freedom, being out of the country gave him plausible deniability. He even went to the length of writing to Kennedy and Johnson to assure them that he wasn't involved in the campaign. Between Peale and Graham, Nixon was aware at some level of the multipronged campaign being waged by Graham and his cohorts on the religion issue. While neither one directly mentioned the Peale meeting itself, it is difficult to believe that Nixon did not know about it ahead of time.

Back in Washington, on the night after the POAU board meeting and the day before the Peale meeting, Stanley Rycroft was feeling pangs of conscience over the electioneering for Nixon he had seen. If Orland K. Armstrong was an unusual character for Nixon's front man on religion, Rycroft was a similarly unlikely candidate for the role of political informant. At the age of 61, he was at the peak of an interesting international career.

Born near Liverpool, England, Rycroft was a member of the Royal Air Force and was shot down three times in World War I.[10] After completing his undergraduate degree at Liverpool University, he moved to Peru as a missionary for the Free Church of Scotland. For the next 18 years, he taught and studied in Peru, eventually earning his doctorate from the University of San Marcos in Lima. In 1940, he moved to New York to become the secretary of the Committee on Cooperation in Latin America, an interdenominational committee of 30 Protestant mission boards. In 1950, he became the secretary for Latin America of the Board of Foreign Missions of the Presbyterian Church U.S.A. It was this connection to the Presbyterian church that may have provided the link between Rycroft and the Kennedy campaign.

Late in the summer of 1960, James Wine, a vice president of the National Council of Churches and a Presbyterian, joined the Kennedy staff as head of religious outreach. Since both Wine and Rycroft were active in mainline ecumenical circles and both were Presbyterians, this may have paved the way for political contact between the two men.

Late on the evening of September 6, 1960, after the POAU board meeting, a person labeled simply "Informant R" dictated a memo to the Kennedy campaign on the various machinations of the Nixon campaign in organizing religious forces against Kennedy, and in the process he confirmed some of the worst fears of the Kennedy apparatus:[11]

> Informant "R" furnished the following information at around 11:15 p.m. on Tuesday, September 6, 1960. This information was given after the informant had been observed leaving the Burlington Hotel in a taxicab with another elderly gentleman. Just before getting in the cab, the informant whispered that they were on the way to the Sheraton Park Hotel.
>
> The informant advised that he was in the company of O. K. Armstrong whom he had earlier identified as the Republican National Committee representative who is dealing with the preachers [in] connection with the religious issue. He stated that Armstrong is a former Republican congressman from the Springfield, Missouri district and was at the luncheon which was held in the Statler Hotel by the group identified as the Board of Trustees of the POAU. He stated that he met Armstrong at the luncheon and was convinced that he was the contact man between A. B. Herman[n]'s office of the Republican National Committee and the various preachers who were attending the conference in Washington on Tuesday and who would be present at the conference on the following day at the Mayflower Hotel.

These paragraphs reveal several important facts. First, Nixon had an operative in the field who was responsible for organizing the likes of POAU and the anticipated gathering of the Peale meeting. Second, the informant was likely a member of the POAU board since most of the people in attendance at the luncheon that day were board members. Rycroft was the only board member whose last name began with the letter *R*. Third, the Nixon operation was being run at the highest echelon of the Republican National Committee, making it virtually impossible that Nixon himself did not know and approve of Hermann's work with Armstrong.

The memo continued:

> The informant stated that when they went to the Sheraton Park Hotel they went to the room of Bill Smith, the individual from the Arkansas Industrial Development Commission. According to information furnished by the informant at an earlier interview, Smith was connected with Winthrop Rockefeller and that Rockefeller's plane was being used by various preachers in transporting them around various states in the southwest in connection with their talks against Kennedy as a Roman Catholic President.
>
> That about three weeks or so ago, Bill Smith had arranged for a meeting with Senator Thruston Morton and A. B. Herman[n] at Jackson, Mississippi, which was to be attended by various southern Baptist preachers. However, it was afterwards called off because it was felt that Senator Morton was being closely followed by the press and it would be impossible for him to meet with the preachers without being observed by the press.
>
> The informant stated that when he met with Armstrong, he then realized that he was the real link between the Republican Committee and the preachers and not as he originally thought, Bill Smith from Arkansas. He was surprised, however, to notice that Smith was listed as a speaker for the conference which was to be held the following morning at the Mayflower Hotel. In this connection, the manual for this so-called National Conference of Citizens for Religious Freedom, shows that at 10:50 a.m., William R. Smith, Commissioner of the Arkansas Development Commission; businessman; planter; from Lake Village, Arkansas, was to talk, "A Layman Looks at the Issue."
>
> The informant advised they went to either L or M-147 at the Sheraton Park and that he found therein another man, whose name he recalls as McLaughlin, an oil man, and a third individual whose name he could not recall.

This offers further confirmation that those at the highest level of the Nixon operation—in this case, Senator Thruston Morton, chair of the Republican National Committee—were involved in outreach to Protestants, in this case, Southern Baptist pastors. It also shows how the increased anti-Catholic drumbeat increased press scrutiny of the campaign and made such high-level clandestine meetings impossible. The Nixon operation clearly knew the incendiary potential of any public leak of their secret organizing work.

The Bill Smith connection was part of the payoff of Armstrong's work. As we saw earlier, Armstrong recruited Smith, an employee of Governor Orval Faubus, Democrat of Arkansas, to help organize the conservative Churches of Christ for Nixon. At first glance, of all the speakers on the program at the Peale meeting, Smith's presence there makes the least sense. Smith was not clergy and he was a Democrat. But he was active in Church of Christ circles and was an early fundraiser for a denomination-wide national television program called *The Herald of Truth*. The oilman named "McLaughlin" was probably a member of a prominent Church of Christ family in Abilene, Texas, named McGlothlin, which funded *The Herald of Truth* and owned the national denominational newspaper the *Christian Chronicle*. The *Christian Chronicle* ran an editorial on the Peale meeting that declared, "We Were There." The unidentified third man was probably James Walter Nichols, editor of the newspaper and one of the people in the Churches of Christ whom Smith recruited to meet Armstrong. One plausible explanation of Smith's presence on the program was that his patron, in this case the member of the McGlothlin family, paid for part of the Peale meeting.

But perhaps the most interesting aspect of the informant's story came near the end of the memo:

> The informant turned over to the writer what was termed as the master copy of the press release which was to be given out at 5:00 p.m. at the close of the meetings of the so-called Citizens for Religious Freedom. It is noted that this master copy is substantially identical to the actual release which was given out at the stated time. There is attached to this memorandum comments as to the changes which were made between the master copy and the actual copy released to the press.
>
> The informant maintained that this master copy was brought over, he believed, by O. K. Armstrong and that it came directly from A. B. Herman[n]'s office in the Republican headquarters. He stated that Armstrong is presently hunting for the master copy.

Here was concrete proof for the Kennedy campaign. The official press release of the Peale meeting was presented to them the day before the Peale meeting itself, and it would prove to be almost identical to the final press release. Its author was someone from within the Republican

National Committee who passed it through Armstrong to the Peale gathering. Whatever illusions the Kennedy brain trust might have harbored about Nixon not manipulating the religion issue were now overthrown. A detailed appendix to the informant memo tracked 18 edits between the final copy of the official press release and the copy the informant gave them, demonstrating that the informant's copy served as the primary document that was subsequently edited in a minor fashion. It had to be a sobering realization for Kennedy that the anti-Catholic forces were now being aided and abetted by the Nixon campaign and its operatives in the field. Given the astonishing range of Protestant leaders at the POAU meeting and at the Peale meeting the next day, the effect must have been powerful.

The memo contained some other interesting tidbits. The informant noted that a group, presumably the POAU board, was perturbed by the fact that Nixon refused to say whether he would send a representative to the Vatican if he was elected president. Kennedy had said that he would not. This would prove to be a huge strategic error on Nixon's part, but that would become apparent only late in the campaign. The group sought to contact Morton by phone to tell him that Nixon needed to give an answer to their question.

The informant also claimed that he was told that Kennedy was going to speak on the religion question in San Antonio, Texas, on September 13, 1960. The informant was amazed that this group had gotten such confidential information about the Kennedy campaign. If it were a member of the Abilene, Texas, McGlothlin family who was in the group, it is entirely possible that this almost-accurate information could have been gleaned from his Texas connections. In fact, Kennedy had received an invitation from the Greater Houston Ministerial Association, as had Nixon, to address the religion issue, but the Kennedy campaign had not yet decided whether to accept. But these Protestants were clearly nervous that Kennedy was about to go on the offensive in a new way in the South, and they were concerned that Nixon was about to make a big mistake by not renouncing the concept of an ambassador to the Vatican.

The informant also reported an attempt to meet with Hermann at the Republican National Committee. Armstrong suggested that a call should be made to Hermann at the RNC (National 8–6800). The informant called the number the next morning, and Hermann reported that it was not advisable for him to be seen in the Republican national headquarters and that he would have one of their men, "Flanagan," and another individual the informant could not remember contact the informant at his hotel. The informant reported that the meeting never materialized.

The informant summarized the comments of Willard Givens, former executive director of the National Education Association and currently director of the Department of Education, Scottish Rite Masons, who pointed out there were 4 million Masons in the country with 2 million of them in the South. Givens stated that he had attended a hearing in the House of Representatives on an education bill. Allegedly, Kennedy later told Givens that he would not vote for the bill even though he was for it because the Catholic bishop in Boston told him not to support it if he wanted to remain in Congress. Givens cited this story to prove Kennedy's nefarious allegiance to the Catholic hierarchy.

One further piece of circumstantial evidence to suggest that Rycroft may have been the informant is Rycroft's letter to POAU employee Stanley Lowell after the board meeting.[12] Writing on October 16, Rycroft lamented to Lowell that Nixon and Lodge favored using public funds for parochial schools while Kennedy was against it. Rycroft insisted that Lowell report this in the POAU magazine *Church and State Review*. POAU had claimed that this issue was the point at which the greatest attack was being made on the doctrine of the separation of church and state. To deny this information to POAU members was shameful.

Rycroft reminded Lowell that two Protestant presidents—Roosevelt and Truman—had sent envoys to the Vatican and that Eisenhower, also a Protestant, took the "non-Protestant" stand on funding birth control programs in foreign countries. He seemed to be signaling his support for Kennedy's candidacy without actually saying it in so many words. But his most revealing comments came at the end of the letter:

> With reference to the September Board meeting, two things gave me concern. First, that Nixon badges were distributed to everyone, and second, that the statement which the Board approved was published in the same column (in the N.Y. Times) as the so-called "Peale Statement." Being linked with that group in this way, and by the attendance of some POAU leaders at the meeting, did harm to POAU, I believe.
>
> I also gained the impression at that Board meeting that perhaps the name should be changed to BAPTISTS AND OTHER AMERICANS etc.

Thus, the likely informant took pains to show that Kennedy was actually right on POAU's main issue—federal aid to parochial schools—and that voting for Kennedy might not be the threat to religious freedom

that most POAU stakeholders feared. But his main concern seemed
to be that POAU had been harmed by the overtly partisan work of its
board and staff. While this does not prove that Rycroft was the informant, it does reveal his discontent.

Early in the next year, Rycroft would chair a group that would
produce a report that took a hard and critical look at POAU's standing in the country in light of the election of Kennedy. He noted that
POAU did not have a glowing reputation and that many thought it
had exploited anti-Catholicism to raise funds. The report indicates the
depth of Rycroft's frustration with how the focus on Kennedy had
undermined POAU's long-term mission of defending the principle of
the separation of church and state.[13]

Despite POAU's prominence in the machinations surrounding the
Peale meeting, the idea for the meeting actually originated within the
brain trust of the National Association of Evangelicals. In an interview
with a reporter for the Associated Press after the Peale meeting, NAE
founder J. Elwin Wright took credit for setting it in motion.[14] The 70-
year-old Wright had contacted Donald Gill, an official with the NAE's
Washington public affairs office, and asked him if he knew of any organization acting as a clearinghouse of information on Kennedy. When
Gill replied that he did not, Wright headed to Washington and set in
motion the plans that would lead Graham to convene the Montreux
meeting. All of this took place within a few weeks of Wright's initial
inquiry. The NAE created Citizens for Religious Freedom to coordinate its efforts to stop Kennedy, and Gill was given leave from his usual
duties at the NAE to run the fledgling organization.

Wright had a long and legendary career in evangelical circles. It was
his vision that led to the creation of the NAE back in the forties. Prior
to that, he had built a robust evangelical umbrella organization in New
England called the New England Fellowship.

A successful businessman, Wright brought formidable organizational skills to the wildly decentralized and unorganized evangelical
bazaar of the mid-twentieth century.[15] The NAE functioned like a trade
association for evangelicals, boasting a complex committee structure
that produced Sunday school literature, promoted foreign missions,
organized congregations for conservative social causes, and lobbied in
Washington on a series of pet conservative issues, all on behalf of the
38 member denominations and tens of thousands of member congregations.

The NAE had been watching Kennedy's rise warily. In January
1960, Clyde Taylor, the NAE's secretary of public affairs, had prepared

a six-page memorandum for the executive committee listing all of the issues which had stimulated policy resolutions at recent NAE annual conferences. The list contained the usual list of the hot-button evangelical issues of the day: alcohol, Communism, gambling, free enterprise, obscene literature, socialized medicine, and tobacco. Yet it also included issues such as religious liberty, religious persecution, an ambassador to the Vatican, and church-state separation. While none of these issues were directly aimed at Kennedy, there was nonetheless an unmistakable sense that these particular issues would take on a renewed saliency with Kennedy's candidacy.[16]

Throughout the fifties, the NAE had produced a lush forest of anti-Catholic tracts. Titles such as *Shall America Bow to the Pope of Rome?* by James Deforest Murch, which included a front-page picture of the U.S. envoy to the Vatican, Myron Taylor, bowing before the pope, as well as *Crimes of Intolerance: The Slaughter of Protestants in Mexico and the Fate of Protestants in Colombia* by Clyde Taylor and *The Truth about the Protestant Situation in Spain* by an anonymous Spanish Christian, kept up a steady anti-Catholic drumbeat. The implication that Catholicism presented a threat to American values was clear.

It is difficult to convey to contemporary readers the significance and power of tracts in American Protestant life in the middle of the twentieth century. Already we have seen that large pan-Protestant groups, such as POAU and the NAE, as well as specific denominations and individual ministers used this medium, exceeded only by the sermon form itself as a mode of serious communication to the faithful. The tract was, for all intents and purposes, the weapon of choice in the Protestant battle to defeat Kennedy. As a genre, tracts served as informal Protestant case law by applying theological principles to ongoing and emerging social issues. It was in this literature that authors made outrageous claims and defended ecclesiastical practices, and, especially for conservatives, it was in tracts that social issues were dissected and un-Christian behavior was proscribed. In the 1960 election, Protestant tract production reached its apex, only to be swept away by the solidifying of television culture later in the decade. To be sure, evangelical and fundamentalist tract production survived the decade, though with greatly reduced cachet. But in 1960, the lowly tract was crucial to Protestant efforts against Kennedy, and their printing presses unleashed a real fury against him. The NAE offered an especially potent strain.

As Kennedy marched through the primary season, the NAE's anxiety increased. At its April board of administration meeting, the NAE passed a five-point resolution called "Catholicism and the Presidency."

The resolution began with the premise that discussion of the separation of church and state is legitimate whenever a candidate for public office is under consideration. It continued that an affirmation of the principle from all presidential candidates would be necessary regardless of their religious affiliation. It was particularly important for Catholic candidates to make this affirmation in light of the church's policy of fostering church establishment and its exertion of political pressure on public officials toward that end. The resolution moved quickly to its conclusions:

4. That the real source of unrest in respect to church-state separation is the total lack of any convincing commitment of the Roman Catholic Church to the principle of church-state separation, which could only come from the highest authority of that organization and could only be evidenced by the realignment of Catholic policy in those countries where Catholicism is now the established religion, and

5. That due to the political-religious nature of the Roman Catholic Church we doubt that a Roman Catholic president could or would resist fully the pressures of the ecclesiastical hierarchy.[17]

The diabolical power of this logic is that it really did not matter what a Catholic candidate such as Kennedy might affirm regarding the separation of church and state. Ultimately, the power of the hierarchy would overwhelm and nullify any such commitment by a Catholic public official.

In May, the prospect of a Kennedy presidency showed up in the pages of the NAE's glossy monthly magazine, *United Evangelical Action*. In his monthly column, "Capital Commentary," Don Gill noted that Vice President Nixon had faced the question of U.S. assistance in providing birth control information to other nations after a speech to the Associated Church Press in Washington. Nixon said that the United States should not interfere with the internal affairs of any nation, but if asked by another country for assistance, the United States should give it to them. This was a clear shot at Kennedy and Catholic opposition to artificial birth control.

Gill also commented on the recent Wisconsin primary results by noting the extensive Catholic bloc voting for Kennedy and concluded that Humphrey had done slightly better and Kennedy slightly worse than predicted. West Virginia would hold the key to the primary season.[18] The cover story in the same issue was "A Catholic President: How Free from Church Control?" by NAE executive director George Ford.[19] The article chronicled the usual set of arguments and concluded, in effect, that Protestants should not vote for Kennedy. The NAE reprinted the article as a tract and distributed it en masse throughout the country. In his June column, Gill noted that with his West Virginia primary victory, Kennedy was the strongest contender for the Democratic nomination. Calling his victory a surprise, Gill predicted that Kennedy would receive extensive scrutiny, and the religion issue would be put to the test in the general election.[20]

In a special report to the NAE executive committee on July 20, Clyde Taylor updated the NAE leadership on several important topics. As chair of the recently completed Billy Graham crusade in Washington, he reported "a very successful campaign." If nothing else, this establishes Taylor's close ties with Graham. He also reported that Glenn Everett of the Religion News Service was compiling a report on the influence of Catholics in the Democratic Party in general and at the national convention in particular. But the last half of the six-page report was dedicated to the NAE's role in publicizing the dangers of having a Roman Catholic in the White House among "our people."[21]

In response to many press inquiries, Taylor had issued statements and had consulted with POAU on its efforts. POAU had a four-part plan to distribute literature, stage mass meetings across the country, set up study groups in churches, and distribute a film. In consultation with NAE board member James Deforest Murch, Taylor thought the NAE should partner extensively with POAU. The two groups would press the same message that the Catholic church had not supported the separation of church and state and that Kennedy could not stop the drift toward tyranny in other Catholic countries from occurring here in America. Taylor concluded that the work of POAU and the NAE must at all costs avoid personal references to Kennedy as a candidate and stay away from the appearance of partisan politics. They should instead promote the separation of church and state as a principle.

Against this background of growing anxiety within the NAE, Wright's suggestion of a Washington pan-Protestant conclave to oppose the Kennedy juggernaut made perfect sense. Billy Graham, perhaps at the urging of Wright and/or Taylor, convened the war council in Montreux and invited Peale to join the deliberations in Switzerland. According to Graham's autobiography, it was Taylor who invited Peale to the meeting in early September in Washington. Graham encouraged Peale to go.[22] The wheels were set in motion to pull the meeting together.

Shortly after the Montreux meeting, a minor kerfuffle erupted among Baptists. On August 24, Kennedy met Dr. C. Emmanuel

Carson, executive director of the Baptist Joint Committee on Public Affairs, which represented the Southern Baptist Convention, the American Baptist Convention, and two large black Baptist conventions, the National Baptist Convention, U.S.A., and the National Baptist Convention of America. Kennedy and Carson agreed to the statement "A frank renunciation by all Churches of political power as a means of religious ends would greatly improve the political climate and would seem to be a legitimate request by both political parties."[23]

Kennedy's press secretary confirmed that the statement reflected the senator's views. Carson was quoted as saying that, although Baptist organizations were not in the habit of participating in elections, he was concerned for the good of the country in the current election—an oblique reference to Baptist activism against Kennedy. He acknowledged that half-truths and sham materials were being circulated in some churches. Carlson stated that the Baptists were seeking a similar meeting with Nixon.

Billy Graham's father-in-law, Nelson Bell, reacted in horror. From his perspective, this meeting amounted to a Baptist endorsement of Kennedy. He believed that, at the grassroots level, there was no support for Kennedy among Baptists. He wrote to a Baptist friend that pressure should be brought to bear on Carson to divest the joint committee of any endorsement of Kennedy.[24] Bell importuned his correspondent to take the day off and come to Washington for the meeting on September 7. He hoped that between 150 and 300 Protestant opinion leaders would come. The prospect of Baptists going soft on Kennedy and Catholicism in the late days of the campaign clearly disturbed Bell and fed his sense of urgency over the upcoming meeting. He was undoubtedly not the only one who was worried. Around the same time, Armstrong wrote that "plans will be developing rapidly now under the leadership of Don Gill and Dr. Bell."[25] Armstrong's groundwork, Peale's and Graham's correspondence with Nixon after the Montreux meeting, and the production of the final press release of the Peale group before the meeting of the Republican National Committee—all point to the Nixon campaign's full knowledge of and cooperation in organizing the Peale meeting.[26]

The National Conference of Citizens for Religious Freedom consisted of seven speeches over the course of September 7, 1960, at the Mayflower Hotel in Washington, D.C.[27] Over 150 people, primarily clergy, from 37 denominations attended. Dr. Norman Vincent Peale, pastor of Marble Collegiate Church in New York City, presided over the day's events. The first speaker was Dr. Daniel Poling, editor of the

Christian Herald and promulgator of the omnipresent story of the Four Chaplains Chapel controversy.

The manual distributed to registrants contained a lengthy discussion of the purpose of the meeting and the methods that the organization would be using during the balance of the campaign. The goal was to convene a working session of people who were concerned with the political aspects of Roman Catholicism and who wanted to deal with the real issues in a spirit of good will. The conference was a means of articulating the concerns of millions of citizens.[28]

The brief introduction struggled to find a route between overt bigotry and apathetic silence. The fact that the meeting was closed to the press and the public showed its delicacy, and yet the acknowledgment that millions of citizens shared their concerns made complete secrecy unwise as well. The subtext here was that, if Kennedy were to be opposed for his Catholicism, the organization would have to find a way to do it that did not leave a heavy footprint. Of course, the Nixon forces could not afford to have their role announced. Public engagement would have to be done in a manner that preserved plausible deniability for various parties, including Billy Graham.

In addition to rallying the faithful, the meeting also aimed to raise funds and distribute literature. Any pamphlets, advertisements, postcards, spot announcements, and other means of communication had to be of the highest caliber and had to be factual. Every attendee was given a kit containing "some of the better material available" along with addresses where individual pieces could be ordered. In addition, Citizens for Religious Freedom produced its own brochure that was available for purchase and distribution.

Press reports indicated that one speaker solicited contributions from attendees to supplement an already existing fund of $5,000. Donald Gill was quoted as saying that $20,000 would be required to stage similar meetings around the country.[29] NAE records reveal that over $23,000 was raised and spent by the end of October for the Citizens for Religious Freedom's Reformation Sunday efforts, but there was no budget line item for the Peale meeting, for funds either raised or expended. The precise source and amount of the funding for the Peale meeting itself remain a mystery.

The manual also contained a "fact sheet," which was a collection of arguments and assertions outlining the message that should go forth from the meeting: "Like Mark Twain's weather, everybody is talking about the 'religious issue' but nobody is doing anything about defining it. It's high time somebody did."

> The key question is whether any church organization should attempt to control the actions of its members in political and civic affairs. While the current Roman Catholic contender for the Presidency states that he would not be so influenced, his Church insists that he is duty-bound to submit to such directives. This unresolved conflict between the position of Mr. Kennedy and his Church leaves doubt in the mind of millions of citizens.
>
> We cannot afford to gamble with freedom. Inform yourself on the facts in the religious issue...and vote your conscience.[30]

The manual then listed 10 facts that were the core of the Protestant argument against Kennedy. The Peale meeting served as a centralizing point for the theologically diverse assembly.

The first "fact" was that Roman Catholicism was not only a religion, to which many good friends and neighbors belong, but also a political force in society. The Vatican was also a secular state, making Catholicism unique among world religions. Since it was often impossible to distinguish between these political and religious roles, many Americans were rightly concerned about Catholic political involvement. With no sense of irony, these Protestants were organizing their faithful to become a political force to keep Kennedy out of office because it was wrong for religion to become a political force.

In addition, Roman Catholic doctrine was ultimately incompatible with the principle of the separation of church and state, which was the cherished foundation of religious freedom in America. Here, the manual cited a 1948 statement of U.S. Catholic bishops that decried the separation of church and state as a "shibboleth of doctrinaire secularism." It also quoted Pope Leo XIII, who in 1885 called for Catholics to "penetrate, wherever possible" into the administrations of their countries' civil affairs. Nothing was said about the American Catholic embrace of American religious freedom and the robust intellectual discussion in American Catholic circles over the previous decade.

The third "fact" expressed the anti-American argument, that is, wherever Catholicism was the majority religion, it attempted to suppress all other religious faiths and used government to impose itself on a country. Spain and Colombia were cited as examples. Since almost all Protestant denominations maintained foreign missionaries in Europe and South America, this argument seemed to have particular force. At some level, this argument implied that Catholics were not true Americans, but were European in their political and theological loyalties.

The fourth "fact" was that the hierarchy of the Catholic church insisted on controlling its lay members in civic and political affairs.

The manual cited a May 17 article in the Vatican newspaper, *L'Osservatore Romano*, which claimed that the church had the power to direct all Catholics to keep their ideas and actions in conformity with the gospel. Any conflict between the individual and the judgment of the church must be resolved by obedience to the church. That Kennedy had vowed to resist any Catholic pressure merely demonstrated the reality of that pressure. If Kennedy denied the pressure, he was lying; if he acknowledged it, then Protestants should not risk voting for him.

The sixth "fact" repeated the now-hoary story of the Chapel of the Four Chaplains, allegedly proving that Kennedy had not resisted Catholic pressure in the past and would not in the future. The seventh conveyed the threat that Kennedy could be excommunicated if he ignored official Catholic advice. The eighth was that some Catholic politicians, such as John McCormack of Massachusetts, had used their influence to pass bills to benefit the Catholic church. The ninth "fact" was that the American Catholic church had used its influence to procure public funds for its schools, hospitals, businesses, and other institutions.

This laundry list of arguments concluded that Americans must decide individually whether it is wise, knowing the political power of the Roman Catholic hierarchy in the United States, to elect a president who had given his allegiance to that system. The final "fact" insisted that Catholics were constantly warned that they must follow the directives of the hierarchy:

> The current situation involves a basic conflict between Senator Kennedy's commitment to resist all ecclesiastical pressures and the position of Roman Catholicism which insists that it has control of his conduct, even in political affairs. On this point the American people *must* render a decision.[31]

The second speaker was William R. Smith, a Church of Christ member whose talk was called "A Layman Looks at the Issue." Smith was apparently a late addition to the roster; O. K. Armstrong's files contain an earlier list of speakers on which his name does not appear. This is perhaps more circumstantial evidence that Smith was added to the speakers list due to financial backing from Church of Christ sources. According to Clyde Taylor's notes on the speech, Smith cited columnist Joseph Alsop that 25% of the voting population was now Catholic compared to 10% in 1928 when Al Smith was defeated. With high Catholic birth rates, the election of Kennedy would represent a Catholic coup.

The next speech was by the Reverend Harold J. Ockenga, an early leader in the NAE and at Gordon College, who was pastor of

New England's flagship evangelical church, Park Street Church, located at the corner of Boston Common. His talk, "Religion, Politics, and the Presidency," was a classic piece of evangelical scholasticism. It is notable for its systematic collection and mastery of the intellectual, political, and theological arguments that various conservative Protestants had assembled against Kennedy. Between the 10 "facts" of the conference manual and this speech, one gets a relatively complete—even encyclopedic—picture of the Protestant case against Kennedy. And it is important to remember that it is a case against Kennedy and not a positive case for Nixon. This flaw may have proved to be decisive in the end for many voters.

The speech began in fine evangelical sermonic fashion by quoting Matthew 22:21, "Render unto Caesar the things that are Caesar's and to God the things that are God's." Ockenga then stated his theme: "The issue discussed in this message is, does a candidate's religion have anything to do with political office, especially the presidency of the United States."[32] The first full paragraph of the speech quoted a litany of Catholic writers who had answered the question affirmatively. Ockenga cleverly established the legitimacy of the topic in order to subvert the charge of bigotry. Even Catholic clergy and intellectuals agreed that the religion of the candidates was worthy of investigation.

Open inquiry in which both sides of the issue could be examined was best, according to Ockenga. Unfortunately, there were two forms of censorship in the Roman Catholic–Protestant issue of the day. The first was self-imposed censorship by Protestants who were afraid of offending their Catholic neighbors. Protestants should not let the threat of misinterpretation of their motives dissuade them from speaking out on the topic. The second form of censorship was brought by "certain elements" in the Roman Catholic church who labeled any criticism of the church as offensive and intolerant. Here, Ockenga was trying to address the difficult public relations problem in which Protestant arguments did appear strained and bigoted to many Americans. He valiantly started the speech by trying to knock down this argument.

From this observation, Ockenga segued to a refutation of the claim that the American Catholic church was different from the church elsewhere when it came to divergence from official Catholic church teachings. The church, he argued, permitted no divergence on its dogma. Liberal American Catholics were wrong to assert otherwise. He cited the case of American Catholic bishops who, in the late nineteenth century, tried to infuse the church with American-style democracy and were condemned by Pope Leo XIII. He argued:

> If we want to know what will happen if a Roman Catholic America ensues, we must understand the official teaching of universal Roman Catholicism. When we have understood that, if America wants the system, that is America's decision but if and when the decision is made it should be an intelligent one with an understanding of the result.

Ockenga did not engage the arguments of contemporary American Catholics like Murray and Weigel, nor those of liberal Protestants such as Niebuhr and Bennett, who argued explicitly against his thesis. He knew these arguments but chose to ignore them; therein lies the major weakness of his case.

From here, Ockenga raised the question, "Does religion make such a difference in a politician's life such that one would be disqualified from certain offices?" He cited Bishop James A. Pike, of the Episcopal diocese of San Francisco, who argued that a Mennonite pacifist could not be the secretary of defense. Likewise, a Christian Scientist could not be the secretary of health, education, and welfare because of his disinclination to use medicine and doctors. In a similar manner, Ockenga argued, it is legitimate to ask whether a Catholic is disqualified to serve in certain political offices because of his religious views. Ockenga hastened to add boldly and in self-contradiction that we must not raise a religious test for a candidate for office, but "we cannot ignore his philosophical commitments which may disqualify him for a particular office."

Ockenga detoured to argue that there was no body of canon law or church teaching in American Protestantism which controlled the political, educational, and professional life of a Protestant politician like there was for a Catholic politician. Thus, there was no a priori disqualification of a Protestant from holding office. Interestingly, Ockenga apparently only applied this disqualification of Catholics for office to the presidency, since the history of the Republic was full of examples of faithful Catholics serving in elected and appointed offices from the local level all the way to the Senate and the Supreme Court with no record of Vatican interference and manipulation.

At this point in his speech, Ockenga cited the canonical texts of separation of church and state from Jefferson's letter to the Danbury Baptist Association and from the Supreme Court decisions—*Everson v. Board of Education* and *McCollum v. Board of Education*—in order to contrast the American doctrine of separation with the Roman Catholic doctrine of papal control of politicians and its alleged repudiation of the separation of church and state. A litany of Catholic citations was given to demonstrate that Catholics did not support the separation of church and state and that Catholic politicians were under the direct control of the church hierarchy.

The upshot for Ockenga was that when Catholics comprised half of the American population, Protestants stood to lose their standing. Given their present rate of growth, it was not implausible that Catholics would become the majority. At that point, Protestantism would be tolerated but not allowed to propagate itself among Catholics. Even more troubling to Ockenga was the doctrine of mental reservation, which allowed Catholics, in effect, to lie when telling the truth would cause innocents to be harmed. Since Catholic politicians are captive to the Catholic view that rejects the separation of church and state, any Catholic politician who affirmed separation was simply trying to lull Protestants into complacency. Once in office and in control of the government, real Catholic doctrine would take over. The doctrine of mental reservation, Ockenga argued, allowed politicians to hide the truth until a later time.

Ockenga zeroed in on three specific policy areas where problems could arise in which Catholics said one thing during a campaign but might pursue a different strategy once in office: federal aid to parochial schools, foreign aid, and appointments to federal government posts. In each case, a Catholic presidential candidate might give the "right" Protestant answer, but once in office, he would reverse field. In order to prevent this Catholic Trojan horse nightmare from coming true, the American Catholic hierarchy must insist that the Vatican embrace the separation of church and state as a doctrine, repudiate the Syllabus of Errors and democratize the church, and renounce its goal of dominating America. Nothing short of those moves would placate Ockenga or relieve his fear of Kennedy's candidacy. He concluded:

> Certain questions must be considered. Are we moving into an era of Roman Catholic domination in America? This is the avowed aim of the Roman hierarchy. If and when this becomes a fact, will the principle of Roman Catholic political theory be applied? Will there be a denial of rights, freedom and privileges for non–Roman Catholics? If so, should we aid and abet this situation by electing a President who has more power to advance such a goal than any other person?
>
> The seriousness of the anomalous position of indifference on the part of Protestants has been recognized by the official actions by many of our Protestant denominations. Hence, the opinion expressed in this message is not isolated but represents a wide segment of American thought on a subject which is dividing the American people in a time when we ought to be united.

> Let the Church be the Church and the State be the State. Let the
> wall of separation continue. Let us render unto Caesar the things that
> are Caesar's and to God the things that are God's.[33]

The remainder of the day's program included luncheon speeches
by Clyde Taylor, secretary of public affairs for the NAE, and Dr.
L. Nelson Bell. Bell's speech was a version of one he had previously
given titled "Protestant Distinctives and the American Crisis." POAU
would later reprint Bell's speech as a tract and distribute thousands of
copies to its constituents. Later in the afternoon, Don Gill, listed as
executive director of Citizens for Religious Freedom, spoke on "Plans
and Materials." After Glenn Archer's closing address, "Clerical Mani-
festations," the agenda stated, "informal planning group sessions will
meet throughout the evening."

Thanks to the enterprising work of a young reporter for the Long
Island, New York, *Newsday*, Bonnie Angelo, the disjunction between
the rhetoric of the private meetings and the public face of the gathering began to emerge.[34] Angelo had arrived at the Mayflower before the
morning sessions along with a handful of other reporters only to learn
that the day's meetings were closed to the press. Not satisfied with this
restriction, Angelo surreptitiously entered a sound room adjacent to the
room in which the meetings took place. She was able to hear the morning
speakers, Smith and Ockenga, as well as Peale's remarks as he presided
over them. At the break before the luncheon, she left the sound room to
contact John Lindsay, a veteran reporter for the *Washington Post* who was
there to cover the story. Angelo feared that if she exclusively broke the
story of what was said in the meeting, people might not believe a young
woman reporter. She negotiated a deal with Lindsay to tell him what she
had heard and allowed him into the sound booth for the remainder of
the day in exchange for his pledge that the *Post* would not publish the
story until the edition of *Newsday* with her story broke first. Lindsay
accepted her terms. Thanks to Angelo's tenacity and ingenuity, Peale
would have a hard time during the subsequent press conference.

At that press conference, Peale distributed a brief press release that
noted that Protestant ministers and laypeople from 37 denominations
had resolved that the religion issue "is a real and vital one, but must
be handled in a spirit of truth, tolerance, and fairness."[35] The release
noted that Peale had presided and that others on the program included
Poling, Ockenga, the Reverend Fred Nader Archer, and Bell. "Those
present," it continued, "a nationwide representation, favored free and
open discussion of the religious issue. They condemned so-called 'hate
literature' and 'whispering campaigns.'"

The document ended on a defensive note: "It was noted that attempts to discuss the issue fairly by raising logical questions based on facts is not 'bigotry' as many try to tag it, since it deals with a pertinent issue." The conference had adopted the statement from the Republican National Committee that the Kennedy campaign had received from its informant the night before. The statement was slightly over two pages long, single spaced, and recycled some of the arguments from the speeches of the day: the Catholic church is both a church and a state, the church has repudiated both Kennedy's stand on his freedom of conscience and the argument of American Catholics who embrace the separation of church and state, the record of Catholics in other countries has not been respect for religious freedom, and under canon law an American Catholic president could not participate in interfaith meetings.[36]

Peale was selected to speak to the press, with the aid of Gill and Ockenga. The press quickly put Peale on the defensive. He acknowledged that no Catholics were on the program and that the majority of those present were conservative Protestants. Far from being a representative group conducting a philosophical discussion, the press saw the gathering for what it was, a rally of conservative Protestants against Kennedy. Gill entered the press conference and tried to stanch the bleeding, with little effect. The result was a public relations nightmare for Peale and for Citizens for Religious Freedom.

Lindsay's article in the *Washington Post* was devastating. It began with a detailed account of Bell's speech, which declared that freedom from Romish influence was the key issue in the momentous decision of choosing a president.[37] It related that those at the gathering were encouraged to contribute to an existing fund of $5,000 to carry the message of the conference to the grassroots. Donald Gill was quoted as saying that about $20,000 would be required to conduct similar meetings across the country with different people. Gill refused to reveal the names of the 150 attendees, but Lindsay reported overhearing participants identify themselves as Baptists, Free Methodists, Wesley Methodists, Bible Presbyterians, Congregationalists, and Unitarians, among others, during a luncheon roll call.

During the press conference, Peale denied that Kennedy's voting record was discussed, but Lindsay reported that Kennedy's voting record on federal aid to parochial schools had been raised. All of these factors severely damaged the credibility of the meeting.

Reinhold Niebuhr and John Bennett of Union Theological Seminary in New York issued a blistering response on behalf of the Liberal

Party in New York in which they accused Peale of "blind prejudice" against Kennedy.[38] They argued that the Peale group showed no understanding of developments within Catholicism that were favorable to religious liberty for all in democratic countries. Citing the freedom of American Catholics who already served in high offices, such as governors, senators, and Supreme Court justices, they argued that denying Kennedy the presidency because of his Catholicism would be an affront to the 40 million Catholics in America and would damage the country.

Peale took the hit particularly hard.[39] Feeling abandoned by Graham, who did not publicly intervene to explain his organizing role, Peale dissembled by saying that he was only the ceremonial presider who just happened to be in Washington that day and not the architect of the event. The ensuing negative press sent Peale into a depression. On September 16, Peale sent a letter to his parishioners at the Marble Collegiate Church and to contributors to his radio program in which he cut off any association with the ongoing work of Citizens for Religious Freedom. He argued that he did not organize the group and he had no role in drafting the statement the group had issued. Both claims were true, but he did not say who did organize the meeting nor who wrote the statement. Neither Graham nor Nixon came to his rescue. The recriminations between Dan Poling and Graham over Graham's manipulation of Peale are revealing. Graham eventually took some responsibility in private for pushing Peale to go to the meeting and failing to come to his aid once the avalanche of criticism fell on him. J. Elwin Wright, the architect of the Peale meeting and of Citizens for Religious Freedom, apparently encouraged Graham to stay out of the public fray in order to protect Graham and let Peale suffer the public consequences.[40]

Peale later resigned his pulpit, but the board refused his resignation. Yet his standing in public was permanently marred by his association with the group that came to bear his name.

Reaction in the press and among liberal religious leaders was overwhelmingly poor. The front page of the *New York Times* carried the story, the press release, the press release from POAU's board meeting the day before, and an opinion piece from Jesuit theologian John Courtney Murray in which Murray decried the anti-Catholic bigotry of the election. Nixon himself had to disavow the meeting the next Sunday on *Meet the Press*. It was nothing short of a media massacre.

The outcry illustrated the explosiveness of the threat to the Nixon campaign if it ever criticized Kennedy in public regarding his faith. The Peale meeting came dangerously close to exposing Nixon's clandestine efforts. Despite the fact that the Kennedy campaign now knew what Nixon was up to, it could not go public with the information perhaps since it came from a source who was not publicly identified. Only with the passage of time would the full effect of the event become clear. On the one hand, it certainly fed the view that Kennedy was a victim of organized bigotry. On the other hand, it reminded a lot of Protestants that many Protestant opinion leaders had doubts about Kennedy. The net electoral effect of these divergent conclusions was not immediately apparent. But both campaigns seemed to realize the dangerous territory they were in and neither was sure what to do about it.

There was a range of reactions among the Citizens for Religious Freedom stakeholders, from outright anger at Peale for backing down, to sympathy for his plight, to scurrying for cover on the part of people like Graham. One sample of the bitter reaction of some at the Peale meeting came from James Walter Nichols, a representative of the Churches of Christ who had been recruited by Armstrong. In the denominational newspaper he edited, the *Christian Chronicle*, Nichols wrote:

> We were there for the National Conference For Religious Freedom in the Hotel Mayflower, Washington, D.C., September 7, 1960.
>
> We were there when Mr. Norman Vincent Peale presided at the conference, and we heard his very pointed statements as he told 150 religious leaders from across the nation, "Our freedom, our religious freedom, is at stake if we elect a member of the Roman Catholic order as President of the United States."
>
> We were there when he approved the statement that was to be released to the press. We were there when he was selected to speak the feelings of this conference to the people of America through the press.
>
> We were not there, however, when the pressures were brought that caused him to back down. We do not know the personalities nor did we hear what he was told, but it was sufficient to cause the recanting of this man who suggested that it might be well for all to imitate his wife who the first thing each morning prayed God would not let America lose her freedom by surrendering to the Roman Catholic state.
>
> Many things could be said about his forthright statements and his later retractions, but one observation is sufficient.
>
> If this man, who avows his opposition to the Roman Catholic system and who pledges no allegiance to it whatsoever, could be pressured to change as he has changed, what will a man who pledges his allegiance to [the] Roman Catholic hierarchy be able to do though he now proudly declares that he will not surrender?[41]

The forces of Citizens for Religious Freedom and its parent, the National Association of Evangelicals, tried to put the best possible spin on the fiasco. In his monthly column in the NAE's magazine, *United Evangelical Action*, Don Gill downplayed Peale's role in the meeting and argued that the substance of the program came from other speakers. By making Peale the scapegoat, the press revealed that it was strongly influenced by vested interests, clearly meaning the Kennedy family, and that Protestants would notice this fact from now on. Gill opined that now the religion issue was out in the open and would get serious attention as a result of the mudslinging against Peale.[42]

In early October, Citizens for Religious Freedom sent out a recalcitrant and unrepentant letter to its supporters, claiming that the enormous pressure brought to bear on Peale was being applied all across the nation. It repeated the old argument that nothing short of papal renunciation of Catholic political pressure would enable Kennedy to serve as president in a manner similar to that of members of Protestant churches.[43]

For his part, Clyde Taylor offered the NAE board of administration a slightly different interpretation. He reported that press coverage of the Peale meeting had allowed falsehood to triumph over truth as bigots got away with calling others bigots. Outside forces, he argued, stimulated the press to keep the religion issue alive, overlooking the fact that Peale had cracked under pressure at a press conference that Citizens for Religious Freedom itself had called.

He went on to argue that, despite the bad press, the meeting had succeeded to bring the religion issue to the nation's attention. In light of the scrutiny, Taylor said, they had decided not to do any more large-city public events and instead to concentrate on voter registration and church outreach within the Protestant community. Avoiding the national press would become part of the ongoing strategy.[44] The final semi-public push would be a coordinated effort among thousands of Protestant congregations on Reformation Sunday in late October. The failed public campaign forced the NAE and its surrogate, Citizens for Religious Freedom, to lower its public profile and pursue a course of action far closer to the grassroots of the Protestant world.

On September 12, Taylor outlined the ongoing work of Citizens for Religious Freedom to the executive board of the NAE. It would continue the dissemination of acceptable literature, in this case tracts prepared by the NAE; it would conduct a get-out-the-vote campaign in NAE member churches; it would buy newspaper ads and circulate a bibliography of available material; and it would encourage Reformation Sunday rallies.[45]

On a far more conciliatory note, Nelson Bell wrote to Peale to thank him for "the grand work that you did." He added, "I sympathize with you in the adverse criticism [that] particularly in the political field, is bound to accrue to us."[46] Bell went on to say that he had been besieged by calls from the press: "This is just part of the price that we have to pay for taking a stand, and I just want you to know that we admire you and thank you for all that you have done."

The "we" here may have included his son-in-law, Billy Graham, who made no effort to rescue Peale from the charge that he, Peale, was the one responsible for "the Peale group" and not Graham himself. As Peale's biographer Carol George has shown, Peale felt abandoned by Graham in the firestorm over the meeting. Bell's letter may not have had a palliative effect on Peale's pain.

Peale's old friend and Kennedy's tormentor, Daniel Poling, wrote to Nixon's operative O. K. Armstrong to say that he, too, was saddened by the outcome of the Washington meeting: "It is never wise, I think, if you have in good faith committed yourself to any proposition, to start a retreat." He went on to tell Armstrong that he no longer had any interest in joining efforts against Kennedy.[47]

Despite the public media firestorm, Bell and POAU's Archer exchanged letters that revealed that the fight was still ongoing. Bell wrote to Archer on September 24 and told him that he had just gotten a phone call asking him why his speech at the Peale meeting, "Protestant Distinctives," was not available in the POAU collection of tracts. Bell said that, so far, 90,000 copies of his speech had been printed. If POAU would like a stock of the tract to distribute, he would happily send them.[48] Archer requested 10,000 copies for POAU to distribute.[49]

Bell closed his next letter with a bitter denunciation of Charles Taft, chair of the Fair Campaign Practices Committee, a public citizens' watchdog group that had promulgated principles of fair campaign practices that both national political parties had signed. Taft had chastised Bell for his claim that the American Catholic bishops were expending funds and circulating statements of support for Kennedy and opposing Nixon. Bell knew that this was true and hoped to show information that could be documented to give to Taft.[50] Thus, these two speakers from the Peale meeting, one from the Billy Graham wing of evangelicalism and the other a mainline Protestant, engaged in a massive distribution of anti-Catholic literature undeterred by the negative fallout from the Peale meeting.

Meanwhile, Kennedy was in the middle of a lackluster whistle-stop train campaign from Portland to Los Angeles. His aide Dave Powers described him as "very mad" about the news about Peale.[51] In his first public comments on the Peale meeting on September 9, he had to be drawn out by a reporter's question.[52] He refused to comment on quotes from Peale or on the statement issued by the group. When pressed, though, he answered at length:

> I have made my position very clear on this question. I am a member of my Church and I know my responsibilities as a citizen of the United States and the support of the [C]onstitution. I have been in the Congress for 14 years and have met those responsibilities. I wouldn't attempt to reply to Dr. Peale or to anyone who questions my loyalty to the United States. I am delighted to respond to those who want to ask what my position is. But for those who are not interested in my position and prefer to state it themselves, it really is very difficult to state it by me and give any answer which would satisfy them.

Another reporter asked him if he believed that Peale had questioned his loyalty. Kennedy replied:

> I would think that he has questioned my ability to fulfill my constitutional oath because he states I would be unable to fulfill it because my Church would place pressure on me which I would succumb to. I don't accept the view that my Church would place pressure upon me. I don't think there is any evidence of that in the United States. The Constitution is very clear on the separation of Church and State. I have been clear and precise in my commitments to that Constitution, not merely because I take the oath which is taken to God but also because I believe that it represents the happiest arrangement for the organization of a society.
>
> Therefore, I believe in that theory strongly, just as strongly as Dr. Peale or anyone else. I don't know what I can do other than state that as my conviction, state that as my record, and state that that is the philosophy which would guide me in the Presidency. Beyond that, then it just becomes a question as to whether in 1960 we are going to carry out the Constitution which says there shall be no religious test for office, or whether we are going to decide because I was born Catholic and lived a Catholic that for some reason I am unfit to hold office. That is the question.[53]

Kennedy was then asked if he thought that the separation of church and state was the wisest arrangement, and he said:

> Yes, I think it is. In many countries in Europe and in tradition there has not been a separation of church and state. They work out their solutions to suit themselves. There isn't in England, in some of the Scandinavian Countries, but that does not mean that Americans who

happen to be members of those same faiths—and in some countries where Catholics are a majority—that there isn't a separation of church and state. Lutherans in the United States believe in separation of church, so do Catholics, so do Jews. We have been able to work this out in our society. But why should something be raised when I run for the Presidency? That is what I cannot understand. It wasn't raised when I ran for the House or the Senate. I know that the Presidency has a great influence, but why should I be questioned in my running for the Presidency of the United States[?][54]

A reporter then asked if he were going to start talking about this in his campaign speeches as he did in West Virginia, and Kennedy replied that he would not unless he were asked, perhaps indicating that the campaign was still struggling with the invitation to speak in Houston the next week on the topic.

Behind the scenes, the Peale meeting had sent a shock wave through the Kennedy camp. Over the summer, anxiety had been growing within the campaign that the West Virginia primary results had not put the religion issue to rest at all. But between the revelation from the informant that Nixon had an operative in the field organizing conservative Protestants against Kennedy and the realization that the Peale group and POAU represented a huge swath of the Protestant world, a renewed sense of urgency struck the brain trust. While the press reaction had been thorny for the Peale group, the meeting had succeeded in raising the religion issue, and it was not abundantly clear that the negative press had actually changed any voters' minds for Kennedy. Reluctantly, Kennedy, his brother Robert, and Sorensen agreed that the issue had to be addressed directly. They agreed to accept the speaking engagement from the Greater Houston Ministerial Association the next week. The stakes could not have been higher.

7

A LION IN A DEN
OF DANIELS

· ·

Kennedy accepted the Democratic Party's nomination on July 15 in
Los Angeles, where he delivered the famous "New Frontier" speech.
Six paragraphs into the speech, he highlighted the role of his faith:

> I am fully aware of the fact that the Democratic Party, by nominat-
> ing someone of my faith, has taken what many regard as a new and
> hazardous risk—new, at least, since 1928. But look at it this way:
> the Democratic Party has once again placed its confidence in the
> American people, and in their ability to render a free, fair judg-
> ment. And you have, at the same time, placed your confidence in
> me, and in my ability to render a free, fair judgment—to uphold
> the Constitution and my oath of office—and to reject any kind of
> religious pressure or obligation that might directly or indirectly
> interfere with my conduct of the Presidency in the national inter-
> est. My record of fourteen years supporting public education—
> supporting complete separation of church and state—and resisting
> pressure from any source on any issue should be clear by now to
> everyone.
>
> I hope that no American, considering the really critical issues
> facing this country, will waste his franchise by voting either for me
> or against me solely on account of my religious affiliation. It is not
> relevant, I want to stress, what some other political or religious leader
> may have said on this subject. It is not relevant what abuses may have
> existed in other countries or in other times. It is not relevant what
> pressures, if any, might conceivably be brought to bear on me. I am
> telling you now what you are entitled to know: that my decisions on

every public policy will be my own—as an American, a Democrat, and a free man.[1]

He returned to religion at the end:

It has been a long road from that first snowy day in New Hampshire to this crowded convention city. Now begins another long journey, taking me into your cities and homes all over America. Give me your help, your hand, your voice, your vote. Recall with me the words of Isaiah: "They that wait upon the Lord shall renew their strength; they shall mount up with wings as eagles; they shall run, and not be weary."

As we face the coming great challenge, we too, shall wait upon the Lord, and ask that He renew our strength. Then shall we be equal to the test. Then we shall not be weary. Then we shall prevail.[2]

While the speech projected hope and optimism, behind the scenes there was growing anxiety among the Kennedy brain trust that the religion issue had not been put to rest. The Harvard advisors were unanimous. Archibald Cox was running a sort of informal Harvard think tank for Kennedy. He had suggested a speech on the separation of church and state as early as April. While Kennedy could not say anything on the topic to move the prejudiced, Cox thought that there was a sizable group of thoughtful people, presumably many of them in the halls of Harvard, who were "seriously troubled about the prospect of having a President whose religion is what they regard as authoritarian."[3] Likewise, John Kenneth Galbraith was alarmed that, during his forays among midwestern farm people, he had discovered severe misgivings about Kennedy's Catholicism. Something—although Galbraith wasn't sure precisely what—had to be done.[4]

Arthur Schlesinger, Jr., was the most loquacious. He, too, worried about liberal anti-Catholicism. And the addition of Johnson to the ticket had further raised suspicions among liberals.[5] After attending the board meeting of Americans for Democratic Action, where a tepid statement of support for Kennedy had been adopted, Schlesinger wrote an anguished, five-page, single-spaced epistle to Kennedy. Many liberals feared that, if Kennedy won, it meant that the Democratic Party would become the Demo-Catholic Party. Schlesinger counseled Kennedy to woo Reinhold Niebuhr to speak on behalf of the campaign. He also suggested that Kennedy go out of his way to help Protestant Endicott "Chub" Peabody to win the Democratic gubernatorial primary in Massachusetts to show his independence.[6]

Immediately after the Peale incident, Schlesinger complained to Robert Kennedy that Nixon was getting the benefit of Peale and company without paying any price for it. He suggested finding a surrogate, perhaps a southerner like Sam Ervin or even Lyndon Johnson, to hector Nixon over the incident.[7] RFK liked the idea and put Senator Henry Jackson, chair of the Democratic National Committee, on the case.[8]

But, as was often the case, it was Sorensen who effectively combined analysis with a plan of action. In a lean, two-page August "Memorandum on the Religious Issue," he diagnosed the problem and laid out a solution.[9] He began with his "present convictions" that, given the normal Democratic majority, assuming that JFK's personal appeal, hard work, and political operation produced as they had in the past, Kennedy should win. Only the religion issue could defeat him.

Sorensen called for the establishment of a "Community Relations" team that would have two parts: one to reach out to Jewish voters and the other to neutralize the religion issue. To neutralize anti-Catholic forces, the group would respond to the flood of mail coming into the campaign on religious topics; assemble a fact book with candidate speeches, voting records, and statements from religious bodies; contact editors of religious publications; establish national clergy committees; plan a national conference for Kennedy and religious leaders; and work with POAU and similar organizations and individuals to reassure them. The Peale meeting would soon pressure the campaign to ramp up this operation and also significantly modify its work, but even at this juncture Sorensen realized that they had to put the religion issue on the front burner.

Sorensen lobbied campaign manager Robert Kennedy to hire James Wine, an attorney then working for the National Council of Churches in Washington, D.C.[10] Sorensen had met Wine earlier in 1960 during a controversy over an air force training manual. The manual had been produced at a single base, and in addition to normal military material, it included allegations against Communist groups, including accusations from fundamentalist preacher Billy Hargis that the National Council of Churches had been infiltrated by Communists. Wine had issued a stinging report rebutting the charges and had sent Kennedy a copy.[11] As early as June, Wine had shared his thoughts with Sorensen on what the campaign might do to address the nexus of religion issues.[12]

Indeed, Wine provided much of the analysis that would end up in Sorensen's August memorandum. Wine offered a cornucopia of advice and observation. He argued for an ad hoc strategy of neutralizing the various anti-Catholic strategies based upon a distinction between hardcore bigots and less extreme mainline Protestant opponents.

In both cases, Wine ruled out direct appeals to religious groups. Kennedy had to maintain a posture consistent with his past record of arguing that his religious affiliation was a matter of private concern, and thus during the campaign he had to avoid "the blandishments of church leaders of any religious group." (The reason to present Kennedy's religion as private was to avoid the Protestant charge of favoritism to Catholics, *not* to portray Kennedy as a secularist.)

Wine felt that Kennedy had been relatively successful early in the campaign at neutralizing the religion issue. The greatest challenge, he thought, was in the South. While certain parts of the Southwest, Northwest, and Midwest were susceptible to anti-Catholic fears, the power of the anti-Catholic rhetoric did not seem strong enough to take any electoral votes away from Kennedy.

On the positive side, Wine argued, large numbers of church leaders of conservative denominations were persons of "probity and intelligence." While their traditions were prone to anti-Catholicism, they could be approached indirectly with appeals to reason, to Christian conscience, and to their obligations as citizens. The most that could be hoped in many cases was to soften them from what otherwise would be an uncompromising opposition. The effect would be to prevent them from being too vociferous in their sermons and writings:

> The point needs to be made with such clergymen that—if Senator Kennedy is to be judged at all on religious grounds—it should be in terms of his Christianity; that only on such a basis can comparison[s] be made with other candidates—past and present—as to how well the Senator has followed the dictates of his Christian concern for others.

For Wine, it was important that Kennedy be presented as a man of high moral and ethical convictions, owing allegiance to no parochial group, who as president would be representative of all people and faithful to his oath under the Constitution. In the process, the campaign should make clear that injecting the religious question into the election could actually undermine the freedom of religion so dearly prized by Protestants. For this strategy to work, Kennedy must not show any favoritism, presumably maintaining some public distance from Catholic leaders.

The second part of the memorandum consisted of more practical recommendations. These included appealing directly to the editors of various religious magazines with Kennedy's stand on standard issues, such as the separation of church and state, representation at the Vatican, aid to parochial schools, and birth control, always citing his voting record. The same material should be sent to religion editors in the mainstream press, to executives of state and local councils of churches, and to denominational judicatory officials.

Wine also advised assembling a roster of surrogates who could respond locally to blunt overt attacks. He was resigned to the reality of extremist attacks from the far Right, but he thought it might be worthwhile to respond even to these attacks by calling for retractions and corrections when they, inevitably, made errors. He advised approaching Monsignor George Higgins of the National Catholic Welfare Conference to write an issue-oriented look at Kennedy for his highly influential column, which ran in 25 diocesan newspapers around the country. Rabbi Arthur Gilbert of the Anti-Defamation League could advise on how to approach Jewish groups.

His final two practical suggestions were to convene a nonpartisan group of church leaders to invite Kennedy to a meeting to discuss the religion issue and to approach the National Conference of Christians and Jews to keep it informed of the campaign's efforts. Wine even suggested having some conversation with POAU, from which "Kennedy may expect the subtlest and the attack most appealing to many persons." Wine's post at the National Council of Churches plus his activity in the Presbyterian church put him in an ideal position to monitor the currents of Protestant thought.

On the strength of this advice, Sorensen convinced Robert Kennedy to hire Wine to run the community relations office. He began work on August 26.[13] Two weeks later, John Cogley, former editor of *Commonweal* magazine and director of the Fund for the Republic's Center for the Study of Democratic Institutions, was hired to assist Wine.[14] Even before the Peale explosion, the campaign was already expending resources and manpower on the religion question.

An early assessment of the Kennedy field operation also noted the high barrier that Kennedy's Catholicism posed. An unsigned July 21 "Memorandum on Texas Political Situation" painted a dire picture of the state in general and the religion issue in particular.[15] The world's largest Baptist, Methodist, and Presbyterian churches were all in Dallas, along with one of the largest Masonic lodges in the country. Opposition to Kennedy was being led by two Baptists, the Reverend W. A. Criswell, the pastor of First Baptist in Dallas, and one of his church members, Carr P. Collins, a wealthy insurance company owner.

Criswell had already publicly denounced Kennedy. The Kennedy campaign predicted that the 12,000 members of his congregation would be active all over the Dallas area and that their money and influence would spread throughout Baptist churches all across the state. Likewise, Collins would be busy working against Kennedy. He had already met with Nixon in Washington on July 16, one day after Kennedy was nominated and before the Republican convention.

The author of the memo suggested that a lot of anti-Catholic sentiment would be masked by expressions of opposition to the national Democratic platform. He also noted that there was no statewide leadership in Texas left from Al Smith's 1928 presidential campaign, so there was no collective political wisdom or experience in dealing with a Catholic nominee in Texas. Nevertheless:

> The sooner Kennedy's religion is brought out into the open, the better, and it should be in Texas before the State Convention. There is no denying that this is an issue, and it is being talked about; therefore, let people talk about it. On the other side of the coin, there are a great many people here who honestly have no opposition to Kennedy's religion. No one but Kennedy himself can or should do this. How best to do it, remains the question. Maybe when Kennedy passes through Dallas or Texas, he can do this through a press conference, or perhaps a T.V. speech.

Press reports from Tennessee, another key state for the Kennedy campaign, were also not encouraging. A front-page story on August 15, 1960, in the *Nashville Banner* proclaimed that many Southern Baptist and Church of Christ preachers would ask their congregations to vote against Kennedy.[16] This was the consensus view of the annual meeting of the Southern Education Reporting Service in Nashville. Ramsey Pollard, president of the Southern Baptist Convention, who had been in communication with Orland Armstrong, was quoted as saying that an overwhelming majority of the over 31,000 Southern Baptist preachers in the South would take to their pulpits to oppose Kennedy. The Southern Baptist church claimed over 750,000 members in Tennessee alone. Likewise, Dr. Carroll Ellis, a prominent preacher in the Churches of Christ and a professor at David Lipscomb College in Nashville, said that most ministers in the Churches of Christ would preach one or more sermons on why their members should not vote for a Catholic.

Lyndon Johnson's experienced advisors were in a unique position to understand the risks attached to any strategy the campaign devised to combat anti-Catholicism in the South. Their viewpoint was an important one as the campaign struggled to craft an effective response. Almost all of the major players in LBJ's circle had opinions on the matter.

George Reedy expressed surprise that the Catholic issue evoked such an extreme reaction. He suggested polling Baptist leaders informally to determine just how deep these sentiments ran. If a number of prominent Baptist laypeople were willing to go on the record with a declaration against religious bigotry in voting, this might stave off the onslaught. That this strategy never emerged is telling.[17] Bill Moyers, Johnson's campaign manager, told Pierre Salinger and Robert Kennedy something that he and LBJ had heard from a prominent Oklahoma Baptist educator. Ninety-five percent of the ministers, he said, are

> vigorously opposed to the ticket, but...their efforts would be coun-
> teracted by voters under 40 who (1) are not prejudiced, and (2) who
> feel that some issues are more important than the religious question,
> and (3) who are interested in building the kind of future for their
> country that will enrich their own personal future.[18]

Moyers advocated pursuing a youth strategy to counteract the clergy-led anti-Catholic appeal.

Walter Jenkins, who was Johnson's eyes and ears for political gossip in Texas, was getting a raft of feedback from his sources all across the state. One source noted a quiet anti-Catholic campaign being waged in his region by the Masons.[19] Another reported that "we are just catching hell" on the Catholic issue there. A Baptist preacher in Waco gave a scorcher of a sermon on it. He identified Carr P. Collins as the organizer of the anti-Catholic forces.[20] Another source elaborated on Collins's efforts. Collins had ordered 52 broadcast slots of 15 minutes each on a radio station in Sherman. He was organizing Baptist and Church of Christ ministers for Nixon in the central part of the state.[21]

Federal judge Byron Skelton, another Johnson advisor, cited religion as the main issue. He counseled the campaign to face the issue directly and seconded the observation that the Baptists and the Church of Christ were the main troublemakers. The best way to combat these forces was for Kennedy to travel for two days through the whole state, but especially the panhandle, where the religion issue was the strongest. Yet Skelton felt that all the talk of Texas being a doubtful state for the ticket was "hogwash."[22] Jenkins also picked up the tip that Albert Hermann of the Republican National Committee was the organizer of anti-Catholic forces for Nixon. It is not clear what, if anything, Johnson did with this particular piece of intelligence, which came from a New York tax attorney with strong Texas ties, Ambrose McCall.[23] At a minimum, Johnson knew that Collins and Hermann, both of whom had direct ties to Nixon, were leading efforts to exploit Kennedy's Catholicism.

Johnson's close political ally Speaker of the House Sam Rayburn sent Johnson a sample letter to show him how he was responding to the flood of mail he was getting on the Catholic question.[24] The letter commended Kennedy's patriotism, noted America's commitment to religious freedom, such that a man's religion should not be held against him, and added a personal note from Rayburn:

> I am glad, being a Baptist of the hard shell type, that I have no religious prejudices. I have served in Congress with hundreds of Catholics. By no speech they ever made, nor vote they ever cast, did they indicate they were a Catholic, Protestant or Jew. I know this statement is true.
>
> Please think again and vote for the man regardless of religion, whom you think can best serve our beloved country.

The best analysis of the situation in Texas came from aide Horace Busby, a member of the Churches of Christ. He told Johnson that Texas church groups had raised anti-Catholicism to a dignified, legalistic, "documented" level.[25] The bigoted Ku Klux Klan approach was not heard, at least in public. Busby said this was subtle and significant, and he was right on both counts. With his finger firmly on the pulse of conservative Texas Protestantism, Busby dissected the situation systematically.

His first point was that Texas Protestant preachers realized that old-style extreme bigotry was unacceptable to present-day audiences. This was a key insight in that it showed that Protestant preachers could not simply be dismissed as extreme right-wing radicals, especially if the campaign wanted to reach the tens of thousands of congregants in these churches. Second, Texas audiences react against ranting and rabble rousing on religion just as they would on race. But they think their preachers are presenting factual information on Catholicism and not fulminations. Busby counseled that, somehow, Kennedy had to discredit this anti-Catholicism by linking it to the kinds of extremism that modern Texas audiences would find repugnant.

It would be a mistake to ignore the problem, and it would also be a mistake to start a debate with the preachers over the history or teachings of the Catholic church. As he put it, accurately, "the anti-Catholic case is thoroughly, although irrelevantly, briefed and documented." Long before this campaign, Protestant preachers had seriously excited themselves about the threat to civil government posed by Romanism. This practice had spread beyond the fundamentalists to mainline Protestants as well. Preachers had a basic belief that their anti-Catholic sermons were justified—even imperative—on the basis of history, and as a result "they sorely resent any accusations of pure bias, of which they honestly feel themselves innocent."

Their chief fear was foreign domination of U.S. civil government. This line of thinking drew heavily on Catholic documents and periodicals, especially from Europe. The specific threat was seen to public education as Catholics would seek federal funding of parochial schools. Busby counseled linking the anti-Catholic issue to the lunatic fringe and not directly addressing the respectable preacher element. He concluded:

> Overall, it would seem likely that the eventual strategy in Texas will be to keep the anti-Catholic from going militantly to the polls as a bloc—rather than trying to persuade them to change their minds. With one or two exceptions the denominations will not vote as a bloc. But in all of them, there are people who would go to the polls aggressively to vote against the ticket because of the Catholic issue, where otherwise—if that issue is not too strong—they would simply not vote at all.

This diagnosis of the situation on the ground was brilliant, even if the counsel on how to respond to it was weak. And that was a much trickier problem. How should the campaign respond? The same day that he received Busby's memo, Johnson had his aide Walter Jenkins call Pierre Salinger to solicit advice on how to handle the religion question in light of the flood of mail that Johnson was getting.[26] Salinger told Jenkins to send out copies of Kennedy's spring speech before the American Society of Newspaper Editors. Jenkins thought the Los Angeles acceptance speech was better. Salinger agreed and noted that this could be excerpted in a letter to inquirers. Salinger said that, based on their experience in West Virginia, the best course of action was to respond to the question as it arose and not to bring it up first. On the whole, Salinger's advice did not amount to much help for Johnson and was representative of the fragmentary response by the Kennedy campaign.

The seriousness of the threat that Johnson felt can be seen in an exchange of letters between the vice presidential nominee and Paul Stevens, head of the Southern Baptist Radio and Television Commission. On August 16, Stevens wrote to Johnson to tell him that, while he had always seen Johnson as an example of "a fine Christian being active in politics," he would now do everything in his power to defeat Kennedy and Johnson. Stevens lamented that he had always voted Democratic as had his father. But he now planned to use "the considerable facilities at my disposal to defeat the Democratic ticket in November. Had you been the presidential candidate, I would have voted wholeheartedly for you. Now, I do not think I can ever do so again."[27]

Johnson penned a blistering response.[28] Noting that he was surprised by Stevens's letter, Johnson went on the attack. What exactly had Johnson done to justify losing his esteem as a Christian in politics? He was particularly surprised that Stevens threatened to use all of his resources to fight Johnson. Did that include the resources of the Southern Baptist Convention's Radio and Television Commission? Johnson suggested that Baptist theology insisted that no Baptist ever try to speak for another, believing that each man is a moral agent free to find his own way before God. He also understood that no head of a Baptist agency should ever try to use that agency as a channel for his own political views. Johnson closed his letter by saying that he respected Stevens's right to believe as he chose. He only asked a reciprocal respect for his own views, at which he had arrived conscientiously.

In the midst of this fusillade of disturbing news from the anti-Catholic forces in his home state, Johnson got a letter from Billy Graham, almost exactly as Graham was holding the meeting in Montreux, Switzerland, to plot against Kennedy. Graham wrote:

> A rumor has been floating about among certain Democratic Party leaders that I intend to raise the religious [issue] publicly. This is not true. I shall be in Europe until just prior to election time and hope to stay as much out of the political campaign as possible. I would appreciate your conveying this to Senator Kennedy at your convenience.
>
> I am deeply grateful that you took time [out] of your busy schedule to attend our last meeting in Washington. Please be assured that I hold you in the highest personal esteem.[29]

Johnson wrote back that he was impressed and grateful for Graham's letter. He had showed the letter to Kennedy, and "he was obviously impressed by your attitude." Johnson told Graham how much he thought of him and how greatly he appreciated his ministry.[30] Graham's duplicitous conduct is now clear.

By early September, the Johnson operation had drafted a standard response letter and packet on religion.[31] In the letter, Johnson argued that no man should be barred from office because of his religion. He cited Kennedy's heroism in defense of the country. He noted that Kennedy had faced the religion question fully, frankly, and courageously. He had answered every possible doubt. The letter enclosed a seven-page packet that included quotes from Kennedy, statements on the relevant policy questions, and favorable quotes from a range of Protestant leaders, including Blanshard, Oxnam, and Archer of POAU.

In late June, Sorensen had called to Robert Kennedy's attention the work of a new social scientific research company, Simulmatics. Sorensen thought that it could do some survey work that might be useful.[32] Simulmatics had been founded by a collection of university professors, including Ithiel de Sola Pool of MIT. By collating 66 polls and 100,000 voter surveys, developing 480 distinct voter types, and using state-of-the-art computer databases, these scientists were able to conduct simulated surveys on discrete political questions, generating analyses for the campaign. By Labor Day, Simulmatics had generated profiles of both Kennedy and Nixon as voters viewed them.[33]

Robert Kennedy was sufficiently intrigued by this early work to ask University of Michigan professor George Belknap, who had been hired by the campaign as a polling advisor, to evaluate the work of Simulmatics. Belknap interviewed de Sola Pool, reviewed Simulmatics' early report, and dismissed its work as the polling equivalent of reading entrails.[34] Nevertheless, Kennedy engaged its services. Its analysis of the religion question may have proved pivotal.

From August 11 through 18, Simulmatics conducted a poll that showed Nixon leading Kennedy 39.5% to 37.5% with 23% of the voters still undecided. De Sola Pool sent preliminary results to Robert Kennedy and then traveled to Washington to present him with the group's full analysis.[35] The 43-page report, "Kennedy before Labor Day," included a comprehensive analysis of Kennedy's image, a simulation on the Catholic issue, the data from the August poll combined with its existing data bank, a discussion of the salient issues, and an assessment of Kennedy's strengths and weaknesses among voters.[36] This survey may have represented the dawn of contemporary focus groups and micro targeting.

The survey summary contained two tantalizing claims: that the religion issue could be turned to Kennedy's advantage and that Republican Catholics were not defecting to Kennedy. Should Kennedy make an issue of anti-Catholicism and religious prejudice, he would lose some reluctant Protestant voters, but gain Catholic and minority voters. Based on Simulmatics' computer simulation, this would be a net gain for Kennedy.[37]

The devil was in the details. At that moment, it looked like the election would turn on three issues: party, religion, and competence in foreign affairs. The religion issue cut both ways, with Catholics more inclined to support Kennedy and anti-Catholic sentiment driving some non-Catholic voters. Yet the voting behavior of Catholics and Protestants was not as predictable as many thought. For instance, 22% of

Protestants were still undecided as were 21% of Catholics and 32% of Jews. In the course of the campaign, voting preference by religion could easily change.

In order to test what might happen if the issue of anti-Catholicism and religious prejudice became more salient, the company ran a simulation that assumed that religion emerged as a full-fledged, embittered dimension of the campaign and became the dominant issue in the race. Its conclusion was that, by mid-August, Kennedy had already lost the bulk of the votes he would lose as a result of anti-Catholicism. The worst had already happened. A rise in the anti-Catholic issue would bring about a reaction against prejudice for Kennedy. The simulation found that, among Jews and African Americans, some anti-Catholicism existed, but many in both groups also saw it as analogous to their own problems in American society. The report concluded:

> It is in Kennedy's hands to handle the religious issue during the campaign in a way that maximizes Kennedy-votes based on resentment against racial prejudice and minimizes further defections. On balance, he would not lose further from forthright and persistent attention to the religious issue, and could gain.
>
> The simulation shows that there has already been a serious defection from Kennedy by Protestant voters.
>
> Under these circumstances it makes no sense to brush the religious issues under the rug. Kennedy has already suffered the disadvantages of the issue even though it is not embittered now—and without receiving the compensating advantages inherent in it.[38]

Simulmatics also presented reports on "Negro Voters in Northern Cities"[39] and "Nixon before Labor Day."[40] The Nixon assessment was the mirror image of Kennedy's. He was holding Republican Catholic voters while gaining some Protestant anti-Catholic voters: "As long as the issue remains relatively quiescent, he stands to gain."[41]

At the press conference in which he first responded to the news of the Peale meeting, Kennedy was asked if he planned to talk more about the religion issue, and he replied that he would only if asked. He was also asked if he believed that Nixon had rejected the support of religious bigots. Kennedy replied that Nixon had been clear in rejecting bigotry and that he, Kennedy, would not disagree with him.

Robert Kennedy lashed out at Peale and Poling, questioning their motives and pointing out their ties to Vice President Nixon: "Their close relationship with Mr. Nixon and the Republican party in the election leads me to question the sincerity of their statement and their judgment in issuing it."[42] He went on to say that Democrats faced an uphill struggle in seven southern states—Virginia, North and South Carolina, Kentucky, Tennessee, Florida, and Texas—because of the religion issue. But he concluded that they had a chance in all of them.[43]

The combination of the polling data about the continued saliency of religion and the fear that the Peale group had generated forced Kennedy to accept the speaking invitation from the Greater Houston Ministerial Association with considerable reluctance.[44] Wine felt that the speech represented a pivotal moment in the campaign and that the stakes were high, but that the risk was worth taking.[45] There seemed to be no alternative to directly addressing the religion issue before a potentially hostile Protestant audience in Texas.

Kennedy had earlier made speeches on the topic of the role of religion in public life. When he began to craft the Houston speech, Sorensen turned to these earlier works and to the *Look* interview. Protestant arguments against Kennedy also influenced the shape of Kennedy's counterarguments. In addition to receiving notes from Cogley and Wine, Sorensen also read a draft of the speech over the phone to the Jesuit theologian John Courtney Murray. Murray in turn dictated a one-paragraph statement that did not ultimately show up in the speech but was used by Kennedy in the question-and-answer period. Murray's advice was to distinguish between faith and morals, where the church's hierarchy was free to instruct all of its members, and public policy, where the Vatican would never coerce Catholic public officials.

The choice of Murray as an advisor is interesting because he was not initially a Kennedy supporter. According to Cogley, who knew Murray well from his time as editor of *Commonweal* and from their work together with the Fund for the Republic, Murray did not like Kennedy and opposed him. He leaned toward Republicans and had twice voted for Eisenhower. He took a dim view of Adlai Stevenson and an even dimmer view of Kennedy, whom he saw as a lightweight.[46] Murray had even counseled Cogley not to go to work for the Kennedy campaign.

The Peale meeting apparently had prompted Murray to rethink his position. On September 9, Murray released to the *New York Times* an excerpt from an article that was scheduled to appear in the September 23 issue of the Jesuit weekly magazine *America* in response to the Peale episode. His words were fiery:

> The brutal fact becomes increasingly clear. The "oldest American prejudice" as anti-Catholicism has rightly been called, is as poisonously alive today as it was in 1928, or in [the] Eighteen Nineties,

or even the Eighteen Forties. Its source is the same—political and religious ignorance. Its result is the same, a disastrous confusion of politics and religion.

Only one difference is discernible. Now the ancient "anti-papist" text is embellished by a new set of footnotes. This is the single concession to the current climate which has altered in only one respect.

Today even religious prejudice feels the need somehow to contrive to itself a semblance of rationality. The footnotes, of course, prove none of the time-worn anti-Catholic charges in the text; they merely serve to cloak the prejudice that long ago wrote the text.[47]

Murray concluded that his fear was that the religion issue might lead to Catholic anger instead of the tradition of reason—which was, in fact, the Catholic tradition.

The two recently hired religion advisors, John Cogley and James Wine, were dispatched to negotiate the arrangements and terms for the Houston speech with the Reverend Herbert Meza, leader of the Houston Ministerial Association, on the day before the speech. Both parties agreed that there would be no screening of questions. The negotiators for the ministers were afraid that extremely anti-Catholic clergy might ask embarrassing questions and give Texas Protestants a bad national image. Cogley noted that the campaign would not have been upset if that happened.[48] Cogley and Wine joined the campaign staffers in San Antonio and debriefed Sorensen on the ground rules they had negotiated. Sorensen was angry that they had allowed any questions to be asked by the audience during the televised event. Kennedy was nervous about the speech and would not be happy about having to field any and all questions. When Kennedy entered the discussion after his speech at the Alamo, he did not seem upset, much to Cogley's relief.[49]

On the way to Houston, Cogley peppered Kennedy with questions that he might get that night. Since Kennedy was saving his voice, he wrote out answers in longhand on a yellow legal pad. This was Cogley's first meeting with Kennedy. He was relieved after the speech that every question that Kennedy was asked had been covered in their practice session.[50]

Cogley noted that there were two primary audiences for the speech: the Protestant audience to which he was going to talk and the large Catholic population that might be sensitive to any perception that he somehow might sell out his religion or church in the name of political expediency. Kennedy sensed that he was walking a tightrope. He had to craft answers that addressed both audiences without alienating either.

Kennedy began the speech by offering a counternarrative to the prevailing Protestant critique that Kennedy's Catholicism was the central issue in the campaign. While he acknowledged that the religion issue was the chief topic that night, he emphasized at the outset that "we have far more critical issues to face in the 1960 election," including the spread of Communist influence to Cuba, the humiliating treatment of the president and vice president by foreign leaders on their recent trips, hungry children in West Virginia, old people who could not afford health care, too many slums, too few schools, and being too late to the moon and outer space. These were the real issues that, he insisted, should decide the election.

By framing the speech in this fashion, Kennedy was arguing implicitly that, if he sufficiently addressed the questions about his religion, he should prevail on the real issues. Yet he recognized the dynamic at work in the campaign:

> But because I am a Catholic, and no Catholic has ever been elected President, the real issues in this campaign have been obscured—perhaps deliberately, in some quarters less responsible than this. So it is apparently necessary for me to state once again—not what kind of church I believe in, for that should be important only to me—but what kind of America I believe in.

This is as close as Kennedy ever came to publicly accusing the Nixon camp of deliberately drumming up the religion issue. After all, he knew from his informant that Armstrong and Hermann were working with the Peale group. Yet he left the charge ambiguous so that it was not a direct challenge to Nixon. It was important also that Kennedy directly affirmed his Catholic faith at the outset of the speech. This was not a secularizing speech in which Kennedy fled his church. Quite the contrary. He embraced his faith while specifically denying that it would be a hindrance in carrying out the constitutional duties of the presidency.

He then launched into the substance of his counternarrative by spelling out his view of the separation of church and state as part of his view of America:

> I believe in an America where the separation of church and state is absolute; where no Catholic prelate would tell the President—should he be Catholic—how to act, and no Protestant minister would tell his parishioners for whom to vote; where no church or church school is granted any public funds or political preference, and where no man is denied public office merely because his religion differs from the President who might appoint him, or the people who might elect him.

Here, Kennedy took the separation of church and state, the most powerful tool being used against him by Protestants, and turned it in his favor. He affirmed it categorically and proceeded to show how his detractors were in fact violating this principle in their attacks on him. He stated that he believed in a country that was not officially Catholic, Protestant, or Jewish. No public official should request or accept instructions on public policy from the pope, the National Council of Churches, or any other ecclesiastical source. No religious body should seek to impose its will directly or indirectly upon the populace or public officials. Religious liberty should be so inviolable that an act against one church should be treated as an act against all.

Here, Kennedy introduced two important concepts. First, religious pressure on officials by church leaders to circumvent democratic and pluralistic values should not be tolerated. As he would note in the question-and-answer session after the speech, citing Murray's distinction without crediting him, religious groups can instruct in terms of faith and morals, but not in terms of public policy. Again, the passage of a half century of history makes this distinction between having influence on public policies, on the one hand, and faith and morals, on the other, truly problematic. We know of many public policy issues where the moral teachings of various religious groups run counter to prevailing law, and there are instances of various religious groups pressuring public officials to follow those teachings despite the contrary state of the law. But Kennedy's position was clear: churches and church leaders should not seek to impose their views on politicians in terms of public policy.

The second point was that the Protestants who sought to limit the religious liberty of Catholic office seekers might someday see their own religious liberty threatened on similar grounds. It was, of course, ironic that many Protestants were arguing that their religious liberty was threatened by Kennedy's Catholicism and thus their only recourse was to deny Kennedy his religious liberty in order to protect their own. Kennedy denied this was true. He noted that in past years, Jews, Quakers, Unitarians, and Baptists had all experienced assaults on their religious liberty.

Pushing the point further, Kennedy envisioned a future America where religious intolerance would no longer exist. It would be a country where all people and all churches are treated as equal, and everyone has the same right to attend or not attend the church of their choice, where there would be no Catholic vote, no anti-Catholic vote, no bloc voting of any kind. He went on to say that he wanted a chief executive who could attend any ceremony, service, or dinner that his office might require him to attend. His oath of office was not limited or conditioned by any religious oath, ritual, or obligation. Here, he was clearly trying to knock down Daniel Poling's Chapel of the Four Chaplains story, which was still making the rounds in Protestant circles.

Kennedy personalized the argument in the second half of the speech, invoking the holiest of Texan holy arguments, the Alamo:

> This is the kind of America I believe in—and this is the kind of America I fought for in the South Pacific, and the kind my brother died for in Europe. No one suggested then that we might have a "divided loyalty," that we did "not believe in liberty" or that we belonged to a disloyal group that threatened the "freedoms for which our forefathers died."
>
> And in fact, this is the kind of America for which our forefathers died—when they fled here to escape religious test oaths that denied office to members of less favored churches—when they fought for the Constitution, the Bill of Rights, and the Virginia Statute of Religious Freedom—and when they fought at the shrine I visited today, the Alamo. For side by side with Bowie and Crockett died McCafferty and Bailey and Carey—but no one knows whether they were Catholics or not. For there were no religious tests there.

After putting himself firmly on the side of the founders of the country and the state of Texas, he asked his audience to judge him on the basis of his 14 years of congressional service and upon his declared stands against a Vatican ambassador, against unconstitutional aid to parochial schools, and against any boycott of public schools—which, he reminded his hearers, he had attended—and not to judge him on the basis of pamphlets and publications filled with selective quotations from Catholic leaders from other countries and other centuries. He also noted that these publications always omitted the 1948 statement of the U.S. Catholic bishops that endorsed the separation of church and state. He elaborated:

> I do not consider these other quotations binding upon my public acts—why should you? But let me say, with respect to other countries, that I am wholly opposed to the state being used by any religious group, Catholic or Protestant, to compel, prohibit or persecute the free exercise of any other religion, and that goes for any persecutions at any time by anyone in any country. And I hope that you and I condemn with equal fervor those nations which deny their Presidency to Protestants and those which deny it to Catholics. And rather than cite the misdeeds of those who differ, I would also cite the record of the Catholic church in such nations as Ireland and France—and the independence of such statesmen as [German chancellor Konrad] Adenauer and [French president Charles] de Gaulle.

Here, too, Kennedy embraced his Catholicism. He argued that it was possible to be a Catholic president and to honor the American constitutional system in a manner that preserved the separation of church and state and religious liberty. By this point he had systematically answered the array of Protestant charges that had been leveled against him in the campaign and also turned some of those very arguments back on their sources. Then came the powerful, dramatic conclusion:

> But let me stress again that these are my views—for, contrary to common newspaper usage, I am not the Catholic candidate for President. I am the Democratic Party's candidate for President who happens also to be a Catholic. I do not speak for my church on public matters—and the church does not speak for me.

Several things were going on in this paragraph. Kennedy was taking pains to undermine the notion that he was a formal representative of the church and thus dependent upon the hierarchy, both in Rome and in the United States. He clearly reminded his Texas and national audience that he was the Democratic candidate, and certainly most southern Protestants were Democrats in 1960. If he could break the link that his anti-Catholic detractors had tried to forge between him and the leadership of the Catholic church and solidify his political independence, he would go a long way in overcoming the force of the anti-Catholic narrative. Yet it is worth noting that he did not deny his Catholic faith in the process, as some have read this speech to say. He did deny that he spoke for the church and denied that the church spoke for him *on public matters*. This is far different from saying he was not a Catholic or that he did not take his faith seriously. He was denying the specific historical argument of his opponents.

The next two paragraphs elaborated the nature of the relationship he had as a Catholic with his faith, his church, and how he would form public policy:

> Whenever an issue may come before me as President, if I should be elected—on birth control, divorce, censorship, gambling, or any other subject—I will make my decision in accordance with these views, in accordance with what my conscience tells me to be in the national interest, and without regard to outside religious pressure or dictates. And no power or threat of punishment could cause me to decide otherwise.
>
> But if the time should ever come—and I do not concede any conflict to be even remotely possible—when my office would require me to either violate my conscience or violate the national interest,

then I would resign the office; and I hope that any other conscientious public servant would do the same.

Again, Kennedy asserted his independence from the Catholic hierarchy on specific policy issues. He would decide those issues based on what his conscience told him was in the national interest, not based on the views of clergy. He directly denied that religious pressure would have an impact on his policy-making processes. He was once again specifically denying a cardinal point of the pan-Protestant critique of his faith.

Critical to this section was the strategy of offering his resignation should he face an irreconcilable conflict between his faith and the duties of his office. While some commentators have suggested that this statement indicated Kennedy's bottom-line secularism, the sentence was crafted to emphasize the power of his faith. In a conflict between his conscience and the duties of the office, he would side ultimately with his faith. But at the same time, he did not believe such a conflict was a real possibility. John Cogley noted that he had suggested this strategy in a column he wrote for *Commonweal* in response to Kennedy's *Look* magazine interview, in which he felt Kennedy had ceded too much ground to his Protestant critics. Cogley was surprised that the line appeared in the Houston speech and did not know how it got there.

Bishop John Wright's claim that he suggested the line to Sorensen is convincing. His argument was that such a declaration from Kennedy would show the world that he was serious about his faith and that he was confident there was no conflict between his Catholicism and the office he sought. It would be a dramatic way to affirm his belief in the compatibility of Catholic duty and public service. Sorensen confessed that it would probably be a tough sell to make to Kennedy, but he was apparently successful. Kennedy closed the speech on a strong note of resistance, perhaps even defiance:

> But I do not intend to apologize for these views to my critics of either Catholic or Protestant faith—nor do I intend to disavow either my views or my church in order to win this election. If I should lose on the real issues, I shall return to my seat in the Senate, satisfied that I had tried my best and was fairly judged. But if this election is decided on the basis that 40 million Americans lost their chance of being President on the day they were baptized, then it is the whole nation that will be the loser, in the eyes of Catholics and non-Catholics around the world, in the eyes of history, and in the eyes of our own people.
>
> But if, on the other hand, I should win this election, then I shall devote every effort of mind and spirit to fulfilling the oath of the Presidency—practically identical, I might add, to the oath I have taken

for 14 years in Congress. For, without reservation, I can "solemnly swear that I will faithfully execute the office of President of the United States, and will to the best of my ability preserve, protect and defend the Constitution, so help me God."

Here, Kennedy reinforced the theme that he was not adapting his views to placate theological critics. He was not running away from his faith; he was explaining it. But even more important, Kennedy had shifted the frame of the debate. Rather than rebut Protestant arguments that he should be disqualified for his Catholicism, he suggested that the real problem was that he was being attacked unfairly and that the Protestant arguments were incorrect and un-American. This played directly into the polling data that suggested that the perception that Kennedy was a victim of religious bigotry would move undecided voters into his column. By reminding his audience that the world, history, and the American people would not look kindly on his rejection solely because of his faith, he reminded the country that fundamental democratic principles were at stake. The issue at stake was bigotry, not his Catholicism.

The speech drew applause from the assembled clergy. While many treatments of the speech stop here, it is important to note that the program segued into an extended question-and-answer session that was also part of the live television broadcast across the state of Texas. The transcript of the speech is 8 pages long, while the question-and-answer session is 26 pages. Clearly, the clergy still had issues to take up with Kennedy.

Kennedy fielded questions on several topics. The first, from a Baptist minister, asked whether or not, as a Catholic, Kennedy could have attended the current meeting if it had been held in a Protestant church, since the Catholic leadership forbade Catholics to attend Protestant services. Kennedy replied that he could attend such an event or any related event, such as a private ceremony, wedding, funeral, or any service that had any connection with his public office.

Then Kennedy took two questions, yet again, about the Reverend Poling and the Four Chaplains Chapel episode. Kennedy painstakingly went through the whole episode and his view of what had transpired, defending himself yet again from a spurious charge that never seemed to go away. He explained his withdrawal from the speaking engagement on the grounds that he was not credentialed to be a representative of the Catholic church. He closed his second long response by noting that he was uncomfortable contradicting the Reverend Poling, for whom he had respect as well as for his son, who was one of the four chaplains who gave his life and was memorialized in the chapel. It was a gracious and touching conclusion to what had to be an infuriating moment.

Kennedy took a question from the president of a local Bible college and pastor, asking him if he would use his influence with Catholic countries that sought to persecute Protestants and limit their ability to propagate their faith. Kennedy responded that he would use his influence as president to encourage the development of freedom all over the world. He believed in the right to free speech, the right of assembly, and the right to free religious practice, and he would stand for those rights all around the world without regard to religious or special beliefs. This response drew applause.

Next, he was asked by another Baptist minister if he would appeal to Cardinal Cushing in Boston to present his views on the separation of church and state to the Vatican so it might authorize Kennedy's views for all Catholics in the United States. If Kennedy answered that he would take the question to Cushing, he would show that he was subservient to the hierarchy. If he refused to do so, it would imply that he knew his views were novel and would not be acceptable to the hierarchy. As an aside, it might be noted that this question bears the marks of several episodes in the New Testament where the opponents of Jesus play "stump the Messiah" by peppering Jesus with questions that offer only bad options. The irony here, of course, is that it was a Christian clergyman who played the role reserved for the opponents of Jesus in the Gospels.

The exchange between Kennedy and the minister is instructive. The pastor read a resolution passed by a group of Baptist pastors in St. Louis. The statement appealed to Kennedy to have Cardinal Cushing—"Mr. Kennedy's own hierarchical superior in Boston"—present to the Vatican Kennedy's sincere statement about the separation of church and state and religious freedom as represented in the Constitution so that the Vatican "may officially authorize such a belief for all Roman Catholics in the United States."

In reply to this challenge, Kennedy noted that, having just said that he did not accept the right of any ecclesiastical official to tell him what to do "in the sphere of my public responsibility as an elected official, I do not propose also to ask Cardinal Cushing to ask the Vatican to take some action." He went on to say that he was confident that his position publicly represented the opinion of an overwhelming majority of American Catholics. When pressed by the pastor that the Vatican had not made such an endorsement, Kennedy, in effect, said that he did not care:

Well, let me say that anyone that I would appoint to any office as a senator, or as a President, would, I hope, hold the same view, of necessity, of their living up to not only the letter of the Constitution but the spirit.

If I may say so, I am a Catholic. I have stated my view very clearly. I don't find any difficulty in stating that view.

In my judgment, it is the view of American Catholics from one end of the country to the other.

Why, because, as long as I can state it in a way which is, I hope, satisfactory to you, do you possibly think that I represent a viewpoint which is hostile to the Catholic church in the United States?

I believe I am stating the viewpoint that Catholics in this country hold towards the happy relationship which exists between church and state.

Later, he added:

I have not submitted my statement, before I gave it, to the Catholic church. I did not submit it to Cardinal Cushing, but in my judgment Cardinal Yaling, who is the Cardinal from the diocese of which I am a member, would approve this statement in the same way he approved the 1948 statement of the Bishops.

In my judgment, and I am not a student of theology, I am stating what I believe to be the position of—my personal position, and also the position of the great majority of Catholics across the United States. I hope that other countries may someday enjoy the same happy relationship of a separation in church and state, whether they are in Catholic countries or non-Catholic countries.

Now it seems to me that I am the one who is running for the office of the Presidency and not Cardinal Cushing and not anyone else.

The clergymen responded with applause.

The final questioner, V. E. Howard, a Church of Christ minister, read a long series of quotations from various Catholic sources. If nothing else, Howard displayed the fundamentalist scholastic skills that not even the Southern Baptists in the audience could exceed. When taken together, these quotes twisted the Catholic doctrine of mental reservation to say that Catholics were able to lie and were even obliged to lie in certain public circumstances. Howard was clearly attempting to imply that Kennedy could lie about his relationship with the Catholic church in order to preserve his electoral chances. Howard was interrupted when several members of the audience stood up and asked the Reverend Meza, the moderator from the Houston clergy, to ask the speaker to stop. Howard paused and posed two questions to Kennedy: Did he subscribe to the doctrine of mental reservation as outlined in the quoted sources? Did he submit to the authority of the pope, whom he quoted?

Kennedy responded effectively by saying that he did not agree with the quotations. He could comment better if he had the entire quotations in front of him, but if the upshot was that a Catholic could take an oath knowing that he did not believe the oath or did not have to tell the truth, he did not agree with that. Kennedy then said that he had not heard Howard's question about the pope.

Howard repeated the line from Pope John XXIII: "Catholics must unite their strength toward the common aid and the Catholic hierarchy has the right and duty of guiding them," and asked if Kennedy subscribed to that. The candidate replied:

> Well now, I couldn't subscribe. Guiding them in what area? If you are talking about in the area of faith and morals, and the instructions of the church, I would think any Baptist minister or Congregationalist minister has the right and duty to try to guide his flock.
>
> If you mean by that statement that the Pope or anyone else could bind me by a statement in the fulfillment of my public duties, I say no. If that statement is intended to mean, and it is very difficult to comment on a sentence taken out of an article which I have not read, but if that is intended to imply that the hierarchy has some obligation or an obligation to attempt to guide the members of the Catholic church, then that may be proper, but it all depends on the previous language of what you mean by "guide."
>
> If you mean "direct" or "instruct" on matters dealing with the organization of the faith, the details of the faith, then, of course, they have that obligation.
>
> If you mean by that that under that he could guide me or anyone could guide me or direct me in fulfilling my public duty then I do not agree.

Howard then moved in for what he must have thought was the kill, thanked Kennedy, and then asked, "Then you do not agree with the pope in that statement?" But Kennedy was not to be cornered by a Church of Christ preacher:

> See, that is why I wanted to be careful because that statement seems to me to be taken out of context that you just made to me.
>
> I could not tell you what the Pope meant unless I had the entire article. I would be glad to state to you that no one can direct me in the fulfillment of my duties as a public official under the United States Constitution, that I am directed to do, to the people of the United States, sworn to on an oath to God.

> Now, that is my flat statement. I would not want to go into
> details on a sentence which you read to me which I may not under-
> stand completely. I think my statement is quite clear.

Kennedy again received applause from the ministers.

His final inquisitor raised the only remaining Protestant shibboleth, the Syllabus of Errors, a series of propositions that had been condemned by Pope Pius IX in 1864. These propositions represented the
chief heresies of the time and were denied to be true. Each error was
refuted with references to past papal documents containing summary
statements of often complex and nuanced positions. The 80 theses were
grouped into 10 sections, including civil society and liberalism. The Syllabus rejected the separation of church and state in thesis 55. Of course,
these theses were particularly controversial in America. And as such,
the Syllabus was the most frequently cited source in the anti-Catholic
literature of the entire campaign. These citations were the backbone of
the theological case against Kennedy.

The Reverend Robert McClaren of Westminster Presbyterian
Church in Houston rose and congratulated Kennedy on his clear
belief in the separation of church and state. But he wanted to follow
up on Kennedy's statement that "if you found, by some remote possibility, a real concrete conflict between your oath of office as President
that you would resign that office if it were in real conflict with your
church."

Kennedy corrected McClaren. He had said if the conflict were with
his *conscience*. McClaren then segued into three specific things that
were condemned by the Syllabus of Errors which, McClaren noted, the
Encyclopedia of Catholicism (written in 1912) said was still binding on
all Catholics. These were denunciations of the separation of church and
state, the freedom to practice other religions other than Catholicism,
and the freedom of conscience. McClaren asked Kennedy, "Do you
feel these as binding you that you hold your oath of office above your
allegiance to the pope on these issues?"

Kennedy marched through the three questions directly. He supported the separation of church and state, as had the U.S. Catholic
bishops since 1948 and as did most American Catholics. He believed
that any faith should be able to propagate itself without limitation by
the state. And he believed in the freedom of conscience. As time was
running out, he gave this conclusion to the evening's session:

> Let me say finally that I am delighted to come here today. I don't want
> anyone to think, because they interrogate me on this very important

question, that I regard that as unfair or unreasonable or that some-body who is concerned about the matter is prejudiced or bigoted.

I think religion is basic in the establishment of the American sys-tem, and, therefore, any candidate for office, I think, should submit himself to the questions of any reasonable man.

My only limit to that would be that if somebody said, "Regard-less of Senator Kennedy's position, regardless of how much evidence he has given that what he says he means, I still won't vote for him because he is a member of that church."

I would consider that unreasonable. What I consider to be rea-sonable in an exercise of free will and free choice is to ask Senator Kennedy to state his views as broadly as possible. Investigate his record to see whether he states what he believes and then make an indepen-dent and a rational judgment as to whether he could be entrusted with this highly important position.

So I want you to know that I am grateful to you for inviting me tonight. I am sure that I have made no converts to my church, but I hope that, at least, in my view, which I believe to be the view of my fellow Catholics who hold office, I hope that it may be of some value in at least assisting you to make a careful judgment.

With that, the meeting ended with applause, bringing to a close perhaps the single most dramatic public moment in the entire cam-paign. In the immediate aftermath, the press hailed the speech as a triumph. Kennedy was pleased. The reaction of Protestant elites, both liberal and conservative, would become clear in short order.

The general election campaign had only just started. By now, the Kennedy campaign knew that the religion issue would not be fully resolved until Election Day. There were still two months of campaigning ahead of them, and anything could happen. On the Nixon side, the shadow strategy of organizing Protestants below the radar had done more harm than good. Frustration was building within the campaign over the failure of the Peale meeting and the success of the Houston speech.

Theodore White gave perhaps the best contemporary summary of the period between the Democratic National Convention through the Houston speech. He noted that round one of the general election had begun for Kennedy with euphoria over the victory in Los Angeles, had swung almost to despair over the Peale meeting, but rose to a point of cautious hope in Houston.[51] White summarized the impact of the speech:

When he had finished, he had not only closed Round One of his election campaign—he had for the first time more fully and explicitly than any other thinker of his faith defined the personal doctrine of a modern Catholic in a democratic society.

How much effect he had that evening no one could tell. He had addressed a sullen, almost hostile audience when he began. He had won the applause of many and the personal sympathies of more; the meeting had closed in respect and friendship. But how far the victory in this hall would extend its glow no one could measure. The national TV networks were to broadcast his performance the next day in fragments around the nation....

Nevertheless the candidate, always happiest as a man when confronting crisis with action, felt better. As if miraculously, his cracking voice began to clear; in a few weeks, he could dispense entirely with the constant attendance of the voice coach who had hitherto accompanied him.

The next day he barnstormed to growing crowds under the patronage of Lyndon B. Johnson and Sam Rayburn; the following day to crowds in St. Louis; and then he was off to New Jersey and New York and ever greater throngs in the industrial Northeast, where he meant to win.[52]

Kennedy had survived a near-death campaign experience. He had turned adversity into triumph with the Houston speech. His faltering West Coast trip was now forgotten, and he entered the general election campaign with renewed momentum. He had directly confronted the issue of his faith and in so doing found his stride. Polls indicated that the race with Nixon was tight. The remainder of the campaign would prove to be tough.

8

THE ENDGAME
··

Coming off the Houston speech, the Kennedy campaign was in good spirits. The speech had created a sense of hope and momentum on the heels of the offensive launched by the Peale meeting.

Yet the staffers faced a massive force of grassroots anti-Catholicism that was just beginning to flex its muscles. Aided and abetted by the Nixon campaign, a spasm of anti-Catholic literature was soaking the country to an extent not seen before or since. The decentralized engines of Protestant bigotry were ramping up for the fall election, and an astonishing array of co-belligerents was plotting Kennedy's defeat. It would be one of the last pan-Protestant moments of cooperation in American history. One thing that could still unite liberal, moderate, evangelical, and fundamentalist Protestants in 1960 was their common foe, the Roman Catholic church.

The sheer size of the effort was extraordinary. Sorensen claimed that over 300 different anti-Catholic tracts were distributed to over 20 million homes along with countless mailings and radio and television broadcasts. He put a price tag of several hundred thousand dollars on the effort.[1] While he had evidence from the Peale meeting that the Nixon campaign was behind some of this, he never directly accused it. It is impossible to determine precisely how much of this effort bubbled up from the Protestant world itself and how much was generated, bought, and paid for by the campaign.

The Fair Campaign Practices Committee, in collaboration with the Democratic National Committee, collected and monitored anti-Catholic literature. They found 360 individual publications and tracts devoted to the campaign. These publications included the work of large national groups, such as POAU, the National Association of Evangelicals, and the Masons, and individual sermons from legions of Southern Baptist and Church of Christ preachers.[2] The titles suggest that the arguments ranged from the salacious to the scholastic. From *Abolish the Nunneries and Save the Girls* to *What If America Becomes 51% Catholic*, no argument, it seems, was too outrageous to find its way into print.

The committee received over 2,000 complaints regarding the religion issue. It divided the literature into four categories: vile, 5%; dishonest, 25%; unfair, 35%; responsible, 35%. The phenomenon was not limited to the South; anti-Catholic literature was circulated in every state. Three states—California, Pennsylvania, and Minnesota—were the origin of one-third of the scurrilous anti-Catholic tracts.[3] From the grassroots to the highest echelons of their leadership, these churches and organizations saw defeating Kennedy as a struggle of historical importance.

Southern Baptist elites were among the most vocal and active. By this point in the campaign, the Southern Baptist Convention had passed a resolution, which Orland Armstrong had helped to engineer, expressing reservations about a Catholic president. Billy Graham had helped to set the Peale meeting in motion and had shared his mailing list with the anti-Kennedy efforts.

Graham also wrote to Kennedy and mentioned a potential bombshell in the form of malicious gossip he had "overheard" about Kennedy.[4] Graham had taken it to two of Kennedy's closest friends, and they had "clarified" it for him. He promised that it had not gone beyond him and expressed that it was unfortunate that political leaders were subject to these ugly rumors. It is tempting to overinterpret Graham's intentions here and see this as a veiled threat. But it is more likely that Graham was just trying to protect his reputation by telling Kennedy that he was not part of any Protestant smear campaign. While he would vote for Nixon, Graham wrote, if Kennedy were elected, he would have Graham's wholehearted loyalty and support.

Other Southern Baptists were hardly as coy or as concerned about their standing with Kennedy. W. A. Criswell, the pastor of First Baptist Church in Dallas, preached and subsequently published a blistering sermon against Kennedy. The NAE published it in its monthly magazine, and Criswell told the *New York Times* that he expected to distribute over 200,000 copies before the election.[5]

The sermon was a classic of the genre. After an impassioned defense of the American tradition of religious freedom, Criswell said that Americans need to get over their reticence to criticize Catholics because Catholicism is not only a religion, "it is a political tyranny." When elected, Catholics sought to overwhelm political systems and force elevation of their Church above all others. Kennedy's election would mark the beginning of the end of religious liberty in America.

The Reverend W. O. Vaught, a vice president of the Southern Baptist Convention, preached a similar sermon at Immanuel Baptist Church in Little Rock. The Arkansas Baptist State Convention announced plans for a statewide campaign against Kennedy, including a public rally in Little Rock on October 3.[6] Ramsey Pollard, the president of the Southern Baptist Convention, likewise preached sermons like these in his home congregation, Bellevue Baptist Church in Memphis.

One of the only discernible hints of Baptist dissent came from the Baptist Joint Committee on Public Affairs. The members of the BJC had been discussing the likelihood of a Catholic presidential candidate since 1957.[7] Throughout the late fifties, they had reminded their constituents of the constitutional provision that no religious test should be required for public office.

When Kennedy emerged as a leading candidate in 1959, the BJC began to express concern about Kennedy's views on the separation of church and state. But through the spring of 1960, the committee established a moderate posture on the possibility of a Catholic candidate. The May–June issue of its *Report from the Capital* featured a long article that came to three conclusions. First, the constitutional prohibition of a religious test for office must be applied. Second, any candidate's religion was relevant to his stance on many policy issues, making it permissible to ask questions of candidates regarding religion. Third, since all of the candidates were politicians, there should be room for the possibility that a candidate might ignore principles set out by his denomination in order to attract votes. At the conclusion of the article, the BJC advocated observing the principles promulgated by the Fair Campaign Practices Committee. Prominent among them was a rejection of "stirring up, fostering, or tolerating religious animosity, or injecting elements of a candidate's faith not relevant to the duties of the office he seeks."[8]

Yet Baptist anxiety over the possibility of a Kennedy victory led the BJC to voice continued concern over the possible conflict between a Catholic president and the church in areas where they disagreed. After the election, the BJC expressed its satisfaction with Kennedy's good record throughout the campaign on church-state issues. While Southern Baptists were at the vanguard of anti-Kennedy efforts, the work of the committee illustrates that Baptists were not a monolithic force.

At the grassroots level, there was an extremely powerful Protestant reaction to Kennedy's Catholicism. Carr P. Collins, the insurance millionaire whom Orland K. Armstrong had approached for funds to spearhead Nixon's work among conservative Protestants, founded a group called Texans for Nixon. Collins was a member of Criswell's large First Baptist Church in Dallas, and he quickly became a controversial figure in the campaign.

On August 11, Collins wrote to Leonard Hall of the Nixon campaign and the Republican National Committee to report that the inaugural meeting of Texans for Nixon had gone exceedingly well. The determination and enthusiasm of the attendees was the strongest he had seen in his 40 years of Texas politics. Collins told the *Dallas Morning News* that Nixon would win Texas by a larger margin than had Eisenhower in 1952 and 1956.[9]

Collins purchased radio time on two 50,000-watt stations in Dallas and ran 15-minute programs Monday through Friday.[10] The vituperative nature of Collins's radio broadcasts soon caught the attention of the Fair Campaign Practices Committee and the national media. On September 7, a Laredo, Texas, resident, Julia Smith, wrote to the committee to complain that she had heard a broadcast in which Collins made vicious attacks on Democrats, including the charges that Kennedy was a socialist, a friend of Communists, and a dishonest man.[11] She had written to Collins and the Republican National Committee to no avail.

Bruce Felknor, the executive director of the committee, replied to Smith in late October that the organization had shared her concerns with both the Republican and Democratic national committees. But Collins had toned down his rhetoric lately, so they would not be taking any formal action.

In the meantime, the national press had picked up the story. On September 15, David Broder wrote a story on Collins's broadcasts for the *Washington Star*. He highlighted Collins's accusations that Kennedy was soft toward Communists and that he was the Democratic nominee only because his Catholic friends had handed him the nomination.[12] Broder quoted a Methodist minister from Dallas, Baxton Bryant, as saying that Collins was the guiding hand in the anti-Catholic campaign. Collins denied injecting religion into the campaign, but Broder had copies of the scripts of the broadcasts and was able to show that

Collins had raised religion, subtly and sometimes not so subtly. Bryant told another reporter that he had attended a clergy meeting in Dallas convened by the Reverend Tom Landers, who claimed to be in contact with political leaders for Nixon's campaign.[13]

The Republican National Committee chair, Senator Thruston Morton, told Broder that, as far as he knew, no Republican funds were being used for Collins's broadcasts. He promised to contact Collins and insist that he remove any attacks on Kennedy's religion from the broadcasts. The DNC chair, Senator Henry Jackson, issued a press statement calling on Nixon to renounce Collins.

Collins hotly denied Broder's charges.[14] While he often quoted editorials mentioning Kennedy's religion, he denied that this was intended to cast doubt upon Kennedy's ability to separate himself from the Roman Catholic church in matters of state. He defiantly said that he would not make changes to the broadcasts: "Jack Kennedy has deliberately set out to make a martyr of himself on the Catholic issue. He started this campaign to get sympathy in his acceptance speech in Los Angeles and has never missed a chance to keep the religious issue alive."

One sign of just how closely the Kennedy campaign followed these sorts of religious flare-ups is that James Wine had his staff compile a dossier on Collins.[15] It contained newspaper excerpts that showed Collins had been a leader against Al Smith in 1928. At the time, he had been accused of being a member of the Ku Klux Klan but denied it. The file also contained Collins's response to a reporter's question about whether he would support Nixon if he were Catholic. There wasn't any use in speculating on anything as hypothetical as that, Collins had said.

Despite Senator Morton's apparent ignorance, there is evidence to suggest that the Nixon campaign was aware of the work of Texans for Nixon. In addition to Collins's letter to Leonard Hall, Nixon himself wrote to Collins after the election, thanking him for his efforts and soliciting his advice for the future, as did campaign manager Robert Finch.[16] Finch in particular thanked Collins for his invaluable work in Texas.

Another conservative Protestant denomination in the South, the Churches of Christ, produced a large volume of anti-Catholic tracts and papered the countryside with them. All of the major periodicals in the Churches of Christ wrote against Kennedy's candidacy with the usual set of arguments.[17] V. E. Howard, one of Kennedy's inquisitors in Houston, printed a 32-page tract called *The White House: American or Roman?* At one point, Howard claimed that 400,000 copies were circulating, and he was aiming for a million. The enterprising David Broder asked Howard how much they cost to print and who was paying for it.[18] Howard refused to answer but said that he offered them to listeners on his radio broadcasts and also sold them in bulk. His largest single order, he said, had been for 10,000 copies, but he refused to divulge its source.

On October 9, Batsell Barrett Baxter, the minister at the Hillsboro Church of Christ in Nashville, Tennessee, preached the sermon "A Dangerous Doctrine." Baxter was a widely revered minister in the denomination for, among other things, his appearances on the nationally broadcast television show, *The Herald of Truth*. The sermon was emblematic of the kind of anti-Catholic rhetoric that permeated conservative Protestant pulpits and tracts in that era. Baxter began by asserting that, in addition to the Communist threat, America faced a threat to religious freedom in the form of the Roman Catholic church. After citing a long litany of Catholic sources, and without mentioning Kennedy's name, Baxter concluded, "[I]t would seem wise and even necessary that all non-Catholics oppose the further growth and spread of the Roman Catholic Church, until such time as the Roman Catholic Church changes its doctrine of intolerance toward other religions."[19]

All of this was unremarkable in terms of the arguments that were advanced. The iconic Baxter was one of the leading ministers in the Churches of Christ at that time, and Hillsboro was an upscale and prestigious congregation. Chet Huntley of NBC News had sent a crew to film Baxter preaching the sermon to an empty sanctuary the day before. NBC also filmed Ramsey Pollard, president of the Southern Baptist Convention, at his church in Memphis. But after the sermon, Congressman Joe Evins, from the Fourth Congressional District in eastern Tennessee, who was in attendance that Sunday, asked Baxter if he might say a few words to the congregation.

Evins entered the pulpit and briefly criticized what he labeled a partisan sermon and called for religious toleration. A firestorm erupted. Evins, a member of the Churches of Christ and a Kennedy supporter, was roundly criticized in church circles, and the local and national media wrote about the event.[20]

The elders of the congregation decided to have Baxter's sermon printed as a tract and distributed throughout the country. A wealthy member of the congregation, William Lipscomb Davis, paid for 60,000 copies to be printed.[21] Davis was a financial contributor to Baxter's national television show, which had been founded by James Walter Nichols, who had been contacted by Orland K. Armstrong when he began organizing conservative Protestants on behalf of the Nixon campaign.

Evins received a great deal of mail from members of the Churches of Christ, castigating him for his nervy impromptu rebuttal of the iconic Baxter. In another sign of how closely and seriously the Kennedy campaign monitored anti-Catholicism in key states, Robert Kennedy wrote to Evins: "I read about your recent action in speaking out so forthrightly on the religious question. I would like you to know that I very much appreciate what you did and I am sure that Senator Kennedy does too."[22]

In addition to Protestant denominations and individual preachers, groups like the National Association of Evangelicals and its spin-off, Citizens for Religious Freedom, were also working against Kennedy.

On September 13, just after Kennedy's Houston speech, CRF sent a letter to its constituents and released a statement. The press release sounded a conciliatory note, commending Kennedy for making "the most complete, unequivocal and reassuring statement which could be expected of any person in his position."[23] But the statement quickly pivoted:

> The only remaining question is whether his statement is acceptable to his Church and, of course, he is in no position to answer on that question. We do hope that endorsement of his position will be forthcoming from sources of authority in the Roman Catholic Church. When such an endorsement is forthcoming, the question will be settled for all thinking citizens.[24]

While the NAE had taken a public relations beating in the national media over the Peale meeting, the political reality was that the millions of congregants in its member churches were not usually swayed by the mainstream press. In the NAE's magazine, Donald Gill, the director of Citizens for Religious Freedom, gave voice to a common view that Kennedy was purposefully raising the issue of his religion as a political tool. Kennedy was portraying himself as the underdog because of his Catholicism, making a subtle pitch for votes by appealing to Americans' sense of fair play.[25] Gill hinted that the attack on Peale revealed the extent to which the press had a vested interest in Kennedy's success. That alone, he argued, should get Protestants' attention.[26] Citizens for Religious Freedom had a plan for a ground war in the general election, and it would not be dissuaded by the debacle of the Peale meeting. Its efforts centered on targeting congregations on Reformation Sunday in late October.

The primary focus of the NAE's work before the election was a massive campaign to distribute anti-Catholic literature to its member denominations. At the executive committee meeting in St. Louis on October 10, NAE director George Ford reported that a full-page ad had been purchased in *Christianity Today* and that approximately 65,000 letters had been sent out.[27] Twenty denominations were cooperating on the distribution of 750,000 bulletin inserts and 400,000 NAE folders and the mailing of 500,000 copies of a reprint of Ford's article on the dangers of a Catholic president. It was a massive distribution of literature across a broad spectrum of the evangelical world.

The next day, the larger board of administration of the NAE adopted "A Statement of Concern," which challenged the thesis that Protestant discussions of Kennedy's Catholicism were bigotry. The board believed that the religion issue had become "distorted" in the campaign. The failure of the Catholic hierarchy to repudiate its interference in the private consciences of citizens and in the political affairs of governments impelled NAE to register its views.[28] The statement called for an end to the emotional attacks in the media against people who were raising legitimate concerns, the threats of reprisal on the part of government, and the boycotts and social pressure against people and organizations who had the courage to speak their minds. It was probably reacting against the work of the Fair Campaign Practices Committee, which threatened to report to the Internal Revenue Service any possible violations of the nonprofit status of groups it believed were engaged in prohibited partisan activities.

In the weeks prior to Reformation Sunday (traditionally, the last Sunday of October), which commemorates the start of the Reformation, the NAE would conduct a Stand Up and Be Counted program. Over 100,000 pastors had been contacted and sent sample material for their congregants. The cover letter to the pastors cut directly to the chase: "If a Roman Catholic is elected President—what then? The Church of Rome will have a new, great advantage and the United States will no longer be recognized as a Protestant nation in the eyes of the world."[29] The letter asked congregations to set aside the first prayer meeting of each month until the election to pray for the nation and to emphasize the danger of a Roman Catholic president and other problems (such as Communist infiltration and the general moral and spiritual decadence in the country). They were also asked to order materials for Reformation Sunday and to take up a special collection for the NAE to underwrite this national campaign. Ford told the administration board that the NAE anticipated reaching millions of churchgoers with this effort.

It is hard to judge what impact these efforts had on the election. The Reformation Sunday activities did not generate much media attention. Yet that was not their purpose. The NAE was narrowcasting its message to a specific segment of American society, not broadcasting it to the general population. It would seem fair to conclude that it might have helped to shore up evangelical opposition to Kennedy.

With all of the activities of various conservative Protestant groups and the ongoing work of organizations like POAU, a formidable array of tactics, people, and money were assembled to defeat Kennedy.

Meanwhile, the Kennedy campaign was hard at work. Immediately after the Houston speech, it began a concerted effort to multiply its message, buying television time on 22 Texas stations, at a cost of almost $10,000, to broadcast Kennedy's speech.[30] The Texas Democratic Party requested 20,000 copies of the speech and 20,000 copies of the campaign's "religious memorandum" for statewide distribution.[31] The campaign produced three different half-hour film versions of the speech, which were shown on television at least 193 times in 40 states.[32]

Lou Harris did a series of polls in the crucial state of Texas, where religion was a huge factor. Texas had voted Republican three times that century, in 1928 against Al Smith and in the previous two elections for Eisenhower. The campaign's ability to meet the religion issue head on would be crucial in this pivotal state.[33]

The first poll showed Kennedy leading Nixon 45%–41%, with 14% of the voters undecided. Harris concluded that Johnson could persuade many of these voters, but the religion issue loomed large. Anti-Catholicism in Texas was as "virulent and rampant" as anywhere in the country: "Nearly everyone knows Kennedy is a Catholic, and what is more, very few members of the electorate have been spared a sermon in church, a lecture by a neighbor, or a mailed piece of extreme anti-Catholic literature."[34] If Nixon were to prevail, it would be because he had been "abetted in heavy measure by religious prejudices against a Catholic becoming President."[35]

Yet there was some reason for hope. Texas Catholics were breaking for Kennedy by huge margins, and Harris believed that anti-Catholic bias had peaked. Plus, Protestants had only just begun to respond, as they had in West Virginia, by rebelling against the excesses of anti-Catholic bigotry. Harris's breakdown of the vote into Baptists and Methodists led him to believe that Methodists might be especially susceptible to persuasion, particularly by Johnson.[36] Harris pushed for congregational outreach, predominantly to Methodists, and counseled Kennedy to hit the religion issue hard.

A month later, Harris noted significant progress. The campaign tour, the Houston speech, and the first debate with Nixon had combined to extend Kennedy's lead to 48%–40%, with 12% undecided. Kennedy continued to lead Nixon among Catholics, but now led among Methodists as well and had closed the gap among Baptists to 8%.[37] But the issue was far from settled, and Harris thought that Kennedy should continue to raise the question of religious bigotry through the national media. Meanwhile, James Wine went to work to implement the plan Sorensen had drawn up. With a staff and an informal advisory committee, the director of community relations would respond to correspondence from voters, assemble a fact book to be mailed in bulk, prepare television films, massage religious and secular media, establish regional and local committees of religious leaders, work with religious watchdog groups to monitor bigoted material, promote a nationwide conference with national religious leaders, and offer reassurance to POAU and similar organizations.[38] It was an ambitious and unprecedented plan. Wine jumped into the fray, employing his network of connections from his time working for the National Council of Churches in Washington.

One of his first products was a memo to all state campaign coordinators. He noted that the religion issue could flare up quickly and without warning, so they needed to remain alert and ready to defend.[39] To help in that effort, Wine gave each of them a list of persons in their states who were willing and able to assist the campaign in responding on religion issues. The heart of the strategy was to be aggressive in responding to outbreaks of religious bigotry but not to raise the issue without provocation. Wine enclosed copies of the "religion kit" and noted that a 30-minute film of the Houston speech was available for use.

The religion kit consisted of a series of statements on religious toleration from a number of committees and individuals. The most important one was a 10-point statement that, among other things, called for resistance to a religious test for elected office, affirmed that a candidate's faith is relevant to his conduct in office, and declared that no religious organization should seek to influence public officials for its own gain. Its 90 signers included John Bennett, Reinhold Niebuhr, Father Robert Drinan, Father John Courtney Murray, Richard Cardinal Cushing, and Bishop Bromley Oxnam.[40]

Wine provided Sorensen with updates on his work. One of the more enigmatic reports from Wine detailed a September 30 meeting in New York with a committee of the Synagogue Council of America, a Jewish umbrella organization.[41] The purpose of the meeting was for the elected and administrative heads of the organization to express their support for Kennedy. At the same time, though, they were alarmed by reports that in several states many Jews were sitting out the election. Nixon had met with some leaders of the Jewish community in New York "in a successful manner." Wine said that the problem was religious in nature and that "certain assurances," if offered by Kennedy himself, could completely allay the problem. Wine suggested that Kennedy meet with a representative group of these leaders in October and give them the assurances they needed. Wine also reported on his efforts to woo Episcopal clergy who were sympathetic to Kennedy and told of an upcoming meeting in Washington with a group of Protestant clergy who were interested in helping the campaign.

Wine also counseled Robert Kennedy on the need for better coordination of the campaign's messaging. Robert Kennedy and Senator Henry "Scoop" Jackson, chair of the Democratic National Committee, had both been attacking Nixon for fomenting religious bigotry. In fact, Jackson came as close as any figure related to the Kennedy campaign to accusing Nixon directly of financing and organizing the explosion of anti-Catholic literature and activity. On September 14, Jackson had pointed out the flood of material being distributed and challenged news organizations to investigate the source and financing of this effort.[42] The next day, he called on Nixon to specifically repudiate Citizens for Religious Freedom, the organizers of the Peale meeting, as well as Peale himself and Carr P. Collins, the Texas millionaire who was making inflammatory charges against Kennedy on the radio.[43]

Wine thought that this stream of communication might prove counterproductive.[44] The campaign needed to coordinate its messages in order to maximize their effectiveness. Wine was working quietly within POAU, the NCC, and other Protestant enclaves. He wanted to make sure that Robert Kennedy and Jackson knew the details of this work so they would not inadvertently alienate the campaign's friends inside these groups. If all three of them were on the same page, that would decrease the likelihood that they would do some harm. Wine's ear for nuance was more finely tuned to Protestant sensitivities than were either Jackson or Robert Kennedy. He recognized the delicate balance between reassuring Protestant leaders in private and attacking Nixon in public.

Wine's effectiveness as a political firefighter can be seen in his management of one crisis that threatened the campaign. Henry Van Dusen, the president of Union Theological Seminary in New York City, was conducting a malicious whispering campaign against Kennedy. On August 2, Van Dusen had written to Adlai Stevenson, relaying his fears that Kennedy was unfit for the office of the presidency due to his sexual promiscuity.[45] These "rumors" had allegedly come to him from none other than his Union colleague Reinhold Niebuhr, who attributed the stories to Kennedy advisors John Galbraith and Arthur Schlesinger, Jr. Once the truth came out, Van Dusen feared, Kennedy would be doomed. John Bennett, also Van Dusen's colleague at Union, had written him to say that the rumors were unsubstantiated. Van Dusen wrote back and said that Kennedy needed to deny the rumors, or put them in the context of his younger life before he was married, or affirm them and admit that he was thus unfit for office. Van Dusen sent a copy of his reply to Bennett to Stevenson.[46]

Stevenson agreed that the rumors were disturbing—but they were rumors nonetheless. "I have some experience with rumors and have become a little cynical, I confess," he wrote to Van Dusen.[47] While Stevenson wanted no part of this episode, he was concerned enough about either the veracity of the rumors or the potential damage that a leading liberal Protestant Christian could do to Kennedy that he alerted the campaign. Schlesinger erupted. He expressed his "extreme impatience" with rumormongering of this sort.[48] Even if the rumors were true, they didn't bear "essentially" on Kennedy's capacity to be president. Private virtue was no substitute for public qualification.

Schlesinger confessed that he had no knowledge of the facts, but it was his impression that the ubiquitous rumors about Kennedy's escapades were greatly exaggerated. He had heard them in Northeast Harbor, in Fisher's Island, in Easthampton, and "in all those circles, where, in the past, vicious and lying stories have been told about Woodrow Wilson, Franklin Roosevelt, Harry Truman, and you." He then supplied Stevenson with the pre-1955 story line that Schlesinger had shared with Van Dusen. Finally, Schlesinger questioned Van Dusen's motives. He asked Stevenson if he had seen Van Dusen's latest "nauseating" book, *The Spiritual Legacy of John Foster Dulles*. Schlesinger thought Stevenson should give Van Dusen hell for circulating rumors that were out of date, largely unsubstantiated, and, even if true, hardly relevant. This was hardly a categorical denial. Schlesinger all but admitted that, in the past, Kennedy had been sexually promiscuous.

But Van Dusen was not placated, as he soon indicated to Stevenson. Van Dusen proposed that Stevenson sit down with one or two leading liberal Protestant leaders to confirm or deny the rumors.[49] Stevenson replied more fully this time to say that he had no interest in such a meeting since he had no direct knowledge of the charges. He went on to indicate that he had heard such rumors and that Kennedy may have been "overactive in that direction" prior to 1955 and during a period of acute trouble with his spine when his long-term survival was in question. After a series of surgeries from which he made a complete recovery and regained a normal life expectancy, "he seems to have settled down to preparing himself for his ambition—the Presidency." Since Stevenson himself had been the victim of such ugly rumors, he found "this whole business distasteful in the extreme!"[50] He closed with the observation that, even if the rumors were true, they were hardly crucial since the alternative was Richard Nixon.

Wine caught wind of Van Dusen's discomfort early on and took it seriously. He pursued John Kenneth Galbraith, who denied ever talking to Niebuhr about Kennedy's sex life, and sent a telegram, apparently to many leading Protestant figures, specifically knocking down the story. Wine sent a telegram to Dr. Franklin Clark Fry, a Lutheran, a World Council of Churches leader, and a major figure in the NCC: "For your information, Galbraith today specifically denied conversation reported by Van Dusen concerning Kennedy. Declared pure fabrication. Is Astounded."[51]

It is hard to assess just what the consequences of this story might have been had Van Dusen successfully introduced it into the mainstream media, but it is clear that the Kennedy operation acted swiftly to knock it down. Wine's efforts were critical to keeping it under wraps.

In a particularly surprising bit of outreach, Sorensen had launched a long-term strategy to blunt POAU's effectiveness by courting its special counsel, Paul Blanshard. While this effort did plant seeds of doubt in Blanshard's mind about POAU's anti-Kennedy strategy, it did not ultimately have even a marginal impact on POAU's singleness of mind. Among Catholics Blanshard was seen as the bête noire of liberal anti-Catholics in the middle of the twentieth century. As the Harvard-educated author of the bestselling *American Freedom and Catholic Power* in 1949 and its follow-up volume, *Communism, Democracy and Catholic Power*, Blanshard served as special counsel to POAU, advising it on legal cases and lecturing nationwide. He was widely hailed in Protestant circles and simultaneously reviled among Catholics.

As early as the summer of 1958, Blanshard had warned Archer and Lowell of POAU that its publications were riding the presidential issue far too much. POAU was in danger of being regarded as the successor to the Know-Nothing movement, and it would be sunk if Kennedy did win the presidency. He argued that the anti-Catholic Protestants who fought Al Smith in 1928 never fully recovered from the fallout of that election. The ongoing work of POAU should take precedence over short-term partisanship.[52]

In the spring of 1959, after *Look* published the profile of JFK in which he stated that nothing should take precedence over an officeholder's oath to uphold the Constitution, Blanshard wrote a letter to the editor of the *Washington Post*, commending Kennedy for his stand "against his bishops."[53] Within weeks, Sorensen arranged a visit between Kennedy and Blanshard. Kennedy told Blanshard that the Catholic press had taken an almost uniformly negative view of his *Look* interview. Kennedy believed that, as a Catholic, he was well suited to stand up to Catholic pressure. Blanshard quizzed the senator on birth control and Catholic clerical pressure on families to boycott public schools and attend Catholic schools. Kennedy had never heard of Canon 1374, which supposedly banned Catholics from attending public schools. He told Blanshard that he personally supported the Catholic teaching on birth control, but he would not block federal birth control aid if legislation were passed. Blanshard was clearly impressed.[54] He told Archer that Kennedy was frank, and while he could not publicly share the conversation, he came away reassured, believing that Kennedy "is at heart reasonably anti-clerical."[55]

A year later, Sorensen asked Blanshard to read a draft of the article that Cardinal Cushing had written as a response to Protestant clergy attacks on Kennedy in some national magazines. Sorensen asked him for his candid confidential assessment of the advisability of printing such an article.[56] Blanshard provided a detailed critique, and while he liked parts of the essay, he ultimately told Sorensen that the piece would do little to meet the anxieties of non-Catholics.[57]

Throughout the summer and fall, Blanshard produced a series of letters to Archer, Lowell, and others, setting out in minute detail his analysis of the campaign. He continued to fear that POAU publications were too hard on Kennedy and failed to hit Nixon adequately on federal funds for parochial schools. While he made it clear that, as a liberal, he could not vote for Nixon, he told one correspondent that he might vote in protest for Norman Thomas instead of Kennedy. He was particularly frustrated with Kennedy's Houston speech, which he believed gave the American bishops far too much credit for their 1948 statement on the separation of church and state. So while Kennedy's and Sorensen's outreach to Blanshard was bold, it only reinforced incipient doubts in Blanshard's mind and did not materially affect POAU's election efforts.[58]

By hiring Wine and John Cogley, the campaign had built an unprecedented staff to handle the issues surrounding Kennedy's Catholicism. In short order, Wine implemented Sorensen's ambitious plans. A professional film was edited, copied, and distributed; a press kit was assembled to distribute on a mass basis; the capacity to respond to voter letters was quickly ramped up; a national list of local surrogates on the topic of religion was sent to state field directors; informal contacts were established across a broad range of sympathetic religious leaders; salacious rumors were quashed; and private meetings were held to shore up support among shaky religious constituents. All in all, it was an impressive flurry of activity that consolidated much of the wisdom gained by the campaign throughout the primary season. With it, the era of modern campaign religious outreach was born.

As Election Day neared, the campaigns kept jousting. Kennedy kept religious bigotry front and center, while Nixon struggled to respond. Perhaps the best concise commentary on Nixon's treatment of Kennedy's religion was Ted Sorensen's pronouncement that the Nixon campaign handled the issue "shrewdly."[59] Much of our understanding of Nixon's perspective comes from his book *Six Crises*, which was published after the election and was aimed in large part at preparing for another run at the presidency.

In an early draft of the manuscript, Nixon, like Sorensen, identified religion as the most important issue in the campaign. The difference between the two candidates was that Kennedy could talk about it and Nixon couldn't.[60] Nixon made clear in the book that he had read a version of the Bailey Memorandum—which, as we saw earlier, Father John Cronin had given to him. He claimed to accept its premises and thought that its predictions had come true. Nixon wrote that he had believed all along that Kennedy's Catholicism would draw more Catholics to his side than it would drive Protestants to Nixon. Early in the campaign, Nixon campaign manager Robert Finch had declared the issue out of bounds. A "confidential memorandum" to campaign staff—which was actually released publicly—quoted Nixon's convention speech: "Religion will be in this campaign to the extent that the candidates of either side talk about it. I shall never talk about it and we'll start right now."[61]

The memo had drawn three guidelines. First, no person or organization conditioning their support on religious grounds would be recognized by the campaign. Second, there should be no discussion of the "religious issue" in any literature prepared by any volunteer group supporting Nixon, and no literature of this sort should be distributed or made available. Finally, staff and volunteers should avoid discussing the "religious issue" informally since it might be construed as part of a deliberate campaign. This was great political theater and a strong attempt to gain the moral high ground.

The Kennedy campaign would soon learn from its informant that Nixon was clandestinely plotting with Protestants. It began to counterpunch by raising the religious bigotry issue, and it struck the Kennedy camp as more than a little cynical that Nixon was calling for a moratorium on discussions of religion. When the Kennedy campaign complained about the rise in anti-Catholic attacks, the Nixon camp would argue that Kennedy was the one keeping the religion issue alive. On September 11, Nixon answered questions at some length on *Meet the Press*. He again called for an end to religion as a topic in the campaign. The best way to keep it out of the campaign was for the candidates to refrain from raising it, he said. He called on Kennedy to do so.[62]

The Republican National Committee chair, Senator Thruston Morton, issued a blistering press statement, saying that Democrats were trying to keep the issue alive by making false and reprehensible charges.[63] Morton believed that the Democrats kept raising the issue because it helped Kennedy. He appealed to Kennedy to set a date for an end to this discussion, preferably right now.

Whatever the import of his disavowal of raising religion as a political issue, Nixon was not above courting religious leaders. In mid-October, Nixon spoke at the Mormon Tabernacle in Salt Lake City and received the endorsement of David McKay, the president of the Church of Jesus Christ of Latter-Day Saints. Despite Kennedy's speech in the same venue three weeks before and his earlier visits with McKay, it was Nixon who received McKay's public blessing.[64] Similarly, the research division of the Republican National Committee tracked Protestant discontent in both Texas and Tennessee and noted that Nixon had a reasonable chance to win both states because of Kennedy's Catholicism.[65] In the late stages of the campaign, Nixon's staff grew frustrated with Kennedy's success in decrying religious bigotry. Republican complaints that this amounted to perpetuating the issue did not seem to be gaining much traction with the public. What could be done? One proposal was for Billy Graham to endorse Nixon in *Life* magazine, but Nixon vetoed that. The staff then lobbied Nixon to make a special address. On the last Wednesday night of the campaign, Arthur Flemming, the secretary of health, education, and welfare, presented Nixon with a draft of a speech on religion. Nixon thought it was a moderate and reasonable speech.

It called for people to vote on the issues and not to be influenced in any way by the religion of the candidates.[66] The staff was unanimously in favor of the speech. But ultimately Nixon rejected the idea, feeling that he would be accused of bigotry and of reneging on his commitment not to talk about religion.

Nixon finally did raise the subject during a nationally broadcast speech on the Sunday before the election.[67] He urged voters not to take his or Senator Kennedy's faith into account. The Kennedy camp undoubtedly saw this as an unvarnished reminder to Protestants that Kennedy was a Catholic. After all, the staff knew that Nixon and his supporters were using religion as a political weapon across the country. And yet, by taking this rhetorical high road, Nixon was publicly repudiating such work and thus inoculating himself against accusations. It was a thinly veiled means of raising Kennedy's Catholicism one last time on the eve of the election.

The final insight into Nixon's general election strategy on religion comes from *Six Crises*. He elaborated on what he wanted to accomplish in the book regarding the role of religion in the election. One purpose was to refute the popular thesis advanced by some academics and pro-Kennedy journalists that if Kennedy had been some religion other than Catholic he would have won by a larger margin.

By the time *Six Crises* went to press, Nixon had changed his mind about expressing public regret for resisting his advisors' counsel. In examining the religion issue in retrospect, Nixon concluded that he could not have handled it any other way. He did mention the Peale meeting and denied he had any advance knowledge of it. He also expressed some sympathy for Peale by saying that he believed Peale's account that he was only a bit player in the meeting. He clearly strained to respond to Kennedy's post–Labor Day strategy of raising religious bigotry as an issue. He did not hit back on the point while expressing his personal frustration that Kennedy and his supporters were exploiting the issue.[68] Nixon wistfully observed that the 1960 election would be the last national election in which the religion issue would be raised.[69] *Six Crises* was ultimately written in anticipation of Nixon's continued presence on the national scene. He was thankful that Kennedy's victory meant that Nixon would not have to deal with Catholicism again.

From a purely Machiavellian perspective, Nixon had managed the issue well. By employing Armstrong to clandestinely aid the native anti-Catholicism of large swaths of the Protestant population, he had fanned those flames in secret. Of course, it was a risky strategy in that, if Armstrong were exposed, Nixon would pay mightily. The Kennedy campaign's reticence to use the knowledge it had gained from its informant prevented this. At the same time, by constantly saying that he would not raise the religion issue, Nixon was able to remind Protestants of their fears while preserving his innocence.

Three incidents late in the campaign may have had a huge impact on the outcome. The first of these took place in October, when three Puerto Rican Catholic bishops issued a pastoral letter instructing Catholics that they could not vote for the reelection of Governor Luis Muñoz Marín and his Popular Democratic Party. Marín eventually won with 90% of the vote, which called into question the power of the bishops.

Sorensen recorded that several advisors attempted to get Kennedy to make a speech on Sunday before the election to address the issue. But Kennedy decided not to feed the issue by calling more attention to it.[70] *Time* magazine reported some outrage in Protestant circles as well as swift renunciation from several Catholic sources. *America* magazine said that such a move was unprecedented in American Catholic history. Cardinal Spellman formally denied that it would be a sin to disregard the Puerto Rican bishops' injunction. The Vatican's apostolic delegate to the United States said that U.S. Catholic bishops had never taken such a position and that he was confident that no such action would ever be taken by the hierarchy in America. Cardinal Cushing said it was totally out of step for any ecclesiastical authority to dictate the voting of citizens.[71] Ultimately, the issue failed to catch fire.

The second episode involved Dr. Martin Luther King, Jr., and the "blue bomb." King had been jailed in Atlanta, and through a series of maneuvers was sentenced by a state judge to serve time in the general population of a rough state prison, where King's life would be in danger. Civil rights leaders reached out to both campaigns. Nixon chose not to respond while the Kennedy campaign did, in a complicated way.[72] In a breach of legal ethics, Robert Kennedy ended up calling the state judge, while JFK called Coretta Scott King to express his good wishes and to say he was doing everything he could to help. After King was released, the Kennedy camp, realizing the public relations coup it had scored, set up a dummy corporation and, working with the Reverend Gardner Taylor's clergy network, printed and distributed over 2 million copies of the story of Kennedy's work to free King. These 24-page pamphlets—printed on blue paper, hence the label "blue bomb"—were given out at African American churches nationwide. Historians Taylor Branch and Nick Bryant make compelling cases that this episode and its publicity may have turned enough African American votes from Nixon to Kennedy to give Kennedy his final margin of victory.

But it was the third episode that was most crucial. Harris's final poll in Texas, on November 3, contained mixed news. Kennedy led Nixon 48%–42% with 10% undecided, enough to swing the final vote either way. Nixon had picked up 2 points on Kennedy since the last survey. Harris noted that the degree of anti-Catholic bigotry remained perilously high, but it had not changed for the worse.[73] At the same time, a confident Carr P. Collins telegraphed Nixon to say, "you may be absolutely assured that Texas will go for Nixon and Lodge by an overwhelming majority. I predict that Texas will give Nixon and Lodge at least fifty five percent of its total vote."[74] While these campaign insiders were plying their trade, a lone religious editor wrestled with his conscience.

E. S. James was the editor of the *Baptist Standard* with a circulation of 340,000 subscribers in Texas. James had attended the Peale meeting but had also corresponded with Kennedy. Kennedy had answered James's questions on policies related to Catholicism. But, inexplicably, Nixon had not replied to identical queries, and Texas Baptists were growing restive.[75] Kennedy had defied the Catholic church by opposing public funding for parochial schools on the grounds that it was unconstitutional and that the separation of church and state was best for the country. By contrast, Nixon, a Quaker, had advocated federal grants to sectarian colleges. His running mate, Henry Cabot Lodge, an Episcopalian, announced on *Face the Nation* that he was in favor of federal aid to parochial schools. Glenn Archer of POAU commented, "We believe that Mr. Lodge will yet discover that most Americans of all faiths believe that churches and their institutions are better in a free, democratic society when they support their own programs with voluntary gifts rather than with tax funds."[76]

It would be hard to overestimate the political damage done by Lodge's admission. It put almost every Protestant anti-Catholic critic in the difficult position of seeing the Republican ticket embrace one of the very policies that they believed Kennedy would support as president.

The staff of the Baptist Joint Committee on Public Affairs expressed to Nixon "uneasiness among Baptist leaders and people" regarding this turn of events. Executive director Emmanuel Carlson wrote to Nixon, "Our people are averse to the use of the power of taxation for the support of churches or religious institutions for the same reason that they oppose the use of police power to impose attendance at worship." Nixon declined to meet with Carlson, but Kennedy did and agreed in a public statement that "a frank renunciation by all churches of political power as a means to religious ends would greatly improve the political climate and would seem to be a legitimate request by both political parties."[77]

Yet Nixon still refused to answer. Herbert Klein, a special assistant to Nixon, wrote in response, "As you know, he [Nixon] has taken the position that the question of religion should not be discussed in the campaign and he has also forbidden his staff to talk about this matter. Under the circumstances, I am sure you will understand that it will not be possible to furnish any statements such as you requested."[78]

Carlson made a third effort to discuss the separation of church and state with Nixon. "We are still concerned for an open discussion of the public policy interpretations which the different candidates ascribe to the broad American principles of Church-State relations," he wrote. He added a stern warning: "If this should become a one-sided discussion it will be subject to a variety of interpretations among our people. Any refusal to admit that public issues exist in this field will also be difficult to explain to our people."[79]

Carlson was alerting Nixon to the huge blunder that was unfolding quickly in the closing days of the campaign. Hundreds of thousands, perhaps even millions, of Baptists would be reading his words. The *Baptist Standard* continued to report that it had been informed that Nixon would be making a statement setting out his position on federal aid to parochial schools, but the magazine had yet to receive it.

Yet when Nixon finally did respond, he managed to dig himself an even deeper hole.

Nixon sent a substantial telegram to James on October 23.[80] He affirmed that no church or religion could be supported by the federal government. In terms of aid to education, Nixon believed that direct federal aid to private and public colleges was allowed. He then dropped a bombshell:

> There is, however, a public responsibility for elementary and secondary education, a responsibility which under our Constitution rests with the States. Therefore, any assistance which the Federal Government wants to give in the field of elementary and secondary education should be given to the States. It will then be up to each State to decide whether Federal funds given to each State should be used for both public and private schools.

With that, Nixon ended.

If Nixon thought that a states' rights argument would appeal to a Texas audience, he was poorly informed. Far from being the absolute rejection of federal aid to parochial schools that Southern Baptists wanted to hear, Nixon left the door open for the widespread use of federal monies for Catholic schools. To make matters even worse in the South, Lodge, speaking in New York City on October 12, announced flatly that "there should be a Negro in the Cabinet."[81]

In a November 2 *Baptist Standard* editorial entitled "Vote Your Convictions," E. S. James wrote words that may well have swung enough Baptist votes to Kennedy to allow him to carry Texas:

> The *Standard* has never attempted to tell the readers how to vote. They would not have listened if we had done so. We hold that Baptist people are thoroughly competent to think for themselves and that they are independent enough to make up their own minds about what ought to be done. However strong may have been our desire to discuss some political aspects of the race, we have declined to do so; but we have not hesitated to give full coverage to all news that is connected with religion and religious freedom. We have not been apologetic for our definitive position or editorial comment on those matters that relate to religious liberty and the separation of Church and State....
>
> So, here are two pictures 10 days before the election. The first is that of a Protestant candidate for the presidency whose church has always supported separation of Church and State, but he makes a statement about it that is vague, evasive, and ambiguous about aid to parochial schools. He favors Federal aid to both public and private schools of higher learning, and he says he would leave it to each state to decide whether or not Federal money allotted to it would be used to aid sectarian schools. The ambiguity in it lies in the fact that many states are Catholic controlled and would no doubt apportion some of our tax money to Catholic elementary and high schools. This is not the clear, unequivocal statement Protestants had a right to expect from him, and many of them, along with the *Standard*, will not be happy with it. After all, aid to secular education is the testing ground now because it is here that the Roman Catholic hierarchy is exerting its pressure for government support.
>
> The other picture is that of a Roman Catholic candidate who affirms again and again that he is definitely committed to the principle of separation of Church and State and that he is opposed to Federal aid to parochial education or the appointment of an envoy to the Vatican. At the same time his church, around the world, continues to prove that she does not agree with him. It is true that prominent Catholic laymen have declared themselves for complete separation, but the laymen do not have a vote in Catholic affairs. The hierarchy does the ruling, and it has not taken one single step since he was

nominated to indicate that it would support his position. Quite to the contrary, it continues to regiment its peoples [*sic*] wherever it can in every area of life....

Perhaps the whole matter now resolves into one big question: Which candidate will be in the better position to resist the pressure of those who would destroy this wall of separation, and which one gives promise of the greater desire and determination in the matter? So far as the *Standard* is concerned, this is the only issue we feel free to discuss; and we have no desire to tell other[s] how they ought to vote. The editor will cast his own ballot on the basis of what he believes to be the greater assurance of immediate and long-term religious free-dom for everyone. If to others there are other issues more important, then that is their own affair; but we would urge everyone to vote for someone. It is a blood-bought privilege.[82]

This is hardly the partisan screed of a bigoted fundamentalist. It is impossible to know with certainty what the electoral impact of it was. But if hundreds of thousands of Texas Southern Baptists read it in the days before the election, they saw a much fairer and balanced analysis of Kennedy's position than was usually the case.

The National Association of Evangelicals sent a telegram to Nixon and Lodge regarding Lodge's stance on federal aid to parochial schools. They, like James, were stunned by the Republican ticket's stand on this issue and declared their "surprise and alarm":

Our constituency, having a membership of 38 denominations, includ-ing 28,000 local congregations and reaching out to more than 10 million evangelical Christians, protests this position on the part of Ambassador Lodge, which would violate the constitutional guaran-tees of separation of church and state. His statement is insupportable in terms of the interests of religious freedom, and in light of the con-trary position taken by the other candidates in the current campaign. We therefore call upon him to reconsider his position.[83]

Lodge had clearly blundered, and Nixon's response to James did little to undo the damage. The NAE leadership was nonplussed at the prospect of the Catholic Kennedy being right on one of their funda-mental issues while Nixon was in the wrong.[84]

Carr P. Collins believed that it was Nixon's response to James, coupled with Lodge's statement about the cabinet, that made the dif-ference. James became "unduly persistent," according to Collins, about getting a statement from Nixon, so insistent that he talked to Collins and another Texas supporter of Nixon, Jack Porter, about the mat-ter. Porter called Finch to insist that Nixon send a telegram stating his position. When Nixon finally did respond, Collins tried to get James not to print the story, but as a newspaper man, James felt he had to print it. "It literally wrecked us," Collins wrote:

> I got calls from all over Texas as soon as the paper was received. Dr. James said the readers could judge for themselves which candidate to vote for and he had made it clear that Kennedy's position was unequivocal and Lodge and Nixon were apparently favorable toward federal aid to parochial schools. He didn't need to go any further. There were literally thousands and thousands of Baptists throughout the state that were just looking for some excuse to change over and vote for Kennedy and this was the excuse they needed.[85]

Collins met Nixon's plane when it landed in Fort Worth a week before the election in order to show Finch all of this material. But Finch was not on the plane, and they never got to speak about the matter. Collins said it was the most bitter disappointment he had ever experienced in a campaign.

Some commentators believe that Kennedy was losing momentum and Nixon was gaining in the closing days of the campaign. The outcome was excruciatingly close as Kennedy defeated Nixon by an incredibly narrow margin, 112,881 votes out of almost 69 million cast. Texas went for Kennedy by just 46,000 votes out of 2,289,000. Almost half of Kennedy's national popular vote margin came from Texas. In the end, had Nixon replied differently to a Texas Baptist editor about his view on federal aid to parochial schools, he might have won the election. The most difficult issue of the campaign, Kennedy's Catholicism, which had cost Kennedy so much, presented him with an opportunity to pull it out at the end. By applying extensive assets to address the issue and by taking seriously the concerns of Protestants—and by virtue of Nixon's failure to understand these issues—Kennedy prevailed.

EPILOGUE

· ·

What, ultimately, was the electoral impact of Kennedy's Catholicism? Did his religion help or hurt him? The short answer is that it depends on what time frame you examine. Gallup polls maintained that Kennedy's early popularity in 1958 and 1959 was undercut as more voters learned that he was Catholic. That is undoubtedly true. Yet Catholic bloc voting in Wisconsin helped him to defeat Humphrey there while at the same time Humphrey's strength in the more Protestant regions of the state kept him in the race long enough to face Kennedy in overwhelmingly Protestant West Virginia. Kennedy's triumph in West Virginia suggested that he might be able to win in the general election by attracting Catholics while holding on to enough Protestants to cobble together a majority.

Yet in the general election, Protestants vastly outnumbered Catholic voters, so winning a large percentage of Catholics while sparking a large Protestant defection would have led to disaster. Fortunately, data from the Center for Political Studies at the University of Michigan on religion and the 1960 election allow us to sharpen our analysis of the results from the general election. Lyman Kellstadt and Mark Noll have examined these data and drawn some conclusions about the effect of Kennedy's Catholicism on the outcome.[1] Kennedy carried 34% of the white Protestant vote. Interestingly, this is almost exactly the same percentage of the white Protestant vote that Adlai Stevenson carried in 1956, when Eisenhower obliterated him 57% to 42%. But Kennedy carried 83% of the Roman Catholic vote while Stevenson had carried just 45% in 1956.

200

So it would appear that Kennedy was able to fulfill the rough prediction of the Bailey Memo. That is, he held 6 of the 7 states that Stevenson carried in 1956 and added another 14, including states with significant Catholic voting populations, such as New York, Ohio, Pennsylvania, Rhode Island, and Louisiana.

Yet it is also clear that Kennedy faced massive defections from Protestants who identified themselves as regular attenders, meaning that they reported attending services weekly or more often. For example, Kennedy carried only 25% of regular-attending Baptists and 31% of regular-attending Methodists. Regular-attending Pentecostals gave Kennedy 0% of their votes while regular-attending northern evangelicals gave him 24% of their vote and southern evangelicals gave him 30%. It is probably correct to conclude from this information that the massive efforts among Protestant churchgoers had a significant impact on the results.

Kellstadt and Noll also note that, among regular-attending black churchgoers, Kennedy won 50% of the vote. This was the lowest percentage of any Democratic presidential candidate from 1948 through 1984. They conclude that the strong anti-Catholic sentiment among white Protestants also spilled over into many black churches.[2]

Thus, Kennedy was able to stave off enough Protestant defectors, apparently among the less frequent church attendees, and attract a sizable enough Catholic vote to narrowly win the election. His faith hurt him with more devout Protestants and helped him immensely with his fellow Catholics. The net result was an extraordinarily close election.

Another interesting—but rarely discussed—question is: What was the nature of Kennedy's Catholicism? Two contemporary trends have tended to prematurely render this question obsolete: the various revelations about Kennedy's marital infidelities and the growing tendency to interpret his Houston speech as a secularizing move in which he declared his religion to be purely private and hence politically irrelevant.[3] While I cannot give a full-blown account of his faith, two of his contemporaries from the 1960 election offered tantalizing evidence. Both Bishop John Wright and John Cogley gave similar accounts of Kennedy's faith.

Cogley argued that Kennedy was as "good" a Catholic as most of his age.[4] He was not an intellectual Catholic politician in the mode of Eugene McCarthy, but there was "a kind of cultural overflow of Catholicism which was very deeply reflected in Kennedy." This meant, for Kennedy, that he was free of the Protestant burden that somehow power and its use were evil or very close to evil. Cogley believed that

Kennedy never worried about power as being evil in itself. Rather, what determined the goodness of the use of power was how it was exercised.

Further, Cogley called Kennedy an old-fashioned, very Boston sort of Catholic who put great emphasis on fish every Friday and mass on Sunday. He did not think Kennedy would have remained a traditional pre–Vatican II Catholic had he lived beyond the council. He also did not think that Kennedy was as theologically illiterate as some portrayed him. He was not a Catholic intellectual, but he was as religiously literate as most Catholic politicians.[5]

Wright gave a similar yet vastly more detailed assessment. Wright, who knew Kennedy from just after World War II until his death, saw Kennedy not as an intellectual but as an activist:

> I mention this a little wistfully, although I've always been aware, and very much aware, of the first class mind that the late President had, I have always been a little dismayed by the pretense that he was an intellectual in any authentic sense of the word. He was not. He was a doer, an extremely eager and passionate doer. He was enamored of ideas and very much liked on occasion, though not on a prolonged occasion, the company of people who [had] ideas and who talked about them, but he was not an intellectual.[6]

Wright noted that Kennedy used the best available talent to get the best available material to use for practical and political purposes, but he did so with little regard for its deeper intellectual significance. This is an apt description of Kennedy's approach to the political problem created by his Catholicism. He built a staff that could create a political response to the vast array of anti-Catholic forces opposing him and that did not require him to master the intricacies of the emerging discussion of Catholicism's role in the American democratic political system.[7]

For Wright, Kennedy was a quintessentially Boston Irish Catholic. By this, he meant that Kennedy was conventional in his observance of typical Catholic rituals, such as regular attendance at mass, but without any metaphysical or philosophical dimensions beyond a strong desire not to die outside of the church. Kennedy's distrust of Catholic clergy was another aspect of this, which Wright believed he inherited from his father. Wright cited the Puerto Rican bishops' opposition to the election of Luis Muñoz Marín as governor of Puerto Rico as an example of how Kennedy believed that Catholic clergy could not be trusted. If they really wanted him to win, why did they go public with their opposition to his politics? He distrusted Catholic clergy since they seemed to be willing to undermine Catholic politicians.

Wright drove home the point that, despite later attempts to classify Kennedy as some sort of new breed of Catholic, he was a conventional Catholic of his day:

> The fact is that for all the years of his political ascendancy Jack Kennedy functioned very definitely within the structures of Catholicism in its highly institutionalized form as found in Boston, Massachusetts, in the 1950's. That is to say, far from being anyone who found uncongenial or unwelcome the sociological structures—represented by things like, oh, say, Knights of Columbus, and Holy Name Communion Breakfast...things to which the more emancipated Catholic of the mid-twentieth century is allergic—Jack Kennedy took to them like a fish to water, or rather like the political, astute guy that he was, to structures, and precisely to structures....Jack Kennedy was a very structured Catholic and a very traditional Catholic whatever the depth of his theology and things of this sort apart.

Contemporary accounts that highlight Kennedy's alleged secularism or disregard for Catholic morality do not account for the side of his religious belief and practice that Wright recalls. The point is not somehow to reconceive Kennedy as a deep Catholic thinker or intellectual; rather, it is to acknowledge the complexity of his personality. The impact of his faith may not have been overwhelming, but it was not negligible either.

In light of the continuing importance of religion in U.S. politics, perhaps the most interesting question for Americans today is whether Kennedy's answers about the role of his faith and his politics in his Houston speech remain viable. The simple answer here has to be no, if for no other reason than that the internal politics of the American Catholic church have changed such that politicians and other laity have come under direct clerical pressure on political issues such as abortion. The sort of pressure from the church to which Kennedy denied he would be subjected has now become routine. There are now stories of Catholic laity being refused communion because they have expressed an intention to vote for presidential candidates who support abortion rights.

Likewise, the meaning of the metaphor of the separation of church and state has now become so vexed that a simple endorsement of the concept by a politician does little to clarify precisely what is being embraced and what is being rejected. The range of meaning runs from attempts to scrub all religious references from public life to proposals to restrict public funding of any religious programs. With the rise of an expanded religious vocabulary in presidential rhetoric beginning in the Reagan era, it would be virtually impossible for a politician to get elected president who deviated significantly from this rhetorical genealogy.[8]

The times cry out for a more sophisticated and satisfactory account of just how a president—or any politician, for that matter—might move from his or her particular faith, or lack of faith, into our increasingly pluralistic political world and successfully forge political consensus on the vexing social and political issues of the day while, on the one hand, not completely sacrificing religious particularity and, on the other hand, acknowledging the religious diversity of the country. I remain deeply skeptical that a recovery of some form of civil religion is adequate to this task.

It was part of Robert Bellah's famous 1967 thesis on civil religion that John Kennedy was, along with Abraham Lincoln, a prime example of the success of this tradition. At that time, Bellah was not sure that American civil religion had the necessary resources to successfully navigate the challenges of the day. It is my belief that it no longer has the philosophical or theological depth to sustain U.S. citizens in the face of contemporary problems, such as global climate change and the so-called war on terror, to name only two pressing issues.[9]

As for political lessons, let me suggest two. First, as Kennedy's listening tour demonstrated: If you do not understand the nature of your opposition, go to the sources and talk to your opponents. As religion has increasingly become connected to the political divide in this country, it has reinforced a gulf among faith communities such that members of the religious Right and the religious Left routinely demonize one another and, in so doing, ape the worst aspects of American political culture.

The result far too often is that Republican politicians only talk to a select group of conservative religious leaders and Democrats only talk to a different set of religious leaders or none at all. Kennedy was not satisfied to accept that Protestant leaders were mostly against him. He and his brother Robert took the time to try and find out why this was the case. They did not seek formal endorsements from Protestant leaders; instead, they sought understanding. It would be a good thing for the U.S. polity if people seeking public office spent less time pandering for public support from religious leaders and more time listening to religious leaders talk about the concerns and aspirations of their organizations' members. If the United States is to make any progress in transcending the current political gridlock, conducting civil discourse across religious divides will be critical to that progress.

The second political lesson is that clandestine organizing among and fundraising from religious communities are bad form. It is worth pondering just what Nixon's religious strategy risked for Nixon and his associates. His use of Orland K. Armstrong contradicted his public stance of taking the high road and not exploiting Kennedy's Catholicism for political gain. Had this strategy come to light at the time, it would have damaged both Nixon and the various religious groups and actors who were helping him. Public knowledge of the fundamental dishonesty attached to this course could have been disastrous.

In many ways, Nixon's religious strategy foreshadowed the rise of the religious Right. He exploited the oppositional nature of much of evangelical Protestantism's historical engagement with American public life in a self-aggrandizing fashion. By playing to Protestant fears about a Catholic president, Nixon chose to fan the flames of intolerance in a manner that he could not publicly acknowledge. The use of election tactics that cannot survive public scrutiny is to be rejected.

And finally, in terms of moral and ecclesiastical lessons, there are two conclusions worth noting. First, the political independence of faith communities is good for both the faith communities and the democratic polity.[10] One of the tasks of faith communities is to remind the state of its proper functions: to provide for the common good of the nation, to uphold justice for all of its citizens, to provide for the welfare of the dispossessed, to strive for peace in the world, etc. Faith communities require a form of independence from the state if they are to perform these functions and to worship without interference from the state. If they forge covenants with the state, all of these functions are compromised.

Politicians, on the other hand, are often tempted to try to lure religious groups into dependent, permanent alliances. It rests primarily on faith communities themselves to maintain their independence from such alliances. The alternative is not sectarian withdrawal, even though that is a time-honored alternative; rather, the best stance is one in which religious communities forge temporary, ad hoc alliances with political movements that are always subject to renegotiation. In that way, faith communities can maintain their long-term independence and integrity while participating in the democratic process.

Last, formal endorsements of politicians by faith communities are usually misguided. It is much better for faith communities to set out principles and rules of engagement, to provide issue education, to allow public space for debate, and to avoid the overt and covert coercion of voters. Certainly, there will be times of extraordinary stress when religious communities must oppose certain political movements. But that should be the exception to the rule. The ease with which so many Protestant groups joined the opposition to John Kennedy is dismaying, especially in light of the lengths to which Kennedy went to demonstrate that he did not support the alleged Catholic positions on hot-button issues.

This complex tale of the election of America's first and only Catholic president yields much for the country to digest. The background of a growing religious diversity makes the issue of the role of religion in democratic politics all the more pressing. John Kennedy's trailblazing victory as a member of a religious minority who won a presidential election despite significant opposition from the majority Protestantism of the day should give Americans hope that they may yet again choose a president who helps them to break down some of the many internal barriers that have been erected in the United States.

Notes

···

Abbreviations

DNCP   Democratic National Committee Papers, John F. Kennedy
Library

GBOP   G. Bromley Oxnam Papers, Library of Congress, Washington,
DC

JFKL   John F. Kennedy Library, Boston, MA

JFKPPP   John F. Kennedy Pre-Presidential Papers, John F. Kennedy
Library

LBJPL   Lyndon B. Johnson Presidential Library, Austin, TX

OKAP   Orland K. Armstrong Papers, University of Missouri / State
Historical Society of Missouri, Columbia

RFKP   Robert F. Kennedy Papers, John F. Kennedy Library

RMNPPP Richard M. Nixon Pre-Presidential Papers, Richard M. Nixon
Presidential Library, Yorba Linda, CA

TCSP   Theodore C. Sorensen Papers, John F. Kennedy Library

Chapter 1

1. Letter, Sargent Shriver to Joseph P. Kennedy, July 18, 1956, John
F. Kennedy Pre-Presidential Papers (hereafter JFKPPP), Box 810, Senate Files,
Candidacies, 1956 Vice Presidency, 11/22/55–7/26/56, John F. Kennedy
Presidential Library (hereafter JFKL). All references to the Shriver-Stevenson
conversation come from this letter.

2. See Robert Dallek, *An Unfinished Life: John F. Kennedy 1917–1963*
(Boston: Little, Brown, 2003), 206.

3. Sorensen chronicled this chain of events four years later in a letter to White. See Letter, Theodore Sorensen to Theodore H. White, April 12, 1960, Theodore C. Sorensen Papers (hereafter TCSP), Box 27, Correspondence Copy Files, 1959–1960, W Folder #1, JFKL.

4. See JFKPPP, Box 810, Senate Files, The Catholic Vote 5/19–8/7/56, JFKL.

5. Ibid.

6. Letter, David Broder to John Bailey, April 27, 1959, TCSP, Box 125, Campaign Files 1959–1960, "Religious Issue Catholic Issue Folder 2," JFKL.; Letter, Theodore Sorensen to Fletcher Knebel, April 6, 1956, JFKPPP, Box 810, Senate Files, Candidacies, 1956 Vice Presidency, 11/22/55–7/26/56, JFKL. Sorensen cautioned Knebel about the delicate nature of these data. He told the reporter that he was "extremely reluctant" to let this personal study out of his hands because he did not want anyone to know that one of Kennedy's aides was preparing or circulating this material, which made it look like Kennedy was campaigning for the vice presidential slot.

7. "The 'Catholic Vote': A Kennedy Staff Analysis," *U.S. News and World Report*, August 1, 1960, 68–72.

8. Letter, Robert L. Reynolds to John F. Kennedy, April 17, 1956, TCSP, Box 3, Articles: *Jubilee* [Catholic publication], 7–8/56, "The Catholic Vote 4/28/54–7/16/56," JFKL.

9. Letter, John F. Kennedy to Robert L. Reynolds, May 3,1956, ibid. See the subsequent correspondence between Sorensen and Reynolds: Letter, Reynolds to Sorensen, May 4, 1956, and Sorensen to Reynolds, May 25,1956, ibid.

10. Sorensen also pressed the case for Kennedy to be chosen for Stevenson's second slot with an aide to Stevenson at about the same time as the Shriver plane conversation. See Dallek, *An Unfinished Life*, 205.

11. Letter, Sargent Shriver to John F. Kennedy, July 22, 1956, JFKPPP, Senate Files, Candidacies, 1956 Vice Presidency, 11/22/55–7/26/56, JFKL. Shriver called Joseph Kennedy's reply "very interesting," and he assumed that John Kennedy had seen a copy of it.

12. David Powers Papers, Box 9, Powers Writing File, "Johnny We Hardly Knew Ye," transcribed tapes, #26–48, 1953–59, up to Ray Miller–Disalle over Ohio, #34, JFKL. For detailed accounts of the Chicago convention's selection of Estes Kefauver over Kennedy, see Dallek, *An Unfinished Life*, 204–210; and Herbert Parmet, *Jack: The Struggles of John F. Kennedy* (New York: Dial, 1980), 372–383.

13. Dallek, *An Unfinished Life*, 209.

14. See November 1956 Memorandum to Files "Catholic Vote in Presidential Election 1956," TCSP, Box 25, Campaign Files, 1959–1960, Religion Issue Campaign Material, Folder 2, JFKL.

15. The other impediments were that, as a frontrunner, a stop Kennedy movement might emerge, the process might lead to a deadlocked convention, a

spoiler might emerge in the primaries like Kefauver, his age might put off some voters, or Kennedy might be typecast as vice presidential material.

16. Speech, Vermont Holy Name Societies, St. Michael's College, Burlington, VT, May 15, 1954, JFKPPP, Speech Files, Box 894, JFKL.

17. Speech, Commencement Address, Assumption College, Worcester, MA, June 3, 1955, ibid.

18. Speech, North Shore United Church Canvass Banquet, November 17, 1955, ibid.

19. Speech, National Conference of Christians and Jews, Boston, MA, February 16, 1956, ibid., Box 895.

20. Oral history interview, Bishop John J. Wright, D.D., Pittsburgh, PA, March 7, 1966, p. 1, JFKL.

21. Ibid., 20.

22. Ibid., 22.

23. Robert Moats Miller, *Bishop G. Bromley Oxnam: Paladin of Liberal Protestantism* (Nashville, TN: Abingdon, 1990).

24. In addition to Miller, *Bishop G. Bromley Oxnam*, see G. Bromley Oxnam, *I Protest* (New York: Harper, 1954); *Bishop Oxnam and the Un-American Activities Committee* (Boston: Beacon, 1953); Wayne Lowell Miller, "A Critical Analysis of the Speaking Career of Bishop G. Bromley Oxnam," Ph.D. diss., University of Southern California, 1961; and David Gillingham, "The Politics of Piety: G. Bromley Oxnam and the Un-American Activities Committee," thesis, Princeton University, 1967.

25. G. Bromley Oxnam Papers (hereafter GBOP), Box 28, Diary entry, June 16, 1958.

26. Ibid.

27. Dallek, *An Unfinished Life*, 231.

28. G. Bromley Oxnam Papers, Box 28, Diary entry, June 16, 1958.

29. See John Wicklein, "Oxnam Questions Kennedy Freedom," *New York Times*, January 4, 1960. Oxnam wrote to Poling to say that he liked Kennedy very much but was troubled by the details of the chapel story. He asked Poling if there were any other information about other similar circumstances. Poling replied that he did not know of other examples of pressure from the Catholic hierarchy on Kennedy. See Letter, Oxnam to Poling, December 7, 1959, and Letter, Poling to Oxnam, December 11, 1950, both in GBOP, Box 36, General Correspondence, "Daniel A. Poling 1938–1960" file.

30. Letter, July 2, 1958, Kennedy to Oxnam, TCSP, Box 8, Subject Files, 1953–60, Catholic Question, 1/6/58–10/31/58, JFKL.

31. Letter, July 14, 1958, Oxnam to Kennedy, ibid.

32. Edward T. Follard, "Methodist Bishops Talk Over Leading Issue with Kennedy," *Washington Post*, April 16, 1959.

33. GBOP, Box 29, Diary entry, April 15, 1959.

34. Ibid., April 16, 1959.

35. GBOP, Box 30, Diary entry, March 27, 1960.

36. Oral history interview, Bishop John J. Wright, D.D., Pittsburgh, PA, March 7, 1966, p. 26, JFKL.

37. Ibid., 33.

38. Ibid., 23.

39. Ibid., 17.

40. Ibid., 21. I can find no other reference to this tour in the primary or secondary literature.

41. TCSP, Subject Files, 1953–60, Box 1, "Agenda, 1957 Schedules, 5/1/57–6/12/58."

42. JFKPPP, '60 Campaign, Campaigns by State, Pre-Convention Political Files, 1959–1960, Texas–Labor–Utah, Box 965, "Utah General (G–W)" file.

43. Ibid.

44. Letter, Anne Baar to Kennedy, December 10, 1957, JFKPPP, Box 998, Religious Issue File, Representative Letters, 12/10/57–11/28/59, JFKL.

45. Letter, January 24, 1958, Kennedy to Baar, ibid.

46. Letter, April 2, 1958, E. Claude Gardner to Kennedy, ibid.

47. Letter, April 24, 1958, Kennedy to Gardner, ibid.

48. Letter, Glenn Archer to Kennedy, April 8, 1958, ibid., General Correspondence, 3/1/58–4/27/58.

49. Letter, Kennedy to Archer, May 20, 1958, ibid.

50. Letter, Archer to Kennedy, November 27, 1959, JFKPPP, Box 1001, 1960 Campaign Files, Religious Issues File, Birth Control Correspondence, JFKL.

51. Robert Dallek cites popular news articles on Kennedy in the late fifties in *Look*, *Time*, the *Saturday Evening Post*, *McCall's*, *Redbook*, *U.S. News and World Report*, *Parade*, *American Mercury*, and *Catholic Digest*. While Kennedy probably courted many of these outlets, there is no doubt that they also sought him out as a new breed of celebrity politician. See Dallek, *An Unfinished Life*, 225.

52. John H. Fenton, "Cushing Defends Kennedy's Views," *New York Times*, March 10, 1959.

53. Dallek, *An Unfinished Life*, 232–233.

54. Austin C. Wehrwein, "Kennedy Regards Religion as Issue," *New York Times*, April 10, 1959.

55. John Wicklein, "Knoxville Pastor to Lead Baptists," *New York Times*, May 22, 1959.

56. Democratic National Committee Papers (hereafter DNCP), Clippings File, JFK Box 1, JFKL.

57. See the 10-page summary memo of this meeting, "Memos: Robert Kennedy, Outgoing, 10/28/59–4/30/60," in Robert F. Kennedy Papers (hereafter RFKP), Pre-Administration Political Files, Box 39, General Subject, 1959–1960, JFKL.

58. Theodore H. White, *The Making of the President 1960* (New York: Atheneum, 1961), 60. I am indebted to White's account of the Hyannisport

meeting throughout this section. White's account gives detailed descriptions of 9 of the 16 attendees. See also Dallek, *An Unfinished Life*, 242–243.

59. White, *The Making of the President*, 61.

60. Ibid., 65.

61. Statement of Senator John F. Kennedy Announcing His Candidacy for the Presidency of the United States, U.S. Senate Caucus Room, Washington, D.C., January 2, 1960, available at http://www.jfklibrary. org/Historical+Resources/Archives/Reference+Desk/Speeches/JFK/JFK+Pre-Pres/1960/Announcement+of+Candidacy+for+the+Presidency.htm

62. Arthur M. Schlesinger, Jr., *A Thousand Days: John F. Kennedy in the White House* (New York: Houghton Mifflin, 1965), 21.

Chapter 2

1. The *Christian Century* published twice as often as *Christianity and Crisis*, and it published over five times as many pages in a year. The scholarly analysis of the influence of the *Christian Century* is sadly thin. See Linda-Marie Delloff, Martin E. Marty, Dean Peerman, and James M. Wall, *A Century of the Century* (Grand Rapids, MI: Eerdmans, 1984), for broad historical essays on the magazine.

2. Harold Fey, "Presentation to Private Luncheon, Congress Hotel, Chicago, December 3, 1958," Christian Century Business Files, Foundation Documents: 1958, Christian Century Foundation Archives, Special Collections, Southern Illinois University Collection 36, Box 214, Folder 7.

3. Harold Fey, "Aims of the *Christian Century*," undated manuscript, ibid.

4. The long and impressive list includes Carlyle Marney, Eugene Carson Blake, Edwin Dahlberg, Bishop G. Bromley Oxnam, and James Wine, to name only a few. See "The Christian Century Foundation," undated draft manuscript for presentational booklet *The Christian Century Foundation: A Program of Ecumenical Christian Journalism*, ibid., Folder 3.

5. "Pope John XXIII Plans a World Church Council," *Christian Century* 76, no. 5 (February 4, 1959): 124. Three weeks later, Franklin Littell chided the Vatican for calling the council ecumenical when it would not include the Orthodox or Protestants. Instead, it would simply be a "denominational synod." See Franklin H. Littell, "The Pope's Ecumenical Council," *Christian Century* 76, no. 8 (February 25, 1959): 224–225.

6. "The Candidates' Religion," *Christian Century* 76, no. 9 (March 4, 1959): 251–253.

7. Ibid., 252–253. In another editorial in the same issue, the magazine noted fearfully that, for the first time in history, Roman Catholics made up the largest single denominational group in Congress. See "Diplomatic Ties with Vatican Again Urged in Congress," *Christian Century* 76, no. 9 (March 4, 1959): 253.

8. Letter, William Coolidge Hart to Senator John F. Kennedy, March 27, 1959, Christian Century Foundation Archives, Special Collections, Southern Illinois University Collection 36, Box 54, Folder 3.

9. Letter, C. Stanley Lowell to Harold Fey, July 29, 1958, ibid., Box 65, Folder 7.

10. Letter, Harold Fey to the Reverend R. D. Frederickson, March 17, 1959, ibid., Box 54, Folder 3.

11. Harold E. Fey, "Christian and State in America," *Christian Century* 76, no. 31 (August 5, 1959): 891–893.

12. Ibid., 893. The very next issue contained a brief review by Schubert Ogden of Henri de Lubac, S.J., *Catholicism: A Study of Dogma in Relation to the Corporate Destiny of Mankind*. De Lubac would be an influential theologian during Vatican II. See *Christian Century* 76, no. 32 (August 12, 1959): 923. So the magazine was monitoring developments within global Catholicism.

13. Jaroslav Pelikan, "The Tragic Necessity of the Reformation," *Christian Century* 76, no. 36 (September 9, 1959): 1017–1020.

14. Ibid., 1019.

15. Paul Blanshard, "Ecclesiastical Justice in Spain: I," *Christian Century* 76, no. 38 (September 23, 1959): 1080–1081; and Blanshard, "Ecclesiastical Justice in Spain: II," *Christian Century* 76, no. 39 (September 30, 1959): 1115–1116.

16. For more on Morrison, see Linda-Marie Delloff, "Charles Clayton Morrison: Shaping a Journal's Identity," in Linda-Marie Delloff, Martin Marty, Dean Peerman, and James Wall, *A Century of the Century* (Grand Rapids, MI: Eerdmans, 1984), 3–16.

17. Charles Clayton Morrison, "The Organization of POAU," n.d., Christian Century Foundation Archives, Special Collections, Southern Illinois University Collection 36, Writings of Charles Clayton Morrison, Box 2, Folder 6. The *Christian Century* published the entire text when it appeared. See Martin Marty, "Peace and Pluralism: The *Century* 1946–1952," in Delloff et al., *A Century of the Century*, 78–80.

18. Morrison, "The Organization of POAU."

19. Letter, C. Stanley Lowell to Harold Fey, July 18, 1958, Christian Century Foundation Archives, Special Collections, Southern Illinois University Collection 36, Box 65, Folder 7.

20. Letter, C. Stanley Lowell to Harold Fey, March 19, 1958, ibid.

21. Harold Fey, "Free from . . . Error," *Christian Century* 77, no. 7 (February 17, 1960): 191–192.

22. Ibid., 191.

23. Victor B. Harris, "An Unhallowed Perversion: A Flagrant Violation of the Constitutional Requirement as to Church-State Separation Is Soon to Be Contested in St. Louis, Missouri," *Christian Century* 76, no. 40 (October 7, 1959): 1143–1145.

24. Ibid., 1144.

25. O. Walter Wagner, "Our Hallowed Preoccupation: The Position of St. Louis University in Mill Creek Redevelopment Dispute Is Contractually Legal, Valid, Above-Board," *Christian Century* 76, no. 45 (November 11, 1959): 1303–1304.

26. Jaroslav Pelikan, "New Light from the Old World," *Christian Century* 76, no. 41 (October 14, 1959): 1182–1183.

27. Ibid., 1183.

28. "Reformation: New Phase," *Christian Century* 76, no. 44 (November 4, 1959): 1267–1268.

29. Ibid., 1268.

30. "Congratulations 'Commonweal,'" *Christian Century* 76, no. 45 (November 11, 1959): 1300–1301.

31. "Catholic Bishops Call Population Explosion 'Propaganda,'" *Christian Century* 76, no. 49 (December 9, 1959): 1247.

32. "Bishop Pike Asks for Candidates' Views," *Christian Century* 76, no. 49 (December 9, 1959): 1247.

33. Robert McAfee Brown, "Rules for the Dialogue," *Christian Century* 77, no. 7 (February 17, 1960): 183–184.

34. *Christianity and Crisis* was born in 1941 under the leadership of Reinhold Niebuhr in rebellion against the pacifist stance of the *Christian Century* at the beginning of World War II. For background on Niebuhr and the founding of *Christianity and Crisis*, see Heather A. Warren, *Theologian of a New World Order: Reinhold Niebuhr and the Christian Realists 1920–1948* (New York: Oxford University Press, 1997); and Richard W. Fox, *Reinhold Niebuhr: A Biography* (New York: Pantheon, 1985). The most thorough analysis of the magazine is Mark Hulsether, *Building a Protestant Left: Christianity and Crisis Magazine 1941–1993* (Knoxville: University of Tennessee Press, 1999).

35. Robert McAfee Brown, "Senator Kennedy's Statement," *Christianity and Crisis* 19, no. 4 (March 16, 1959): 25–26. Through the forties and early fifties, the magazine had maintained a reactionary anti-Catholic stance that only began to moderate in the late fifties. See Hulsether, *Building a Protestant Left*, 61–64.

36. Arthur Schlesinger, Jr., "Senator Kennedy and His Oath," *Christianity and Crisis* 19, no. 7 (April 2, 1959): 52.

37. Gustave Weigel, S.J., "Inside American Roman Catholicism," *Christianity and Crisis* 19, no. 10 (June 8, 1959): 79–81.

38. Ibid., 81.

39. Thomas F. O'Dea, "The Ideologists and the Missing Dialogue," *Christianity and Crisis* 19, no. 10 (June 8, 1959): 81–84.

40. William Clancy, "A Roman Catholic View of American Protestantism," *Christianity and Crisis* 19, no. 10 (June 8, 1959): 85–87.

41. C. Stanley Lowell, "A Word for Father Weigel," *Christianity and Crisis* 19, no. 11 (June 22, 1959): 96.

42. Henry P. Van Dusen, "American Catholicism: Grounds for Misgivings," *Christianity and Crisis* 19, no. 14 (August 3, 1959): 115. Hulsether argues that Van Dusen was the most reluctant of the Union Seminary crew on the magazine to abandon the earlier anti-Catholicism of the publication. See Hulsether, *Building a Protestant Left*, 64.

43. Ibid., 116.

44. Claud Nelson, "The Dialogue Continued," *Christianity and Crisis* 19, no. 14 (August 3, 1959): 117–118.

45. Francis J. Lally, "Double Soliloquy Is Not Dialogue," *Christianity and Crisis* 19, no. 16 (October 5, 1959): 143. Lally was present at the Columbia University Four Cs conference (see below) and was also active in Fund for the Republic activities, so he had more than a casual acquaintance with many leading Protestant thinkers.

46. Ibid., 143.

47. C. Stanley Lowell, "A Word from the Pope Requested," *Christianity and Crisis* 19, no. 18 (November 2, 1959): 160.

48. Ibid., 160.

49. William Clancy, "Gratitude, Disappointment, Despair," *Christianity and Crisis* 19, no. 19 (November 10, 1959): 166–167.

50. Ibid., 167.

51. John C. Bennett, "Universal Religious Freedom," *Christianity and Crisis* 19, no. 18 (November 2, 1959): 155.

52. See Mark Massa, S.J., *Anti-Catholicism in America: The Last Acceptable Prejudice* (New York: Crossroad, 2003).

53. Ibid., 7.

54. Ibid.

55. Ibid., 10.

56. John McGreevy, "Thinking on One's Own: Catholicism in the American Intellectual Imagination, 1928–1960," *Journal of American History* 84, no. 1 (June 1997): 97–131.

57. Massa, *Anti-Catholicism in America*, 14.

58. Ibid., 17.

59. John T. McGreevy, *Catholicism and American Freedom* (New York: Norton, 2003), 168. I am indebted to McGreevy's analysis throughout this section.

60. Ibid., 173. McGreevy also cites the rise of Father Charles Coughlin as another example of liberal fear of Catholic links to fascism.

61. Ibid., 175.

62. Ibid., 179.

63. Ibid., 180.

64. Ibid., 183–184.

Chapter 3

1. Each entity invited guests to participate in the conference. The attendance lists from 1959 and 1960 are quite impressive and include H. Richard Niebuhr, John Bennett, William Clancy, Ed Dowey, Nathan Glazer, Rabbi Arthur Hertzberg, the Reverend Monsignor Francis Lally, Martin Marty, Liston Pope, Gustave Weigel, Emil Fackenheim, Paul Lehmann, and Harold Weisberg. See "Participants in Conference" and "Agenda," *Christian Century* Foundation Archives, Special Collections, Southern Illinois University Collection 36, Box 61, Folder 4.

2. Letter, Wayne Cowan to Harold Fey, January 13, 1960, ibid.

3. See Adlai Stevenson, "The Survival of the Free Society," *Christianity and Crisis* 19, no. 23 (January 11, 1960): 204–208.

4. John C. Bennett, "The Candidacy of Mr. Nixon," *Christianity and Crisis* 19, no. 24 (January 25, 1960): 209.

5. Ibid., 210.

6. John C. Danforth, "Mr. Nixon Defended: Dr. Bennett Questioned," *Christianity and Crisis* 20, no. 4 (March 21, 1960): 31.

7. Ibid., 31–32.

8. Reinhold Niebuhr, "Why Christianity and Crisis?" *Christianity and Crisis* 20, no. 1 (February 8, 1960):1–2.

9. John C. Bennett, "A Roman Catholic for President?" *Christianity and Crisis* 20, no. 3 (March 7, 1960): 17–19.

10. Ibid., 17.

11. Ibid., 19.

12. For more background on this episode, see Phyllis Elaine Alsdurf, "*Christianity Today* Magazine and Late Twentieth-Century Evangelicalism," Ph.D. diss., University of Minnesota, 2004, pp. 135–141. I am indebted to her analysis throughout this section.

13. Letter, Oxnam to Poling, December 7, 1959, GBOP, Box 36, General Correspondence, Daniel Poling, 1938–1960.

14. Letter, Poling to Oxnam, December 11, 1959, ibid.

15. John Wicklein, "Oxnam Questions Kennedy's Freedom," *New York Times*, January 4, 1960.

16. "Editorially Speaking…Nov. 8," *Christian Herald*, October 1960, 26.

17. E. S. James, *Baptist Standard*, February 17, 1960.

18. Letter, Kennedy to James, February 29, 1960, TCSP, Box 25, Campaign Files, 1959–1960, "Religious Issue Catholic Issue Folder 2."

19. Letter, James to Kennedy, March 11, 1960, ibid.

20. "Excerpts from Remarks by Theodore C. Sorensen February, 1960: The Catholic Issue in American Politics," David F. Powers Papers, JFKL, JFK Political Organization and Campaigns, Box 27, Religious Issue, 1959–1960.

21. "Political Pots Begin to Boil," *Christian Century* 77, no. 2 (January 13, 1960): 37–38.

22. An *Economist* Correspondent, "John F. Kennedy: An Overseas View," *Christian Century* 77, no. 3 (January 20, 1960): 76–77.

23. "Why Senator Kennedy Withdrew as Speaker," *Christian Century* 77, no. 4 (January 27, 1960): 93.

24. Ibid.

25. Dave Powers Papers, Powers Writing File, "Johny We Hardly Knew Ye," transcribed tape #47, p. 6.

26. Letter, Pat Lucey to Ted Sorensen, December 22, 1959, RFKP, Box 39, Pre-Administration Political Files, General Subject, 1959–1960, Memos: Theodore Sorensen, 10/19/59–6/1/60.

27. RFKP, Box 45, Pre-Administration Files, General Subject, 1959–1960, Poll: Preferences in the Democratic Presidential Primary in Wisconsin, 2/13/60 (Harris), p. 2.

28. Ibid., 4.

29. Ibid., 6.

30. Ibid., 10–12.

31. Ibid., 18.

32. Ibid., Poll: The Democratic Primary Election in Wisconsin 3rd, 9th, and 7th Congressional Districts (Harris).

33. Ibid., 9.

34. Ibid., 10.

35. Transcript, "What Happened in Wisconsin," CBS Television Network, April 5, 1960, p. 6, ibid., Box 50, State Files: Wisconsin, Primary, Miscellaneous, 12/31/58–4/30/60.

36. Ibid., 19–21.

37. Dave Powers Papers, Powers Writing File, "Johny We Hardly Knew Ye," transcribed tape #50, p. 14.

38. The practice of trying to "spin" the press is not a recent invention. The Kennedy campaign issued a press sheet entitled "Analysis of the Wisconsin Returns" that put the best possible light on the results. See David F. Powers Papers, JFK Political Organization and Campaign, Box 27, Primary: Wisconsin (4/5/60), Schedules and Plans.

39. Robert Michaelson, "Religion and the Presidency: I," *Christian Century* 77, no. 5 (February 3, 1960): 133–135, and Michaelson, "Religion and the Presidency: II," *Christian Century* 77, no. 5 (February 10, 1960): 159–161. In his astonishing epistolary zeal, C. Stanley Lowell of POAU penned a letter to the editor that was critical of Michaelson for not seeing that there were many current issues where the Catholic church claimed absolute authority over Catholic politicians: "There is an inescapable fear that in voting for him [a Catholic] one may be voting partly for a man and partly for a church." C. Stanley Lowell, "Church and Presidency," *Christian Century* 77, no. 10 (March 9, 1960): 289.

40. Letter, Harold Fey to Rev. Graham R. Hodges, March 28, 1960, Christian Century Foundation Archives, Special Collections, Southern Illinois University Collection 36, Box 61, Folder 4.

41. "Religion Plays Part in Wisconsin Vote," *Christian Century* 77, no. 16 (April 20, 1960): 460.

42. Martin Marty interview, January 2000, Pepperdine University, Malibu, CA.

43. W. H. Lawrence, "'Stop Kennedy' Drive Led by Byrd of West Virginia," *New York Times*, April 11, 1960.

44. "Candidate Prospects in West Virginia," *Christian Century* 77, no. 16 (April 20, 1960): 460–461.

45. "Moratorium on Bigotry," *Christian Century* 77, no. 17 (April 27, 1960): 499.

46. Ibid.

47. Memorandum, April 27, 1959, Sorensen to Kennedy, JFKPPP, 1960 Campaign Files, Pre-Convention Political Files, West Virginia Organization, Box 968, 2/18/59–4/27/60.

48. William L. Long, "The John F. Kennedy Library Oral History Project: The West Virginia Democratic Presidential Primary, 1960," Ph.D. diss., Ohio State University, 1982, p. 55.

49. David F. Powers Papers, Powers Writing File, "Johnny We Hardly Knew Ye," transcribed tape #47, p. 9.

50. West Virginia Polls, David F. Powers Papers, JFKL, JFK Political Organization and Campaigns, Box 27, Primary: West Virginia (5/10/60).

51. Memorandum, Chuck Daly to Mike Feldman, April 6, 1960, JFKPPP, 1960 Campaign Files, Box 989, West Virginia Primary, Data Campaign Issues.

52. Memorandum, Ted Sorensen and Ralph Dungan to Senator John F. Kennedy and Robert F. Kennedy, April 18, 1960, JFKPPP, Box 997, 1960 Campaign Files, Feldman Subject File, 1960 Religion, 5/23/59–4/2/60 and undated.

53. Ibid. The draft text of the letter and brochure rehearse a number of specific arguments that Kennedy had already used in other contexts to address the religion issue as well as themes that would emerge later. This dry run, while not used in this instance, shows the ongoing deliberation on the issue in Sorensen's mind.

54. Background Materials, David F. Powers Papers, JFK Political Organization and Campaigns, Box 27, Primary: West Virginia (5/10/60).

55. Press Release, "The Religious Issue in American Politics," April 21, 1960, JFKPPP, Box 908, Senate Files, Speech Files, American Society of Newspaper Editors, Washington, DC, April 21, 1960.

56. Ibid., 5.

57. Ibid., 7.

58. Ibid., 7–8.

59. Ibid., 9.

60. Long, "John F. Kennedy Library Oral History," 78–79.

61. Memorandum, Robert Wallace to Robert F. Kennedy and Theodore Sorensen et al., April 23, 1960, RFKP, Box 50, Pre-Administration Papers,

Political Files, General Subject State Files: West Virginia Primary Correspondence, 10/26/59–5/10/60 and undated.

62. See Nancy Carol Arnett, "John F. Kennedy's 1960 Presidential Campaign: Rhetorical Strategies and Image Projection," Ph.D. diss., Florida State University, 1983, p. 299.

63. An Outline of Remarks and Questions, TCSP, Box 25, Campaign Files, 1959–60, Religious Issue Campaign Material, Folder 2.

64. Dave Powers Papers, Box 9, Powers Writing File, transcribed tape #50A, p. 19.

65. Ibid., 14.

66. "West Virginia Kills a Myth," *Christian Century* 77, no. 21 (May 25, 1960): 629–630.

67. "Will Catholics Give Up Bloc Voting?" *Christian Century* 77, no. 21 (May 25, 1960): 630.

68. William Lee Miller, "Profiles in Power," *Christianity and Crisis* 20, no. 13 (July 25, 1960): 109–110.

69. Ibid., 110.

70. Reinhold Niebuhr, "Stray Thoughts on the Political Scene," *Christianity and Crisis* 20, no. 14 (August 8, 1960): 124.

71. Ibid.

72. Ibid.

73. "Planned Politics Pays Off," *Christian Century* 77, no. 30 (July 27, 1960): 867–868.

74. Ibid., 867. A few issues later, the magazine reported that two-thirds of the delegates to the Democratic convention were Protestant. It concluded that the delegates did not vote according to religion but according to political expediency. See "Democratic Delegates Were Two-Thirds Protestant," *Christian Century* 77, no. 32 (August 10, 1960): 916.

75. Ibid., 867.

76. "No Political Messiahs," *Christian Century* 77, no. 32 (August 10, 1960): 915–916.

Chapter 4

1. Richard M. Nixon, *Six Crises* (Garden City, NY: Doubleday, 1962), xii.

2. Ibid., xv.

3. Further evidence of the anticipatory nature of the book can be seen in a staff memo from Chuck Lichenstein to Nixon that assessed Theodore White's *The Making of the President 1960*. This eight-page critique of White's book ends by predicting that White's book will age rapidly and that, when *Six Crises* appears, it will have its own audience, "ready, willing, and malleable." Memorandum, Lichenstein to Nixon, September 14, 1961, "1960 Election Chapter," Richard M. Nixon Pre-Presidential Papers (hereafter RMNPPP), Series 258, *Six Crises* Manuscript, Box 1 of 2.

4. The other crises were the Alger Hiss case, his speech defending his use of a spending fund as vice president, Eisenhower's heart attack, Nixon's visit to Caracas, and the kitchen debate in Russia.

5. Memorandum, Richard Nixon to Chuck Lichenstein and Agnes Waldron, September 12, 1961, "Book Memos," RMNPPP, Series 258, *Six Crises* Manuscript, Box 1 of 2.

6. Nixon, *Six Crises*, 305.

7. Ibid., 421.

8. Letter, Cronin to Nixon, November 13, 1950, RMNPPP, Series 320, Vice President General Correspondence, Cronin, J. F. (1959)–Cronin, J. F. (1960), Box 191, "Cronin, Rev. John F., 1956 2/2."

9. Letter, Cronin to Nixon, December 3, 1952, ibid.

10. Letter, Cronin to Nixon, September 15, 1953, ibid.

11. Letter, Cronin to Nixon, January 10, 1955, ibid.

12. List, Cronin to Nixon, January 21, 1955, ibid.

13. Letter, Wright to Cronin, November 1, 1955, ibid., 1/2.

14. Letter, Nixon to Cronin, October 3, 1955, ibid., 2/2.

15. Letter, Cronin to Nixon, July 13, 1956, ibid., Box 192, Cronin, John F., Speech Drafts, "Catholic Vote Data."

16. "Random Thoughts on the 1956 Campaign: J.F.C.," RMNPPP, Vice President General Correspondence, Series 320, Cronin, J. F. (1960)–Cronin, J. F. (1959), Box 191, "Cronin, Rev. John F., 1956 1/2."

17. "Ideas for Proposed Talk: Defense of Record," ibid.

18. "Memorandum of Conversation at Lunch, May 22, 1956," ibid.

19. Letter, Cronin to Rose Mary Woods, July 26, 1956; Memorandum, Cronin to Nixon, August 7, 1956; "Summary of R.N.–J.F.C.," all in ibid.

20. Memorandum, Cronin to Nixon, August 14, 1956, ibid.

21. "Memorandum on Post-Convention Speeches," Cronin to Nixon, n.d., ibid., 2/2.

22. Letter, Cronin to Nixon, October 29, 1956, ibid., 1/2.

23. Letter, Nixon to O'Boyle, March 31, 1956, ibid.

24. Letter, Woods to Staff, September 13, 1956, ibid.

25. Letter, Cronin to Nixon, January 27, 1957, ibid., 2/2. It is not clear exactly when Waldron first went to work for Nixon. But by his presidential years, she was a fixture in his press office.

26. Letter, Cronin to Nixon, March 18, 1957, ibid.

27. Letter, Cronin to Nixon, June 18, 1957, ibid. Cronin felt that it was suitable for publication in *Harper's* or the *Atlantic* if she enlarged it and removed "a few of the franker expressions."

28. Memorandum on Race Relations and Proposed Southern Visit, Cronin to Nixon, July 12, 1957, ibid., Box 192, Cronin, John F., Speech Drafts, "Cronin, J. F., 1957–1958."

29. Memorandum, Cronin to Nixon, July 22, 1957, RMNPPP, Vice President General Correspondence, Series 320, Box 191, Cronin, J. F. (1960)–Cronin, J. F. (1959), "Cronin, J. F., 1957–58 2/2."

30. "Suggestions for the Next Two Years," Memorandum, Cronin to Nixon, n.d., ibid.

31. "On Suggested Harvard Lectures," Memorandum, Cronin to Nixon, July 22, 1957, ibid.

32. Letter, Cronin to O'Connor, April 1, 1957, ibid.

33. Letter, Nixon to Rev. James Cronin, April 29, 1957, ibid.

34. Memorandum, Cronin to Nixon, June 23, 1957, ibid., Box 121, Cronin, J. F. Speech Drafts, "Cronin, J. F., 1957–1958."

35. Letter, Cronin to Nixon, November 12, 1958, ibid.

36. "Racial Discrimination and the Christian Conscience Confidential Draft," ibid.

37. See "Report on Religious Leaders' Conference, President's Committee on Government Contracts, May 11, 1959," apparently authored by Cronin, in RMNPPP, Vice President General Correspondence, Series 320, Box 191, Cronin, J. F. (1960)–Cronin, J. F. (1959), "Cronin, J. F., 1959 2/2."

38. Letter, Cronin to Nixon, June 23, 1958, RMNPPP, Vice President General Correspondence, Series 320, Box 192, Cronin, J. F. Speech Drafts, "Cronin, J. F., 1957–1958."

39. Memorandum, Cronin to Nixon, October 17, 1958, ibid., Box 192, Cronin, J. F. Speech Drafts, "Cronin, J. F., 1957–1958."

40. "Comment upon Birth-Control Statement of Catholic Bishops," RMNPPP, Vice President General Correspondence, Series 320, Box 191, Cronin, J. F. (1960)–Cronin, J. F. (1959), "Cronin, J. F., 1959 1/2."

41. "Memorandum on R.H.F.–J.F.C. Conversation on Research, Advisory, and Speech Drafting Problems," January 16, 1960, ibid., Box 192, Cronin, J. F. Speech Drafts, "Cronin, J. F., 1957–1958."

42. Cronin to Nixon, "Suggestions for Nebraska Talk, March 28, 1960, on a True Conservatism," ibid. See also John J. Daly, Jr., "Nixon Urges Catholic Editors to Help Develop Public Grasp of Moral Issues Underlying Law," National Catholic Welfare Conference News Service, May 16, 1960, ibid.

43. Letter, Cronin to Nixon, July 29, 1960, ibid., Cronin, J. F. Speech Drafts, "Cronin, J. F., 1960 1/2."

44. Claude Robinson to R.H.F., February 16, 1960, ibid., Box 258, Invitations (Personal), RHF: Finch, Robert H., 1959 Letters (copies), "Finch, R. H., 1960 Letters 1/2."

45. Ibid., 2.

46. Ibid.

47. Telegram, Nixon to Ockenga, February 25, 1959, ibid., Box 567, "Ockenga, Rev. Harold John."

48. Letter, Ockenga to Nixon, March 2, 1959, ibid.

49. Letter, Ockenga to Nixon, July 13, 1959, ibid.

50. Letter, James D. Hughes, Aide to the Vice President, to Billy Graham, November 17, 1959, ibid.

51. Letter, Gigliotti to Nixon, July 15, 1960, ibid., Box 547, "National Association of Evangelicals."

52. Letter, Gigliotti to Nixon, August 6, 1960, ibid., Box 567, "National Association of Evangelicals."

53. Letter, Howard M. LeSourd to Nixon, May 12, 1955, ibid., Box 583, Peale, Norman Vincent–Pearson, Drew (Articles, Newscasts, 1961), "Peale, Norman Vincent."

54. Memorandum, "rmw" to "PJ," May 20, 1955, ibid.

55. Letter, Nixon to Dillon, May 20, 1955, and Letter, Nixon to Aldrich, May 20, 1955, both in ibid.

56. Letter, Peale to Nixon, April 5, 1960, ibid.

57. Memo, Nixon to Bob Finch, Jim Shepley, and Herb Klein, April 11, 1960, ibid.

58. Memorandum, Nixon to Finch, n.d., with sample letter from Peale dated May 20, 1960, to friends attached, and Letter, Nixon to Peale, July 11, 1960, all in ibid.

59. Letter, Peale to Nixon, June 23, 1960, and Letter, Nixon to Peale, July 15, 1960, both in ibid.

60. Letter, Graham to Nixon, December 2, 1957, ibid., Box 299, Grady, Daniel B.–Grainger, Isaac B., "Graham, Dr. Billy 3/3."

61. Ibid.

62. Memorandum, "CKMcW" to Nixon, December 18, 1957, ibid.

63. Memorandum for File, "CKMcW," February 3, 1958, ibid.

64. Letter, Armstrong to Nixon, January 24, 1959, ibid., Box 50, Armour, Albert–Arnall, Ellis, "Armstrong, O. K."

65. Memorandum to File, Robert Finch, February 10, 1959, ibid.

66. The International Christian Leadership was the forerunner of the stealthy evangelical organization known as the Fellowship.

67. Letters, Armstrong to Nixon, April 15, 1959, and April 27, 1959, RMNPPP, Vice President General Correspondence, Series 320, Box 50, Armour, Albert–Arnall, Ellis, "Armstrong, O. K."

68. Letter, Nixon to Armstrong, May 30, 1959, ibid.

69. Letter, Armstrong to Klein, July 16, 1960, ibid.

70. Letter, Armstrong to Nixon, July 16, 1960, ibid.

Chapter 5

1. Speech text, Robert H. Finch, RMNPPP, Vice President General Correspondence, Series 320, Box 258, "Finch, Robert H., 1960 Personal," Invitations (Personal) RHF: Finch, Robert H., 1959 Letters (copies).

2. "G.O.P. Shifts Staff to Spur Campaign," *New York Times*, June 6, 1960, and "G.O.P. Names Coordinator," *New York Times*, September 24, 1960.

3. Letter, July 12, 1960, Hermann to Armstrong, and Letter, July 16, 1960, Armstrong to Hermann, both in Orland K. Armstrong Papers (hereafter OKAP), Western Historical Manuscript Collection, University of Missouri, Accession 4881, Box 137.

4. Republican National Convention Employee Pass, signed by A. B. Hermann, and Letter, July 16, 1960, Armstrong to Hermann, both in ibid., Box 69.

5. Letter, July 16, 1960, Armstrong to Hermann, ibid., Box 137.

6. "O. K. Armstrong: Memo on Qualifications," n.d., ibid., Box 69.

7. SBC Convention Bulletin: Fourth Day: May 20, 1960, Resolution No. 4: Christian Citizenship, ibid., Box 138.

8. Ibid.

9. Ibid.

10. Confidential Memo to AB, n.d., ibid. While this memorandum is not dated, it does list denominational activity through June 2, 1960; therefore, it is logical to conclude that it is an early communication between Armstrong and Hermann.

11. Confidential Memo for All Leaders of the Campaign, n.d., ibid.

12. Ibid., 2.

13. Ibid., 4.

14. "Expense Account, August: (15th to 31st)," October 1, 1960, ibid., Box 69. His total expense for travel for this period was $741.22.

15. George N. Green, "Collins, Carr P.," *Handbook of Texas Online.* Available at http://www.tsha.utexas.edu/handbook/online/articles/view/CC/fc090.html (accessed February 20, 2001).

16. Handwritten note, OKAP, Box 138.

17. William R. Smith interview, June 8, 2000, Columbia, MO.

18. Letter, Vaught to Armstrong, October 20, 1960, OKAP, Western Historical Manuscript Collection, University of Missouri, Accession 4881, Box 137.

19. Letter, Armstrong to Pollard, October 6, 1960, ibid.

20. Proposed Statement by Dr. Ramsey Pollard, President, Southern Baptist Convention, ibid.

21. Letter, Pollard to Armstrong, October 24, 1960, ibid.

22. Summary of Activities: [August 15 to October 9], ibid., Box 138.

23. This section is drawn from *The Birth of POAU* by Joseph M. Dawson, POAU Pamphlet, n.d., Americans United for Separation of Church and State Papers, Princeton University, 13th Annual Meeting of the Board of Trustees, Box 3.

24. Of course, POAU would feel these pressures itself within a decade and a half and reconstitute itself as Americans United for Separation of Church and State; its evangelical and fundamentalist members left and formed their own parallel organizations.

25. "Officers, Executive Committee, Board of Trustees, and National Advisory Council, Protestants and Other Americans United for Separation

of Church and State, January 19, 1961," Americans United for Separation of Church and State Papers, Box 3, 13th Annual Meeting of the Board of Trustees.

26. "Report on the Editorial Program of POAU to the National Advisory Council, Portland, Oregon, February 15, 1961," ibid.

27. "Literature Distribution," ibid., "Board of Trustees and National Council Semi-Annual Meeting."

28. "Meeting, Board of Trustees, Tuesday, September 6, 1960," ibid.

29. Letter, Archer to Mackay, May 18, 1959, ibid., Box 5, "Mackay, John, 1956."

30. "An Analysis of Catholic 'Power Politics' and Other Factors of Political Pressure in the First Ballot Nomination of Sen. John F. Kennedy for President," ibid., Box 7, "Mailings to Board of Trustees."

31. "Minutes of Executive Committee POAU, June 6, 1960," ibid., Box 3, "Executive Committee of Board of Trustees 1960." The date in the title is an error as the document itself gives July 6, 1960, as the date of the meeting.

32. "Statement Regarding Morrison Manuscript 7/6/60," ibid.

33. Letter, Southgate to Archer, July 15, 1960, ibid.

34. Letter, Newton to Archer, July 18, 1960, ibid., Box 5, "Newton, Louie, Chairman, Board of Trustees, 1960."

35. Letter, Archer to Newton, July 20, 1960, ibid.

36. Ibid.

37. Memo, Archer to CSL [C. Stanley Lowell] and JCM [John Mayne], August 4, 1960, ibid., Box 3, "Board of Trustees and National Council Semi-Annual Meeting."

38. Letter, Archer to Givens, August 4, 1960, ibid.

39. Letter, Hitt to Archer, August 23, 1960, ibid.

40. Letter, Allen to Archer, August 8, 1960, ibid.

41. Letter, Allen to Archer, August 23, 1960, ibid.

42. Letter, Vaught to Archer, August 24, 1960, ibid.

43. Letter, Newton to Archer, August 15, 1960, ibid., Box 5, "Newton, Louie, Chairman, Board of Trustees 1960."

44. Letter, Hall to Archer, August 26, 1960, ibid., "Dick Houston Hall, Jr., Vice President."

45. Ibid.

46. Letter, C. Stanley Lowell to Newton, August 25, 1960, ibid., Box 3, "Board of Trustees and National Council Semi-Annual Meeting."

47. Letter, Archer to Newton, August 25, 1960, ibid., Box 5, "Newton, Louie, Chairman, Board of Trustees 1960."

48. Letter, Archer to Board, August 9, 1960, ibid., Box 3, "Board of Trustees and National Council Semi-Annual Meeting."

49. "Roster, POAU Board Meeting, September 6, 1960," ibid.

50. "Meeting, Board of Trustees," ibid.

51. Ibid.

52. Ibid.

53. Ibid.

54. "News for Release, Wednesday, September 7, 1960," ibid.

55. Ibid.

56. Letter, Rycroft to Lowell, October 16, 1960, ibid., Box 5, "Rycroft, W. Stanley, Jr., 1958."

Chapter 6

1. The most comprehensive treatment of this episode is Carol V. R. George, *God's Salesman: Norman Vincent Peale and the Power of Positive Thinking* (New York: Oxford University Press, 1993). See especially chapter 7, "The Demise of Tribal Politics 1955–1985." In addition, George provides illuminating background material on Peale's relationship with the NAE and with Nixon. I am dependent on her account and insights throughout this chapter. See also Thomas Carty, *A Catholic in the White House? Religion, Politics, and John F. Kennedy's Presidential Campaign* (New York: Palgrave Macmillan, 2004); Mark Massa, *Anti-Catholicism in America: The Last Acceptable Prejudice* (New York: Crossroad, 2003); Paul Blanshard, *Personal and Controversial: An Autobiography* (Boston: Beacon, 1973); William Martin, *With God on Our Side: The Rise of the Religious Right in America* (New York: Broadway, 1996); Billy Graham, *Just as I Am: The Autobiography of Billy Graham* (San Francisco: HarperSanFranciso, 1997); William Martin, *A Prophet with Honor: The Billy Graham Story* (New York: Morrow, 1991); Theodore Sorensen, *Kennedy* (New York: Harper and Row, 1965); Robert Dallek, *An Unfinished Life: John F. Kennedy 1917–1963* (Boston: Little, Brown, 2003); Nancy Gibbs and Michael Duffy, *The Preacher and the Presidents: Billy Graham in the White House* (New York: Center Street, 2007),

2. Letter, Peale to Nixon, August 19, 1960, RMNPPP, Vice President General Correspondence, Series 320, Box 583, Peale, Norman Vincent–Pearson, Drew (Articles, Newscasts 1961), "Peale, Norman Vincent."

3. Letters, Graham to Nixon, June 21, 1960, and August 22, 1960, ibid., Box 299, Grady, Daniel B.–Grainger, Isaac B., "Graham, Dr. Billy 2/3."

4. Letter, Graham to Nixon, May 27, 1960, ibid.

5. Letter, Graham to Nixon, August 22, 1960, ibid.

6. Letter, Graham to Nixon, August 23, 1960, ibid.

7. Letter, Graham to Nixon, September 1, 1960, ibid.

8. Ibid.

9. Letter, Nixon to Graham, September 8, 1960, ibid.

10. William Stanley Rycroft biography, William Stanley Rycroft Papers, Presbyterian Historical Society, Philadelphia, PA, Box 3, "From Witness to New York."

11. Robert F. Kennedy Pre-Administration Papers, Political Files, General Subject File, 1959–1960, Religious Issue: Memo 9/9/60.

12. Letter, Rycroft to Lowell, October 16, 1960, William Stanley Rycroft Papers, Presbyterian Historical Society, Philadelphia, PA, Box 3, "Swomley Report POAU."

13. Statement on Policy and Strategy for POAU, March 24, 1961, ibid., Box 1, "WSR Report on LA 1947."

14. "He Helped Start 'Peale Group,'" *Charlotte Observer*, September 17, 1960, p. 12A.

15. See J. Elwin Wright, "Historical Statement of Events," in *Evangelical Action! A Report of the Organization of the National Association of Evangelicals for United Action* (Boston, MA: United Action Press, 1942), reprinted in Joel A. Carpenter, ed., *A New Evangelical Coalition: Early Documents of the National Association of Evangelicals* (New York: Garland, 1988).

16. Memorandum, Taylor and Gill to the NAE Executive Committee, January 15, 1960, NAE Collection, Wheaton College Archives, Wheaton, IL, Box 30A, "Policy."

17. "Catholicism and the Presidency," ibid., Box 34, "Original Minutes 1960."

18. Don Gill, "Capital Commentary," *United Evangelical Action* 19, no. 2 (May 1960): 4.

19. Ibid., p. 5.

20. Don Gill, "Capital Commentary," *United Evangelical Action* 19, no. 3 (June 1960): 4.

21. "Report to the NAE Executive Committee from the Secretary of Public Affairs," July 20, 1960, NAE Collection, Wheaton College Archives, Wheaton, IL, Box 34, "Original Reports 1960."

22. Graham, *Just as I Am*, 391–392.

23. "Kennedy Confers with Baptists," Religion News Service, August 24, 1960.

24. Letter, Bell to W. Maxey Jarman, August 26, 1960, Nelson Bell Collection, Box 19, Folder 16, "General Correspondence: The Citizens Committee for American Religious Freedom 1960."

25. Letter, Armstrong to Caradine Hooten, August 24, 1960, OKAP, Box 138.

26. The Nixon campaign itself, not just the Republican National Committee, knew of Armstrong's work. A memorandum for the files in Nixon's papers dated September 19, 1960, simply states, "O. K. Armstrong participated in the Norman Vincent Peale Group." See "Armstrong, O. K.," in RMNPPP, General Correspondence Vice President, Series 320, Box 50, Armour, Albert–Arnall, Ellis.

27. See the National Conference of Citizens for Religious Freedom Manual, NAE Collection, Box 46B, "R.C. Candidates." The handwritten notes on the various speeches seem to be those of Clyde Taylor. I draw this inference from the fact that there are no notes taken on Taylor's speech in this copy of the manual.

28. Ibid.

29. John J. Lindsay, "Pastors Raise Church Issue Here," *Washington Post*, September 7, 1960.

30. National Conference of Citizens for Religious Freedom Manual, NAE Collection, Wheaton College Archives, Wheaton, IL, Box 46B, "R.C. Candidates."

31. Ibid.

32. Rev. Harold J. Ockenga, "Religion, Politics, and the Presidency," in OKAP, Box 138.

33. Ibid.

34. Bonnie Angelo interview, March 2006, Washington, DC.

35. See News Release, September 7, 1960, OKAP, Box 138.

36. Statement of the Conference on Religious Freedom, Mayflower Hotel, Washington, DC, September 7, 1960, NAE Collection, Box 46B, "R.C. Candidates."

37. Lindsay, "Pastors Raise Church Issue Here."

38. See "Liberal Party Assails Peale View on Kennedy," Associated Press, September 9, 1960.

39. George, *God's Salesman*, 203 ff.

40. Ibid., 208 ff.

41. "We Were There," *Christian Chronicle*, November 4, 1960, p. 2. Nichols had maintained a vociferous anti-Catholic and anti-Kennedy editorial stand throughout the fall campaign.

42. Don Gill, "Capital Commentary," *United Evangelical Action* 19, no. 8 (October 1960): 8.

43. Letter, W. K. Harrison to Dear Friend, October 10, 1960, OKAP, Box 138.

44. Report of the Secretary of Public Affairs to the Board of Administration, the National Association of Evangelicals, October 11, 1960, NAE Collection, Box 34, "Original Reports 1960."

45. See Minutes, Executive Committee NAE, Monday, September 12, 1960, ibid., "Original Minutes 1960."

46. Letter, Bell to Peale, September 9, 1960, Nelson Bell Collection, Box 41, Folder 12, "General Correspondence: Peale, Norman Vincent 1957–1964."

47. Letter, Poling to Armstrong, October 21, 1960, OKAP, Box 137.

48. Letter, Bell to Archer, September 24, 1960, Nelson Bell Collection, Box 13, Folder 19, "General Correspondence: Archer, Dr. Glenn 1960."

49. Letter, Archer to Bell, September 27, 1960, ibid.

50. Letter, Bell to Archer, September 30, 1960, ibid.

51. Dave Powers Papers, Box 9, Powers Writing File, transcribed tape #52.

52. See Press Conference of Senator John F. Kennedy, Lockheed Air Terminal, September 9, 1960, Burbank, California, JFKPPP, '60 Campaign Press

and Publicity, Press Secretary's Speech and Statement File 1960, Speeches by Date, Box 1057, "Speeches by Date 9/9/60–9/13/60."

53. Ibid.

54. Ibid.

Chapter 7

1. "The New Frontier: Remarks of Senator John F. Kennedy Accepting the Nomination, Democratic National Convention, July 15, 1960," Theodore H. White Papers, *The Making of the President 1960*, Subject Files: Kennedy, Box 27D, "Kennedy 2 of 4."

2. Ibid.

3. Letter, Cox to Kennedy, April 8, 1960, TCSP, Campaign Files 1959–60, Box 25, "Religious Issue Catholic Issue Folder 1."

4. Letter, Galbraith to JFK, August 25, 1960, Box 993, JFKPPP.

5. Letter, Schlesinger to Kennedy, August 26, 1960, RFKP, Pre-Administration Political Files, Box 26, 1960 Campaign and Transition Correspondence, 1959–1960, "Schlesinger, Arthur M., Jr."

6. Letter, Schlesinger to Kennedy, September 8, 1960, ibid.

7. Letter, Schlesinger to Robert Kennedy, September 10, 1960, ibid.

8. Letter, Robert Kennedy to Schlesinger, September 15, 1960, ibid.

9. Memorandum on the Religious Issue, August 15, 1960, TCSP, Box 25, Campaign Files 1959–1960, "Religious Issue Campaign Materials Folder 2."

10. Memorandum, Sorensen to Robert Kennedy, July 23, 1960, ibid., "Sorensen Campaign Memos Folder 2."

11. Letter, Wine to Kennedy, March 31, 1960, ibid., Box 24, "Religious Issue Air Force Manual Controversy."

12. Letter and Memorandum, Wine to Sorensen, June 20, 1960, James Wine Personal Papers, JFKL, Series 1, Kennedy Campaign, Box 1, Statements, 1959–1960, Folder 2 of 2.

13. Press Release, August 26, 1960, DNCP, Press Releases, Box 18 B-2183, Appointment of Dr. James W. Wine, Special Assistant for Community Relations 8/26/60.

14. Press Release, September 8, 1960, ibid., Box 19 B-2310, Appointment of John Cogley: Kennedy-Johnson Campaign Staff 9/8/60.

15. Memorandum on Texas Political Situation (as of July 21, 1960), JFKPPP, 1960 Campaign Files, Post Convention to Election Files, Box 987, "Texas Organizational 6/21/60–9/26/60."

16. James Talley, "Ministers See Pulpit Attacks on Kennedy Bid," *Nashville Banner*, August 15, 1960, p. 1.

17. Memorandum, Office Files of George Reedy, LBJPL, Box 10, "1960 Campaign."

18. Memorandum, Moyers to Salinger and Kennedy, August 19, 1960, DNCP, Box 135, 1960 Campaign, "Citizens for Kennedy/Johnson: Byron

White Texas 8/19/60–9/22/60," Democratic National Committee Collection, JFKL.

19. "Telephone Conversation between Lou Bouldes and Walter Jenkins, August 13, 1960," Office Files of Walter Jenkins, LBJPL, Box 2, "Transcript of Walter Jenkins Telephone Calls, August 1960."

20. "Telephone Conversation between Irving Goldberg and Walter Jenkins, August 16, 1960," ibid.

21. "Transcript of Conversation between Elmer Parish and Walter Jenkins, August 16, 1960," ibid.

22. "Transcript of Conversation between Byron Skelton and Walter Jenkins, August 20, 1960," ibid.

23. "Transcript of Conversation between Ambrose McCall and Walter Jenkins, September 9, 1960," ibid., "Transcript of Walter Jenkins Telephone Calls, September 1960."

24. Letter, Rayburn to Johnson, August 9, 1960, Lyndon Johnson Papers, Lyndon B. Johnson Presidential Library (hereafter LBJPL), Senate Political Files, Box 262, Political Files, 1959–60, "Religious Issue Form Letters."

25. Memorandum, Busby to Johnson, August 2, 1960, ibid., "Memos: Horace Busby to LBJ."

26. "Telephone Conversation: Walter Jenkins Called Pierre Salinger, Tuesday, August 2, 1960," ibid.

27. Letter, Stevens to Johnson, August 16, 1960, ibid., "Religion."

28. Letter, Johnson to Stevens, August 19, 1960, ibid.

29. Letter, Graham to Johnson, August 8, 1960, ibid., "Famous Names G."

30. Letter, Johnson to Graham, August 16, 1960, ibid., "Famous Names G."

31. Letter, Johnson to Dear Friend, and "The 'Catholic Question,'" ibid., "Religion: The Catholic Question."

32. Memorandum, Sorensen to Kennedy, June 27, 1960, TCSP, Box 25, Campaign Files 1959–60, "Sorensen Campaign Memos Folder 2."

33. Simulmatics Corporation, DNCP, 1960 Campaign, Box 212, "Simulmatics Corporation Public Opinion Analysis."

34. Memorandum, Belknap to Robert Kennedy and Steve Smith, August 29, 1960, RFKP, Box 45, Pre-Administration Political Files, General Subject, "Poll: George Belknap 6/20/60–8/29/60 & Undated."

35. Letter, de Sola Pool to Kennedy, August 21, 1960, ibid., Box 48, General Subject 1959–60, "Simulmatics: Miscellaneous 5/15/60–9/13/60."

36. "Kennedy before Labor Day," August 25, 1960, DNCP, 1960 Campaign, Box 212, "Simulmatics Report #2."

37. Ibid., 2.

38. Ibid., 25. The survey also found that anti-Catholicism was concentrated among older voters and was more prevalent in rural areas and in the South.

39. DNCP, 1960 Campaign, Box 212, "Simulmatics Report #1, May 15, 1960: Negro Voters in Northern Cities."

40. Ibid., "Simulmatics Report #3, August 25, 1960: Nixon before Labor Day."

41. Ibid., 3.

42. Claude Sitton, "Peale Is Criticized," *New York Times*, September 8, 1960.

43. Ibid.

44. Sorensen, *Kennedy*, 189.

45. James Wine, interviewed by John Stewart, January 26, 1967, p. 62, JFKL Oral History Program.

46. John Cogley, interviewed by John Stewart, February 20, 1968, p. 31, ibid.

47. "Priest Sees Bias as Bad as in 1928," *New York Times*, September 10, 1960, p. 8.

48. John Cogley, interviewed by John Stewart, February 20, 1968, p. 7, JFKL Oral History Program.

49. Ibid., 10.

50. Ibid., 11.

51. White, *The Making of the President 1960*, 293.

52. Ibid., 313.

Chapter 8

1. See Theodore C. Sorensen, *Kennedy* (New York: Harper and Row, 1965), 194.

2. Campaign Material in DNC Files, Fair Campaign Practices Committee Papers, Georgetown University Archives, Box 4, Folder 59.

3. Associated Press, "Survey Finds Anti-Catholic Tracts Used in Every State in Campaign," *Washington Post*, February 18, 1962.

4. Letter, Graham to Kennedy, August 10, 1960, JFKPPP, Box 550, Senate Files, President's Office Files, "Religion."

5. W. A. Criswell, "Religious Freedom and the Presidency," *United Evangelical Action* 19, no. 7 (September 1960): 8–9; John Wicklein, "Anti-Catholic Groups Closely Cooperate in Mail Campaign to Defeat Kennedy," *New York Times*, October 17, 1960.

6. W. O. Vaught, "The Issue of a Roman Catholic President," Fair Campaign Practices Committee Papers, Box 3, Folder 19. See also "Baptist Group against Kennedy," *Baltimore Sun*, September 7, 1960.

7. I am indebted throughout this section to Stan Hastey, "A History of the Baptist Joint Committee on Public Affairs, 1946–1971," Ph.D. diss., Southern Baptist Theological Seminary, 1973.

8. *Report from the Capital*, May–June 1960, p. 4.

9. Hilton Hagan, "Texans for Nixon Drive Launched by Carr Collins," *Dallas Morning News*, August 12, 1960.

10. Letter, Collins to Hall, August 11, 1960, RMNPPP, Vice President General Correspondence, Series 320, Box 163, Collingwood, Charles–Colt's Patent Fire Arms Company, "Collins, Carr P."

11. Letter, Smith to Fair Campaign Practices Committee, September 7, 1960, Fair Campaign Practices Committee Papers, Box 2, Folder 67.

12. David Broder, "Anti-Kennedy Drive Gets Rough in Texas," *Washington Star*, September 15, 1960.

13. Mike Quinn, "Rally for Nixon Angers 2 Clerics," *Dallas Morning News*, September 10, 1960.

14. Associated Press, "Texan Denies Using Religion in Campaign," *Washington Post*, September 18, 1960.

15. Dossier, Carr P. Collins of Dallas, Texas, JFKPPP, '60 Campaign Issues, Religious Issue, Files of James Wine 1960, Box 1018, Aberree–Collins, Carr P., "Collins, Carr. P."

16. Letter, Nixon to Collins, January 19, 1961, and Letter, Finch to Collins, November 29, 1960, both in RMNPPP, Vice President General Correspondence, Series 320, Box 163, Collingwood, Charles–Colt's Patent Fire Arms Company, "Collins, Carr P."

17. See Richard Hughes, *Reviving the Ancient Faith: The Story of the Churches of Christ in America* (Grand Rapids, MI: Eerdmans, 1996), 263–266. I am indebted to Hughes's account throughout this section.

18. David Broder, "Texas Clergy Plunges into Political Battle," *Washington Star*, September 21, 1960.

19. Dr. Batsell Barrett Baxter, "A Dangerous Doctrine," Batsell Barrett Baxter Papers, Lipscomb University Archives.

20. James Talley, "Evins Mounts Pulpit, Answers Political Sermon," *Nashville Tennessean*, October 11, 1960.

21. Letter, Davis to W. E. Fentress, October 10, 1960, Batsell Barrett Baxter Papers, Lipscomb University Archives.

22. Letter, Robert Kennedy to Evins, October 14, 1960, Joe Evins Papers, Tennessee Tech University Archives, Box 477, Folder 4.

23. "Statement: 9/13/60: For Release Tomorrow," OKAP, Accession 4881, Box 138. It is possible that Armstrong himself drafted this release, but it is not clear if that is the case.

24. Ibid.

25. Don Gill, "Capital Commentary," *United Evangelical Action* 19, no. 7 (September 1960): 4.

26. Don Gill, "Capital Commentary," *United Evangelical Action* 19, no. 8 (October 1960): 8.

27. "Minutes of the Executive Committee, National Association of Evangelicals, Monday, October 10, 1960," NAE Collection, Box 34, "Original Minutes 1960."

28. "A Statement of Concern," ibid.

29. Letter, Thomas Zimmerman, President, National Association of Evangelicals, to Pastors, Fair Campaign Practices Committee Papers, Box 3, Folder 55.

30. "Television Stations to Carry Statewide Telecast, Saturday, September 12, 1960," Lyndon B. Johnson Papers, LBJPL, Senate Political Files, 1949–1961, "JFK–LBJ Texas Democratic Campaign Headquarters Publicity and Public Relations, 1 of 2."

31. Letter, Mac Roy Rasor to Jim Hackett, September 26, 1960, ibid., 2 of 2.

32. Confidential Special Report, "Houston Ministers" for Bob Kennedy, RFKP, Pre-Administration Political Files, Box 37, General Subject File 1959, "1960 Media Campaign: Film of Houston Ministers Conference (Schedules)."

33. "A Survey of the Presidential Election in Texas in 1960: September 14, 1960, Louis Harris and Associates," ibid., Box 45, General Subject, 1959–1960, Poll #828: The Presidential Elections in Texas, 9/14/60 (Harris).

34. Ibid., 9.

35. Ibid., 1.

36. Ibid., 12.

37. "A Survey of the Presidential Election in Texas in 1960 II: October 17, 1960, Louis Harris and Associates," ibid., Poll #829: The Presidential Elections in Texas, 10/17/60 (Harris).

38. Theodore Sorensen, Memorandum on the Religious Issue, August 15, 1960, James Wine Personal Papers, Series 1, Kennedy Campaign, Box 1, "Personal Correspondence 1 of 2 March–August 1960" folder.

39. RFKP, Pre-Administration Files, Box 47, General Subject 1959–1960, "Religious Issue: 9/4/60–10/29/60 Correspondence."

40. LBJ Papers, Senate Political Files, 1949–1961, Box 221, JFK–LBJ Texas Democratic Campaign Headquarters, Religious Issue.

41. Memorandum, Wine to Sorensen, October 1, 1960, TCSP, Box 15, Subject Files, Religion 1/24/58–10/1/60.

42. Press Release, Democratic National Committee, September 14, 1960, DNCP, Press Releases, Box 19 B-2363, Executive Committee Press Conference 9/14/60.

43. Press Release, Democratic National Committee, September 15, 1960, TCSP, Box 15, Subject Files, Religion 1/24/58–10/1/60.

44. Memorandum, Wine to Robert Kennedy, September 19, 1960, James Wine Personal Papers, Series 1, Kennedy Campaign, Box 1, Personal Correspondence, Folder 2 of 2.

45. Letter, Van Dusen to Stevenson, August 2, 1960, Adlai Stevenson Papers, Box 84, Folder 6, Princeton University Archives.

46. Letter, Van Dusen to Bennett, August 1, 1960, ibid.

47. Letter, Stevenson to Van Dusen, August 11, 1960, ibid.

48. Letter, Schlesinger to Stevenson, September 4, 1960, ibid., Box 74, Folder 1.

49. Letter, Van Dusen to Stevenson, August 28, 1960, ibid., Box 84, Folder 6.

50. Letter, Stevenson to Van Dusen, September 13, 1960, ibid.

51. Telegram, Wine to Fry, n.d., James Wine Personal Papers, Series 1, Kennedy Campaign, Box 1, "Personal Correspondence 1 of 2 March–August 1960" folder.

52. Letter, Blanshard to Stanley Lowell, July 27, 1958, Paul Blanshard Papers, Box 3, Folder 3–29.

53. Letter, Blanshard to editor, *Washington Post*, March 22, 1959, ibid., Folder 3–38.

54. "Conversation with Senator Kennedy, April 29, 1959," ibid.

55. Letter, Blanshard to Archer, May 2, 1959, ibid.

56. Letter, Sorensen to Blanshard, March 14, 1960, ibid., Folder 3–45.

57. Letter, Blanshard to Sorensen, March 18, 1960, ibid., Folder 3–46.

58. Memorandum, Blanshard to Archer and Lowell, July 26, 1960, ibid., Folder 3–47; Memorandum, Blanshard to Archer and Lowell, September 26, 1960, ibid., Folder 3–49; Memorandum, Blanshard to Archer and Lowell, October 18, 1960, ibid., Folder 3–50; Letter, Blanshard to Mrs. Pickens, September 18, 1960, ibid., Folder 3–49.

59. Theodore C. Sorensen, *Kennedy* (New York: Harper and Row, 1965), 193.

60. "Religious Issue," RMNPPP, Series 258, "Memos and Drafts 1 of 2," *Six Crises* Manuscript, Box 2 of 2.

61. Confidential Memorandum, 8/16/60, RMNPPP, Series 77, Box 28.

62. *Meet the Press*, Sunday, September 11, 1960.

63. "Senator Morton Says Democrats Are Exploiting Religious Issue Deliberately," September 15, 1960, Republican National Committee News Release.

64. Thomas Ross, "Mormon Leader Endorses Nixon," *Chicago Sun Times*, October 14, 1960.

65. Status of States, Tennessee, September 23, 1960, and Status of States, Texas, October 28, 1960, Research Division, Republican National Committee.

66. Nixon, *Six Crises*, 367.

67. Nationwide Television Speech of the Vice President Originating at Los Angeles, Calif., November 6, 1960. In *Freedom of Communications: Final Report of the Committee on Commerce, United States Senate*, part II, *The Speeches, Remarks, Press Conferences, and Study Papers of the Vice President Richard M. Nixon, August 1 through November 7, 1960* (Washington, DC: U.S. Government Printing Office, 1961), 1059.

68. Nixon, *Six Crises*, 365 f.

69. Ibid., 421.

70. Sorensen, *Kennedy*, 209.

71. "The Religion Question," *Time*, November 7, 1960.

72. For different accounts of this episode, see Taylor Branch, *Parting the Waters* (New York: Simon and Schuster, 1988), 351–378; Nick Bryant, *The Bystander* (New York: Basic, 2006), 179–224; Nixon, *Six Crises*, 362–363; Sorensen, *Kennedy*, 215–216.

73. "A Survey of the Presidential Election in Texas in 1960 III: November 3, 1960, Louis Harris and Associates," RFKP, Pre-Administration Political Files, Box 45, General Subject, 1959–1960, Poll #830: The Presidential Elections in Texas, 11/3/60 (Harris).

74. Ibid.

75. Lyndon B. Johnson Papers, LBJPL, Senate Political Files, 1949–1961, LBJ for Vice President, Subject Files *Baptist Standard*.

76. "Baptists Disturbed by Nixon-Lodge Statements," *Baptist Standard*, October 19, 1960, p. 6.

77. Ibid.

78. Ibid.

79. Ibid.

80. Telegram, Nixon to James, October 23, 1960, Drew Pearson Papers, Box G281, 2 of 3.

81. Statement by Henry Cabot Lodge, Republican Vice Presidential Nominee, New York, New York, October 12, 1960, Lyndon B. Johnson Papers, LBJPL, Senate Political Files, 1949–1961, LBJ for Vice President, Subject Files, Lodge, Henry Cabot.

82. E. S. James, Editorial, "Vote Your Convictions," *Baptist Standard*, November 2, 1960.

83. "Minutes of the Board of Administration, National Association of Evangelicals, Hotel Statler, St. Louis, Missouri, October 11, 1960," NAE Collection, Box 34, "Original Minutes 1960."

84. "Report of the Executive Director to the Board of Administration, National Association of Evangelicals, October 11–12, 1960," ibid.

85. Letter, Collins to Finch, November 14, 1960, RMNPPP, Vice Presidential General Correspondence, Series 320, Box 163; Charles Collingwood, Colt's Patent Fire Arms Company, "Collins, Carr P."

Epilogue

1. Lynn Kellstadt and Mark Noll, "Religion, Voting for President, and Party Identification, 1948–1984," in Mark Noll, ed., *Religion and American Politics: From the Colonial Period to the 1980s* (New York: Oxford University Press, 1990), 355–379. All citations of CPS data are from this chapter.

2. Ibid., 366.

3. For an interesting account of Kennedy's infidelities, see Ted Sorensen, *Counselor: A Life at the Edge of History* (New York: HarperCollins, 2008). See especially chapter 10, "My Perspective on JFK's Personal Life."

4. John Cogley Oral History, February 20, 1968, p. 28, JFKL.

5. Ibid., 29.

6. Bishop John J. Wright Oral History, March 7, 1966, p. 2, JFKL.

7. Ibid., 5.

8. For a detailed and fascinating account of this shift in presidential rhetoric, see David Domke and Kevin Coe, *The God Strategy: How Religion Became a Political Weapon in America* (New York: Oxford University Press, 2008). On the metaphor of separation of church and state, see Philip Hamburger, *Separation of Church and State* (Cambridge, MA: Harvard University Press, 2002).

9. See Robert N. Bellah, "Civil Religion in America," *Daedalus* 96, no. 1 (Winter 1967): 1–21.

10. For an interesting proposal for making evangelical political engagement more independent and less beholden to any single political party, see David Gushee, *The Future of Faith in American Politics: The Public Witness of the Evangelical Center* (Waco, TX: Baylor University Press, 2008).

INDEX

···

Note: Unless otherwise specified, "Kennedy" refers to John F. Kennedy.

235